Each volume of this series of companions to major philosophers contains specially commissioned essays by an international team of scholars, together with a substantial bibliography, and will serve as a reference work for students and nonspecialists. One aim of the series is to dispel the intimidation such readers often feel when faced with the work of a difficult and challenging thinker.

Francis Bacon (1561–1626) is one of the most important philosophers of the early modern era. His plan for scientific reform played a central role in the birth of the new science. The essays in this volume offer a comprehensive survey of his writings on science, including his classifications of sciences, his theory of knowledge and of forms, his speculative philosophy, his idea of cooperative scientific research, and the providential aspects of Baconian science. There are also essays on Bacon's theory of rhetoric and history as well as on his moral and political philosophy and on his legacy. Throughout, the contributors aim to place Bacon in his historical context.

New readers and nonspecialists will find this the most convenient and accessible guide to Bacon currently available. Advanced students and specialists will find a conspectus of recent developments in the interpretation of Bacon.

THE CAMBRIDGE COMPANION TO

BACON

The Cambridge Companion to
BACON

Edited by Markku Peltonen
Academy of Finland

Published by the Press Syndicate of the University of Cambridge
The Pitt Building, Trumpington Street, Cambridge CB2 1RP
40 West 20th Street, New York, NY 10011-4211, USA
10 Stamford Road, Oakleigh, Melbourne 3166, Australia

© Cambridge University Press 1996

First published 1996

Printed in the United States of America

Library of Congress Cataloging-in-Publication Data

The Cambridge companion to Bacon / edited by Markku Peltonen.
    p.   cm.
    Includes bibliographical references (p.   ) and index.
    ISBN 0-521-43498-X. – ISBN 0-521-43534-X (pbk.)
    1. Bacon, Francis, 1561–1626.   I. Peltonen, Markku.
B1198.C265   1996
    192 – dc20
                                                            95-26405
                                                               CIP

A catalog record for this book is available from the British Library

ISBN   0-521-43498-X Hardback
       0-521-43534-X Paperback

CONTENTS

v

vi   Contents

CONTRIBUTORS

IAN BOX teaches political science at Mount Allison University in New Brunswick, Canada. He has written articles on Bacon for a number of journals including *History of Political Thought* and *The Seventeenth Century*. He is currently preparing a study of the social criticism of Henry David Thoreau.

JOHN CHANNING BRIGGS is Associate Professor of English at the University of California, Riverside. He received his B.A. from Harvard University and his Ph.D. from the University of Chicago. He is the author of *Francis Bacon and the Rhetoric of Nature* (Cambridge, Mass., 1989), winner of Harvard University Press's Thomas J. Wilson Prize.

SACHIKO KUSUKAWA is a research fellow at Christ's College, Cambridge. She is the author of *The Transformation of Natural Philosophy: The Case of Philip Melanchthon* (Cambridge, 1995).

MICHEL MALHERBE is Professor of Philosophy at the University of Nantes. He has published several books on Hobbes and Hume. He has copublished a French translation of Bacon's *Novum organum* and has written several articles on Bacon's theory of science and influence on the seventeenth- and eighteenth-century philosophy.

MARKKU PELTONEN is a researcher at the Academy of Finland. His publications include *Classical Humanism and Republicanism in English Political Thought 1570–1640* (Cambridge, 1995).

ANTONIO PÉREZ-RAMOS is Assistant Professor of Philosophy at the University of Murcia, Spain. He holds a Ph.D. from the University of Cambridge and is the author of *Francis Bacon's Idea of Science and the Maker's Knowledge Tradition* (Oxford, 1988).

vii

GRAHAM REES is Senior Lecturer in the History of Science at the University of Wolverhampton. He has written exclusively on Francis Bacon and is a General Editor of the Oxford English Texts critical edition of Francis Bacon's work, the first volume of which was published in 1996. In connection with his researches on Bacon Dr. Rees has been a Wellcome Trust Leave Fellow (1993–4) and a British Academy/Leverhulme Trust Senior Research Fellow (1995–6).

PAOLO ROSSI is Professor of the History of Philosophy at the University of Florence and President of Florence Center for the History and Philosophy of Science. In 1985 he was awarded the Sarton Medal for the history of science. In 1988 he was appointed member of the Accademia dei Lincei and of Academia Europaea. Among his publications are *Francis Bacon: from Magic to Science* (1957; English and Japanese translation, 1968), *Clavis universalis: arti della memoria e logica combinatoria da Lullo a Leibniz* (1960; Japanese, Spanish, and French translations, 1983, 1989, 1993), *Philosophy, Technology and the Arts in the Early Modern Era* (1962; English translation, 1970), *The Dark Abyss of Time: The History of the Earth and the History of Nations from Hooke to Vico* (1979; English translation, 1984), *La scienza e la filosofia dei moderni: aspetti della rivoluzione scientifica* (Torino, 1989), *Paragone degli ingegni moderni e postmoderni* (Bologna, 1989), and *Il passato, la memoria, l'oblio* (Bologna, 1991).

ROSE-MARY SARGENT is Assistant Professor of Philosophy at Merrimack College. She has published a number of articles on philosophy of science and on the history of seventeenth-century English science. Her book *The Diffident Naturalist: Robert Boyle and the Philosophy of Experiment* was published by The University of Chicago Press in 1995.

JOHN F. TINKLER has worked extensively on Renaissance humanism, the history of rhetoric, and rhetorical invention. Since moving to the United States, he has taught in both Rhetoric and English departments at the University of California at Berkeley, Towson State University, and the University of Virginia.

BRIAN VICKERS has been Professor of English Literature and Director of the Centre for Renaissance Studies at ETH Zürich since 1975.

He is the author of *Francis Bacon and Renaissance Prose* (Cambridge, 1968), editor of *Essential Articles for the Study of Francis Bacon* (Hamden, Conn., 1968; London, 1972), of *English Science, Bacon to Newton* (Cambridge, 1987), and of the volume on Francis Bacon in "The Oxford Authors" series (Oxford, 1996).

TEXTUAL NOTE

All references (unless otherwise stated) to Bacon's writings are to
The Works of Francis Bacon, ed. James Spedding, Robert L. Ellis, and
Douglas D. Heath (London: Longman, 1857–74), 14 vols. References
to volume and page of this edition are given in parentheses in the
text.

CHRONOLOGY

1561 Born at York House, London, 22 January, the youngest son of Sir Nicholas Bacon, Lord Keeper of the Great Seal, and Ann, second daughter of Sir Anthony Cooke.

1573 Goes to Trinity College, Cambridge with his elder brother Anthony in April; matriculated in July.

1575 Leaves Cambridge in December.

1576 Admitted to Gray's Inn. Travels to the Continent and stays in France for almost three years in the embassy of Sir Amias Paulet.

1579 Returns to England after his father's death; commences his studies at Gray's Inn.

1581 Sits for the first time in Parliament for Bossiney in Cornwall.

1582 Admitted to the bar as an utter barrister.

1584 Sits in Parliament for Weymouth and Melcombe Regis. Writes his earliest political tract, *A Letter of Advice to Queen Elizabeth.*

1586 Becomes a bencher of Gray's Inn; sits in Parliament for Taunton.

1588 Gives his first reading at Gray's Inn on Advowsons. Appointed to a committee of lawyers to review existing statutes.

1589 Sits in Parliament for Liverpool. Writes *An Advertisement Touching the Controversies of the Church of England.*

1592 Writes *Of Tribute, or Giving That Which Is Due* [*A Conference of Pleasure*] and *Certain Observations Made upon a Libel Published This Present Year, 1592.*

1593 Sits in Parliament for Middlesex; opposes the subsidy bill.

1594 Appointed Deputy Chief Steward of the Duchy of Lancaster and made Queen's Counsel Extraordinary. Writes *A True*

xiii

Report of the Detestable Treason, Intended by Dr. Roderigo Lopez, A Promus of Formularies and Elegancies, and *Gesta Grayorum.* Argues in Chudleigh's case.

1595 Writes *Of Love and Self-love.*

1596 Writes *Maxims of the Law.*

1597 Sits in Parliament for Ipswich. Publishes the first edition of *Essayes. Religious Meditations. Places of Perswasion and Disswasion.*

1600 Gives his reading on the Statute of Uses.

1601 Sits in Parliament for Ipswich. Publishes *A Declaration of the Practices and Treasons Attempted and Committed by Robert, Late Earl of Essex.*

1602 Writes *A Confession of Faith.* Argues in Slade's case.

1603 Knighted. Publishes *A Brief Discourse Touching the Happy Union of the Kingdoms of England and Scotland.* Writes *De interpretatione naturae proemium, Temporis partus masculus,* and *Valerius Terminus of the Interpretation of Nature.*

1604 Sits in Parliament for Ipswich. Publishes *Apology in Certain Imputations Concerning the Late Earl of Essex* and *Certain Considerations Touching the better Pacification and Edification of the Church of England.* Writes *Cogitationes de natura rerum* and *Cogitationes de scientia humana.*

1605 Publishes *The Advancement of Learning.*

1606 Marries Alice Barnham.

1607 Appointed Solicitor General. Writes *Cogitata et visa, Filum labyrinthi,* and *Partis instaurationis secundae delineatio et argumentum.*

1608 Argues in Calvin's case. Writes *Certain Considerations Touching the Plantation in Ireland, In felicem memoriam Elizabethae, Of the True Greatness of the Kingdom of Britain,* and *Redargutio philosophiarum.*

1609 Publishes *De sapientia veterum.*

1611 Writes *Phaenomena universi, De viis mortis,* and *De fluxu et refluxu maris.*

1612 Publishes the second edition of *Essays.* Writes *De principiis atque originibus, Descriptio globi intellectualis,* and *Thema coeli.*

1613 Appointed Attorney General.

1614   Sits in Parliament for Cambridge University. Publishes *The Charge Touching Duels.*

1616   Becomes a member of the Privy Council. Writes *Proposition Touching Amendment of Laws.* Argues in the case of *de non procedendo Rege inconsulto.*

1617   Appointed Lord Keeper of the Great Seal.

1618   Granted the title of Lord Chancellor. Created Baron of Verulam.

1619   A. Gorges's translation of *De sapientia veterum* published.

1620   Publishes the preliminary material of *Instauratio magna* as well as *Novum organum* together with *Parasceve ad historiam naturalem et experimentalem.*

1621   Created Viscount of St. Albans. Impeached.

1622   Publishes *The History of the Reign of King Henry the Seventh* and *Historia ventorum* in a volume entitled *Historia naturalis et experimentalis.* Writes *Advertisement Touching a Holy War* and *Abecedarium novum naturae.*

1623   Publishes *Historia vitae et mortis* and *De augmentis scientiarum.* Writes *Historia densi et rari.*

1624   Writes *Considerations Touching a War with Spain, New Atlantis, Magnalia naturae, praecipue quoad usus humanos,* and *Sylva Sylvarum.*

1625   Publishes the third edition of *Essayes or Counsell, Civill and Morall, Apophthegms New and Old,* and *Translation of Certain Psalms.*

1626   Dies at London, 9 April. *Sylva Sylvarum* and *New Atlantis* posthumously published.

THE CAMBRIDGE COMPANION TO
BACON

William Marshall's title page to Gilbert Wats's translation of the *De augmentis*, 1640. Reproduced by permission of the Syndics of Cambridge University Library.

Introduction

I

Francis Bacon has always had a central but controversial place in historical accounts of early modern philosophy. For some, he was the first spokesman of modern science in general and the father of its inductive method in particular. For others, he was an immoral charlatan who had nothing original to say. In the seventeenth and especially in the eighteenth century, when Bacon's reputation was at its peak, he was widely seen as the originator of modern science and philosophy. In the middle of the nineteenth century William Whewell could still bestow fulsome praise on Bacon – "the supreme Legislator of the modern Republic of Science." The tide, however, was turning apace, and it soon became a commonplace to ridicule Bacon's philosophy and criticize his moral outlook.

Both of these negative assessments have proven surprisingly tenacious. While moral denunciation continues,[1] the main contemporary criticism of Bacon concerns the shortcomings of his grand philosophical schemes and methodological views. But there has been little consensus as to where precisely Bacon's philosophical failure lay. For some present-day epistemologists, Bacon was a spokesman for a hopelessly naive induction by enumeration, and had thus nothing to do with the development of modern science. In striking contrast, the Frankfurt School criticized Bacon for being the very epitome of the modern scientific domination of nature and humankind.[2] However, although these censures are still occasionally repeated, tremendous strides have been made in Bacon scholarship. New and important material has been turned up and anachronistic criteria for assessing Bacon's philosophy have been abandoned. Sev-

I

eral ghosts of nineteenth-century interpretation have been exorcised and a new detailed account of Bacon's philosophy has started to emerge. There has been, in fact, something of a transformation in Bacon studies during the last few decades.

This transformation has first of all meant that new areas of Bacon's philosophy have come under close scrutiny. His moral, political, and legal philosophy as well as his conception of rhetoric, for instance, have recently attracted some of the attention they deserve. Similarly, his speculative philosophy has been thoroughly excavated. But the transformation of Bacon scholarship has also meant that his importance in early modern philosophy has been restored. His plan of scientific reform has been given a central place in historical accounts of the birth of the new science. Bacon declared that a new era in the history of humankind was at hand and that therefore traditional philosophy should be refuted. By replacing contemplative science, interested in words rather than works, with an active or operative science, humankind would have power to produce effects and thus to transform its conditions.

II

Bacon's life was integrally linked to the political, courtly, and cultural elite of late–sixteenth- and early–seventeenth-century England and London. Apart from his youthful stay in Paris, he rarely left the world of privilege and position into which he was born at York House, in London on 22 January 1561. His father, Sir Nicholas Bacon, Lord Keeper of the Great Seal, had come from a modest social background, but had made his way to the uppermost rungs of Elizabethan society. Francis's mother, Sir Nicholas's second wife, Ann Cooke, was a well-educated Calvinist who tried to guide her two sons (Francis and his elder brother Anthony) with a firm hand. She was the sister-in-law of William Cecil, Lord Burghley. The most powerful statesman in Elizabethan England was thus Bacon's uncle.

Little is known of Francis's early life. He seems to have been precocious though fragile of body. He received his early education at home, where he and his elder brother Anthony were tutored by John Walsall.[3] It has been suggested that Sir Nicholas's household, where work and public service as well as political and religious reform were emphasized, must have had a profound effect on Francis's later thought.[4] In 1573 Sir Nicholas sent Anthony and Francis to his own college, Trinity College, Cambridge, where they were put under the personal tutelage of the Master, Dr John Whitgift, the future archbishop of Canterbury. They resided there until Christmas 1575 (with an interval from August 1574 to March 1575 occasioned by an outbreak of the plague). The education Bacon received was largely in Latin language and in the medieval curriculum, consisting of the trivium (grammar, rhetoric, and dialectic), quadrivium (arithmetic, geometry, astronomy, and music), and the three philosophies (moral, natural, and metaphysical). But the impact of humanism had drastically changed the way in which this curriculum was taught. A particular emphasis was placed on practical problems at the expense of logical subtlety. Indeed, just at the time Bacon arrived in Cambridge, Petrus Ramus's attack on Aristotle's philosophy was being fiercely debated. We have Bacon's later literary secretary and first biographer Dr William Rawley's evidence of the impact of this humanist culture on Bacon. At Cambridge, he wrote, Bacon "fell into the dislike of the philosophy of Aristotle; not for the worthlessness of the author, to whom he would ever ascribe all high attributes, but for the unfruitfulness of the way" (I, 2).[5]

As Sir Nicholas had designed his sons' education to be suitable for a public career, the next step was entrance to Gray's Inn. Before assuming his studies, however, Francis was sent to serve with Sir Amyas Paulet, ambassador to France. He stayed in Paris for almost three years, and there has been some speculation of the possible impact on his intellectual development of the French courtly *académie* and of Bernard Palissy (an apprentice potter whose experiments on ceramics brought him brief renown), whose public lectures on agriculture, mineralogy, and geology Bacon could have attended.

Francis returned to England after his father's death in February 1579. Without a position or income, he commenced the study of law at Gray's Inn, where he made rapid progress: he was admitted to the bar as an utter barrister in 1582, became bencher in 1586, reader in 1588, and double reader in 1600. Although he professed the law, "his heart and affection was more carried after the affairs and places of estate," as Rawley put it (I, 6). Accordingly, in the by-elections of 1581, at the tender age of twenty, Bacon was returned to Parliament for Bossiney, Cornwall. Three years later in 1584, he was returned to Parliament, and in this period he wrote his earliest political tract –

"A letter of Advice to the Queen" – where he discussed the danger of the Catholic population of England and pondered political alliance with other enemies of Spain. Bacon's political star was clearly rising: he was employed in investigating of English Catholics and was visible for the first time in the parliament of 1586–7; in 1588, at the age of twenty-seven, he was appointed to a committee of lawyers which was to review existing statutes; in 1589 he was an active participant in the Commons, appearing as a reporter of committee business and drawing up a political treatise, "An Advertisement Touching the Controversies of the Church of England," where he exhibited moderate views in support of the government.

Early in the next decade, Bacon was drawn close to the young earl of Essex, and they soon struck up an intimate friendship. Essex tried to secure first the Attorney Generalship and, failing this, the Solicitor Generalship for Bacon. Both suits were prolonged and exhausting, but they came to naught, partly because of Bacon's opposition to the subsidy bill in 1593, which had offended the queen, and partly because of Essex's perseverance, which had annoyed her. Yet, although the queen did not give Bacon a significant office, she employed him as a member of her legal counsel.

Important as Bacon's friendship with Essex is from a biographical point of view and for accounts of Bacon's supposed moral failure (Bacon was made to act as a prosecutor in his onetime patron's trial), for our present purposes the most important development of Bacon's career in the early 1590s is his intellectual gestation. For, at the beginning of the 1590s, Bacon quite suddenly broached two topics which would preoccupy him for the rest of his life. First, as befitted a precocious and aspiring lawyer, he began to ponder the idea of reform of English law. In a 1593 parliament speech he noted that "[t]he Romans appointed ten men who were to correct and recall all former laws, and set forth their Twelve Tables, so much of all men to be commended" (VIII, 214). This concern was also evident in a masque he wrote for the Christmas festivities at Gray's Inn in 1594, where Bacon had the counselor advising the prince in "Virtue and a gracious Government" assert: "purge out multiplicity of laws, clear the incertainty of them, repeal those that are snaring, and press the execution of those that are wholesome and necessary" (VIII, 339). Two years later Bacon wrote his *Maxims of the Law* which was meant as an example of how English law should be restructured.

Secondly, and more importantly, from the early 1590s we have the first proper evidence that Bacon had grand schemes of philosophical reform in mind. In 1592 he wrote his oft-quoted letter to Lord Burghley: "I wax now somewhat ancient; one and thirty years is a great deal of sand in the hour-glass" (VIII, 108). He expressed a youthful determination to serve the queen, not as a soldier, nor a statesman, but as a philosopher. Eloquently, Bacon wrote:

I confess that I have taken all knowledge to be my province; and if I could purge it of two sorts of rovers, whereof the one with frivolous disputations, confutations, and verbosities, the other with blind experiments and auricular traditions and impostures, hath committed so many spoils, I hope I should bring in industrious observations, grounded conclusions, and profitable inventions and discoveries; the best state of that province. This, whether it be curiosity, or vain glory, or nature, or (if one take it favourably) *philanthropia*, is so fixed in my mind as it cannot be removed. And I do easily see, that place of any reasonable countenance doth bring commandment of more wits than of a man's own; which is the thing I greatly affect. (VIII, 109)

At approximately the same time Bacon composed a masque in which it was argued that "[a]ll the Philosophie of nature" is governed either by "the Gretians," who focus on "words" and "disputacons," or by "the Alchimists," whose arguments are governed by "imposture . . . auricular tradicons, and obscuritie." In contrast, Bacon acknowledged "[t]he in[dustrie of] artificers" which had made "some smale improuments of things invent[ed]," and listed printing, artillery, and the compass as the most important inventions (VIII, 123–6).[6] Two years later in the masque for the Christmas festivities at Gray's Inn, Bacon spoke about "the conquest of the works of nature" (VIII, 334–5).

These briefly expressed opinions, appearing within two years of one another, are of great importance, for they sketch so many of Bacon's philosophical themes. He argued against the barrenness of scholastic philosophy and against the preposterous claims of alchemy. He promised to form a new method, which would replace both exploded schools, and produce not just words but works. He pointed to the mechanical artificers, who created printing, artillery, and the compass, as his forerunners, and expressed his confidence that, once his method was applied, it would enable men to make new discoveries that would benefit humankind. It is extremely significant that Bacon called knowledge "the worthiest power," since it shows that he was already, at the beginning of the 1590s, making his novel link between science and power: science could become an operative action. Finally, his letter to Lord Burghley and his masque of 1594 reveal the idea that science is not a task for a solitary *magus*. Cooperation was the only way in which Bacon's scientific schemes could be put into practice, and they needed the help of political authorities if they were to materialize.

Several scholars have rightly emphasized the fact that all these writings occurred in a political rather than in a philosophical context.[7] But this was inevitable, since Bacon needed patrons, and patronage could only be attracted via the court. In other words, this political context should not prompt us to belittle the historical and philosophical importance of Bacon's plans. Despite the fact that they were presented for the first time in a political context, they contained a number of philosophical novelties, which represented a radical break with received traditions.

Although the appearance of both these themes – law reform and science – during the 1590s is of great importance to our understanding of Bacon's thought and its development, his first venture into print was a modest collection of the *Essays* (together with *Religious Meditations* and *Places of Perswasion and Disswasion*) printed in 1597. The slim volume was dedicated to his brother Anthony, and its ten essays treated personal and courtly issues in a terse, aphoristic style, which Bacon conceived as a genre setting down discrete observations on life, and aspiring to some kind of objective validity.

In 1603, James VI, the king of Scotland, ascended the English throne, and Bacon made a strenuous effort to gain his favor. He wrote to several Scottish gentlemen who were likely to be influential with the new king, went to meet James before he arrived in London and, like many others, published a treatise on the designed union between England and Scotland – *A Brief Discourse Touching the Happy Union of the Kingdoms of England and Scotland*. Bacon's efforts quickly bore fruit. In July 1603 he was knighted, though, to his great disappointment, so were three hundred others. He was immediately involved in the scheme for the union of the two kingdoms, appearing as the crown's advocate of the union in the several sessions of the Parliament which met for the first time in 1604. At the same time Bacon advised James on religious problems and published a tract – *Certain Considerations Touching the better Pacification and Edification of the Church of England* – in which he reiterated his former views on religion and church government. In 1607 Bacon was appointed Solicitor General.

Bacon's active involvement in politics during the first decade of the seventeenth century was channeled into two somewhat different intellectual pursuits. On the one hand, he continued to work for legal reform, which was closely linked with the plan to unify English and Scottish laws. On the other hand, from this period came Bacon's first serious writings on political theory. As a close counselor to James, he was involved in several ideological disputes on behalf of the king. More importantly, the union debate prompted Bacon to explore the theme of civic greatness. This theme also surfaced in his second edition of the *Essays*, published in 1612, as well as in some of his writings of the early 1620s. It is no exaggeration to argue that it formed a central theme in Bacon's political philosophy.

The first decade of the new century turned out to be one of the most productive periods in Bacon's entire life. Political business started to pile up; he developed his ideas on law reform and composed important tracts on political theory. On top of all this, Bacon wrote a number of philosophical treatises. If his general idea of a new, productive natural science had started to take shape in the early 1590s, it was a decade later that its final form appeared in outline.

From these productive years comes *The Advancement of Learning*, published in 1605. It was Bacon's first published philosophical work, and the only one which he published in English. All the other published philosophical works were written in Latin – an indication of the international scope of his project. *The Advancement of Learning* was divided into two books. The first was an eloquent defense of the importance of learning to every field of life. The second book, much longer and more important, was a general survey of the contemporary state of knowledge, pointing out deficiencies in contemporary knowledge and supplying Bacon's broad suggestions for the ways of improvement. The importance of *The Advancement of Learning* (and its expanded edition in Latin, the *De dignitate et augmentis scientiarum* [1623]) is that it presents Bacon's views on many philosophical issues and also serves as a central source for his views on history, rhetoric, moral philosophy, and civil philosophy.

More generally, it is an exposition of Bacon's classification of knowledge. Another work from this tremendously productive period is the *De sapientia veterum*, published in 1609, a collection of ancient fables complete with Bacon's interpretations. Although traditionally listed under literary works, the *De sapientia veterum* treats various philosophical issues and has more recently been seen as an important contribution to both his natural and civil philosophy.

At the same time that Bacon composed and published these two works, he was engaged in writing several other philosophical pieces, all published only after his death. These include: *De interpretatione naturae proemium*, *Temporis partus masculus*, *Valerius Terminus of the Interpretation of Nature*, *Cogitationes de scientia humana*, *Cogitata et visa*, *Partis instaurationis secundae delineatio et argumentum* and *Redargutio philosophiarum*. The exact dates of these writings are difficult to ascertain (the chronological list of the principal events of Bacon's life at the beginning of the present volume gives the most probable, though by no means conclusive dates for all these writings). But even if their exact dates of composition are in doubt, their general significance cannot be questioned. They show that by the beginning of the seventeenth century Bacon had a definitive picture of his scheme of the *Instauratio magna* ("Great Instauration").

De interpretatione naturae proemium ("A Preface to the Interpretation of Nature") was a short tract in which Bacon asserted his grandiose plans: "Now among all the benefits that could be conferred upon mankind, I found none so great as the discovery of new arts, endowments, and commodities for the bettering of man's life" (X, 84). He expressed his disappointment that his former attempts – his "zeal" – to acquire political backing for his philosophical schemes had been "mistaken for ambition" (X, 85). In the *Temporis partus masculus* ("The Masculine Birth of Time"), Bacon summoned all the schools of ancient and modern philosophy to the bar and heaped scorn on them. A similar discussion was repeated in the *Cogitata et visa* ("Thoughts and Conclusions") and in the *Redargutio philosophiarum* ("The Refutation of Philosophies"), where Aristotle and Plato were roundly criticized; a more favorable account was given of Empedocles, Heraclitus, and Democritus. At the same time, Bacon criticized traditional philosophy for its sterility, for its uncooperative nature, and for its lack of proper method. To remedy all this, he expounded his ideas of an operative science. Moreover, Bacon attempted to offer a historical explanation for the failures of natural philosophy in earlier civilizations. The *Valerius Terminus of the Interpretation of Nature* – yet another plea for an active science – offered an exposition of Bacon's famous doctrine of idols and formulated his scientific method, while the *Cogitationes de scientia humana* provided first signs of the centrality of natural and experimental histories to Baconian science.

On the whole, these tracts show that Bacon's thinking about science had developed considerably since the early 1590s. Not only are many of his central ideas present, but he put them forward in a manner which makes it possible to call these writings the origins of his most famous philosophical work, the *Novum organum* (1620) (though he called the methodological part of his work at this time "*Clavis interpretationis*" – "The Key of Interpretation") (XI, 64). Sending a copy of the *Cogitata et visa* to Lancelot Andrewes in 1609, Bacon pointed out that he was about to write "a just and perfect volume of philosophy" (XI, 141). In the *Partis instaurationis secundae delineatio et argumentum*, an overall description of his plan for the interpretation of nature (possibly written in 1607), Bacon talks about his whole philosophical plan as consisting of six parts.

There has been much scholarly discussion about the exact relationship between Bacon's published works and his manuscript treatises: why, for example, did he publish *The Advancement of Learning* and the *De sapientia veterum*, but decide to leave the other works of this period unpublished? Some scholars have sought an explanation in the historical context in which these writings were produced. By the turn of the century, they have argued, Bacon had become disenchanted with the possibility of advancing his philosophical plans through a political medium. He thus divorced his philosophical ambitions from politics, became an obsequious politician and, employing an enigmatic style, confined his philosophical message to an exclusive audience.[8] Bacon himself hinted that whilst he would publish those parts of his work "which have it for their object to find out and bring into correspondence such minds as are prepared and disposed for the argument, and to purge the floors of men's understandings," some other parts he would just pass "from hand to hand, with selection and judgment" (X, 87).

Another and equally imaginative solution to the same problem has recently been located in Bacon's "social circumstances" (as opposed to his "intellectual interests"). Underlying this explanation is the conviction that the form of writing (whether in manuscript or in print) was used as "social self-definition." To publish was to act as a professional author. From an aristocratic point of view, this was too degrading. For an aristocrat, the only respectable means of publicizing was to circulate a manuscript privately. Bacon's manuscript treatises can, according to this interpretation, be seen as an indication of a "gentlemanly disdain of professional authorship." But when he ventured into print with *The Advancement of Learning*, he assumed "a new social stance" and appealed "to a new audience, 'times succeeding,' posterity, rather than the immediately accessible figures of the court."⁹

Ingenious as both of these explanations are, we should bear in mind the fact that philosophy, though clearly important to Bacon, was only one facet of his life. It follows that his philosophical writings were the product of his spare time. This might account for the unfinished character of many of Bacon's writings, as well as for his habit of constantly revising them. Perhaps he simply did not find some of these treatises polished enough to be published.

If the decade from 1603 to 1612 (when Bacon published the much enlarged second edition of his *Essays*) was extremely productive, after 1613 (when he was appointed Attorney General) the amount of public business began to take a heavy toll. After the death of his cousin, Robert Cecil, the earl of Salisbury, in 1612, Bacon became one of James's most important advisors, and the increased amount of advisory work is evident from the growing number of letters and memoranda written to James. As an indication of his importance, Bacon became a member of the Privy Council in 1616, and was appointed Lord Keeper of the Great Seal, which made him head of the Court of Chancery in 1617. A year later he was granted the title of Lord Chancellor, which was the highest legal position under the crown. At the same time he was elevated to the House of Lords as Baron Verulam. When Bacon turned sixty in January 1621, he was created Viscount St. Albans. As Attorney General and Lord Chancellor, he took part in several state prosecutions for treason as well as in many minor trials. In Chancery, he worked hard to reduce the backlog of cases he inherited.

Despite being busy with law and politics, Bacon continued his philosophical work, and the second decade of the seventeenth century saw the maturation of his major philosophical work – the *Novum organum*. It was published together with the preliminary material of his whole philosophy – the *Instauratio magna* – in October 1620. It consisted of a preface, a plan of the whole work, an incomplete second part of the work (*Novum organum*) and a preparative to the third part of natural and experimental histories. Bacon's political position is well attested in the volume. It was printed by the king's printer and dedicated to the king and Bacon's post in the royal government is mentioned in the title.

In sending a copy of the book to the king, Bacon claimed that he had been working on the book "near thirty years" (XIV, 120). Rawley confirmed this, recalling that Bacon accounted the *Novum organum* as "the chiefest of his works," and pointing out that it was "the production of many years' labour and travel." Rawley claimed that he had seen at least twelve different versions of the work (I, 11). Although these remarks cannot be taken literally, it must be borne in mind that it was indeed nearly thirty years since Bacon had first called for a new natural philosophy and that his unpublished writings from the early years of the seventeenth century were in many respects the real precursors of the *Novum organum*.

Bacon explained his overall scheme and the particular intention of the *Novum organum* to the king: "The work, in what colours soever it may be set forth, is no more but a new logic, teaching to invent and judge by induction, (as finding syllogism incompetent for sciences of nature,) and thereby to make philosophy and sciences both more true and more active." The ultimate goal, he told the king, was nothing less than "to enlarge the bounds of Reason and to endow man's estate with new value" (XIV, 119–20).

The *Novum organum* is divided into two books. The shorter first book is a refutation of the impediments which hinder the embracement of the new method. Its intention is thus to prepare the reader to accept the new method presented in the much longer though incomplete second book. Bacon excused the publication of an "unperfect" book partly on the grounds that "I number my days, and would have it saved," but mainly because he wanted to move on to the next part of his *Instauratio*, the compiling of natural histories, for which he was expecting to find help (XIV, 120; IV, 8). He firmly believed that an exhaustive completion of natural and experimental histories rather than a new logic would rapidly change the destinies of humankind.

At the turn of the year 1620–1 Bacon was at the pinnacle of his career. In October he had published the *Novum organum* and in January he was created Viscount St. Albans. At the same time, he was busily engaged in the preliminary work for a new parliament. This parliament was assembled on the 30th of January 1621 and Bacon took his seat in the House of Lords. Bacon had forty years of experience in the House of Commons, but this was the first time he sat in the Lords. It proved to be a fatal parliament for him. Within a few weeks charges of bribery were brought against him (he had taken gifts from two men whose cases he had tried in court) and on the third of May he was removed from office by the High Court of Parliament, having pleaded guilty to these charges. (Bacon was not impeached because of the gifts he had taken. Rather, he was a victim of a political campaign directed against monopolies and the king's chief favourite Buckingham.) He was imprisoned at the king's pleasure (he was actually imprisoned for only three days), was to pay a fine of £40,000, was barred from any office or employment in the state and forbidden to sit in parliament or come within the verge (twelve miles) of the court.

Terrible as the shock of his impeachment must have been for Bacon, it is this tragedy that we have to thank for the tremendous intellectual output of the last five years of his life. After his short imprisonment Bacon went to Gorhambury, his country seat near St. Albans, and almost immediately set himself to writing his only historical work – *The History of the Reign of King Henry VII*. He wrote with breathtaking speed and the work came out in March 1622. Although a similar history of the reign of Henry VIII was both planned and expected, Bacon turned his attention to more philosophical issues. The first fruits of this were two case histories for the third part of the *Instauratio*. The *Historia ventorum* (*History of the Winds*) was published in 1622 in a volume entitled *Historia naturalis et experimentalis*, and the *Historia vitae et mortis* (*History of Life and Death*) was issued early in the next year. In 1623 Bacon also wrote a third case history – *Historia densi et rari* (*History of Dense and Rare*) – (published only in 1658), and published an expanded translation of *The Advancement of Learning*, entitled *De dignitate et augmentis scientiarum*, which formed the first part of Bacon's six-part plan. His work rate showed no slackening. He planned a political comeback, wrote some political tracts and worked on his reform of English law. But he also continued to work on his natural history project, which he deemed the most urgent one and whose fruit was posthumously published in 1626 in the *Sylva Sylvarum*. In addition, Bacon planned to revise the *De sapientia veterum*, and he found the time to write his utopia – the *New Atlantis* – which presented an unfinished picture of an ideal scientific community. In 1625 he published a collection of *Apophthegms, Translation of Certain Psalms* and, most importantly, his third and final edition of the *Essays*, which brought their number to fifty-eight.

Bacon died in poignant circumstances, which come clear in his last letter addressed to the earl of Arundel:

I was likely to have had the fortune of Caius Plinius the elder, who lost his life by trying an experiment about the burning of the mountain Vesuvius. For I was also desirous to try an experiment or two, touching the conservation and induration of bodies. As for the experiment itself, it succeeded excellently well; but in the journey (between London and Highgate) I was taken with such a fit of casting, as I knew not whether it were the stone, or some surfeit, or cold, or indeed a touch of them all three. But when I came to your Lordship's house, I was not able to go back, and therefore was forced to take up my lodging here, where your house-keeper is very careful and diligent about me. (XIV, 550)

In spite of the hospitality, he contracted either bronchitis or pneumonia and died on Easter Sunday, 9 April 1626.

Although the number of Bacon's surviving letters, speeches, and notes is copious, his personality remains obscure. Despite the obvious intimacy with such men as his elder brother Anthony and close friend Toby Matthew, Bacon seemed to some people rather cold and arrogant. His experiences of friendship with the earl of Essex in the 1590s and with George Villiers, the duke of Buckingham, in the 1610s and 1620s might account for his observation in the essay "Of Followers and Friends" that "[t]here is little friendship in the world, and least of all between equals" (VI, 495). His marriage with Alice Barnham (they were married in May 1606, he being forty-five and she only fifteen) does not match modern sensibilities of ideal marriage, and Bacon's dispassionate comments about marriage in his essay "Of Marriage and Single Life" are often taken to reflect his own experiences.

It has aptly been said that Bacon's own career was "very un-Baconian." "Boldness, innovation and imagination had little place in" it, for it was governed by a deference to authority.[10] Bacon himself thought his life akin to that of a Roman senator. He emphasized throughout his life the values of the *vita activa* and chose as his first title a Roman town – Verulam. At the moment of his impeachment he compared himself with Demosthenes, Cicero, and Seneca (XIV, 372). And toward the end of his life he not only planned to erect by his will a lecture in both universities on "natural Philosophy, and the sciences thereupon depending," but also decided to imitate "Cicero, Demosthenes, Plinius Secundus, and others" by preserving his orations and letters (XIV, 546).

What emerges in any account of Bacon's life is the exceptional talent by which he could combine a busy political career with a productive literary and philosophical career. Politics was an unsteady employment, but there is little doubt that he pursued his philosophical ambition with consistency and perseverance. What had started off in the early 1590s as a purge of knowledge from "two sorts of rovers" had thirty years later become nothing less than a comprehensive plan "to commence a total reconstruction of sciences, arts, and all human knowledge" (IV, 8).

III

Bacon firmly believed that a new era was imminent. His natural philosophy thus began with a thorough criticism of prevailing schools: their classifications of knowledge were inadequate, their methods of acquiring knowledge were flawed, their idea of science as a solitary enterprise was misleading, and, above all, their conceptions of the aims of science were flatly wrong. As Paolo Rossi demonstrates in the opening chapter of this volume, Bacon was perhaps the most important constructor of the modern image of science and the scientist. He wanted to replace the Aristotelian image of science as a contemplation and organization of eternal truths long since discovered with a conception of science as a discovery of the unknown. More importantly, he wanted to unite the rational and empirical faculties, theory and practice, and to create a truly active or operative science. Science was to be seen not so much as a contemplative *episteme* as part of the practical, active life. In his attempt to link human science (*scientia*) and human power (*potentia*), Bacon was making a novel claim which altered the function of science in human life. As Rossi emphasizes, the crucial importance of operation in Baconian science should not prompt us to see him as a utilitarian. He did not claim that utility is the guarantor of truth. Rather, he argued that only by getting to things as they really are, to the truth, can we achieve usefulness, produce faithful works – which will alter the course of natural phenomena.

In order to accomplish the "total reconstruction of sciences" and to replace the old nonproductive conception of science with his new operative science, Bacon constructed a six-part plan, which he presented at the beginning of the *Instauratio magna*:

1. Division of the Sciences.
2. The New Organon; or Direction concerning the Interpretation of Nature.
3. The Phenomena of the Universe; or a Natural and Experimental History for the Foundation of Philosophy.
4. The Ladder of the Intellect.
5. The Forerunners; or Anticipations of the New Philosophy.
6. The New Philosophy; or Active Science (IV, 22).

In the first part of his plan – the classification of knowledge – Bacon mapped out the whole field of knowledge in general and pointed out in particular the inadequately cultivated areas. The division was based on what he took to be the main functions of the human understanding: memory, imagination, and reason. These corresponded to history, poetry, and philosophy respectively. This division was hardly original but, unlike his predecessors, as Sachiko Kusukawa points out (Chapter 2), Bacon used it to present the entire realm of human knowledge. His classification, in other words, was universal in its scope. Furthermore, unlike for instance Aristotle, Bacon tried to place all the branches of human knowledge under one umbrella: they were all intended to be parts of the same comprehensive system. And he firmly held that there was a *philosophia prima* – first philosophy – a cluster of axioms shared by all the individual branches of science. His classification of knowledge reveals the closeness of theoretical and practical parts in his conception of science; they were, in Kusukawa's apt phrase, "two sides of the same coin, rather than independent types of *scientia*." Bacon's classification thus confirms his general idea of science as an operative science.

The seond part of Bacon's *Instauratio magna* consisted of his scientific method, which is the topic of Michel Malherbe's essay (Chapter 3). By the very title of this part – the *Novum organum* – Bacon announced his aim. He wanted to replace the Aristotelian method of syllogism with an entirely new scientific method. According to Bacon, a crucial weakness in the old Aristotelian logic was that it jumped from empirical particulars to first principles (axioms), which formed the premises of deductive reasoning. But Bacon believed that the most general axioms should form the end rather than the beginning of scientific inference, and his own methodology was designed to avoid Aristotle's mistake. Bacon's method proceeds along a strict hierarchy of increasing generality; a central place is assigned to natural histories – systematic accounts of natural phenomena – which will form the basis of all natural philosophy. For Bacon, it was a serious mistake to assume (as Aristotle had done) that experience gives the human mind things as they are: our senses are unreliable – our mind is "like an enchanted glass" (III, 395). Rather than becoming a skeptic, however, Bacon took the skeptics' arguments in his stride, insisting that in order to yield reliable information, human senses needed methodical assistance.

According to Bacon's hierarchic methodology, knowledge rises from lower axioms or propositions to more general ones, becoming less and less empirical and more and more theoretical. A key role in this process is played by the induction of exclusion. As Malherbe shows, the whole process is only completed when the fundamental laws of nature (the knowledge of forms) have been reached and, from there, new experiments or works have been derived by practical deduction.

If induction belongs to the more technical part of Bacon's philosophy, so does his theory of forms. Although retaining the Aristotelian term *forma*, Bacon's theory of forms, as Antonio Pérez-Ramos shows (Chapter 4), is radically different from the Aristotelian notion of substantial forms. The Baconian form is, in fact, a transitional notion between the Aristotelian substantial form and the seventeenth-century Corpuscularian theory of internal structures: it opens the door for a purely mechanical or materialistic type of explanation in natural philosophy.

In order to fully understand Bacon's concept of *forma*, we should bear in mind his notion of operative science – the idea that natural philosophy includes both "the Inquiry of Causes and the Production of Effects" (IV, 346). *Forma* is a nonperceptible arrangement which accounts for our list of fundamental properties or natures of a phenomenon, which can only be reached by true Baconian induction. It is, therefore, the attainment of the knowledge of these *formae* which perfects human power and fully converts speculation into operation. As Pérez-Ramos observes, Bacon's operative science belongs to the maker's knowledge tradition: true knowledge can be had only of what can be made. But, in order to achieve a truly operational science, the ancient gap between the products of Nature and those of human art had to be bridged. It was precisely this task that the Baconian *forma* was meant to accomplish: a perfect knowledge of the inner structure of nature not only makes our operation possible; it also makes it perfectly natural.

Of the six parts of the *Instauratio magna* Bacon more or less finished only the first part (the classification of knowledge). The second and third parts (the new method and the natural histories) were left unfinished at his death, but we have enough evidence to have a good idea what they might have looked like had he had time to finish them. The last three parts, however, were left almost wholly untouched. The fourth part – "the Ladder of the Intellect" – was meant "to set forth examples of inquiry and invention according to my method, exhibited by anticipation in some particular subjects" (IV, 31).[11] If the fourth part was going to be an example of Bacon's method in action, the fifth part was meant to offer some anticipatory results. He never produced a proper account of this part of the *Instauratio* but, as Graham Rees argues (Chapter 5), his other writings yield enough material to enable us to reconstruct his speculative philosophy. It was based on a geocentric universe, divided into three zones. The core of the Earth consisted of passive, tangible matter, the heavens of active, pneumatic matter. The zone between these two was an area where the two forms of matter mixed and thus created terrestrial phenomena. Revealing his indebtedness to Paracelsus, Bacon divided these three zones into two quaternions – that of mercury and that of sulphur. Later on, he added an intermediate quaternion in order to integrate plants and animals into his theory.

Bacon's speculative philosophy represented an odd hodge-podge of ideas taken from various sources and put together in a way which would have surprised the originators of these ideas. Indeed, in his attempt to draw up these "Anticipations of the New Philosophy," Bacon sometimes stretched analogical reasoning to its very limits. Nonetheless, his was not a system borrowed from someone. Rather, it represented a genuine, if eclectic, attempt to form an independent theory of the universe and nature. Rees's excavation of Bacon's speculative science serves as a valuable reminder of the doubleness of his natural philosophy: it comprised a program for the advancement of learning and a strange corpus of speculative science.

These five parts of the *Instauratio magna* were meant to be but "subservient and ministrant" to the sixth part – "the New Philosophy; or Active Science." Bacon was, however, aware of the fact that the completion of this last part (and thereby the whole *Instauratio magna*) was "a thing both above my strength and beyond my hopes" (IV, 32). The idea that the whole secret of nature and the universe could be disclosed by one genius had of course been central to the magico-alchemical tradition in the Renaissance. Bacon utterly rejected this view. For him, the only way learning could advance from the collecting of natural histories to the completion of the new operative science was by openness and cooperation. In her exploration of this theme (Chapter 6), Rose-Mary Sargent suggests that Bacon's account of cooperation was partly due to his attempt to seek political backing for his reform plans. But he was also convinced that without the wide cooperation of scientists with one another learning could not be advanced. Bacon conceived this cooperation on three different levels. It was cooperation between the past and the present, between illiberal and liberal arts (philosophy and practical arts), and, most importantly, within the whole community of scientists.

Bacon's cooperative scheme imitated his classification of knowledge and methodological ideas and was thus hierarchical in character. This hierarchy was clear in his scientific utopia – the *New Atlantis*. The society described there is wholly dominated by its scientific community, which is organized as a strict hierarchy – from empirical observation to the formation of theories. Moreover, science is cloaked in secrecy: the scientific community is clearly separated from the rest of the society and in certain dangerous cases (e.g., destructive weapons) it is up to the scientists to decide which results of their research are made public and which are not. Bacon's mid–seventeenth-century followers did not heed his strictures. The tensions inherent in Baconian science between democratic coopera- tion and hierarchy, between openness and secrecy, became increas- ingly clear, as Sargent shows at the close of her article, in their attempts to found scientific communities modeled on the Baconian ideology.

One of the central tenets of Bacon's defense of learning was his strict separation of science and religion. Yet, in his essay "Bacon's Science and Religion" (Chapter 7), John C. Briggs argues that there were several religious overtones to Bacon's philosophical writings. The *Novum organum* has a significantly religious cast: Bacon was "relying on divine assistance," and natural histories, he believed, should be collected with "religious care." For Bacon, man had re- nounced his original power with the Fall. The true end of knowledge was therefore nothing less than "a restitution and reinvesting . . . of man to the sovereignty and power . . . which he had his first state of creation" (III, 222). Whereas faith would repair the fall from inno- cence, science would restore dominion over nature. Similarly, the Christian virtues of humility and charity play a prominent role in Baconian natural philosophy: the lack of vanity was a measure of the truth of scientific works, and man's scientific works were consid- ered to be charitable blessings. Furthermore, Bacon's doctrine of idols suggested that opposition to the new science was a form of heresy which needed to be smashed by Baconian induction – "as if by divine fire." And, as Briggs observes, Bacon argued that the new sciences resembled religion by being cryptic: both were disclosed only to initiates. Bacon even suggested that the new science could attain both full knowledge of the natural laws and knowledge of the kingdom of glory.

Although Bacon's natural philosophy has always attracted great scholarly attention, it is clear that his philosophical interests were not confined to it. Bacon was after all a politician as well as a lawyer, and his classification of knowledge embraced natural and human philosophy alike. An important role both in his public career and in his classification of knowledge was played by rhetoric. His eloquence was praised as well by Elizabeth I as by Ben Jonson and they earned him the cognomen "our English Tully."[12] Since Bacon argued that rhetoric was "a science excellent, and excellently well laboured" (III, 409), his contribution to rhetoric, as Brian Vickers points out (Chapter 8), is not so much to be sought in the form of a general theory of rhetoric as from his more specific account of how rhetoric actually works.

In Bacon's scheme, rhetoric was closely linked to logic. Together they formed training in thinking and arguing. Furthermore, for Bacon, as for many humanists, rhetoric carried an important ethical element. In true Ciceronian fashion, Bacon argued that although wisdom won greater admiration, only eloquence could bring about a desired result and thus create and reinforce social harmony. Rhetoric, in other words, had an important task in insinuating into men a preference for truth and the good. In his attempt to explain how rhetoric performed its task in practice, Bacon turned, as Vickers demonstrates, to Aristotelian and faculty psychology. For him, imagination was an autonomous faculty between reason and will, acting as a "messenger" between them and helping the reason to reach truth and the will to reach moral good. The task Bacon assigned to rhetoric was "to apply Reason to Imagination for the better moving of the will" (III, 409). Together with logic and moral philosophy, rhetoric aided reason which, if left to its own devices, was at the mercy of the affections. Bacon's mingling of faculty psychology and ethics in his account of rhetoric is truly original, offering "a model of persuasion that has considerable explanatory power," as Vickers puts it.

A discipline which was particularly close to rhetoric in the Renaissance was history. They were both members of the *studia humanitatis* and they had epistemological and even moral similarities. As far as Bacon's concept of civil history is concerned, scholars have often attempted to interpret it as a precursor of modern scientific historiography. But, as John F. Tinkler demonstrates (Chapter 9), the development of humanist historiography set the terms for Bacon's idea of history. He agreed with his humanist predecessors that history, like demonstrative rhetoric, should aim at bestowing praise and blame. Bacon's *History of the Reign of Henry VII* attempted "to do honour to the memory" of Henry (VI, 25). But Bacon's indebtedness to humanist historiography emerges most clearly in his keen interest in the conventional topics of virtue and fortune. As Tinkler argues, however, Bacon was unconventional in placing a much stronger emphasis on fortune than virtue. Bacon's concept of history, therefore, comes close to Francesco Guicciardini's skeptical attitude: history is the realm of unpredictable accidents. Rather than being a pioneer in a new method of historiography, Bacon, Tinkler concludes, rearranged conventional humanist topics.

Where natural histories were intended to form the experimental basis of natural philosophy,[13] civil history was to form a similar basis for moral and civil philosophy. This remained, however, a plan, for Bacon never completed a systematic moral or political philosophy. Yet, his classification of knowledge contains surveys of both, and they were further treated in his literary and professional writings. Bacon divided moral philosophy into two parts. The first part treated the question of the nature of the good. As Ian Box's account of Bacon's moral philosophy (Chapter 10) shows, Bacon stressed the crucial importance of the public good as the ultimate aim of morality. It followed that *negotium* was more valuable than *otium*. Bacon roundly criticised both Aristotle and skeptics (who were particularly fashionable at Bacon's time) for preferring contemplation and self-preservation to action. The other part of Bacon's moral philosophy – the Georgics of the mind – aimed at showing how the lofty aim of the public good could be attained in practice. This did not occur by transforming human nature, but, as Box notes, by making "practical use of our knowledge of it." The aim was to collect histories of human characters and passions, which, when completed, would act as the foundation of the moral health.

There is an obvious link between Bacon's moral philosophy and his conception of operative science. Both emphasized the priority of action over contemplation and thus the public good over the private one. And both did this by appealing to Christian charity and the values of the *vita activa*. There remain, however, crucial divergences, as Box stresses at the close of his article, between Christian charity and the *philanthropia* of Baconian science on the one hand and the concept of the public good of his moral philosophy on the other. These discrepancies emerge most conspicuously in the *New Atlantis* where, for instance, the values of domesticity, criticized in the *Essays*, are held in an exceptionally high esteem.

Bacon was a politician for most of his life and, given his interest in intellectual activities, it comes as no surprise that he also wrote about political philosophy. After the accession of James I in 1603, Bacon acted as an important counselor to the king and presented himself as "a perfect and peremptory royalist" (XI, 280). Nonetheless, I suggest (Chapter 11) that Bacon's main political ideas cannot be identified with absolutism. On the contrary, he subscribed to the idea of the ancient constitution and sometimes even accepted the right of resistance. His strong arguments for the active life, his sincere respect for the republican and aristocratic forms of government, and his Machiavellian conception of civic greatness attest to his thorough familiarity with and indebtedness to the classical republican strand of political thought. Most importantly, his theory of civic greatness was a genuinely Machiavellian theory of war, vigor and instability, and set an important precedent for the militaristic aspects of mid–seventeenth-century English republicanism.

As we have seen, a legal reform formed a lifelong aspiration for Bacon, and he devoted the final part of civil philosophy to jurisprudence.[14] He argued that the remedy for the defects in contemporary law was to be sought from Roman law, and he often related his own project of legal reform to Justinian's *Corpus Iuris Civilis*. As his project developed, the influence of Roman law became more marked. Whereas in his early work – *Maxims of the Law* – he had sought to integrate Roman law concepts into a common law context, by the early 1620s he was assimilating his common law experience into a Roman law context. His terminology was thoroughly Roman, and Justinian's sixth-century reform of the Roman law provided the model for a text-based legal reform. Common law and statute law were to be separately reduced and recompiled just as in "the plan followed by Trebonianus [Justinian's chief assistant] in the Digest and Code" (V, 100). Bacon further suggested a set of auxiliary texts – "Institutions; a treatise *De regulis iuris*; and a better book *De verborum significationibus*, or terms of the law" – all drawn from Justinian's *Corpus Iuris*.[15]

Bacon's strong Roman law bias did not entail a replacement of the English common law by the Roman civil law.[16] Rather it served to emphasize the universal scope of his project. Although many of Bacon's ideas reflected his common law experience, he sought to find the universal axioms of all different legal systems and focused on methods of legal reasoning to remove uncertainty and ambiguity from the positive law.[17] But he was also interested in the human origin of laws, arguing that in every civil society there is a legislative authority – "an absolute power (*suprema potestas*)" – which makes and revokes the law.[18]

Two main strands can be distinguished in Bacon's impact on Western philosophical tradition. First, as Antonio Pérez-Ramos observes in his article on the reception of Bacon's philosophy (Chapter 12), his theory of scientific method in general and induction in particular was much commented on in subsequent epistemological debate. Second, and more importantly, Bacon's impact on Western philosophy is to be found in the ideological part of his philosophy – the active ethos with which he infused modern science.

The Continental philosophers of the seventeenth century saw in Bacon an eloquent critic of scholasticism, but it was in England that he had his greatest impact. On the one hand, Bacon's conviction that the advancement of science was an effective means to assuage humankind's sufferings and improve its state found eager response in republican England. But his followers also focused their attention on the institutional aspects of his philosophy. The full translation of these ideas into action, in the founding of the Royal Society after the Restoration of 1660 represents, as Pérez-Ramos points out, Bacon's deification as a philosopher and the final victory of the Baconian project of collaboration, utility, and progress. Another high point in Bacon's fortune occurred in the eighteenth century, when the French *philosophes* revered him as the most important propagandist of science (although they largely ignored the more technical parts of his philosophy). Bacon's methodological precepts received an enthusiastic response from the English epistemologists of the early nineteenth century, but a reaction soon followed, and by the latter part of the century Bacon was ridiculed as an ignorant *Wunderdoktor*, as Justus von Liebig put it in the most extreme formulation.

Perhaps the most obvious consequence of this nineteenth-century denigration, which has continued in some circles to the present day, was the fact that Bacon's more technical philosophy lost much of its relevance. At the same time, however, it is widely acknowledged that his boldly ambitious ideal of the leading role of an operative science in the transformation of the conditions of humankind's life became, soon after his death, a central part of the Western philosophical heritage. And it is not too much to say that there remains today much that Bacon would recognize as part of the program he inaugurated.

NOTES

I am deeply grateful to Erkki Kouri, Graham Rees, Quentin Skinner, and Brian Vickers for their advice and help in preparing this volume. I should also like to thank Graham Rees and Brian Vickers for commenting on an earlier version of this Introduction. I owe particular thanks to Vaughan Hart, Tony Hasler, Steven Huxley, Walter Johnson, M. Grazia Lolla, and Soili Paananen. My research has been funded by the Academy of Finland and Ella and Georg Ehrnrooth's Foundation.

1 E.g., Marwil 1976, pp. 22, 84, 98.
2 See Paolo Rossi's Chapter 1, and Rossi 1984; Pérez-Ramos 1988, pp. 29–31. For correctives of recent bewildering misreadings of Bacon, see Vickers 1991a and Vickers 1992, pp. 499–507.
3 Heltzel 1948.
4 Kocher 1958.
5 For the context of Bacon's education, see Levine 1987, pp. 123–54.
6 "Of Tribute or Giuing that which Is Due," in Frank Burgoyne (ed.), Collotype facsimile & Type Transcript of an Elizabethan Manuscript Preserved at Alnwick Castle, Northumberland (London, 1904), pp. 13–15.
7 Neustadt 1987, pp. 82–97; Martin 1992, pp. 61–71.
8 Neustadt 1987, pp. 107–76.
9 Elsky 1989, pp. 184–208.
10 Box 1989b, pp. 20–1.
11 The introduction to part IV of the Instauratio exists in manuscript, Bibliothèque Nationale, manuscript col. Dupuy no 5.
12 Stephen Jerome, Englands Ivbilee, or Irelands Ioes Io-paean, for King Charles His Welcome (Dvblin, 1625), p. 32.
13 It should be remembered that in Bacon's natural history the term "history" did not have a synchronic meaning as in civil history; it simply referred to a collection of natural phenomena.
14 For a fuller account, see Neustadt 1987, Coquillette 1992, Martin 1992, pp. 106–29, Kocher 1957, and Helgerson 1992, pp. 65–104.
15 Neustadt 1987, pp. 131–4, 79–80; Helgerson 1992, pp. 74–5.
16 Coquillette 1992, pp. 114–15; Neustadt 1987, pp. 208–9.
17 Coquillette 1992, pp. 237–41, 47, 85–6; Neustadt 1987, pp. 130–43.
18 Neustadt 1987, pp. 138–41. See also the recently unearthed manuscript entitled Aphorismi de iure gentium maiore sive de fontibus justiciae et juris, in Neustadt 1987, pp. 247–99.

1 Bacon's idea of science

I HERALD

When we pronounce the word *science* many things come to our minds: the theories and the experiments, the laboratories and places of research, the scientific communities and congresses, the journals and the manuals, the academies and scientific societies, the institutions and the languages of science.

Sometimes, when we speak of science in reference to Bacon or Mersenne or Galilei we are drawn to forget that that which we call science (in the form in which *we* know it) did not exist in the first half of the seventeenth century. The two great historic processes which gave life to *our* science, and which the sociologists have called *institutionalization* and *professionalization* of science, took place between the middle of the seventeenth and the middle of the nineteenth centuries. The question that the historians of philosophical and scientific thought ask themselves (must ask themselves) is the following: what idea or what image of science made those processes possible? On what terrain were they born?

In trying to answer these questions, we cannot refer to the philosophers of science. They have manifested a strong interest in scientific theories and their logical structure and in the methods (for example, in the case of Bacon, for his theory of induction), but tend to take into consideration the already constructed edifices rather than the ways and the techniques of their construction, the already realized styles rather than the emergence of new styles, the already adult individuals rather than the processes of their birth and formation.

When they emerge in history, ideas and social figures also bring with them elements of the past and anticipations of future. Bacon

25

dedicated to the future many of his pages; he listed with great care the rationale on the basis of which the men of his time could derive hope; he compared his undertaking to that of Columbus, and his philosophy to an adventurous voyage on the ocean:

And therefore it is fit that I publish and set forth those conjectures of mine which make hope in this matter reasonable; just as Columbus did, before that wonderful voyage of his across the Atlantic, when he gave the reasons for his conviction that new lands and continents might be discovered besides those which were known before; which reasons, though rejected at first, were afterwards made good by experience, and were the causes and beginnings of great events. (IV, 91)

Bacon assigned himself the task of trumpeter (*bucinator*), the herald, the messenger, not that of combatant: "For I am . . . one perhaps of those of whom Homer speaks: *Hail, heralds, messengers of Jove and men* and such men might go to and fro everywhere unhurt, between the fiercest and bitterest enemies" (IV, 372).

None of the great discoveries which, at the beginnings of the modern era, have modified in depth the knowledge of the natural world (for example: heliocentrism, the principle of inertia, blood circulation) can be traced to Francis Bacon. And yet (notwithstanding the assertions of some of Bacon's "fiercest enemies" of the nineteenth and twentieth centuries) he made a decisive contribution to the birth and affirmation of modern science. Not only by refusing finalism and giving force to the mechanical philosophy, not only by constructing a new encyclopedia of knowledge, but by facing certain decisive themes destined to remain at the center of modernity.

Bacon is one of the constructors – perhaps the greatest – of that which can be called a modern image of science. His discourse on this theme is ample, articulated, full of intellectual force, literarily efficacious, rich in inimitable metaphors. His discourse does not concern only the method of science (everyone knows that he made an important contribution to the discussion on induction). It concerns above all the function of science in human life, the ends and values that must characterize scientific knowledge; it concerns that which today we would call an ethics of scientific research; it concerns, finally, the ways in which this form of knowledge must present itself in comparison to the other forms of cultural life: poetry, history, religion, ethics, politics.

II WHAT SCIENCE MUST NOT BE

An image of science has, in general, descriptive and normative intents. It tells what science *is* and what it *must be*, it makes regulations and imposes prohibitions. On the basis of that image (and there are in the history many different images) boundaries can be drawn between science on the one side and the other forms of knowledge (including the so-called pseudosciences) on the other.

Men – Bacon thought – have a strong desire to know. They are pushed to know for a multiplicity of reasons: natural curiosity, the desire to distract the spirit, the search for fame, the ambition of holding primacy in discussions. Too rarely are they disposed to use the gift of reason for the good of all men

as if there were sought in knowledge a couch, whereupon to rest a searching and restless spirit; or a terrace, for a wandering and variable mind to walk up and down with a fair prospect; or a tower of state, for a proud mind to raise itself upon; or a fort or commanding ground, for strife and contention; or a shop, for profit or sale; and not a rich storehouse, for the glory of the Creator and the relief of man's estate. (III, 294)

Contemplation and action, knowing and intervening must be conjoined more than ever before: in other words, a conjunction similar to that which can occur between Jupiter, the planet of quiet and contemplation, and Saturn, the planet of civil society and action. Knowledge must resemble a bride destined to procreation and happiness. It must not be like either a courtesan in the service of pleasure or a slave who works for the utility of the master (III, 259).

In the philosophical tradition and in the learning of his time Bacon recognizes three wrong kinds of philosophy which correspond to three vices of learning and give rise to three false images of science: *phantastical* or *superstitious* learning, *contentious* or *sophistical* learning and *delicate* learning.

Bacon does not consider only the philosophies, but the entire culture of his time. He finds next to him many forms of knowledge and places them in one of three categories: (1) the *Empirics* (alchemists, magicians, chemists, dyers, artisans in general), who manipulate substances and transform them and are in general bound to forms of knowledge which have some relationships with what today we call the Hermetic tradition; (2) the *Reasoners* or *Philosophers*, who identify all knowledge with altercation and dispute; (3) finally the *Humanists* who identify knowledge with vain affectations and who present a tendency to identify knowledge with words and the beauty of oratory style (III, 282–3).

This tripartition which is present in *The Advancement of Learning* (1605), is substituted by Bacon in the *Novum organum* (1620) by a new one (IV, 63–4). There are now three kinds of false learning: the sophistical, the empirical, the superstitious. The controversy with the tradition of Humanists now appears to Bacon less important and less urgent. In all probability he does not think that all the Empirics were *necessarily* involved with the tradition of magic.

The philosophy of mediaeval Schools is the most emblematic form of the Sophistical type of philosophy which is, in general, the embodiment of a *litigiosa subtilitas* (quarrelsome subtlety) or of a contentious learning. The Schoolmen have had the temerity to incorporate the contentious philosophy of Aristotle into the body of religion; thus favoring the acceptance of consecrated traditional theories and precluding invention and discovery (III, 596).[1]

Like many substances in nature, which are solid, do putrefy, and corrupt into worms, so it is the property of good and solid knowledge to putrefy and dissolve into a number of subtile, idle, unwholesome, and vermiculate questions, which have indeed a kind of quickness and life of spirit, but no soundness of matter or goodness of quality (III, 285). The Reasoners have a sharp and strong wit, abundance of leisure, and small variety of reading. Their wit was shut up in the cells of a few authors as their persons were shut up in the cells of monasteries and colleges. They knew little history either of nature or time. Out of no great quantity of matter and infinite agitation of wit, they spin out unto us those laborious webs of learning which are extant in their books (III, 285). The Scholastic method is the following: to frame objections upon every particular assertion, and solutions to these objections, which solutions are for the most part not confutations, but distinctions. On the contrary, the strength of all sciences is, as the strength of the old man's faggot, in the bond (III, 286).[2]

In this kind of philosophy man's mind works upon itself. The philosophy of Reasoners, who exert their brains in a vacuum, is a purely intellectual game. If the Scholastics had possessed, in addition to their inexhaustible thirst for truth and their incessant spiritual agitation, a variety and universality of reading and contemplation, they might have contributed considerably to the advancement of learning (III, 287).[3]

The empirical kind of philosophy gives birth to opinions more deformed or monstrous than the sophistical type. It has its foundations in the narrowness and darkness of a few experiments. To those who are daily busied with these experiments and have infected their imagination with them, such a philosophy seems probable and all but certain; to all men incredible and vain (IV, 65). The manner of making experiments which men now use – Bacon writes after few pages – is blind and stupid. Wandering and straying as they do with no settled course and taking counsel only from things as they fall out, they fetch a wide circuit and meet with many matters, but make little progress, and sometimes are full of hope, sometimes distracted (IV, 70–1).

The mechanics, being by no means interested in the investigations of truth, rise their minds and stretch out their hands only for those things which bear upon their particular work (IV, 95). Bacon's protest is twofold: against the inadequacy of the operations of Empirics and against the arbitrary character of the doctrine of the Dogmatists. The Empirics are like ants who only collect and use. The Reasoners resemble spiders who make cobwebs out of their own substance. The true *opificium* of philosophy neither relies solely or chiefly on the powers of mind, nor takes material from natural history or mechanical experiments and stores it in the memory whole, as it finds it. Like bees, the true philosophy takes a middle course: it gathers its material from the flowers of garden and the field, but transforms and digests it by a power of its own (IV, 92–3; cf. III, 616).

Bacon thinks that the twin attitudes (the Empirical and the Rational or Philosophical) have not up to now been properly mingled and combined (III, 616).[4] The two could be joined not only by mutual hatred but in a closer and holier union.[5] Bacon thinks that his *Instauratio* has established forever a true and lawful marriage between the empirical and rational faculty, the unkind and ill-starred divorce and separation of which has thrown into confusion all the affairs of the human family (IV, 19). What is important is to open a middle way between experience and theorizing (*via media inter experientiam et dogmata*) and in this way to rescue the human mind from the obscurity of tradition, the giddy whirl of arguments, the waves and roundabout ways of experience (III, 573).[6]

The middle way, as a remedy to the unkind divorce and separation, is a marriage. This marriage is not a mere addition, and *sublates* the original position. Compared to ants and spiders, bees are undoubtedly something entirely new. They have the diligent industry of ants, but they do not only collect material; they produce honey. Bees have the constancy of spiders and give out a substance from their own bodies. But the honey they give out is the result of transformation and digestion.

In opposition to the opinion expressed in this century by Karl Popper and all his followers (until Peter Urbach's book published in 1987), the *digestion* of experience is a basic notion in Bacon's philosophy: experience, according to him, must be duly ordered and digested, not clumsy or erratic (I, 190; IV, 81).

The superstitious kind of philosophy gives rise to vain imaginations, that is to the pseudosciences, like astrology, natural magic, alchemy which have "better intelligence and confederacy with the imagination of man than with his reason" (III, 289). The natural magic "is as far differing in truth of nature from such a knowledge as we require, as the story of King Arthur of Britain, or Hugo of Bordeaux, and such like imaginary heroes, differs from Caesar's Commentaries in truth of story" (IV, 367). Bacon argues fiercely against the Hermetic image of the scholar as an *enlightened* man, against the Hermetic notion of learning leading to results that must be kept secret and withheld from the profanes, against a mentality that is completely dominated by what is extraordinary, astonishing, secret. When in the midst of innumerable falsities, magic does accomplish something – he writes in the *Redargutio philosophiarum* and in the *Novum organum* – then it does so not in the service of mankind, but for the sake of novelty, or to arouse admiration for the figure of the scholar.

I wrote many years ago about the condemning of magic and also about the heritage of magic in Bacon's philosophy.[7] But I cannot agree with Frances Yates's opinion according to which Bacon presented in a more up-to-date language aims and values that had been characteristic of the Hermetic tradition.[8] According to Bacon, magic and alchemy could never be counted as sciences precisely because of the excessive importance they attach to the authority of individuals and their over-hasty judgments. The *rules* contained in the procedures of magic and alchemy can never reach the level of a *method* because their codifiable character can never be established. They will always remain secret rules, formulated in a symbolic language that has nothing to do with the symbolism of modern chemistry, but which refers, through a series of analogies and correspondences, to the Whole, to Universal Spirit, to God. The alchemist cannot codify his method, nor make it a *public* knowledge, available for others and to be used by others. He proceeds on the basis of few texts, that are held to be infallible. His over-large and over-ardent hopes go hand in hand with a continual state of self-accusation for he ends by blaming himself for the errors into which he is led by the texts held to be infallible (IV, 84).

III WHAT SCIENCE MUST BE

Bacon condemned magic and alchemy on ethical grounds. He accused them of imposture and of megalomania. He refuted their non-participatory method and their intentional unintelligibility, their attempt to replace human sweat by a few drops of elixir. But he borrows from the magico-alchemical tradition the idea that man can attempt to make himself the master of nature. Bacon understands knowledge not as contemplation or recognition, but as a *venatio*, a hunt, an exploration of unknown lands, a discovery of the unknown. Nature can be transformed from its foundations. Bacon's definition of man as "the servant and interpreter of Nature" (IV, 47) is the same definition we find in the magico-alchemical tradition, for instance in the texts of Cornelius Agrippa von Nettesheim.

But for all the exponents of magic and alchemistic culture, the texts of ancient wisdom take the form of sacred texts which include secrets that only a few men can decipher. The truth is hidden in the past and in the profound. Like when dealing with sacred texts, it is necessary continuously to go *beyond the letter*, in search of a message which is more and more hidden. The secret message expresses a Truth which is at the Origins and which is always the same.

In the Hermetic tradition, as in the tradition of Platonism, the natural world is conceived as the image or living manifestation of God. Understanding nature can reveal the presence in the world of

divine ideas and archetypes. Bacon's rejection of any natural philosophy founded on allegorical interpretations of Scriptures meant a
withdrawal from exemplarism and symbolism, both common features of mediaeval philosophy and still flourishing in the seventeenth century. As all works – says Bacon – show the power and
ability of their maker, but not his image, so God's work "do shew
the omnipotency and wisdom of the maker, but not his image" (III,
350). The distinction between the will and power of God, so fully
and subtly present in Baconian texts, is very important. "The heavens declare the glory of God, and the firmament showeth his hand-
works": this verse from the Psalms (18,2) is quoted by Bacon several
times. The image of the world, immediately after the Word, is a sign
of the divine wisdom and power, and yet the Scriptures do not call
the world "the image of God," but regard it only as "the work of his
hands," neither do they speak of any image of God other than man.
Theology is concerned with knowing the book of the word of God;
natural philosophy studies the book of God's works. The book of
Scripture reveals the will of God, the book of nature, his power. The
study of nature has nothing to say about God's essence or his will
(IV, 340–3).

Bacon proposed to the European culture an alternative view of
science. For him science had a public, democratic, and collaborative
character, individual efforts contributing to its general success. In
science, as Bacon conceives it, truly effective results (not the illusory achievements of magicians and alchemists) can be attained
only through collaboration among researchers, circulation of results,
and clarity of language. Scientific understanding is not an individual
undertaking. The extension of man's power over nature is never the
work of a single investigator who keeps his results secret, but is the
fruit of an organized community financed by the state or by public
bodies. Every reform of learning is always a reform also of cultural
institutions and universities.

Not only a new image of science, but also a new portrait of the
"natural philosopher" took shape in Bacon's writings. This portrait
differed both from that of the ancient philosopher or sage and from the
image of the saint, the monk, the university professor, the courtier,
the perfect prince, the magus. The values and the ends theorized for
the composite groups of intellectuals and artisans who contributed in
the early seventeenth century to the development of science were

different from the goals of individual sanctity or literary immortality and from the aims of an exceptional and "demonic" personality.

A chaste patience, a natural modesty, grave and composed manners, a smiling pity are the characteristics of the man of science in Bacon's portrait of him. In the *Redargutio philosophiarum* Bacon wrote:

Then he told me that in Paris a friend had taken him along and introduced him to a gathering, 'the sight of which', he said, 'would rejoice your eyes. It was the happiest experience of my life'. There were some fifty men there, all of mature years, not a young man among them, all bearing the stamp of dignity and probity. . . . At his entry they were chatting easily among themselves but sitting in rows as if expecting somebody. Not long after there entered to them a man of peaceful and serene air, save that his face had become habituated to the expression of pity . . . he took his seat, not on a platform or pulpit, but on level with the rest and delivered the following address . . . (III, 559)[9]

Bacon's portrait doubtless resembles Galileo or Einstein more than it does the turbulent Paracelsus or the unquiet and skittish Cornelius Agrippa. The titanic bearing of the Renaissance magus is now supplanted by a classical composure similar to that of the "conversations" of the earliest Humanists. Also in Galileo's *Dialogo* and in Descartes's *Recherche de la vérité* we find the same familiar tone and style of conversation in which (Descartes wrote) "several friends, frankly and without ceremony, disclose the best of their thoughts to each other."[10] But there is besides, in Bacon, the quiet confidence that comes from knowing the new powers made available to man by technology and collaboration.

The new kind of learning, for which Bacon is searching, must get away from touches of genius, arbitrary conclusions, chance, hasty summaries. The emphasis laid by Bacon on the social factor in scientific research and in determining its ends, places his philosophy on a radically different plane from that of the followers of Hermetic tradition. Bacon's insistence on the organizational and institutional aspects of science stemmed from his own definition of learning, which is often hindered by "the nature of the society and the policies of the state":

That there is no composition of estate or society, nor order or quality of persons, which have not some points of contrariety towards true knowledge.

That monarchies incline wits to profit and pleasure, and commonwealths to glory and vanity. That the universities incline wits to sophistry and affectations, cloisters to fables and unprofitable subtilty, study at large to variety; and that it is hard to say, whether mixture of contemplations with an active life, or retiring wholly to contemplations, do disable and hinder the mind more (III, 252).

In the only piece of autobiography and self-analysis in which Bacon indulged (*De interpretatione naturae proemium*, III, 518–20), he says that the discovery of new arts for the bettering of human life is a better ambition than politics, but he allowed himself to be deflected into politics for family and patriotic reasons and because he hoped that "if I rose to any place of honour in the state, I should have a larger command of industry and ability to help me in my work" (III, 519).[11] Like no other philosophers of his time, Bacon vividly sees that scientific enterprise is a collective effort that concerns all society and requires institutions specific to it. The relation between science and politics, in spite of his personal psychological doubts and incertitudes, has for him a structural character. The solution he offers in the *New Atlantis* was a clear, firm *separation*. The men of science, in the New Atlantis, lived in solitude. Their place reminds us of a university campus cut off from the daily concerns of common mortals. But there is something else: the scientists of the New Atlantis held meetings to decide which of the discoveries that had been made should be communicated to the public at large and which should not. Some of the discoveries that they decided to keep secret were revealed to the state; others were kept hidden from political power. On the uses that might be made of scientific and technological discoveries he was no optimist. The wise men who decided to keep some of their dangerous discoveries to themselves did not live in the society of Elizabethan England nor in our corrupt world, but within the imaginary civilization of the New Atlantis, an extremely peaceful and tolerant society.

Bacon's major claim for his science was that it would be a *scientia operativa* (IV, 22, 32) that is, productive of works. What Bacon vigorously refused and what made traditional philosophy appear to him like an infertile desert was the fact that from Socrates to Bernardino Telesio a disjunction had been introduced between knowledge and operation, theories and experiments, theory and practice, truth and utility. One of the "topical" aspects of Bacon's philosophy is the attempt he made to show how these oppositions came about and were reinforced in the history of Western civilization.

In the *Partis instaurationis secundae delineatio* (III, 549), in the *Cogitata et visa* (III, 612), and later in the *Novum organum* (IV, 110), Bacon replies to a very foreseeable objection which could easily be raised from the viewpoint of traditional philosophy:

It will be thought, no doubt, that the goal and mark of knowledge which I myself set up (the very point which I object to in others) is not the true or the best; for that the contemplation of truth is a thing worthier and loftier than all the utility and magnitude of works; and that this long and anxious dwelling with experience and matter and the fluctuations of individual things, drags down the mind to earth, or rather sinks it to a very Tartarus of turmoil and confusion; removing and withdrawing it from the serene tranquillity of abstract wisdom, a condition far more heavenly. (IV, 110)

Those who have talked about "Baconian utilitarianism" have often based their arguments precisely on the questions to which Bacon earnestly endeavored to give a reply. The answers given by Bacon preclude even the possibility that his position could be mistaken as "utilitarian." In the *Cogitata et visa* he wrote:

It may be that there are some on whose ear my frequent and honourable mention of practical activities makes a harsh and unpleasing sound because they are wholly given over in love and reverence to contemplation. Let them bethink themselves that they are the enemies of their own desires. For in nature practical results are not only the means to improve well-being but the guarantee of truth. The rule of religion, that a man should show his faith by his works, holds good in natural philosophy too. Science also must be known by works. It is by the witness of works, rather than by logic or even observation [*ex argumentatione aut etiam e sensu*], that truth is revealed and established. Whence it follows that the improvement of man's mind and the improvement of his lot are one and the same thing. (III, 612)[12]

So Bacon accepts as entirely legitimate the question about the relation between contemplation and utility. But the question does not constitute an objection because the value of theories is wholly realized into the reform of knowledge.

The aphorism 124 of the first book of the *Novum organum* is very important, and must be extensively quoted:

Now to this I readily assent; and indeed this which they point at as so much to be preferred [the contemplation of truth] is the very thing of all others which I am about. For I am building in the human understanding a true model of the world, such as it is in fact, not such as a man's own reason would have it to be; a thing which cannot be done without a very diligent dissection and anatomy of the world. But I say that those foolish and apish images of worlds which the fancies of men have created in philosophical systems, must be utterly scattered to the winds. Be it known then how vast a difference there is (as I said above) between the Idols of the human mind and the Ideas of the divine. The former are nothing more than arbitrary abstractions [*abstractiones ad placitum*]; the latter are the creator's own stamp upon creation [*vera signacula Creatoris super creaturas*], impressed and defined in matter by true and exquisite lines. Truth therefore and utility are here the very same things: and works themselves are of greater value as pledges of truth than as contributing to the comforts of life [*atque ipsissimae res sunt, in hoc genere, veritas et utilitas: atque opera ipsa pluris facienda sunt, quatenus sunt veritatis pignora, quam propter vitae commoda*]. (IV, 110)

Bacon knew Latin well enough to use *idem* correctly in place of *ipse*. The term *ipsissimus*, much used in Scholastic terminology, recurs in other passages of the *Novum organum* with a precise technical meaning. The translation "truth and utility are the very same things," broadly diffused among English and American scholars,[13] is undoubtedly wrong, as I demonstrated in 1962.[14] The "Ideas of the divine," as we can read in the *Novum organum*, are "the true signatures and marks set upon the works of creation as they are found in nature" (IV, 51). The expression *ipsissimae res* and the term *ipsissimus* were used by Bacon in reference to the "objective reality of the things" or to "things in their reality," or simply to "essence" (in the particular meaning that Bacon gives to this term). In the aphorism 20 of the second book of the *Novum organum* heat is considered not in relation to the man (*ex analogia hominis*) but in relation to the universe (*ex analogia universi*). According to Bacon's view, heat is a species of genus "motion." It is not to be thought that heat generates motion or is generated by it; rather, the very essence of heat, or the substantial self of heat, is motion and nothing else (*ipsissimus calor sive quid ipsum caloris motus et nihil aliud est*).

The meaning of that Baconian statement can be summed up as follows: things as they really are, considered not from the viewpoint of appearance but from that of existence, not in relation to man but in relation to the universe, offer conjointly truth and utility. A literal, correct translation is: "the very things themselves are, in this kind, both truth and utility."

From this point of view, the question as to whether scientific truth depends on the procedures employed to affirm them, or on their fruitfulness in practice, is a meaningless dilemma: a scientific truth is always fruitful and this fruitfulness depends precisely and exclusively on its characteristic of full truth: "The chain of causes cannot by any force be loosed or broken, nor can nature be commanded except by being obeyed. And so those twin objects, human Knowledge and human Power, do really meet in one; and it is from ignorance of causes that operation fails" (IV, 32).

IV HOW SCIENCE GROWS

All of Bacon's work calls for a revolutionary reform which was supported by a conviction of radical changes occurring in European history and by the belief that a new epoch was about to be born. These changes *do not depend on philosophy* and do not derive from the philosophical schools or sects. They are connected with a series of material factors which have modified man's way of life. The course of history, according to Bacon, was completely changed by mechanical inventions, oceanic voyages, geographic discoveries. A new world requires a new kind of philosophy: "It would be disgraceful if, while the regions of the material globe, – that is, of the earth, of the sea, and of the stars, – have been in our times laid widely open and revealed, the intellectual globe should remain shut up within the narrow limits of old discoveries" (IV, 82). Since the conditions of time are ripe, Bacon presents his own work as a masculine child of the time (*Temporis partus masculus*) rather than of the mind of a genius.

Three great inventions, the compass, the printing press, and gunpowder, have changed the world of human space, the world of communication, the world of politics. No empire, no philosophical sect, no star has exerted greater power in human affairs. For two thousand years philosophy and the intellectual sciences "stand like statues, worshipped and celebrated, but not moved or advanced"

(IV, 14). They "did and remain almost in the same condition; receiving no noticeable increase, but on the contrary, thriving most under their first founder, and then declining" (IV, 74). "Whereas in the mechanical arts, which are founded on nature and the light of experience, we see the contrary happen, for these (as long as they are popular) are continually thriving and growing, as having in them a breath of life; at first rude, then convenient, afterwards adorned, and at all times advancing." In the mechanical arts "many wits and industries have contributed in one," in the liberal arts and sciences "many wits and industries have been spent about the wit of some one" (IV, 74–5).

Several typical categories of technical knowledge – collaboration, progressiveness, perfectibility, and invention – became categories to which Bacon attributed a universal value. Taking the mechanical arts as a *model for culture*, it is then possible to bring to birth a type of learning which, unlike the ancient kind, is capable of progress. The Baconian revaluation of technology and the mechanical arts entailed the rejection of that conception of science which had remained alive for centuries: an "Aristotelian" science which can be born only when the necessities of life have already been procured and which then develops into a disinterested contemplation of truth. Knowing is for Bacon a kind of making.[15] Although the "baroque phrase" that Antonio Pérez-Ramos wrongfully ascribes to me ("a kind of making that involves making")[16] was written by Rodolfo Mondolfo and not by me (as clearly comes out from my own text),[17] I entirely agree with Pérez-Ramos's well-grounded and admirable portrait of Bacon as an exponent of the "Maker's knowledge tradition: a tradition which postulates an intimate relationship between objects of cognition and objects of construction, and regards knowing as a kind of making or as a capacity to make (*verum factum*)."[18]

But Bacon never thought of reducing science to technology and cannot be interpreted as a philosopher of "industrial revolution."[19] The *works* and the *opera* do not mean, in Bacon's philosophy, "artefacts or tools" or "technical achievements" like gunpowder or the printing press. Bacon's science is directed toward *opera* not in the sense of making artefacts, but in searching for "Nature *effects*, phenomena such as heat, colour, or motion."[20]

As we have seen, the Lord Chancellor drove home a double critique, for which he fought (so to speak) "on two fronts": against the inadequacies of the work of *Empirics* and the arbitrariness of the doctrines of the *Rationales*. The methods, the procedures, the language of mechanicians and artisans have grown outside the world of universities, in the communities of the engineers and architects and skilled artisans and makers of machines and instruments. These procedures, these operations must become subject matter of reflection and study. Natural History is conceived by Bacon not only of "nature free and at large," but much more

of nature under constraint and vexed; that is to say, when by art and the hand of man she is forced out of her natural state, and squeezed and moulded. Therefore I set down at length all experiments of the mechanical arts, of the operative part of the liberal arts, of many crafts which have not yet grown into arts properly so called. (IV, 29)

Only in this way the *experientia erratica* of the mechanics, the daily labors of those who transform nature by their hands can be rescued from chance and pure empiricism.

The so-called faith in progress (as we find it in Condorcet, Turgot, Herbert Spencer, Auguste Comte) was principally supported by three beliefs: (1) there is a law in history that tends, through gradations, or phases or steps, toward the perfection and the happiness of the human race; (2) such a process of perfecting is generally identified with the development and growth of scientific knowledge; (3) science and technology are the principal source of moral and political progress and also constitute the confirmation of such progress.

We continue to project these three convictions into the past and to attribute the nineteenth-century idea of progress to all the authors who have variously written about the growth and advancement of learning. The image of progress (and of scientific progress) present in Europe between the age of Giordano Bruno and that of Isaac Newton has characteristics quite different from those imagined by philosophers who love great "epochal" classifications. I know of no author who, between the sixteenth and early eighteenth centuries, would have been willing to subscribe to the three affirmations that I have now listed.

We can begin with the so-called exaltation of technology. Many critics of Bacon's enthusiasm for the technology and for the industrial society cannot have read his interpretation of the myth of *Daedalus sive mechanicus* in the *De sapientia veterum*. Daedalus was an abominable man of the greatest genius (vir ingeniosissimus sed execrabilis).

He . . . supplied the machine which enabled Pasiphae to satisfy her passion for the bull; so that the unhappy and infamous birth of the monster Minotaurus . . . was owing to the wicked industry and pernicious genius of this man. Then to conceal the first mischief he added another, and for the security of this pest devised and constructed the Labyrinth; a work wicked in its end and destination, but in respect of art and contrivance excellent and admirable. Afterwards again, that his fame might not rest on bad arts only, and that he might be sought to for remedies as well as instruments of evil, he became the author likewise of that ingenious device of the clue, by which the mazes of the labyrinth should be retraced. . . . Certainly human life is much indebted to them [mechanical arts], for very many things which concern both the furniture of religion and the ornament of state and the culture of life in general, are drawn from their store. And yet out of the same fountain come instruments of lust, and also instruments of death. (VI, 734–5)

I think that in the whole history of philosophy it is very difficult to find a text so efficacious in underlining the "ambiguous" character of technology.

Francis Bacon, as everyone knows, firmly believed in the advancement of learning, but his belief has nothing to do with a "progressive" philosophy of history. In the Redargutio philosophiarum and in The Advancement of Learning, Bacon places the "pre-Socratic" philosophy (particularly that of Democritus) at a level superior to that of Aristotle, the destroyer of philosophical pluralism. In that very ancient philosophy, where many of his contemporaries saw only sparse fragments, Bacon saw a solidity of thought that, precisely because of its extraordinarily high quality, had sunk in the depths of time.

In the Praefatio to the Novum organum we can read the general affirmation according to which "Time is like a river, which has brought down to us things light and puffed up, while those which are weighty and solid have sunk" (IV, 15).

In the De sapientia veterum Bacon presented a general view on the course of history. A cyclical vision of the flourishing and decadence of states and political bodies becomes the main point of the consideration of historical events. There is present the image of the depraved conditions of man's nature that opens, in the intervals, ages of desolation. The theme of the vicissitudes of things, to which Bacon was to dedicate one of his essays, is also present:

But howsoever the works of wisdom are among human things the most excellent, yet they too have their period and closes. For so it is that after kingdoms and commonwealths have flourished for a time, there arise perturbations and seditions and wars; amid the uproars of which, first the laws are put to silence, and then men return to the depraved conditions of their nature, and desolation is seen in the fields and cities. And if such troubles last, it is not long before letters also and philosophy are so torn in pieces that no traces of them can be found but a few fragments, scattered here and there like planks from a shipwreck; and then a season of barbarism sets in, the waters of Helicon being sunk under the ground, until, according to the appointed vicissitude of things, they break out and issue forth again, perhaps among other nations, and not in the places where they were before. (VI, 722)

In the *Cogitata et visa* and in the *Novum organum* Bacon says that out of the five and twenty centuries over which the memory and learning of men extends

you can hardly pick out six that were fertile in sciences or favourable to their development. In times no less than in regions there are wastes and deserts. For only three revolutions and periods of learning can properly be reckoned; one among the Greeks, the second among the Romans, and the last among us, that is to say, the nations of Western Europe. (IV, 77)

As Bernard Cohen has shown, Bacon uses the term *revolution* in astronomical meaning, in every way traditional, of a motion that continually repeats itself.[21] He does not think *revolution* as a traumatic event that generates new situations. As in many other passages, a "marine" image completely gives us the sense of Bacon's perspective: the ebb and flow of ocean, which motion is placed alongside the term revolution: "For wise and serious men [suppose] . . . that in the revolution of time and of the ages of the world the sciences have their ebbs and flows; that at one season they grow and flourish, at another wither and decay, yet in such sort that when they have reached a certain point and condition they can advance no further" (IV, 90).

Bacon, who attributes this thesis to "wise and serious men," does not find it acceptable. It is not true that one cannot go further. Bacon does not believe that there is no reason for hope. He knows very well that he who reveals his hopes is immediately judged to be powerless and immature. The enthusiasm for the undertaking should not brake the severity of judgments. We must leave aside "the light winds of hope" and probe the reasons that authorize us to nourish it. To avoid sin of ingenuity, it is opportune to adopt "that political wisdom that is diffident in principle and always expect the worst in human doings." The discourse on the reasons to hope, the so-called *ostensio spei*, is a part which is not secondary to the preparation of minds and to the Great Instauration. Hurried readers often forget this. But from the middle of aphorism 92, through aphorism 114, the text of the first book of the *Novum organum* is entirely dedicated to numbering the twenty-one reasons that authorized us to nourish "reasonable hopes" in a difficult and uncertain future. Without the *ostensio spei*, the great reform would serve only to sadden human beings, to harden them to an ever lower and more vile opinion than they at the present have (IV, 90–1).

It has always been clear to all interpreters, since the seventeenth century, that Bacon's philosophy has something to do with the theme of advancement of learning and with the history of the idea of progress. Our times, he frequently emphasizes, have the advantage of making use of almost two thousand years of events, of experience, and of knowledge of the once unknown two-thirds of the surface of the Earth (III, 564). But, like that of many great moderns, Bacon's philosophy cannot be easily outlined. In the thought of Bacon whom many have considered to be the advocate of technological progress, the enthusiastic apostle of industrial civilization, strong themes arise that are close to the tradition of Lucretius and Machiavelli: the wheel of time and the river of time, the "revolutions" and the ebb and flow of time, its flowering and its "desolate tracts," the ages propitious to learning and those which are barren, the shipwrecks of cultures and the planks of the shipwrecks that have reached our shores, the possible return of barbarism. Only by referring to this context can we understand what Bacon said about the advancement of learning and about the growth of the sciences.

The Baconian idea of the *advancement* does not presuppose a "progressive" view of history, but it expresses a dimension that had become an essential trait of modern science. Forgetting the past and going beyond all that has been said in the past are positive values for scientific knowledge. Science is an exploration of unknown lands and is like a hunt. The quarry is in the future. The light of nature lay ahead. Behind there is the darkness of the past. Scholars' interests should be turned toward the future, not to the past. What remains to be done is more important that what had been done: *"Nec refert quid factum fuerit. Illud videndum quid fieri potest"* (III, 535).

V DENIGRATIONS

During our century two different negative appraisals centered on Bacon's philosophy. According to some neopositivists and many Popperian epistemologists, Francis Bacon was a model or a champion of what science has never been and will never be: a kind of knowledge obtained by observation, a process of accumulation of data, an illusory attempt to free the human mind from theories and presuppositions. "The inductivist logic of discovery" – wrote Imre Lakatos – "is the Baconian doctrine according to which a discovery is scientific only if it is guided by facts and not misguided by theories."[22]

According to Max Horkheimer, Theodor Adorno, and other representatives of the Frankfurt School, Francis Bacon was precisely the opposite – the symbol of what science has been up until now and should no longer be: the impious will to dominate nature and tyrannize mankind. The old thesis of Bacon as a "vulgarly utilitarian," proposed by reactionary nineteenth-century thought, was thus restored in this century, in much subtler form, by the proponents of the so-called critical theory of society. Taking up again the themes of Edmund Husserl's criticism of Galileo in the *Krisis*, Adorno and Horkheimer in the *Dialektik der Aufklärung* (1942) (and Herbert Marcuse about twenty years later) saw in Bacon the typical *animus* of modern science. Modern science, as Martin Heidegger theorized in the *Holzwege*, is indistinguishable from technology and Francis Bacon is the symbol of this nefarious identification. It is the scientific and technological enthusiasm of the Lord Chancellor that leads to materialism, the mercantilization of culture, to modern industrial society, which is the realm of alienation and conformism, of the standardization and destruction of all human values. "The infertile happiness of knowledge" – Horkheimer and Adorno wrote – "is lascivious according to Bacon as according to Luther. Not that kind of satisfaction that men call truth is important, but only the operation, the successful procedure."[23]

According to the philosophers of our century who extolled scientific knowledge against the nonsensical propositions of metaphysicians, Bacon has nothing to do with science. According to the Continental philosophers who criticized or blamed scientific knowledge for its many sins, Bacon is the very *essence* of science. Being at disagreement over every philosophical problem, the two philosophical parties (who respectively dominate the Anglo-American and Continental philosophy) completely agree on rejecting Bacon's idea of science and Bacon's philosophy but for completely opposite reasons.

Once again, Bacon was reduced to a *symbol*. The "plumb and the weight" of the texts was avoided. "So must we likewise from experience of every kind first endeavour to discover true causes and axioms; and seek for experiments of Light, not for experiments of Fruit" (IV, 71). Bacon's precise distinction between "experiment of light" (yielding valuable information) and "experiments of fruit" (yielding immediate profit) was disregarded. So, too, were ignored the many pages Bacon wrote against the utilitarian desire of immediate results and the foolish habit of abandoning the natural course of scientific enquiry turning aside, like Atalanta, after profit and commodity (VI, 744). "Knowledge that tendeth but to satisfaction is but a courtesan, which is for pleasure and not for fruit or generation. And knowledge that tendeth to profit or profession or glory is but the golden ball thrown before Atalanta, which while she goeth aside and stoopeth to take up she hindereth the race" (III, 222).

As Mary B. Hesse pointed out, "it was a favourite pastime in the nineteenth century to criticize Bacon for not being a Galileo or a Newton."[24] And as Brian Vickers shows in an admirable essay,[25] this kind of pastime continues to be practiced in our century. After the second world war, L. C. Knights found Bacon responsible for the rise of "scientific materialism" and industrial civilization.[26] In more recent years Jonathan Marwil wrote about Bacon's ineptitude and his "failure as a scientist,"[27] Michael Hattaway presented Bacon as "essentially a conservative thinker,"[28] Charles Whitney denied any claim to originality in Bacon's philosophy;[29] Mary Slaughter[30] and R. E. Larsen[31] transformed Bacon into an Aristotelian, Brian Copenhaver[32] into a follower of Ficino's magic. After about thirty years Peter Urbach[33] puts an end to the imaginary Bacon which was invented by Popper and Popperian epistemologists. However, having the tendency to take the community of epistemologists for the whole scholarly community, Urbach holds the Popperian interpretation as a *standard interpretation* ("standard" for what, we are tempted to ask) and does not care to compare this interpretation with other comments, articles, or books published outside the parochial community of English-speaking epistemologists, during the fashion of such interpretation.

General philosophers and epistemologists do not busy themselves very much with the textual analysis of the writings of the past. The "seventeenth century specialists" (as Brian Vickers pointed out, connecting the *works* of Bacon with the ancient and humanistic ideal of the *vita activa*) "all too often do not enquire what happened before 1600."[34]

Perhaps Francis Bacon was right: it is impossible to eradicate all the idols from men's minds (IV, 27). Among the idols we have so far been unable to eradicate are undoubtedly the following: the propensity not to read the original (particularly Latin) texts; the tendency to reduce the philosophies of the past to some seemingly brilliant slogans; the construction on the basis of these of mythical philosophical portraits.

NOTES

1 Translation by Farrington 1964, p. 78.
2 Translation by Farrington 1964, p. 118.
3 Cf. Rossi 1968, pp. 53–63.
4 Translation by Farrington 1964, p. 97.
5 Farrington 1964, p. 98.
6 Farrington 1964, p. 120, revised translation.
7 Rossi 1968, pp. 11–35.
8 Yates 1984, pp. 60–6, 237. Cf. Rossi 1975.
9 Translation by Farrington 1964, pp. 104–5.
10 *Oeuvres de Descartes*, ed. Ch. Adam et P. Tannery, 11 vols. (Paris, 1897–1913), X, p. 498.
11 Translation by Farrington 1964, p. 31.
12 Translation by Farrington 1964, p. 93.
13 Cf. Jardine 1974a, p. 115; Webster 1975, pp. 75, 337; Hacking 1983, p. 242; Cohen 1985, pp. 85, 150; Pérez-Ramos 1988, p. 136.
14 Rossi 1970, pp. 157–60. Italian edition was published by Feltrinelli in 1962.
15 Rossi 1970, pp. 136–45.

16 Pérez-Ramos 1988, p. 156.
17 Rossi 1970, p. 148.
18 Pérez-Ramos 1988, pp. 48–62; 148, 150–6, and see his Chapter 4.
19 Farrington 1949.
20 Pérez-Ramos 1988, p. 142.
21 Cohen 1985, pp. 500–5.
22 Lakatos 1974, p. 259.
23 Horkheimer and Adorno 1972, p. 242.
24 Hesse 1964, p. 149.
25 Vickers 1992.
26 Knights 1946, pp. 92–111.
27 Marwil 1976, pp. 138, 140.
28 Hattaway 1978, p. 184.
29 Whitney 1986, pp. 10–11, 88, 121–2, 154.
30 Slaughter 1982, p. 94 and passim.
31 Larsen 1962.
32 Copenhaver 1988b, pp. 298–9.
33 Urbach 1987.
34 Vickers 1984b, p. 307. Cf. Rossi 1984.

2 Bacon's classification of knowledge

I INTRODUCTION

Francis Bacon set forth his idea for reforming the entire realm of knowledge in *The Proficience and Advancement of Learning Divine and Human* (first published in 1605), which he offered as a "fixed memorial" and "immortal monument" to the magnificence of James I (III, 261–4). It was divided into two books, the first dealing with the merit of augmenting learning, and the second with mapping out parts of knowledge, indicating which parts were extant, absent, or in need of revision in order to facilitate the advancement of learning explained in the first book. It is in the second book that we find Bacon's classification of knowledge. He revised parts of it in 1612 (*Description of the Intellectual Globe* V, 503–44), and further in 1623, when he translated *The Advancement of Learning* into Latin as the *De dignitate et augmentis scientiarum* (*The Dignity and Advancement of Learning*). Bacon now reviewed the entire scope of learning in eight books.

The main aim of this chapter is to explain how and why Bacon classified knowledge in the way that he did. Some of the realignments, renamings, and revisions Bacon made between *The Advancement of Learning* and the *De augmentis* have been noted insofar as they seemed germane for this purpose.[1] As Bacon himself stressed, his classification, however, was not intended merely to establish separate and independent branches of knowledge, but it should rather be considered as "veins and lines" running across a sphere. The realm of knowledge as a whole needed to be kept in sight (III, 366f.). For Bacon, all sciences were, in fact, closely tied to each other (IV, 79). It will therefore be equally important to consider how the

47

branches of knowledge are related to each other and what the kinds of knowledge, classified as such, amount to, as it will be necessary to understand what each branch was assigned to investigate. Bacon also claimed that his classification of knowledge was different from previous ones and necessarily so because he took the realm of knowledge to be much larger than what traditional classification schemes were based on – there were "waste lands" that needed to be cultivated (IV, 23). Compared to previous kinds of classification of knowledge, as I shall be arguing, Bacon's ordering and the scope of knowledge were indeed quite different, most significantly in the goal that his knowledge thus classified was to achieve. For the sake of comparison, I shall begin with a brief summary of some schemes of knowledge preceding that of Bacon.

II CLASSIFICATION OF KNOWLEDGE BEFORE BACON

In the *Posterior Analytics*, Aristotle understood *scientia* as knowledge of necessary causes. For him, demonstration depended on an axiom (not demonstrable within that science) which is true, immediate, more familiar than, prior to, and explanatory of the conclusion.[2] The predicates of demonstrative propositions need to be true of every instance of the subject (e.g., "animal" holds of every man); the predicate belongs to the subject essentially (e.g., "straight" belongs to line essentially, but "musical" belongs to animal incidentally); and the predicate belongs to the subject generally (e.g., summing to two right angles is universal to a triangle as triangle, but does not hold universally for any other kind of figure which contains a wider range of members, i.e., some, but not all, isosceles figures have angles equal to two right angles).[3] Each science thus establishes what the particular *kind* of being is which it is investigating, and then makes inferences concerning other properties of its *kind*.[4] Aristotle's concept of *scientia* thus necessarily implied the independence among different branches of *scientia*: each treats a different *kind* (genus) of objects. Thus Aristotle considered demonstration in general as not transferable from one *scientia* to another.[5]

An exception to this independence and separation amongst the Aristotelian *scientia* is what was called "subalternation" in the Latin West. Aristotle had given the example of geometry and optics; arithmetic and harmonics. One science is "under" another when the former deals with the "fact" of knowledge (*quia*) and the reason why that "fact" is the way that it is (*propter quid*) belongs to the latter science. The former *scientia* is "subalternated" to the latter.[6] Since the subalternated *scientia* takes its "fact" from the external world, but its theoretical reasoning from the subalternating *scientia*, the subalternated *scientia* (which for Aristotle were mathematical sciences), later came to be called *scientia media*, a middle science between natural philosophy and mathematics.

Although Aristotle himself never gave a systematic account of classification of knowledge, he did distinguish certain types of knowledge in the context of determining the kind of knowledge he was about to discuss. In the *Metaphysics*, for instance, he explains that there are three theoretical branches of philosophy: the natural (dealing with neither independent nor immovable entities); the mathematical (which deals with immovable objects not entirely independent of material reference), and the theological (treating entities both independent and immovable).[7] In his *Nicomachean Ethics* Aristotle further distinguishes between theoretical *scientia*, productive art (which brings into existence something which may or may not exist) and prudence, an intellectual virtue which produces action.[8] The theoretical sciences are preferable to others and metaphysics (theology) to the other theoretical sciences.[9]

In the wake of the introduction into the Latin West of Aristotle's *Posterior Analytics* and other philosophical works as well as Arabic scientific works, several authors in the thirteenth century wrote on the classification of knowledge in an attempt to assimilate the new works into existing or more refined frameworks of knowledge.[10] The order, distinction, and scope of knowledge were frequently discussed as part of metaphysics,[11] while topics such as subalternation and the unity of the sciences were often discussed in the fourteenth century in the *Sentences* commentaries, in the context of establishing the nature of theology as knowledge.[12]

It should be noted, however, that in the Latin West, Aristotelian *scientia* was assimilated into an essentially Christian framework.[13] Robert Kilwardby (c. 1215–79) in his *De ortu scientiarum*, for instance, followed Aristotle in dividing speculative philosophy into three kinds: natural philosophy, mathematics, and divine philosophy.[14] He considered, however, the entire speculative philosophy as divine because it dealt with the nature of the divine and with nature as created by God himself.[15] Speculative philosophy, with knowledge useful for human life (ethics, mechanics, and grammar), constitutes philosophy proper.[16] Philosophy in turn is part of a tripartite distinction Kilwardby draws upon knowledge: Divine knowledge is knowledge necessary for salvation; philosophy does not suffice for salvation but teaches truth and a way of living honestly; magical knowledge snatches honest living away from salvation and truth and brings them to pleasure and vanity. Philosophy is useful, universal, and should be cultivated, while magical knowledge is superstitious, injurious, and should be discarded.[17] Written at a time when Kilwardby, a renowned arts master, had just joined the Dominican order and begun his study of theology (c. 1250), his view of knowledge exhibits a decidedly Christian orientation.[18] Indeed pursuit of knowledge was for many a way to acquire Christian wisdom (sapientia).[19] As Honorius of Autun (d. 1156) had portrayed them, the scientia were like towns cleaving along the path to the spiritual Jerusalem, sapientia.[20]

During the fourteenth and fifteenth centuries a different kind of knowledge came to be valued and vigorously promoted by the humanists, who were concerned with the study and emulation of classical antiquity.[21] These humanists promoted studia humanitatis, which comprised grammar, rhetoric, poetry, history, and moral philosophy, as essential and useful for the active life of a citizen.[22] These humanists' criticism of preceding curricula as linguistically unsophisticated, corrupted by commentators and useless for practical life, was soon extended to all areas of education. Juan Luis Vives (1492–1540), for instance, leveled his criticism against speculative philosophy for lacking utility. For Vives, learning was useful to curb human passions and bring individuals to conduct proper moral action. He considered a selected group of classical literature as the most potent source for inculcating moral behavior. The reformed education as he envisaged it in his De disciplinis was reform of education and consequently of society to achieve moral goodness. This was to be achieved without direct intervention from the Church. Vives's scheme of knowledge was thus based on classical literature, and was pragmatic and secular in its orientation.[23] Like Vives, humanists' discussion of the goal and scope of knowledge frequently occurs in the context of reforming education, and most of the time they were concerned with how best to teach an existing body of knowledge.[24]

Bacon in one way or another drew on all these preceding schemes of knowledge I have roughly and briefly summarized – the Aristotelian, the medieval, and the humanist types. Yet, from all these, Bacon created a unique picture of knowledge. And it is to Bacon's own words that we now ought to turn.

III HISTORY, POESY, AND PHILOSOPHY

Bacon divided knowledge into three parts according to the functions of the human "Understanding": history, poesy, and philosophy corresponded to memory, imagination, and reason respectively. In the *De augmentis* (IV, 293), Bacon emphasizes that this partition is the best and that there are these three parts only. These three parts are applicable both to human learning (*doctrina humana*) and to divine learning (*theologia* in the *De augmentis*). The difference Bacon draws between human and divine learnings is in the source of their knowledge, the one takes information from the senses, the other from divine inspiration. Bacon nevertheless claims that it is the one and the same mind which deals with information variously acquired.[25] The main concern for Bacon, however, is the domain of human learning.[26]

Bacon was not the first to identify memory, imagination, and reason as the three dominant faculties of the rational soul.[27] The choice was readily available in Nemesius Emesenus's *De natura hominis*, a commentary on Galen.[28] Nor was Bacon the first to relate mental faculties with areas of knowledge. Juan Huarte (1529–88), in his *Examen de Ingenios. The Examination of Men's Wits* (1575) (published in English in 1594), for instance, linked memory with grammar, theory of law, professional theology, cosmography, and arithmetic; the understanding with teaching divinity, medical theory, logic, natural and moral philosophies; the imagination with poetry, music, medical practice, mathematics, astrology, military art, and painting.[29] Huarte's book was intended as a guide to discover one's aptitude, and thus educate children effectively. His assumptions were that there was one, and only one, type of temperament befitting each science or art; that men had an aptitude for one

science only; and that aptitudes for theoretical and practical knowledge were different.[30] There is no effort on Huarte's part to relate
branches of knowledge or map out the entire realm of knowledge
according to a psychological order.[31] Bacon may well have concurred
that some people had more aptitude and talent for certain things
than others,[32] but he was concerned with mapping out the entire
realm of human knowledge, which he equated with all the functions the rational soul was capable of.

In Bacon's classification, the functions of the rational soul not
only indicate the basic differentiations of disciplines, but more significantly, they explain how the branches were related to one another. The workings of the human mind were then commonly understood on the basis of Aristotle's *De anima* and *Parva naturalia*.[33]
Although the subtlety and complexity with which Aristotle was
understood varied to a great extent, it was generally agreed that the
senses perceive the forms of individual objects (just as the wax takes
the sign from a signet ring without the iron or gold); that this form is
retained as an image in memory (which in a way is a lasting state of
the impression of the signet ring); that with imagination, one can
make use of these images whenever one wishes to, without using
the senses ; that such imaginings are for the most part false; and that
the Intellect takes as its object the forms that are perceived, and
deliberates upon them, forms veridical thoughts, and makes judgments.[34] The relationship between Bacon's three parts of knowledge
is based on the workings of the mind as traditionally understood
according to Aristotle:

The sense, which is the door of the intellect, is affected by individuals only.
The images of those individuals – that is, the impressions which they make
on the sense – fix themselves in the memory, and pass into it in the first
instance entire as it were, just as they come. These the human mind proceeds to review and ruminate; and thereupon either simply rehearses them,
or makes fanciful imitations of them, or analyses and classifies them.
Wherefore from these three fountains, Memory, Imagination, and Reason,
flow these three emanations, History, Poesy, and Philosophy; and there can
be no others. (IV, 292–3)

The mental process leading up to ratiocination is reflected in the
relative significance Bacon attached to the three branches of knowledge. As we shall see further, Poesy is superior to History, Philoso-

phy to Poesy, and Philosophy draws upon History. To this Bacon adds that imagination (Poesy) is useful for (moral) Philosophy.

While Bacon divided history into natural, civil, ecclesiastical, and literary in *The Advancement of Learning*, he begins in the *De augmentis* with the two distinctions of Natural and Civil, the latter now encompassing the other three, namely civil, ecclesiastical, and literary.[35] Bacon divides Natural History in both editions into three: of Generations (or of nature in course), of Pretergeneration (or of Marvels, of nature erring and varying), and of Arts (of nature altered or wrought). In the *De augmentis* the Natural History of Arts is identified with Mechanical and Experimental History (IV, 294), previously discussed as part of the operative part of natural philosophy (III, 361).[36] This transfer was probably meant to demarcate more properly the realm of history and philosophy: both Experimental History *and* Natural History disappear from the partitions of Natural Philosophy in the *De augmentis*. Bacon nevertheless considers Natural History more important as the "primary matter" of natural philosophy (Inductive use of natural history) rather than "for the sake of the knowledge themselves committed to history" (Narrative use of Natural History). It should be noted that as "primary matter" for Natural Philosophy, Natural History for Bacon seems to require some rationale of ordering rather than a haphazard collection: the cases of Natural History need to be arranged and ordered in the form of the *Tables and Arrangements of Instances*, "in such a method and order that the understanding may be able to deal with them" for the Interpretation of Nature (IV, 127).[37]

Bacon found Literary History wanting in both *The Advancement of Learning* and in the *De augmentis*. It is a history of the state of learning, namely the kinds of learning and arts that have flourished and decayed in various parts of the world at various times, origins and transmissions of inventions, sects, principal controversies, authors, books, schools, academies, societies, colleges, and so on. The use Bacon envisages for this History is quite different from Polydor Vergil's enterprise to revive the classical genre of heurematology in the *De inventoribus rerum* or from Johannes Kepler's use of history of astronomy as legitimation of his practice of astronomy.[38] For Bacon, Literary History leads to knowledge not only about the state of learning, but also to knowledge conducive to civil government. He claims that it "would exhibit the movements and perturbations, the virtues and vices, which take place no less in intellectual than in civil matters; and that from the observation of these the best system of government might be derived and established" (IV, 301).

Bacon next discusses knowledge pertaining to imagination, namely Poetry. In renaissance schemes of knowledge, poetry was usually coupled together with rhetoric, invested with an ethical value.[39] Bacon retains this ethical orientation of poetry but also gives it a status independent of rhetoric.[40] He considers poetry an "imitation of history at pleasure" (IV, 315). Poetry is superior to history because the former compensates for and supplies the moral values that history fails to teach. Narrative (or Heroic) Poetry for instance renders acts and deeds more "heroical" while history wears down the mind with "satiety of ordinary events" (IV, 315f.). Dramatic poesy (in the theatre) can educate men's minds to virtue more effectively than when people are on their own. This, Bacon claims, is because "men are more open to impressions and affections when many are gathered together than when they are alone" (IV, 316). Parabolical poesy may teach religion by illustration or cover the mysteries of religion, policy, and philosophy. "But we stay too long in the theatre," Bacon says, and moves on to philosophy which should be treated with "more reverence and attention" (IV, 335).

For Philosophy, Bacon identifies three objects: God (Natural Theology), Nature (Natural Philosophy) and Man (Human Philosophy). He also posits a "universal science" which is like a trunk of a tree where the three "branches" meet (IV, 337). He calls this *Philosophia prima*. It is a "receptacle for all such axioms as are not peculiar to any of the particular sciences, but belong to several of them in common" (III, 347; IV, 337). A mathematical axiom "if equals be added to unequals the wholes will be unequal" may be applicable to distributive justice in ethics, for instance (IV, 337). This is a definition of philosophy quite different from Aristotle's. Unlike Aristotle's metaphysics which was supreme because it dealt with an object of the highest categorical abstraction (being *qua* being), and unlike Aristotle's belief in the nontransference of demonstration across the sciences, Bacon considers his *Philosophia prima* to be a collection of axioms which may be useful to more than one (though not necessarily to *all*) *scientia*. That certain statements of a general nature could be fruitfully applied to more than one case may well be a conviction deriving from his belief in the power of maxims in Jurisprudence.[41] It also reflects Bacon's conviction that individual sciences are not separate but form parts of a whole. *Philosophia prima* also considers what Bacon calls the Adventitious Conditions of Essences, for example, why there can be in nature things so plentiful (iron for instance) and others so few (like gold). Much, Little; Like, Unlike; Possible, Impossible; Being and Not-being are some of the paired conditions he has in mind (IV, 339). Bacon calls this *Philosophia prima* "*sapientia*." By *sapientia*, Bacon says that he does not mean the entire realm of philosophy usually defined as "knowledge of things divine and human."[42] Instead it is the "universal science" which guides the progress of knowledge in general (IV, 337).

Bacon calls the knowledge concerning God Natural Theology, a knowledge "obtained by light of nature and the contemplation of his creatures" (IV, 341). We may recall that at the outset, Bacon had made a distinction between human learning and divine learning (theology). Natural Theology nevertheless belongs to the domain of *human* learning because the former understands God's creatures as perceived through the senses (as opposed to through divine inspiration). Through the contemplation of God's creatures as perceived through the senses, one can learn the "omnipotency and wisdom" of God, but, Bacon cautions the reader, one cannot learn about God's image or will. The use of this Natural Theology is thus limited: it can convert an atheist (somebody who denies that there is a God), but not idolaters or the superstitious (errant believers). For the latter miracles are necessary. Natural Theology in other words does not "establish" religion (IV, 341; III, 349). As an appendix to Natural Theology, Bacon adds the study of Angels and Spirits.

Bacon's definitions of Natural Theology and *Philosophia prima* form an interesting parallel to the *fortuna* of metaphysics and the reemergence of natural theology as a discipline in the late sixteenth century.[43] Toward the late sixteenth century both Protestants and Catholics began to consider dividing metaphysics into the science of being and the science of God. Reacting to the claims of the secular Aristotelians such as Pietro Pomponazzi (1462–1525), the Jesuit Benito Pereira (1535–1610) divided metaphysics into a science of being (first philosophy), which dealt with transcendental predicates such as one, true good, act, and potency, and a divine science which dealt with God, intelligences, and the human soul as species of reality. In divine science, Pereira could still argue for the immortality of the soul, while conceding that Aristotle had not proved the immortality of the soul.

After initially rejecting scholastic metaphysics as a useful form of philosophizing about God, Protestants also returned to metaphysics in the 1570s in order to establish precise definitions of terms such as substance, nature, and accident in the debate (between Calvinists and Lutherans) over the exact nature of Christ and of justification. At the beginning of the seventeenth century, Lutherans who were further faced with the agnosticism of Socinians (followers of Faustus Socinius) and other threats from Epicureanism and Stoics, also saw the need for a revealed theology. Thus Lutherans too came to distinguish between a traditional metaphysics which treated general terminology and principles, and a discipline which dealt with the properties and activities of spiritual beings, often called *pneumatologia*.[44]

Bacon's natural theology and *Philosophia prima* reflects this Continental trend to split metaphysics: he acknowledged the apologetic function of natural theology to which he added the study of the spirits, while he allotted to *Philosophia prima* treatment of abstracted terms and principles. The significant difference is that Bacon's *Philosophia prima* is in no way intended to exhibit the "scientific" character of the *Metaphysics* of Aristotle. As for "Metaphysic" itself, Bacon gives an entirely new meaning (and he is well aware that he is doing something new here) as a part of *Natural Philosophy*.

IV NATURAL PHILOSOPHY

Bacon first divides Natural Philosophy into Theoretical and Operative parts (IV, 343). The Theoretical part inquires the causes and the Operative part produces effects. As is well known, Bacon considered the Theoretical and Operative parts of Natural Philosophy as two sides of the same coin, rather than independent types of *scientia*. That is, the degree of abstraction of a proposition about a given nature in the theoretical part *is* the degree of freedom from material one possesses in reproducing that nature in the operative part. It is precisely this operative element that constitutes the essence of Bacon's concept of Forms and his Natural Philosophy.[45]

The identification of operative production with causal investigation is clearly quite divergent from the Aristotelian concept of *scientia*: for Aristotle neither ethics (which produces action) nor art (which produces artefacts) can legitimately be called *scientia* because they do not pursue necessary causal investigation. Nor does Aristotle consider the operative part of human action as essential to *scientia*. Here, Bacon may well be drawing on a different kind of classical tradition, the "Maker's knowledge tradition" – one knows it because one made (or did) it.[46] It should also be added that in the context of humanist legal reforms of the sixteenth century, causal enquiry and "production" (of law) were closely connected. Johannes Corasius (1513–72), for instance, identified the efficient cause of law with sovereign legislators ("makers" of law); the formal cause with the legislated public law which had a binding force on judges and citizens (the "work" made), and which also gave order to the existing law which was disordered and fragmentary (material cause); and the final cause of law with guarding and defending the state by natural justice.[47] Bacon's ideas for reform of law stem from a different concern and therefore take a different shape, but the application of an "Organon" (rules and procedures whereby certain kinds of knowledge are attained) to a field hitherto unintended for – such as law – was certainly possible and plausible by the end of the sixteenth century.

Of the Theoretical part, Bacon defined Physic as dealing with material and efficient causes, and Metaphysic with formal and final causes. Physic deals with causes which are variable and dependent on matter, and not constant: for instance it investigates fire as a cause of induration in clay or as a cause of melting wax (IV, 346). Physic may further be divided into the first principles of things; the structure of the world; the varieties and smaller structures of things. Another division may be into Concrete and Abstract Physic. Concrete Physic investigates the substance of things with all the variety of their accidents, whilst Abstract Physic deals with accidents as found in every variety of substances (IV, 347).

For Metaphysic, Bacon assigns the knowledge of Forms, a theoretical knowledge of natures of the first class (like dense, rare, hot, cold, heavy, light, tangible, pneumatic, volatile, fixed, and configuration of motions) which allows one to superinduce a given nature to any given material.[48] The study of final causes should also be reserved for Metaphysic. Bacon's main reservations against arguments from final causes is that it has hitherto obscured arguments in Physic. In

Physic, instead of seeing an argument that "the hairs about the eyelids are for the safeguard of the sight," Bacon wants to see the argument "that pilosity is incident to orifices of moisture" (IV, 364). This, Bacon insists, does not denigrate God's Providential plan. Drawing an analogy with a "greater and deeper" politician who governs without letting all his employees know about his intentions, Bacon claims that the wisdom of God shines forth "more admirably when nature intends one thing and Providence draws forth another, than if he had communicated to all natural figures and motions the characters and impressions of his providence" (IV, 364–5).

Bacon's distinction between Physic and Metaphysic brings out the character of his natural philosophy which is quite different from other contemporary natural philosophy. For Philip Melanchthon (1497–1560), whose natural philosophy textbooks were widely read across Europe, nature was a "footprint" of God's Providential design. In his commentary on Aristotle's De anima and the Initia doctrinae physicae, Melanchthon sought to establish that every single part of the physical universe, including the human body and civil governments, was made by God. Melanchthon's goal was to prove that human beings were created for the purpose in civil life to abide by divinely instituted civil order and governments. Teleological explanations of every part of nature which pointed to God's Providential design thus constituted the essence of Melanchthon's natural philosophy.[49] For Bacon, in contrast, final cause understood as Providence had little role to play in his natural philosophy. Instead, Bacon was interested in the power of operation his natural philosophy could attain. It was also in terms of this power of operation that Bacon believes that there can be a knowledge of God at the end of natural philosophy.

Bacon explains how Natural Philosophy is ordered in his famous example of a pyramid. Natural History is at the base of the pyramid; midway between the base and the apex is Physic; and the part nearest to the apex is Metaphysic. The apex is called the "summary law of nature," the knowledge with which God created. Thus, we may not only understand from the diminishing volume of the pyramid toward the apex the degree of abstraction (or freedom) from matter (i.e., the generality of axioms), but we may also identify a hierarchy through which one ascends toward a knowledge held by God. It is the supreme knowledge of creation. The attainability of such a knowledge, however, is not guaranteed (IV, 362).[50]

The parts of Operative Natural Philosophy are called "Mechanic" and "Magic," corresponding to the Theoretical parts of Physic and Metaphysic respectively. Bacon defends his use of the word "magic" as meaning application of hidden forms to the production of nature (IV, 369) and not superstitious practices such as alchemy or astrology. Bacon also distinguishes "Mechanic" from the "merely empirical and operative" kind (now included in Natural History). Mechanic proper is produced through the knowledge of the efficient and material causes understood in "Physic." Bacon was of the generation for whom mechanics had already emerged as a new discipline. In the sixteenth century, mechanics (hitherto considered as a manual art) had received new impetus first by the rediscovery and assimilation of (pseudo-)Aristotle's *Questions of Mechanics* and then by a widening of its scopes by assimilating other types of problems. Humanists such as Leonico Piccolomini considered the *Questions of Mechanics* as dealing with a theoretical and mathematical science, similar in status to astronomy, optics, and harmonics, the traditional *scientia media*.[51] Bacon in contrast exalts the value of Mechanic as part of Natural Philosophy. In fact, the category of *scientia media* as a science *between* the mathematical and natural sciences does not hold in Bacon's scheme of knowledge, mainly because mathematics does not have the status of a theoretical science (dealing with its own kind of objects) equal to that of natural philosophy.

Bacon instead considers mathematics auxiliary to natural philosophy. In the *De augmentis*, Bacon revised the passages on mathematics which, as Graham Rees has shown, suggest some knowledge on Bacon's part of John Napier's logarithm, the debate between Robert Fludd and Johannes Kepler over the transcendental value of mathematics, and a possible knowledge of contemporary developments in algebra.[52] The auxiliary status of mathematics, however, remains essentially the same. Quantity abstracted from matter (the object of mathematics) is for Bacon one of the Essential Forms which should properly be investigated in his Metaphysic. Although Bacon acknowledges that mathematics could also be useful for all parts of Natural Philosophy, nowhere does he indicate that it could be directly useful for the discovery of Forms, the goal of Natural Philosophy.[53]

Mathematics may be divided into pure and mixed. Pure mathematics, which is Geometry and Arithmetic, considers "quantity" as entirely severed from matter and from axioms of natural philosophy (IV, 370). In *The Advancement of Learning*, Bacon added that this pure mathematics was useful to train the wit and intellectual faculties (III, 360). Bacon here largely echoes what had become a commonplace in the sixteenth-century humanist educational reforms, namely that mathematics was useful as preparatory to logical, dialectical, or Aristotelian learning.[54] Mixed mathematics treats quantity insofar as it helps to "explain, demonstrate, and actuate" some axioms in natural philosophy. Traditional *scientia media* such as music, astronomy and perspective as well as cosmography, architecture and machinery belong to this Mixed mathematics (IV, 371). Music and perspective also have the function of pleasing respectively the ears and eyes.[55] Bacon thus does not see in mathematics an autonomous *scientia* either in its object (which is part of Metaphysic) or its use (except for training the mind, pleasing the senses, or illustrating natural philosophical axioms). Nor is it considered as furnishing the essential explanatory structure for Natural Philosophy.[56] This, as Rees has also argued, is because Bacon's actual picture of the workings of nature is essentially a qualitative one, namely a semi-Paracelsian cosmology.[57]

V   HUMAN PHILOSOPHY

As with Natural Philosophy, Bacon continued in the section of Human Philosophy (Philosophy concerning man) to divide, realign, rename, and place his own emphasis on traditional subjects. Human Philosophy comprised all and sundry types of knowledge Bacon considered to have relevance to human beings, such as medicine, logic, rhetoric, ethics, politics, and divination. Bacon divided Human Philosophy according to the conditions and nature of human beings, first by humans as species (Philosophy of Humanity) and then as members of society (Civil Philosophy).

The Philosophy of Humanity considers the "nature and state" of man; the body of man; and the soul of man. The doctrine of the "nature and state" of man considers the Miseries and Prerogatives of human beings (the Person of man), as well as how the body and soul are linked to each other (the League of body and soul). Bacon wishes to catalog in the "Prerogatives" of human beings the magnanimity of humanity by collecting cases of people who excelled in one way or another in the powers and virtues of both mind and body. The League of body and soul is about how knowledge of one leads to knowledge of the other. There are two types of inferences – one is called "Indication": through the study of the lineaments of body (Physiognomy), disposition of the mind may be ascertained, while through natural dreams, which are the result of the agitation of the mind, the state and disposition of the body may be known (IV, 376). The other type of inference between the body and the soul is called "Impression": it investigates how humors and temperaments of the body affect the mind and how passions and apprehensions of the mind affect the body (IV, 377). As Bacon himself points out, such knowledge was readily available in medical regimens, as in the case where physicians prescribed drugs to heal mental diseases (IV, 377f.).[58]

The doctrine on the body of man contributes to the good of man's body in four ways, through Medicine (dealing with health), Cosmetic (beauty), Athletic (Strength), and Voluptuary (pleasure). Bacon further identifies three functions of medicine – preservation of health, cure of diseases, and prolongation of life. By cosmetic, he means cleanliness of the body, but denounces "adulterate" decoration which uses dyes and pigments (IV, 379–94). By Voluptuary arts, Bacon means mainly painting and music. These are the more desirable arts than those which please the other senses because the eyes and the ears are esteemed the most "liberal" and purest (IV, 395). Painting also has reference to memory and demonstrations, while music relates to morality and the passion of the mind. Their sciences are considered most "learned" because it makes use of mathematics (IV, 395). For unguents, pleasures of the table, and lust, Bacon thinks that laws to repress them are needed rather than arts that teach them (IV, 395).

For the doctrine of the soul of man Bacon first divides the soul into the rational and the irrational. The rational soul is divine and the irrational soul subserves the former and is common to all animals. These will be investigated in two ways: concerning the functions of the soul (Substance or Faculties of the soul) and how to use those functions (Use and Objects of the Faculties). Questions as to the substance of the rational soul, such as whether it is native or adventive, separable or inseparable, mortal or immortal, Bacon leaves to religion, since the rational soul itself is "inspired" directly from God, while philosophy investigates knowledge which can be derived from the senses (III, 379; IV, 398). On the sensible soul, Bacon wishes to see more inquiry into its substance, which he considers to be some form of medical spirits (IV, 398). Bacon identifies six functions of the rational soul, namely understanding, reason, imagination, memory, appetite, and will. Two other possible kinds of functions are dealt with in the appendixes, namely Divination and Fascination. Divination either makes predictions by argument from external signs and tokens (Artificial Divination) or makes predictions without external signs due to some kind of innate prenotion (Natural Divination). Fascination is the power of imagination resulting on another body. Divination needs to be separated from various superstitions and Fascination ought to be outlawed as contradicting God's decree in Genesis 3.19 (In the sweat of thy face shalt thou eat bread) (IV, 399–401). For the functions of the sensible soul, Bacon recommends two points to be investigated further: voluntary motion (how nerves and muscles, imagination, etc. are required for motion) and the Sense and the Sensible (how sense-perception works) (IV, 401–4). Bacon here rehearsed what was traditionally treated in the commentaries on Aristotle's De anima and Parva naturalia. It should be noted that Bacon leaves to religion and does not discuss the most frequently and fervently argued topic in those commentaries, the immortality of the soul, while he continues the tradition of examining medical spirits as instruments of the human soul.[59]

The doctrine of the Use and Objects of the faculties follows the subdivision of the rational soul into the Intellect and Will. The use of Intellect is the realm of Logic, the use of the will, Ethic. Although Bacon notes the necessity of Imagination for both the rational and ethical functions (i.e., Imagination provides the Intellect with the images to judge upon and voluntary action is stimulated by Imagination) and even notes its predominant role in divine illumination, he does not think that Imagination produces sciences (III, 382; IV, 405f.) What rational order Bacon can impose on Imagination is treated later on in his discussion of rhetoric.

Logic as the use of the Intellect inquires into four domains: the art of Inquiry or Invention; the art of Examination or Judgment; Art of Custody or Memory; and Art of Elocution or Tradition. These roughly correspond to traditional steps of rhetorical composition, namely inventio, dispositio, elocutio, pronuntiatio, and memoria.[60]

The Art of Invention is invention either of arts and sciences, or of speech and arguments. Against the common assertion that all arts first sprung up haphazardly through experience, Bacon wants to offer some orderly ways whereby some things can be found. Art of Indication and Direction is a somehow orderly way of guessing and borrowing results from other arts. This can proceed either from one experiment to another (Learned Experience), or from experiments to axioms and then from these axioms to new experiments (Interpretation of Nature, the New Organon) (IV, 407–21).

Bacon considers Discovery of Arguments not exactly a discovery of things unknown, but a way of recalling from a mass of knowledge. There are two ways of doing this: one by Topics (where a thing to be looked for is marked), the other by Promptuary (precomposed arguments). Topics can be either general or particular. General topics are useful not only for recalling arguments but also for guiding one's investigation.[61] Particular topics are acquired by application of general questions to specific fields of inquiry. Bacon offers a list of questions applied to the investigation of the nature of heavy and light (IV, 421–7). As Paolo Rossi has noted, Bacon considered these topics which are rhetorical in origin as regulative in the investigation of nature.[62]

The Art of Examination and Judgment is about the nature of proofs and demonstration. Bacon briefly discusses the difference between his Induction and traditional syllogism: syllogism is a reduction of propositions to principles in middle terms and the discovery of those middle terms is a different mental operation from judging the validity of the consequence; Induction in contrast discovers and judges at the same time (IV, 428f.).[63] There are also rules of drawing out true conclusions (Analytic) and detection of fallacies. Detection of fallacies are of three kinds – sophistical fallacies, fallacies of Interpretation, and the Idols (false appearances). Detection of sophistical fallacies are explained in Aristotle's *Sophistical Refutations*, while fallacies of Interpretations are misunderstandings of transcendental terms such as Greater, Less, Much, Little, Identity, Diversity, and so on. Examination of the proper properties of these terms is left to *Philosophia prima* or Metaphysic. The Idols are the famous prejudices and preconceptions of the human mind – Idols of the Tribe (according to the nature of man in general), Cave (individual nature of each man), the Market-place (or of communicative nature) and Theatre (through false laws and philosophies) (IV, 428–34).

For the Art of Memory, Bacon notes the usefulness of writing in the form of common places for helping the memory. He also briefly repeats the traditional elements of place memory[64] – a vague Prenotion of what one is looking for, the "place of memory," and a way to reduce intellectual concepts into images (Emblem) (III, 399; IV, 435–7).

Art of Elocution or Transmission is the art of delivering speech. It considers the Organ of discourse, the Method of discourse and the Illustration of discourse. The Organ of discourse includes notations of speech and writings (grammar) and notation of things (hieroglyphics and real characters in Chinese). Grammar may either teach the use of a language (Literary) or the relative merits of various languages (Philosophical). A section of Ciphers is added here (IV, 438–48).

By the Method of Discourse, or Wisdom of Transmission, Bacon means how best to present matters that need to be communicated. This area is *dispositio*, traditionally dealt with in both dialectics and rhetoric. Depending on the material at hand, Bacon considers that the manner of *dispositio* may vary. Bacon thus objects to the Ramist claim of the "one and only method" of dichotomies as the universally effective way to present topics (III, 406; IV, 449). Indebted though he was to the humanist-dialectic tradition, Bacon did not believe (unlike Ramus) that dialectic rules corresponded to the laws governing the world of nature.[65] Of the various ways of display Bacon lists for various types of delivery, Bacon instead singles out Aphorisms as of "great consequence to science" (IV, 450). Aphorism requires the writer to have solid knowledge in order to give directions in practical life. Precisely because of its abstracted and fragmentary way of representation, it does not give the impression of completed comprehensiveness (which Methodical Display does), but encourages others to contribute and add something (IV, 451).

The Illustration or adornment of discourse is considered the domain of rhetoric. Here, Bacon stresses the importance of the role of imagination and the ethical orientation of rhetoric.[66] Human affections, which grasp what appears good in the present, frequently override human reason, which should look beyond to the future and knows what good one really ought to do. Through rhetoric, imagination can render future and remote things (even if these are incorporeal "virtues") appear to the present vividly as if in a picture, and make reason prevail and excite the appetite and will to good action

(IV, 456f.). The office of rhetoric, therefore, is "to apply and recommend the dictates of reason to imagination, in order to excite the appetite and will" (IV, 455). Bacon concurs with Aristotle[67] that rhetoric should be placed between logic and ethic (IV, 457). This section on rhetoric is thus placed at the end of the discussion on the Use of Reason and before the section on the Use of Will.

In the knowledge concerning the Use of the Will (Ethics), Bacon finds lacking the method of educating and training the mind for the attainment of good. Thus this doctrine may be divided into examples of the nature of good one ought to aspire to (Exemplar or Platform of Good) and the rules whereby the will of man is accommodated to that good (the Regiment or Culture of the Mind). The Exemplar or Platform of Good may be divided into Simple (the kinds of good) or Comparative (the degrees of good). The kinds of good may be divided into Self-good (good of something in itself) and Good of Communion (good of something as a member of a greater body). Self-good may be active (to multiply and propagate oneself) or passive (to preserve and continue oneself). Passive self-good may further be divided into Conservative (to preserve a thing in its existing state) and Perfective (to raise a thing to a higher or greater nature). Perfective self-good is superior to Conservative self-good, but self-good is inferior to Good of Communion. Good of communion is duty either common to every man as a member of a state (General) or of every man with respect to their special profession, vocation, rank, and character (Respective). Bacon thus stresses the superiority of ethical value of society to the good of the individual.

The Culture of the Mind consists of inquiring what is in our power and what is not (Characters of the mind), what kind of affection and perturbation the mind is susceptible to (Affections of the mind), and the Remedies for such perturbation. The Remedies are listed as precepts such as: don't undertake a task that is either too great or too small for the case required; train acquired habits both when the mind is and is not occupied; the mind finds it more agreeable to obtain something as if it were found incidentally rather than intentionally and necessarily (V, 3–30). Bacon's "Culture of Mind" (Cultura animi), it should be noted, is individual self-knowledge oriented toward ethical conduct, an aim Vives also recognized as the goal of learning. The difference between Vives and Bacon was that for the former, it was the primary aim and function of learning to curb human passions and thereby conduct moral good. Bacon's "Culture of Mind," the means to check and control one's passion, was only one of the numerous parts of ethical knowledge which in turn was part of a larger realm of knowledge. Bacon's "Culture of Mind" was also different from the "culture of wit" (*Cultura ingenii*) promoted by Antonio Possevino (1533–1611) who considered the process of reading (selected) books a salvific process by which the wit (*ingenium*) acquired piety.[68] Whilst the whole realm of learning was considered by Possevino to be a cultivation of mind into (Counter-Reformation) orthodox faith, for Bacon, cultivating the mind is only a small part of a secular, ethical self-knowledge.

Thus far Bacon has considered man as man (Philosophy of Humanity), and now in Civil Philosophy he considers man as part of society. Bacon claims that this branch is most difficult to reduce to axioms because they are most "immersed in matter" (V, 32; III, 445). There are three kinds of good one ought to seek in society: comfort against solitude (knowledge of conversation); assistance in business (knowledge of negotiation); and protection against injuries (knowledge of empire or government). The doctrine of negotiation is divided further into the doctrine concerning Scattered Occasions (comprising all variety of business) and doctrine concerning Advancement of Life (suggestions to improve one's own fortunes). Again, several precepts are given. The secret nature of government and empire found in *The Advancement of Learning* (III, 473f.) is partly eliminated in the *De augmentis*. Instead, Bacon mentions two areas where defects can be detected – the extension of the empire and universal justice (V, 78–110). To expand the empire, Bacon lists factors such as courageous citizens, taxation by consent, liberal naturalization of aliens, employment of just laws, swift attendance to the needs of allies, and building up military might, especially naval power. Bacon also offers aphorisms on Universal Justice, because he thinks that nobody has so far laid down the foundations of universal justice from the point of view of a "statesman": philosophers who have written on laws have had no conception of how imaginary laws could be implemented, and lawyers themselves are too caught up with the particularities of their own country. Bacon believes that there is a set of universal laws – in what way can laws be certain and if uncertain how to rectify them, for instance – but he also believes that it should be implemented in such a way that benefits a particular nation best (III, 475–7; V, 88).

Compared to the section on Natural Philosophy, Bacon's discussion on Human Philosophy may come across as less well organized or unified. We should, however, take heed of Bacon's own intention that he was trying to map out both cultivated and uncultivated areas of knowledge. That is, Natural Philosophy and Human Philosophy may well have been at different stages of their advancement. By 1620, Bacon had mapped out in more detail and partially carried out the reform of Natural Philosophy in the *Instauratio magna*, the *Novum organum*, the *Parasceve*, and in many other fragments. Thus in the *De augmentis* he could afford to give the bare skeleton of how Nature was to be studied – the first principles of things; the structure of the world; the varieties and smaller structures of things (IV, 347). He then explained how the parts of Natural Philosophy were related to each other in the pyramid metaphor. In Human Philosophy, in contrast, Bacon was at the stage of laying out the aspects of human beings which were to be investigated (human nature, human body, human soul, body and soul, the Intellect and the Will, man as species, man as members of society, and so on) and allotting to each aspect a field of study. Bacon was thus occupied with mapping out Human Philosophy, but did not give a systematic account (as in the pyramid metaphor) of how the parts are related to each other. Modern scholars have, however, detected some structure in Bacon's Human Philosophy. It has been argued for instance that Bacon's civil history constituted the "prime matter" for his ethic and moral philosophy.[69] His examination of the soul in terms of its substance and its use indeed reflects a concern similar to that in his Natural Philosophy with establishing theoretical and operative knowledge. In Human Philosophy the operative knowledge would have meant ethical behavior and manners and it is surely in this ethical sense that we should understand Bacon's label of Human Philosophy as "self-knowledge."[70] Significantly, it is this knowledge that Bacon called "the end and term of knowledges" (IV, 373).

VI DIVINE LEARNING

The last part of learning to be discussed was Divine Learning or inspired Divinity. Bacon had claimed that the tripartite partition holds for Theology also, namely Sacred History (including Prophecy), Parables (divine poesy), and Doctrines and Precepts (perennial philosophy) (III, 329; IV, 293), but he does not elaborate on further divisions or subdivisions of those disciplines. Instead, he enumerates areas to be augmented. The substance of the argument does not change between *The Advancement of Learning* and the *De augmentis*, though the argument is much compacted in the latter. In the *De augmentis*, Bacon adds three appendixes which he finds absent: the Legitimate Use of Human Reason in Divine Subjects, on the degrees of Unity in the kingdom of God, and Emanations of Scripture. Human reason may be used in religion for either explaining mysteries or deducing arguments from the principles and axioms of faith. By the degrees of Unity in the kingdom of God, Bacon means to establish how much room there is to be divergent in matters of ceremony and faith and where the threshold for being excommunicated should lie. By Emanation of Scripture, he means a collection or annotation of Scriptural texts which are neither apologetic nor reduced to commonplaces severed from their original context. Bacon does not, however, give concrete examples in axioms as he was wont to do throughout the realm of philosophy. Instead, he leaves the task to the theologians (V, 111–19).

VII   CONCLUSION

From a comparison with other schemes of knowledge, one readily notices that Bacon's concerns are emphatically comprehensive, practical, and civil – how to unify all sciences under one comprehensive system; how to unify theoretical and practical parts of science; how to govern and control people through Literary History; how to map out human knowledge as primarily an ethical self-knowledge; how to inculcate ethical behavior in people as members of a society; and how to legislate universal justice. It is as if Bacon mapped out the realm of knowledge following Aristotle's advice in the *Politics* that all the realm of the working of the mind was a proper concern of a statesman.[71]

At the end of the *De augmentis*, Bacon claimed that he had "made as it were a small globe of the intellectual world, as faithfully as I could; with a note and description of those parts which I find either not constantly occupied, or not well cultivated by the labour and industry of man" (V, 118). This intellectual globe is an image that

Bacon's Classification of Knowledge (from the *De augmentis*)

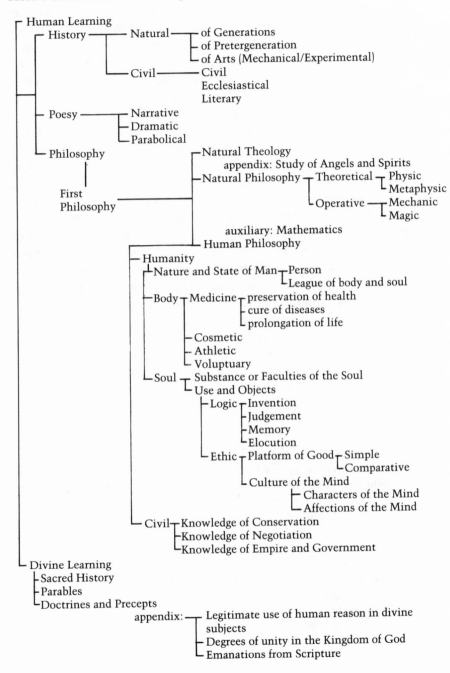

persists with Bacon's program of learning. For instance, in the title page of the 1640 edition of the *De augmentis* engraved by William Marshall (see the frontispiece at the beginning of the present volume), the terrestrial globe and the intellectual globe are firmly tied together, signifying that knowledge is bound by reason and experiment: *"ratione et experientia foederatur."*[72] The pillars are the two universities of Oxford and Cambridge, and at its base is the knowledge as classified by Bacon. It is a picture which should further be contrasted with Conrad Gessner's enterprise to order the realm of knowledge by bringing order to a "library." For Gessner, the sum of human knowledge was represented in books, and the world to be understood was a huge library – a *respublica litteraria.*[73] For Bacon, a library was one of the many institutions which preserved existing knowledge (IV, 284f.).[74] His enterprise, in contrast, was to go out and find the unknown lands, the unwritten books, to enlarge the bounds of the human empire on the intellectual globe, which implied expansion in the territorial globe also. Bacon's classification of knowledge served as an introduction to and a basis of this ambitious and optimistic enterprise. In sum, Bacon's was a unique journey through the intellectual globe leading to unknown territories, not a metaphysician's guide to a spiritual Jerusalem, or a humanist's guide to the ideal of classical learning. Bacon's classification of knowledge was to have a variegated *fortuna* of its own, providing much inspiration, for instance, to the Puritan intellectuals and the compilers of the *Encyclopédie.*

NOTES

1 For details of the difference between the two, see James Spedding's notes to *The Advancement of Learning*, III, 321–491. For the *De augmentis* as following more explicitly a Ramist prescription of establishing dichotomies, see Rees 1986, p. 402.
2 *Posterior Analytics*, I.2.
3 *Posterior Analytics*, I.4.
4 *Metaphysics*, XI.7.
5 *Posterior Analytics*, I.7.
6 *Posterior Analytics*, I.9, 12, 13.
7 *Metaphysics*, VI.1.
8 *Nicomachean Ethics*, VI.4.
9 *Metaphysics*, VI.1.
10 Weisheipl 1965.

11 For instance, Roger Bacon, *Communia naturalium*, "A noble part of metaphysics, since it is common to all science, is to show and demonstrate the origin, distinction, number, and order of all the sciences and what is characteristic of each." As translated in Weisheipl 1978, p. 479.

12 See the example of John of Reading in Livesey 1989.

13 For Christian classification schemes before the reintroduction of Aristotle's *Posterior Analytics* and other philosophical works, see Weisheipl 1978, pp. 461–74.

14 Robert Kilwardby, *De ortu scientiarum*, ed. Albert G. Judy (Oxford and Toronto, 1976), ch. 5, pp. 13f.

15 "Scientia speculativa est pars philosophiae humani aspectus perfectiva per cognitionem rerum divinarum, id est naturae divinae et naturarum a Deo per seipsum conditarum." Kilwardby, *De ortu scientiarum*, ch. 4, p. 13.

16 Kilwardby, *De ortu scientiarum*, ch. 3, pp. 10f.

17 Kilwardby, *De ortu scientiarum*, ch. 1, pp. 9f.

18 Introduction by Albert G. Judy to Kilwardby, *De ortu scientiarum*, p. xvi. For the status of the mechanical arts in a salvationary framework, see Ovitt 1983, esp. pp. 101–4 for Kilwardby.

19 Rice 1958, pp. 1–29.

20 See Honorius of Autun, *De animae exsilio et patria, alias, de artibus*, in *Patrologiae cursus completus*, tom. CLXXII, ed. J-P. Migne (Paris, 1854), p. 1243.

21 The following is a compacted and simplified description of humanism, which is explained in more detail in Kristeller 1988.

22 For the teaching of humanist educators in secondary schools, see Grafton and Jardine 1986.

23 Noreña 1970, pp. 228–53.

24 Jardine 1974a, p. 26.

25 "The information derived from revelation and the information derived from the sense differ no doubt both in the matter and in the manner of conveyance; but the human mind is the same, and its repositories and cells the same. It is only like different liquids poured through different funnels into one and the same vessel." IV, 293; see also III, 346.

26 Note that Natural theology is knowledge about God which falls under "human learning." See below, pp. 55–6.

27 See further a comparison of the ordering of knowledge amongst Bacon, Huarte, Pierre Charron, and d'Alembert by Vleeschauwer 1958.

28 Olivieri 1991. Note that Nemesius Emesenus's *De natura hominis* frequently circulated under the authorship of Gregory of Nyssa. See Wicher 1986 for the transmission and editions of this text.

29 Huarte, *Examen de Ingenios. The Examination of Men's Wits*, trans.

R[ichard]. C[arew]., (London, 1594), p. 103. The Latin edition was placed on the Index of prohibited books in 1581, Zedelmaier 1992, p. 202.

30 Huarte, *The Examination of Men's Wits*, Epistle to the Reader, fol. Avi^{r}f.

31 Relationships between mental faculties are cursorily discussed when Huarte needs to distinguish aptitudes for theoretical and practical parts of knowledge (law and medicine).

32 See for instance the elite "brethren" in the *New Atlantis* who have exclusive control over knowledge, Martin 1992, pp. 137–9.

33 For Renaissance commentaries and readings of Aristotle's concept of the soul, see Park and Kessler 1988, and for the Arabic commentators, see Harvey 1975.

34 *De anima*, II.6, 12; III.1, 3–8; *De memoria*, I.

35 The subsumption of ecclesiastical history (Church History) under Civil History in the *De augmentis* is considered unique by Nadel 1966, pp. 278f.

36 For a list of Experimental History, see no. 127 of *Catalogue of Particular Histories*, IV, 270.

37 Such ordering may belong to the part of Physic concerning "nature manifold or diffused," which is a "gloss or paraphrase attending upon the text of natural history" (IV, 347). Rossi explains that it is a (rhetorical) topical method which is at work here; Rossi 1991, p. 83.

38 For Vergil's assimilation of preceding sources, see Copenhaver 1978. For Kepler's unique use of the history of astronomy as a theoretical validation of the kind (and method) of astronomy he professes, see Jardine 1984, pp. 258–86.

39 Vickers 1988b, p. 715.

40 Rhetoric retains a connection with poetry in that it requires the faculty of imagination, but in Bacon's eyes Rhetoric is different from poetry in that the former applies reasoning to the workings of imagination and therefore becomes a part of philosophy. See Chapter 8.

41 Kocher 1957.

42 For the changing concepts of *sapientia* in the Renaissance, see Rice 1958.

43 For a study of the classical concept of "natural theology," see Jaeger 1947. The following section on Late Renaissance metaphysics is a summary of Lohr 1988, pp. 606–30.

44 Lohr 1988, p. 629.

45 For Bacon's theory of forms, see Pérez-Ramos's Chapter 4.

46 Pérez-Ramos 1988, esp. pp. 48–64 for the Maker's knowledge tradition.

47 For Corasius, the Aristotelian four causes not only furnished law with a character of *scientia*, but also represented the unifying *ars* of law as

proposed in Cicero, *De oratore*, I, 42. For Corasius, I have summarized Fell 1973, pp. 130–302.

48 Note also that forms to be investigated, like alphabets, are finite in number (III, 355f.; IV, 361) and therefore Natural Philosophy may potentially be completed at some point.

49 See Kusukawa 1995.

50 See a survey of ideas of the limits of knowledge in the sixteenth and seventeenth centuries in Ginzburg 1976.

51 For the emergence of Renaissance mechanics and its widening of scope, see Laird 1986.

52 Rees 1986.

53 Cf. the more positive assessment of mathematics for natural philosophy by Clavius in Ariew 1990.

54 Dear 1988, pp. 43f.; Gilbert 1960, pp. 83f.

55 See the "Voluptuary Arts" below, p. 61.

56 Cf. the inferior status of mathematics to natural philosophy in Albertus Magnus and Thomas Aquinas, Weisheipl 1965, pp. 80–9.

57 Rees 1986, and for Bacon's semi-Paracelsian Cosmology, see Rees 1975a, and his Chapter 5.

58 For a concise description of medical regimens and complexional diagnosis, see Siraisi 1990, pp. 120–4.

59 For Bacon's theory of Spirits, see further Walker 1972.

60 For example, Cicero, *De inventione*, I. vii. 9.

61 "[T]his kind of Topic is of use not only in argumentations, where we are disputing with another, but also in meditations, where we are considering and resolving anything with ourselves; neither does it serve only to prompt and suggest what we should affirm and assert, but also what we should inquire or ask." IV, 423; cf. Cicero, *Topica* II. 6–8.

62 Rossi 1991. For the significance of rhetorical *topoi* as organizing universal knowledge in later encyclopaedias, see Schmidt-Biggemann 1983. Cf. the medieval tradition of "topics" as serving mainly as headings under which *differentiae* of substances were discussed, Green-Pedersen 1984.

63 For Baconian method, see Michel Malherbe's Chapter 3.

64 The classic account of the explanation of memory places is by Yates 1966. See now also Carruthers 1990 and Coleman 1992.

65 This is in keeping with the English common law tradition which never submitted to the claims of "natural reason" propounded by Agricola and Ramus, Giuliani 1962, pp. 237–41. For Ramus, see Ong 1958, pp. 180–2.

66 See further Brian Vickers's Chapter 8 below.

67 *Rhetoric*, I.2.

68 For Possevino, see Zedelmaier 1992, pp. 174–224

69 Nadel, 1966.

70 See the humanist transformation of the idea of wisdom into a secular and ethical knowledge in Rice 1958.

71 "The legislation of the true statesman . . . must cover the different parts of the soul and their different activities; and in this field it should be directed more to the higher than the lower, and rather to ends than means." *Politics*, trans. Ernest Barker (Oxford, 1946), VII, 13, p. 317.

72 For Marshall, see Hind 1964, pp. 102f. I owe the reference to this picture to Dr. Frances Willmoth.

73 For an analysis of Gessner's ordering of knowledge in his *Bibliotheca universalis*, see Zedelmaier 1992, pp. 51–124.

74 The library is also "a place where relics of the ancient saints full of true virtue are preserved." IV, 285.

3 Bacon's method of science

I INTRODUCTION

It is a historical fact that Bacon's philosophy is contemporaneous with the birth of modern thought. But it is also a fact that modern thought has developed in a way which does not accord with the idea that Bacon gave of the new science. Of course, we can praise the Chancellor's sense of reformation, his critique of false sciences, his comments on academic institutions and the politics of science; we can even say, as the French Encyclopedists did, that he was the herald of experimental philosophy. But the fact remains that the Baconian concept of science, as an inductive science, has nothing to do with and even contradicts today's form of science. As far as the method of science is concerned (and by method we mean the rules and formal processes of knowledge, and not only a general sense of experience), Bacon's *instauratio* went to a dead end, as early as the first progress of science in the seventeenth century. Members of the Royal Society claimed kinship with the author of the *Novum organum*, but ignored Baconian induction as a scientific method. In a word, from Bacon to our time, there is a gap that cannot be filled up. And it would be no good pretending the contrary; or, at least, that would not serve Bacon's fame.

It does not follow, however, that Bacon's theory of science does not deserve a philosophical analysis and even our praise. But in order to understand his importance for the philosophy of science, we have to see him as a philosopher of his own time. For one should not suppose that modern science, as successful as it may be, is free from any epistemological difficulties. And once one has accepted the idea that Bacon's induction is not the method of modern science, one can discover that this induction, although it is an alternative way which leads nowhere, expresses the real and lasting problems of the method of modern science.

II THE GENERAL IMPORT OF BACON'S METHOD OF SCIENCE

The main and most characteristic feature of Bacon's epistemology is that it rests upon a single method, which is *induction*. The *Novum organum* does not use this word very frequently, but it always uses it to qualify an intellectual behavior and a logical procedure that are both supposed to be entirely new. This method is a kind of conceptual plot, very simple in its principle, but rather intricate in its application, because it is applied to all the stages of knowledge, and at every phase the whole process has to be kept in mind. Knowledge starts from sensible experience, rests upon natural history which presents sense data in an ordinate distribution, rises up from lower axioms or propositions to more general ones, tries to reach the more fundamental laws of nature (the knowledge of forms) and, from there, by a practical deduction, derives new experiments or works. "For I consider induction to be that form of demonstration which upholds the sense, and closes with nature, and comes to the very brink of operation, if it does not actually deal with it" (IV, 24–5). Even if induction is more specifically the ministration of the understanding, it justifies the reduction of the senses, is the active motive of natural history, is the core of demonstration and the only way of establishing first propositions and first notions and provides the operative means to create works. Thus, not only do all parts of the whole process hold together, but the same methodical device operates at the various stages, either in the collecting and ordering of experience in the natural and experimental history or in the establishing of the tables of presentation or in the abstraction of notions and the intellectual induction of axioms.

This method also has a single purpose: to answer the question of invention. How is it possible to invent truth and produce works methodically, and not by chance, since either we do not know what is to be found, and therefore we do not know where to search, so that any discovery is merely fortuitous, or we do know what is to be found and therefore there is nothing to search for? And the metaphysical solutions to this old problem, such as the Platonic idea of reminiscence or the Aristotelian essentialism, which reduces invention to the almost immediate substitution of a noetical apprehension for the empirical perception of things, are to be ruled out.

Let us follow the first aphorisms of the second book of the *Novum organum*. Bacon distinguishes between the speculative and the operative ends of science and, although the invention of causes comes before the production of practical effects, he inverts the order and rests on a first comprehension of practical rules, to make clear the speculative rules of the mind. When we want a practical rule to direct our action, we ask for three things: first, that this rule enables us to reach a result that is not disappointing; secondly, that it does not tie up our operative power to this or that means that could be too restrictive; thirdly, it must make the action easier and must not be more difficult than this action. Therefore "for a true and perfect rule of operation then the direction will be that it be certain, free, and disposing or leading to action" (IV, 121); that is to say, the rule must be efficacious enough, but not too enslaving, and easily leading to action. These three criteria are another expression of the problem of invention: the precept must suggest the means of action and anticipate the result, but without the action being tied up to the means that have been taken up, or being so limited that it becomes impossible.

In a similar manner, the inductive method should be neither blind nor imperative. It must help the understanding on its way toward truth, by giving it some sureness when it is going on, but also a real liberty when it makes a pronouncement. Such is the rule of certainty and liberty. "The fulness of direction to work and produce any effect consisteth in two conditions, certainty and liberty. Certainty is when the direction is not only true for the most part, but infallible. Liberty is when the direction is not restrained to some definite means, but comprehendeth all the means and ways possible" (III, 235). Certainty prospectively restricts the open field of research, but is always limited in extension and perfection, so that it must be overcome by what remains to be found out. The rule will not be an impediment and will be such that things may free the mind of itself. Thus, true knowledge will go from a lower certainty to a higher liberty and from a lower liberty to a higher certainty, and so on. This rule is the basic principle of Bacon's theory of science; prepared in the natural and experimental history, determining the relationship between the tables of presence, it governs the induction of axioms and the abstraction of notions and ordains the divisions of sciences within the general system of knowledge.

III THE CRITIQUE OF THE OLD LOGIC

It is well known that this rule of invention originates in Ramus's methodology and, more formerly, in Aristotle's *Posterior Analytics*.[1] To characterize the nature of the premises required for the foundation of true demonstrations, Aristotle had set down three criteria: the predicate must be true in every instance of its subject; it must be part of the essential nature of the subject; and it must be universal, that is, related to the subject by itself and *qua* itself. Aristotle was defining first propositions as being essential propositions; and he referred universality to necessity and extension to comprehension. These three criteria were much commented upon during the whole scholastic period, and were transformed, or rather extended, by Ramus and others in the sixteenth century. Whereas in Aristotle they had expressed the initial conditions of any conclusive syllogism, in Ramus they became the conditions of every systematic art: within a system, methodically organized for the exhibiting of knowledge, any statement must be taken in its full extension, it must join things which are necessarily related and it must be equivalent to a definition. But these rules for syllogistic or dialectic art in Aristotle or Ramus become rules for inductive invention in Bacon: and their meaning is quite different. With the rule of certainty and liberty, Bacon aims at directly opposing the old logic, infected by syllogistic or rhetoric formalism.

By its title, the *Novum organum* makes Bacon's ambition clear: to replace the Aristotelian organon, which has governed all knowledge until the end of the sixteenth century, with an entirely new logical instrument, a new method for the progress and profit of human science. And the Chancellor proclaims that he has achieved his aim, if posterity acknowledges that, even if he has failed to discover new truths or produce new works, he will have built the means to discover such truths or to produce such works (III, 520). He insists that his method has nothing to do with the old one nor does it try to improve it. And he puts out the choice in these terms:

There are and can be only two ways of searching into and discovering truth. The one flies from the senses and particulars to the most general axioms, and from these principles, the truth of which it takes for settled and immoveable, proceeds to judgment and to the discovery of middle axioms. And this way is now in fashion. The other derives axioms from the senses and particulars, rising by a gradual and unbroken ascent, so that it arrives at the most general axioms last of all. This is the true way, but as yet untried. (IV, 50)

When it is left to itself, the understanding follows the first way, hastily applies itself to reality and generates *anticipations of nature*. But "that reason which is elicited from facts by a just and methodological process, I call *Interpretation of nature*" (IV, 51).

Taken as a whole, Bacon's critique comes to this: from a formal point of view, Aristotle's syllogism is essentially a logic for deductive reasoning, which goes from the principles to the consequences, from the premises to the conclusions. And, of course, in this kind of reasoning, the truth of the conclusions is necessarily derived from the truth of the premises, so that knowledge will start with primary truths that are supposed to be necessary and universal, that is, essential. Now, Bacon asks, how does the mind acquire the knowledge of these primary truths, since, as it is allowed by Aristotle himself, all knowledge starts with experience, which experience is always contingent and particular? How does the mind go from the empirical knowledge of facts or sensible effects (phenomena) to the knowledge of the very nature of things? The formal necessity of the syllogism (or deductive reasoning) makes the old logic forget the pre-judicial question of how we set up first principles. Therefore, any attempt to define the valid form of theories must go through the inquiry upon how we establish truth.

From this general critique, it is easy to understand Bacon's various comments on the old organon. First, since such a logic induces a kind of double start, the empirical one and the rational one, and since it confuses the origin of knowledge with its foundation, the mind is condemned to jump immediately from empirical particulars to first principles (or axioms, in Bacon's terms) and to render superfluous the required induction which would gradually lead from one point to the other. This instantaneous slip from empirical data to rational and essential dogmas is made possible by the very nature of the human mind. Left to itself, the mind hurries toward certainty; it is prone to gain assent and consent; it fills the imagination with idols, untested generalities. And it is this natural haste and prejudice which gives mental activity its anticipative form. By themselves, anticipations draw the most general principles from immediate experience, in order to proceed, as quickly as possible, to the formal deduction of consequences. Therefore, however paradoxical it may appear, the old logic is unduly empirical and unduly logical. And the critique of formalism (formalism draws the conclusions from the premises without inquiring upon the truth of the premises) must be attended by the critique of the nature of the human mind.

The human mind is so disposed that it relies on the senses, which provide it with the rudiments of all knowledge. Of course, Bacon argues, we cannot get any information about things except with the senses, and skeptics are wrong when, questioning them, they plunge the mind into despair. "But by far the greatest hindrance and aberration of the human understanding proceeds from the dulness, incompetency, and deceptions of the senses" (IV, 58). On the one hand, they are too dull and too gross, and let the more subtle parts of nature escape our observation: their range is limited to the most conspicuous information. On the other hand, they are misleading, by a fundamental illusion: they offer things to the mind according to the measure of human nature. "For it is a false assertion that the sense of man is the measure of things. On the contrary, all perceptions as well of the sense as of the mind are according to the measure of the individual and not according to the measure of the universe" (IV, 54). In order to have access to reality, we have to rectify their information and reduce a double delusion: the illusion that the sensible qualities offered by them are the real determinations of things and the illusion that things are divided according to our human sensibility (IV, 194 et sq.).

Thus we can understand a third critique against the old method: the Aristotelian logic rests upon a metaphysics which believes that sensible experience gives the human mind the things as they are, with their essential qualities, and that philosophy can be satisfied with taking empirical phenomena for the true reality of nature, thanks to a mere generalization that erases the particular circumstances of existence. Nevertheless, empirically qualified existences are not to be mistaken for the things themselves. So far, Bacon is undoubtedly a modern, since he claims that the object of knowledge is reality and that reality, if it can be inductively known from empirical data, cannot be reduced to the matter of experience.

Bacon's fourth censure of the old logic follows from this. He agrees with the sixteenth-century dialecticians that Aristotle was wrong when he thought that understanding could skip, without the hard work of induction, from what is immediately given to the senses to what is posed in the first principles of science. Aristotle wanted to know the truth, but did not explain the method of invention. On the other hand, the dialecticians, giving up the attempt to set up the first principles (and thereby the traditional Aristotelian demonstrative science), gave up any attempt to reach the truth. They only retained the deductive and systematic form of discourse to introduce order into men's opinions, and maintained that invention could be reduced to the mere search for arguments, that is, for probable reasons invented to persuade or convince.

Bacon, however, wants to promote the idea of an inductive science and argues that Aristotle's mistake affects the syllogistic form. In the fourth chapter of the fifth book of the *De augmentis*, Bacon develops a remarkable critique of the syllogism and is partly responsible for the widespread disregard of formal logic in the seventeenth and eighteenth centuries.

According to Bacon, "in all inductions, whether in good or vicious form the same action of the mind which inventeth, judgeth" (III, 392). One cannot find without proving, nor prove without finding. But this is not the case in the syllogism: "for the proof being not immediate but by mean, the invention of the mean is one thing, and the judgement of the consequence is another, the one exciting only, the other examining" (III, 392). The syllogism needs the means (the middle term) so that the derived conclusion amounts to a proof. But since the syllogism is incapable of inventing the middle term, it must have been known before. In other words, syllogistic form leaves the invention of the middle term to the natural shrewdness of the mind or to good fortune. Thus, it is because of its own demonstrative form that the syllogism is unable to provide a method of truth and is useless for science.

By now it is clear why the old logic and the knowledge which is built on it are unable to produce works or why the extant works "are due to chance and experience rather than to sciences" (IV, 48). To deduce practical effects, the mind must know real causes or laws of nature. Since the old method does not supply the mind with the means of inventing causes and does not set up the scale of the intermediate propositions that are needed to reduce sensible experience and reach the real science, or to derive rightly and by degrees the consequences from the principles, it is not surprising that invented works are too few and not very useful for men's lives. Thus, from the start in sensible experience to the end in practical deduction, this old method is of no use. And an entirely new one must be proposed, which will be able to carry the human mind from empirical data to the real causes, to supply it with the means of invention, to justify the position of first truths and to manage a secure deduction of practical consequences. And, as the critique of the old logic has to be understood as a whole, so the interpretation of nature has to be conceived as a continuous attempt, proceeding by degrees, by successive stages, to invent truth and to derive works.

IV THE REDUCTION OF THE SENSES AND NATURAL AND EXPERIMENTAL HISTORY

Bacon has very often been described as the philosopher of experience, of an experience so absorbed in collecting facts and so busily preoccupied with utility, that he totally ignored the theoretical essence of knowledge. This portrait is flatly wrong. For the Chancellor frequently criticizes those *Empirici* who "are like the ant; they only collect and use" (IV, 92–3). For to be an empiric is either to commit oneself to the stream of a vague and fortuitous experience, to compile sensible information and link them by hasty resemblances, or to decide "on the authority of too few cases" (IV, 63). In opposition to the rational philosophers, the empiric school is made up with the authors of natural histories or with chemists and blind experimentalists. They not only are in a great hurry to discover new facts, but they also and chiefly fail to understand what is given by nature in experience. Bacon does not naively think that nature immediately tells the senses what things are and what their causes are. We have seen that one of the consequences of his critique of the Aristotelian logic is the claim that there is no possible ontology of common sense and that, if the empirical world is made up with things and qualities, the real world, discovered by science, is a world of causal laws and operations. And the first act of the method, and its most fundamental act, is precisely to make us understand that if it is true that knowledge begins with sensible experience, it must obtain access to the invisible processes and structures of nature.

This is the reason why the first step of the method is the critical "ministration" or assistance afforded to the senses. Although reliance on the senses acts as a bulwark against metaphysical systems and rhetorical uses of language, the empirical information thus gained is itself unreliable. We know that the immediate character of perception leads the mind too easily to consider the sensible content, which is given, as the real nature of things. Therefore, senses should be helped with a methodical assistance: first, to correct their testimony and rectify their information which is biased by human receptivity; secondly, with the help of experiments, of substitutions or graduations, to try to submit to the senses themselves what escapes them because of their too narrow limits; at last, to extend and improve the collecting of facts, the content of which is very hazardous, by an experimentation that provokes nature where it has not yet informed the mind. Therefore, although it is the case that all true science depends on the senses, we should not forget that their information must be corrected and enlarged. Method penetrates sensible experience itself, and stipulates the conditions according to which the senses can judge of the reality of things.

Methodized experience is collected in a renewed natural history, which is the foundation of natural philosophy. Bacon not only reproaches his predecessors for not having collected a natural history which would be large and plentiful enough, but he aims at changing the intention of such a history. "A natural history which is composed for its own sake is not like one that is collected to supply the understanding with information for the building up of philosophy" (IV, 94). Till now, natural history has been made to satisfy curiosity; henceforth, it has to be ruled by the idea of physical and metaphysical knowledge, with a view to the right abstraction of notions and the due invention of general propositions.

If natural history has to obey an inductive logic, it must be enlarged to any particular, natural or artificial, observable or experimental. It is the same nature that operates in individuals, species, or practical experiments of human arts, according to the same laws, the same order of forms realized in matter. Even more, the history of the experiments in which nature is submitted to the violence of human arts will be promoted, since "the nature of things betrays itself more readily under the vexations of art than in its natural freedom" (IV, 29). By doing this, arts dispel the mist of appearances and urge the understanding to disclose the secret structures and the subtle motions of nature.

Thus enlarged to all particulars, natural and experimental history is to be taken for experience itself. "For I consider history and experience to be the same thing, as also philosophy and the sciences" (IV, 293). Of course, Bacon still identifies observation with the action of the senses, and distinguishes it from experiment. But he demands that observation be learned enough to seize invisible things and he contests that it is enough to provoke experiments, as chemists do, to escape the vice of the mere experience that is groping in the dark. "The true method [ordo] of experience on the contrary first lights the candle, and then by means of the candle shows the way; commencing as it does with experience duly ordered and digested, not bungling or erratic, and from it educing axioms, and from established axioms again new experiments" (IV, 81). In general, experience is the collection or the exhibition of such objects as have a theoretical import. And to name these natural or experimental data, Bacon borrows the old word *instance* from Aristotle. An instance is neither an illustrative example, nor a particular case, but any information rich in inductive power, either by the place that it occupies in a table or by some prerogative or methodical virtue.

Thus the method changes and enriches the meaning of experience. Experience, taken from corrected and extended sense-data, ordered and disposed into tables or classifications, is more than mere experience, just as an experience informed by the inductive reasoning itself will be more than mere natural history. It could be opposed that it is contradictory to want knowledge to begin with the things themselves, without any logical or theoretical conditions or presuppositions, and at the same time to require a method that decides what is to be known. How can science have access to reality (and the test for reality is that it is given by the senses) and at the same time ask for a method that will say what reality is? Bacon is very conscious of this question and answers: "I contrive that the office of the sense shall be only to judge of the experiment, and that the experiment itself shall judge of the thing" (IV, 26). Common experience cannot be taken for the experience of the reality itself as it is determined by causes and forms. To move from the sensible to the real requires the correction of the senses, the tables of natural history, the abstraction of propositions and the induction of notions. In other words, the full carrying out of the inductive method is needed.

As the first step of this continuous process of knowledge, natural history is ruled by several requirements. Since it provides the understanding with its information, it must be certain and reliable. Besides the critical demands (one should discard false experiences, marvelous phenomena or unbelievable testimonies, authorities, fallacious narrations, etc.), it has to select fruitful instances, supply a plentiful experience, and train the mind to the subtlety of nature. Fruitfulness means inventiveness:

At first and for a time I am seeking for experiments of light [lucifera experimenta], not for experiments of fruit [fructifera experimenta]; following therein, as I have often said, the example of the divine creation; which on the first day produced light only, and assigned to it alone one entire day, nor mixed up with it on that day any material work. (IV, 107)

Plentifulness does not mean the mere and blind heaping up of data, but the possibility of enlarging or dilating the human understanding to the size of the world, so that it be able to become its exact and polished mirror. This same first attempt to change the measure of man for the measure of the universe is still to be made about subtlety: natural history should free itself of the false subtlety of the mind to get open to the subtlety of nature. One has to collect experiments that can initiate the inductive conversion of the mind and push it from what is apparent to what is latent, from phenomena to the invisible, to the real order of things.

Order is the principle of any natural history. But Bacon is well acquainted with the traditional problem: where does the order come from? Does it come from the understanding itself? Or is it extracted from the things themselves? Now, Bacon on the one hand criticizes any anticipation of the mind, and on the other hand considers that empirical things cannot be taken for real things. His solution is original enough, and concerns both the order within each natural history and the order of the catalog of various natural histories. He entertains an evolutive concept of method: order changes according to the degree of abstraction. A first order can collect the data and it will be empirical, immediately drawn from things, as they appear.

Such a history is still mainly narrative. But if instances are collected that are endowed with an inventive power, the mind can set down a second order, which will be no longer the order of sensible things, but the order of qualities (what Bacon calls natures); and after some labor, this order of concrete natures will be changed into the order of abstract natures, an order much more informative about the causes producing phenomena. Thus, the true method of natural history is to invent an order that can change step by step, each change meaning a more exact and subtle, and a less phenomenal approach of nature by the mind. And this is the fundamental reason why the method of natural history, in its very essence, is inductive. In general, the method is not to be understood as an imperative: it is an indication, a direction, something like a compass (to use Bacon's metaphor). It is a way through or the effort toward the next step of knowledge. We could say that the method of induction is itself ruled by induction. "For we have laid it down that the art of invention must augment the things invented and that the industry and fortune of men must not be forced into an artifice of immobile and immune invention" (III, 635–6).

V   THE TABLES OF PRESENTATION

Thus, there is plainly only one method, from the first step to the last step of knowledge, and the previous step is already the start of the next step, even if the next step, once reached, makes the previous one unnecessary. It has often been said that there were two methods in Bacon's philosophy: the method of natural history, which is a help for the memory (the faculty which registers and arranges data), and the inductive method of the understanding. This is the way in which his successors (for instance Boyle, but also the French encyclopedists) understood his methodical lesson, at a time when the method of theory had become mathematical. Since modern science is mathematical and experimental, one could be Galilean or Cartesian as far as theory is concerned, and Baconian in the experimental field. Bacon would have made clear the conditions and the rules of experimentalism and, willingly or not, would have limited the ambition of an experimental science to the setting up of general facts, that is to say, to the determination of correlated phenomena on a more or less abstract level. In that sense, his main contribution to modern science would not include his attempt to justify an inductive form of theory. Such a reading is possible but somewhat anachronistic, since it was not the purpose of the author of the *Novum Organum*. And it is much more interesting to delineate the Baconian project as opposed to the methodical form of modern science.

When he presents the main partitions of the interpretation of nature in the *Novum organum* (IV, 126–7), Bacon divides the theoretical moment (how to educe and form axioms from experience) "into three ministrations; a ministration to the sense, a ministration to the memory, and a ministration to the mind or reason." Then, he distinguishes three progressive levels: the preparation of a natural and experimental history which is the foundation of all, "for we are not to imagine or suppose, but to discover, what nature does or may be made to do"; then the constitution of "Tables and Arrangements of Instances," because natural and experimental history, left to itself, confounds and distracts the understanding, by its variety, and because understanding needs an order or a method to deal with it; at last, "even when this is done, still the understanding, if left to itself and its own spontaneous movements, is incompetent and unfit to form axioms, unless it be directed and guarded. Therefore, in the third place we must use *Induction*, true and legitimate induction, which is the very key of interpretation." This last phase of method in its turn gives rise to several distinctions: we shall at first consider the tables of presentation and then the process of exclusion which leads to an affirmative; and once the mind has been provided with this methodology, which makes up the essential part of the inductive operation, we can study different aids to the understanding (the prerogative instances), in order to shorten or facilitate induction.

Several things must be noticed in this aphorism (part II, aph. 10). First, the unambiguous affirmation that the core of the method is induction and that the core of induction is the formation of axioms, that is to say, general propositions expressing the causes of phenomena. Secondly, the place of the tables in this general arrangement is unstable: now they are pushed toward natural history, now they are drawn back toward the theoretical part of induction (IV, 126–8, 145). But this instability can be easily explained: the tables present before the understanding all the known instances related to some nature that is the object of investigation. "And such collection must be made in the manner of a history, without premature speculation, or any great amount of subtlety" (IV, 127). And, once these instances have been presented before the understanding, "Induction itself must be set at work" (IV, 145), going to the affirmative through the negative. For, if the mind attempts to get to the affirmative "from the first, as when left to itself it is always wont to do, the result will be fancies and guesses, and notions ill defined, and axioms that must be mended every day" (IV, 145).

But this progress from a first and still empirical presentation to the negative, and from the negative to the affirmative, is already at work in the tables themselves. For, there are three tables: the first one, which still pertains to natural history, exhibits the quality or given nature (for instance, heat, whiteness) that is studied in the common experience of things: the given nature appears as the quality of various substances which will be as dissimilar as possible to enlarge the range of the inquiry. This is the table of presence where the ontological status of substances is still empirical. In order to move from this to the table of absence, it is necessary to break with the Aristotelian notion that a quality is an accident of the substance or something which belongs to its essence. By an abstraction, a quality is correlated with another quality, which is always present or absent when the first quality is present or absent. Once this second quality is discovered and submitted to the due process of induction, it will be known as the form or the real cause of the initial given nature.

Thus, the table of absence starts the extraction of forms from the table of presence (or natural history). It is this table that, by unloosing the given nature from the empirical matter in which it appears, rectifies phenomena, turns the understanding toward causes and forms, and initiates the process of induction. And since the number of instances where the given nature is absent is indefinite, the table will be set up by proximity, that is to say, in such a way that, although the similitude of matters would make the mind wait for the nature that is studied, nevertheless this nature is absent. As for the third table, the table of comparison, it confirms the results of the previous ones, varying the degrees of presence and absence in the two natures henceforth related, the given nature and the invented nature (the form). Of course, such a method, at the beginning, is still engaged with the empirical matter of a still slightly rectified experience and belongs more to concrete physics than to abstract physics.

But it is a first and rough sketch of the induction that operates in the abstraction of axioms and notions; and the law of exclusion is already at work, since exactly the same relationship between the negative and the affirmative prevails in both cases.

VI THE METHOD OF FRUITFUL EXPERIENCE

The end of the exclusion is the invention of causes, and supreme causes are forms. Since human science cannot immediately jump from experience to the knowledge of first causes (that is the method of anticipation, which was used by the old logic), it must go through intermediate stages of knowledge less and less empirical and more and more theoretical, so far as invention proceeds. But the success of the whole enterprise will not be definitely confirmed as long as the ultimate knowledge of forms is not acquired. And it is doubtful whether the human understanding will ever be able to reach such a perfection. Shall we say, then, that, because the ignorance of causes makes any practical deduction impossible, a perfect knowledge is the necessary condition of the welfare and industry of men? But everybody knows that life cannot wait, that men have to get the means of their lives now, not tomorrow. And the one who would require such a condition, would fall into despair and skepticism regarding the possibility of a real knowledge and of a fruitful practice. Therefore, even if our science of causes is imperfect, it must already be taken for a knowledge in progress, instructing the mind and leading to practical consequences.

Bacon repeatedly lays out such truncated proceedings that, in a way, defer the inductive influx in order to get an immediate benefit. First, there is what he calls *learned experience*. The invention of sciences "either proceeds from one experiment to another; or else from experiments to axioms; which axioms themselves suggest new experiments. The one of these I will term Learned Experience [*experientia literata*], the other Interpretation of Nature, or the New Organon. But the former . . . must hardly be esteemed an art or a part of philosophy, but rather a kind of sagacity" (IV, 413). Once a large store of data and experiments has been collected by natural history, it may be expedient, instead of having the understanding to deal with the matter immediately, to weigh this compiled matter and, in a way, to appreciate its fruitfulness as a historical matter. But the condition for such an appreciation is that history be registered in writing: "no course of invention can be satisfactory unless it be carried on in writing. But when this is brought into use, and experience has been taught to read and write, better things may be hoped" (IV, 96). Learned experience tries to go from the known to the unknown particulars, without appealing to general causes. It joins together several empirical devices, the principle of which is transposition: all these procedures rest on analogical extension by proximity, variation, connections, and aim at the transfer of fruitful results to fields not yet explored or to experiments not yet tested. The rule of such analogical strategy, since it cannot be the knowledge of causes which is the true foundation of the real (if not always apparent) similitude of the effects, is the order or method of natural history itself. Of course, things that are discovered this way are not totally certain. But the true method, in the interval between mere ignorance and perfect knowledge, disposes definite degrees of certainty, to relieve the effort of the mind and obtain some practical advantages, before reaching the full understanding of causes.

The same kind of procedure is allowed after the tables of first presentation have been displayed and carefully examined. This is based on the first application of the exclusion principle, a principle which is more inventive and more theoretical than the mere order of natural histories. If the mind duly proceeded on its way toward forms, it would submit the affirmative conclusion, obtained by the application of the exclusion principle, to a new negative process. And even if the mind must "remember withal (especially at the beginning) that what it has before it depends in great measure upon what remains behind" (IV, 149), nevertheless, "I think it expedient that the understanding should have permission, after the three Tables of First Presentation (such as I have exhibited) have been made and weighed, to make an essay of the Interpretation of Nature in the affirmative way" (IV, 149). Bacon calls this first essay of interpretation the "First Vintage." In this way we may, for instance, obtain a first definition of heat that contains what can be said about this nature, on the basis of the tables which have collected and worked out a certain amount of experience, and thus have a first tentative knowledge of the causes of this phenomenon; and we may set forth a first practical rule on how to create heat.

VII THE PRESENCE/ABSENCE RULE AND THE INDUCTION OF AXIOMS

Of course, neither learned experience nor first vintage is the last word of science, and induction must be carried on. A key role in this is played by the process of exclusion. It aims at reducing the empirical character of experience. Mere experience gives the mind concrete things or substances endowed with qualities that are supposed to be essential or accidental. And the Aristotelian epistemology had developed a causal system where changes, motions, were ultimately related to the nature or essence of things themselves. According to Bacon, such a metaphysical explanation of our experience of Being is wrong. Of course, beings are all individual and one must not imagine a separated world, where more perfect beings would exist, such as the Platonic forms. Nevertheless, the concrete character of empirical things, that is to say, the fact that various qualities are melted together into one being that seems to be the reason for them, stands in the way of science. For instance, if one wants to explain why the sun burns, common sense will answer that the sun is a kind of fireball and that it burns because burning belongs to the essence of the sun – which is, of course, to explain nothing. So the first step is to dissect substances and make the various qualities or natures that are entangled distinct. So far, method will be an analysis that makes the anatomy of things. "A separation and solution of bodies must be effected, not by the fire indeed, but by reasoning and true induction, with experiments to aid; and by a comparison with other bodies, and a reduction to simple natures and their Forms, which meet and mix in the compound" (IV, 125). The table of presence already prepares this analysis, since it presents a nature or quality (for instance, the hot) in things as dissimilar as possible, so that it cannot be taken for the mere property of these things. The result is drawn by the second table, the table of absence which presents things where the nature that one wants to study would be expected and is actually absent. This means that this nature is correlated with another nature or quality that is present when it is itself present, and absent when it is itself absent. Thus, one does not examine any longer the essential or accidental link between things and properties, but focuses research on the relationship between two natures or qualities, the given one and the one that is discovered by this process. Of course, the given nature is still empirical and it will have to be analyzed by degrees; and likewise the invented nature may still be compound and need a further resolution. Analysis is a continuous process, the end of which will be simple natures.

But there is another aspect of the method of science than analysis: abstraction. It could seem that Bacon goes back to Plato in his fight against Aristotle, since knowledge must bear on the relationship between natures or forms. According to Bacon, Plato rightly understood that forms are the object of investigation, but he misunderstood the meaning of induction when he did not "consider the first matter as united to the first form" but wanted to abstract forms from matter (V, 468). Forms are real, but they are not beings. Therefore, analysis is to be taken as the means of rising by degrees from particular existences to simple natures and it must save the inductive tension between matter and form, empirical evidence and abstract knowledge. Exclusion is a process of determination, by which science progressively slides from the material determination that is apparent in empirical evidence, to the formal determination of real causes. It is not only a means of comparative determination, by presence and absence, but also the progressive abstraction from matter (matter cannot be entirely neglected) and the progressive generalization of causes. In other words, exclusion must be the way from a less abstract affirmative to a more general affirmative. (Bacon is still working on the Aristotelian pattern of a division or determination by genus and species.)

The best example of this rather sophisticated methodical contrivance (it was more easily understood in the seventeenth century by people brought up in an Aristotelian culture) is provided by the *Valerius Terminus* (III, 235–49), which for the first time sets forth the rule of certainty and liberty. Let the nature to be explained or operatively produced be *whiteness,* and the initial empirical field comprise white objects: snow, the breaking waves of the sea, and the like. A first analysis leads to the first affirmative proposition that whiteness is produced by air and water broken into small pieces and mixed up together. This proposition is roughly true, but limited to two substances, water and air, empirically known (we do not know their invisible structure). And we cannot account for the whiteness of glass beaten to fine powder or for the whiteness of beaten egg-white. So, one must enlarge the empirical field and at the same time proceed to a more determinate conception of the two substances that are mixed up. And here exclusion is at work, if, for instance, instead of water, we say that air is mixed up with an uncolored and more grossly transparent body than air itself. By such a substitution, we have excluded properties which were intermingled with transparency in water (for instance, liquidity) and extracted a quality that can be found in water, in eggs, and the like. And when we refer to an uncolored transparent body, we have to do with an idea which is more abstract than the idea of water. Of course, one can repeat this argument and observe that the powder of crushed amber or sapphire is white and that, therefore, the previous explanation or affirmative is too restricted and inadequate so far as amber and sapphire are not uncolored bodies. Therefore, we must remove the confusion of the uncolored and the transparent, discard the first property and say that whiteness is produced by the mixture of any transparent body with air. And so on.

This remarkable reasoning is many-sided. First, at each step the empirical basis gets larger: more and more substances are covered by the explanation and the phenomenal evidence is relied upon less and less. Secondly, we have a scale of abstraction where the successively invented predicates are gradually and continuously losing their empirical import and, so to speak, say less and less of what could be the essence of bodies or beings and make more and more intelligible a nature that itself gets simpler and simpler. Thirdly, what was at the beginning taken as a cause (the connection between two existing bodies), has become the connection between two predicates or abstract natures, that is to say a law. Fourthly, if we consider the relationship between the empirical phenomenon to be explained (whiteness, such as it appears as a property of various bodies) and the law or the invented cause (according to Bacon, whiteness is produced by the fine mixture of two bodies that are unequal in a simple proportion) and how the law comes to be invented, we find an exemplary application of the rule of certainty and liberty.

If therefore your direction be certain, it must refer you and point you to somewhat which, if it be present, the effect you seek will of necessity follow, else may you perform and not obtain. If it be free, then must it refer you to somewhat which if it be absent the effect you seek will of necessity withdraw, else may you have power and not attempt. (III, 235–6)

Let us take the first explanation of whiteness as being the mixture of air and water: it is certain that if you make this mixture, you will get whiteness. But you will obtain this nature only in snow or in foam, and not in crushed glass. So that certainty means a restriction to a narrow field of experiments. Concerning snow and foam, the explanation is universal and necessary, since when the cause is present or absent, the effect is present or absent. But, of course, it is not good for crushed glass, since here the given nature can be present, and the cause absent (there is no water in glass). So we have to liberate our mind from the first explanation which is too restricted, and to proceed to a more abstract explanation, universally and necessarily valid for snow, foam, crushed glass, and so on. And, at each level, the same dynamic argument is repeated. Of course, the first explanation is not invalidated, but it is strictly confined to its empirical field. The subsequent explanation covers a larger experience and includes the previous one, but in a more abstract way. And it is more subtle and closer to the real and full explanation of the phenomenon. Thus, the rule of presence corresponds to the rule of certainty, the rule of absence to the rule of liberty. And, the rule of presence affirms the universal relationship between the cause and the effect, the form and the phenomenon, the *natura naturans* and the *natura naturata*. The rule of absence confirms this relationship by making it necessary, but this determination itself makes it obvious that the explanation is too narrow, that it is appropriate only for a certain empirical field; and therefore, by the work of exclusion, we must proceed to a more universal, and a more formally determinate explanation. And perfect science will be reached, when causes are strictly adequate to effects.

Thus, induction results from the correlative action of universality and necessity. These criteria were the requirements for premises or first propositions in Aristotle's *Posterior Analytics*. Bacon differs from Aristotle by taking them not as a formal description of every scientific proposition, but as the dynamism of the invention of propositions. When one compares Aristotle's three criteria and Bacon's two laws of certainty and liberty, one easily observes that the rule of certainty plainly corresponds to the law of the universal attribution of the predicate to the subject. The rule of liberty seems to correspond to the third Aristotelian law, which says that the predicate belongs to the subject *qua* itself (being what it is). For Aristotle, however, the second law (that the predicate belongs to the essence of the subject) is the most important one, since it founds the universality and the validity of propositions and syllogisms on the necessity derived from the essence of things.

In Bacon's *Novum organum*, it appears to be changed into a rule of convertibility: "For a true and perfect axiom of knowledge then the direction and precept will be, that another nature be discovered which is convertible with the given nature, and yet is a limitation of a more general nature, as of a true and real genus" (IV, 121–2). And the change is crucial. In Baconian interpretation of nature, convertibility is generated by the application of the rule of absence to the rule of presence: if, when the form (the cause) is present or absent, the given nature (the phenomenon) is present or absent, then the form and the given nature are convertible. The form is the causal definition of the given nature, but only in the limits of the given nature (which means that explanation itself is still imperfect). Therefore, this convertibility does not entail an exact identity. For, the invented form is the cause of the given nature, so far as it draws it from a more general nature, best known by nature (not by ourselves) and of which it is the limitation or the true difference; so that it is a kind of ratio between two degrees of generality, still to be renewed on a higher level, until induction arrives to the affirmative of a simple form. Remarkably, Bacon borrows from Aristotle the species/genus structure: it is when one confirms the determination of species, that genus is invented. By defining convertibility by this structure, by attributing a discursive function to the rule of absence, when applied to the rule of presence, Bacon hopes to solve the problem of induction or invention.

VIII FROM INDUCTION OF AXIOMS TO PRACTICAL DEDUCTION

It will be observed that Bacon is much more concerned by propositions than by reasonings. His main problem is: how can we methodically form true propositions? And he reproaches the old logic for forgetting this question and spontaneously supposing the truth of propositions, for turning quickly to deductive reasonings. But reasoning is primarily the way to pose true propositions; and (causal) definitions are the result of science, not its start. The core of knowledge is invention. The main exertion of the mind is the induction of more and more general axioms expressing the real nature of things.

Moreover, an axiom or a proposition is made up with notions. And the same inductive procedure prevails for notions. "Propositions consist of words, words are symbols of notions. Therefore if the notions themselves (which is the root of the matter) are confused and over-hastily abstracted from the facts, there can be no firmness in the superstructure. Our only hope therefore lies in a true induction" (IV, 49). The mind begins with empirical notions that are ill determined and do not follow the exact and subtle divisions of nature. By a due abstraction, then, we must reduce their sensible meaning. But since both Platonism and nominalism are unacceptable, the real meaning of notions must be invented. And when the meaning becomes more universal and thereby more necessary, the real meaning can gradually be determined: negatively by the rejections and exclusions which remove the restrictions attached to individuals; affirmatively by the knowledge of the formal cause of the nature conceived in the notion. In other words, the induction of notions cannot be separated from the induction of propositions: to think is to know. Thus, the union between the mind and nature can be realized: if the determination of notions requires the knowledge of forms, and if forms are the necessary causes of a given nature, then it is clear that the intellectual determination of notions (which at first are only perceptions in the mind) gradually assumes the real necessity of causes and that the boundaries drawn by the mind fade away in favor of the true divisions of things such as they are prescribed by nature itself. This must be the aim of the mind: to owe nothing to itself, but everything to nature.

In many respects, Bacon's induction still depends on the ancient conception of definition, of species and genus, of matter and form, and generally speaking on the idea that the theory of science must rest on a metaphysical foundation. And it is true that Bacon's conception of induction is metaphysical, since his intention is to promote a method that gives access to nature itself, in such a way that this artificial device of method gives way to reality. But his critique of the Aristotelian essentialism and of the syllogistic logic makes him a modern. In a way, we are caught between the Ancients and the Moderns.

This has to be borne in mind when we come to the last step of the method, the practical deduction. Deduction goes from principles to consequences, and practice from causes to effects. And Bacon retains the Aristotelian identification between first principles and first causes. But there is no deduction without induction, no operation without speculation. We can understand this if we translate the inductive scheme into causal terms. Aristotle distinguished among four kinds of causes: material, formal, efficient, and final. Let us discard the final cause. In Bacon's philosophy, the progress of explanation can be described as the way from the material cause to the formal cause, via the efficient cause. We are empirically acquainted with causes: we say that a body can push another one, when it has acquired a certain force. Such causes are material, since they are related to various bodies and properties that are given by experience. Now, if we use the rule of certainty, according to which when the cause is present, the effect infallibly follows, material causes appear to be efficient. In the restricted field where this universal and necessary connection between cause and effect prevails, we are able to explain and generate the effect from the cause. But we do not yet have a distinct conception of the power which is at work. If we remove the restriction and proceed to a higher level, we will have a more determinate conception of the cause; and our operative power will be more extended, more subtle and more efficient. Thus, we progress in the knowledge of causes, that is to say of forms. And if we were able to know the first formal causes (in metaphysics), we would be able to produce such and such an effect on any matter (in magic). To know causes is to gain a greater power on things, so that the degree of practical power acquired is proportionate to the level of induction. "Human knowledge and human power meet in one; for where the cause is not known the effect cannot be produced. Nature to be commanded must be obeyed; and that which in contemplation is as the cause is in operation as the rule" (IV, 47).

But we said previously that true induction gives way to nature. Consequently, the greater the power of man is, the more nature acts in human operation. The power of men over nature is artificial so long as it is imperfect. At the lower stage of physical knowledge, we are able to set efficient causes into action (for instance, in mechanics). But the full conversion of speculation into operation will be made at best in the metaphysical knowledge of forms, where our human power will become perfectly natural (in magic). Therefore, if man is able to be the true interpreter of nature and if he knows how not to mix up his own nature with the nature of things, then he will be the master of nature, but so far as he is its minister. "For man by the fall fell at the same time from his state of innocence and from his dominion over creation. Both of these losses however can even in this life be in some part repaired; the former by religion and faith, the latter by arts and sciences" (IV, 247–8).

NOTE

1 *Posterior Analytics*, I.4.73a25 et sq.

4 Bacon's forms and the maker's knowledge tradition

I INTRODUCTION

Induction and Form belong to the most "technical" core among the concepts elaborated by Francis Bacon in his reflections on human knowledge, as counterdistinct from the more "ideological" tenets concerning his ideal of collective utility or his desideratum of a state-sponsored model for scientific research. Yet, a mere glance at Bacon's fortunes reveals a profound discontinuity between the reception of inductivism and experimentation on the one hand and of his theory of Forms on the other. Though not paramount among the canonical version of Baconianism presented by Thomas Sprat in his *History of the Royal Society* of 1667 (where the notions of natural history and theory-free experimenting seem to enjoy pride of place), reflections on inductive processes have been traditionally linked to the doctrines expounded in the *Novum organum* and, more generally, to the overall orthodox mapping of modern physical science. But the Baconian Forms seem to have attracted a purely historical (or antiquarian) interest, both from the point of view of what near contemporaries adopted of Bacon's philosophy and from the almost universal verdict that students have pronounced on that concept – a verdict amounting to an uncompromising dismissal of the Form as a totally useless tool in the construction of modern science.

There is a fair amount of Whiggism in this, however; the Baconian Form fell into oblivion very soon as far as a historically recognizable corpus of physics is concerned, but there is perhaps a deeper level of philosophical analysis which, as I shall try to show, transcends the explicit use of a term such as this (or "essence" or "cause") and helps

99

us to unearth certain patterns of thought which are present in both its "modern" and "archaic" expressions.

Now even in the period of Victorian deification in which the standard edition of Bacon's works was finally completed, R. L. Ellis wrote apologetically that "the doctrine of Forms is in some sort an extraneous part of Bacon's system" (I, 28), largely by virtue of the ambiguous use of the term, of its gradual appearance in the Baconian *oeuvre* and of its mostly belonging "not to natural philosophy but to metaphysics" (I, 29). Further yet, Ellis stipulated that Bacon's "peculiar method may be stated independently of this doctrine, and he has himself so stated it in one of his earlier tracts, namely the *Valerius Terminus*" (I, 28). This is a line of defense that can legitimately be adopted if one seeks somehow to complement or to refurbish Bacon's methodological insights in the way a Herschel, a Whewell, or a J. Stuart Mill tried to do, that is, by taking Bacon as an almost contemporary figure. For example, since no concept in nineteenth-century science corresponded to the Baconian notion of Form, Whewell sought to salvage the prestigious link between Bacon's and Newton's method by arguing that the Lord Chancellor had hit upon one of the key notions of modern scientific rationality, that is, Nature's lawlikeness:

Bacon and others had used *form* as equivalent as *law*. If we could ascertain that arrangement of particles of a crystal from which its external crystalline form and other properties arise, this arrangement would be the internal form of the crystal. If the undulatory theory be true, the *form* of light is transverse vibrations: if the emission theory be maintained, the form of light is particles moving in straight lines, and deflected by various forces. Both the terms, form and law imply an ideal connection of sensible phenomena; form supposes matter which is moulded to the form; law supposes objects which are governed by the law. The former refers more precisely to existences, the latter to occurrences.[1]

Recent research has tried to document Whewell's interpretation against the background of the matter theory against which Bacon reacted and whose defeat led to the undisputed sway of Corpuscularianism in European philosophy. Dwelling on his relation both to Aristotelianism and to the oncoming particulate doctrines, N. E. Emerton has argued that

Bacon understood the form in terms of an ordered disposition of matter and also as a law, the divine *fiat* . . . [It was] expressed in terms of law rather than as some easily visualized mode of material structure, but at the same time it was more practical, suggesting ways in which the activity of the form might be investigated experimentally. Bacon was able to combine a critical attitude to scholasticism with an appreciation of Aristotelian insights; indeed he was often close to Aristotle in his approach. From this tradition he obtained his emphasis on the material involvement of the form; his understanding of the form as law, as order, and as act; his use of internal configuration; his recognition of the material and efficient causes as vehicles of the form; and his hierarchy of lower and higher forms.[2]

This is a highly documented way of putting historical flesh onto the philosophical bones of Whewell's sympathetic analysis, as Emerton is able to trace this linking of the notion of form with the internal disposition of bodies to insights already present in the Aristotelian persuasions of an Ockham, an Oresme, or a Nifo. Yet the search for ideal precedents ought not to obscure the fact of Bacon's undisputed claim to novelty and how this claim can be articulated in terms of the style of thought and the paradigm of human knowledge which he so enthusiastically adopted with his conception of a *scientia operativa*, wholly bent on subduing rather than contemplating Nature. A philosophical hermeneutic worth its salt has to reconstruct the semantics of this ideal as it manifests itself in one of Bacon's most perplexing key concepts, whose critical target may be succinctly outlined before we proceed.

In its various versions as a key concept of Peripatetic matter theory, the notion of substantial form recaptures the main import of Aristotle's hylomorphism. Yet in Aristotle's own texts we may distinguish between those parts in which the Greek philosopher was predominantly dealing with the problem of change *qua* physical alteration[3] and those in which he tried to discriminate between epistemologically acceptable definitions in terms of the genus/species differentiation.[4] Aristotle's Scholastic followers failed in general to keep these two fields apart, and so their doctrine lent itself to great complexity and elaboration, as well as to much confusion and verbosity. Briefly put, the substantial forms accounted for the essential characteristics of a thing (in Scholastic jargon, its *nota* or defining traits or marks) and for the specific behavior or function which that thing exhibits (in Latin, its *vis effectrix*). For instance, it is the substantial form of an orange tree which supposedly makes that lump of timber and heap of leaves something qualitatively different from a cactus or an oak. And the essential characteristics of that species in terms of its behavior – for example, its budding season, its requirements of sun exposure, temperature, humidity, and the rest – are also the result of its having received that particular substantial form *and no other*, as it is the business of the substantial form of magnet to attract iron and of fire to melt it. Hence substantial forms seem to resemble tiny souls attached to matter, intentional agents of sorts and principles of physical action: without them matter would be a merely passive lump (precisely, *un*informed matter). Now the fact that neither Bacon nor Descartes (to cite the two standard-bearers of modern anti-Scholasticism) did develop a sustained and systematic argument against the exacting complexities of these doctrines reflects the uncompromisingly different projects of physical inquiry that both embraced with regard to Scholasticism and its general matter theory. Lexical continuities, however, may obscure this point.

II THE ELEMENTARY COMPONENTS OF NATURE

No seventeenth-century author seems to have seriously objected to Bacon's use of the term Form. Nor did the various definitions of the Form that he offered in his major works appear whimsical or eccentric. Let us review two significant passages:

> The Form of a thing is the very thing itself [*Forma rei sit ipsissima res*] and the thing differs from the form no otherwise than as the apparent differs from the real, or the external from the internal, or the thing in reference to man from the thing in reference to the universe [*aut in ordine ad hominem et in ordine ad universum*]. (IV, 137; I, 248)

> The Form . . . [is] true specific difference, or nature-engendering nature, or source of emanation (for these are the terms which come nearest to a description of a thing [*ad indicationem rei proxime accedunt*]). (IV, 119; I, 227)

Our construal of the Baconian Form may take this kind of definition as its starting point. We notice first that, contrary to purely phenomenologist approaches to matter theory, Bacon holds that the inquiry into natural beings ought not to stop at the level of sense perception.[5] Rather, it should introduce a fundamental distinction between that which is apparent and that which is postulated as real. What sort of man-independent reality is this? The context suggests that true reality is only duly unveiled when the human perceiver, whose cognitive equipment Bacon has already declared faulty (I, 163–79; IV, 53–69), is put into brackets or, so to speak, abstracted from the very process of cognition. Now, what kind of metaphysical commitment is this phrasing suggesting? Obviously one in which, amongst the qualities that the human perceiver can get hold of, some are granted a higher ontological status than others – a position which mirrors the so-called scale or hierarchy of Forms *qua* theoretical counterparts of any such high-ranking "natures" or perceptible qualities. This metaphysical presupposition conveys the idea of, in Bacon's own phrase, an *abecedarium Naturae*, that is, a list or canon of fundamental physical properties which, by combining and recombining themselves in various modes, give rise to the manifold of sense experience. Such privileged set, however, does not depend on any empirical information, but appears to be posited a priori. Nature, as a collection of individuals conceptually ordered into classes, may be infinite; the number of its minimal components is not (IV, 122, 126; V, 209, 426). And such minimal components are postulated as physically retranslatable in terms of some essential or elemental qualities (heat, cold, texture, etc.); these in turn are supposed to be the result of some further elements that are not substantively qualitative themselves: figure, bulk, and motion. In Bacon's own magisterial English in *The Advancement of Learning* (1605):

The Forms of Substances . . . (as they are now by compounding and transplanting multiplied) are so perplexed, as they are not to be enquired; no more than it were either possible or to purpose to seek in gross *the forms of those sounds which make words*, which by composition and transposition of letters are infinite. But on the other hand, to enquire *the form of those sounds or voices which make simple letters* is easily comprehensible, and being known, induceth and manifesteth the forms of all words, which consist and are compounded of them. In the same manner to enquire the Form of a lion, of an oak, of gold, nay of water, of air, is a vain pursuit: but to enquire the Forms of sense, of voluntary motion, of vegetation, of colours, of gravity and levity, of density, of tenuity, of heat, of cold, and all other natures and qualities, which like an alphabet are not many, and of which the essences (upheld by matter) of all creatures do consist; to enquire . . . the *true forms* of these is that part of Metaphysic which we now define of. (III, 355–6; cf. I, 364–6; IV, 361)

The comparison of the limited number of letters that we find in a given language and make up the great variety of its words with the multiplicity of physical things is an image of venerable ancestry. It already appears in Aristotle's *Metaphysics* and in Lucretius's *De rerum natura*.[6] As such it constitutes one of oldest illustrations employed by the atomists in order to explain how the manifold of sensible qualities could be analyzed in terms of elementary units. Though no atomist himself, Bacon is here advocating a brand of pluralist ontology in which the Aristotelian resonance of the term "form" does not commit him to any of the contemporary versions of Peripatetic matter theory.[7] The substantive content of Bacon's theory can be postponed till we elucidate the hermeneutically relevant motivations which led him to adopt this particular approach.

III FORMS AND OPERATIVE SCIENCE

The aim of the whole project of Baconian science is untiringly referred to as the *Inquisitio Formarum* which leads to "works" or *opera* (I, 227, 462; III, 354, 793), and Bacon defines natural philosophy as "the Inquiry of Causes and the Production of Effects" (IV, 346). There is nothing to object to the first part of this definition of knowledge from the standpoint of the old epistemologies. Yet, the crucial complement that knowledge ought to guarantee the "production of effects" cannot be easily accommodated within the general matrix of Western philosophical discourse. It mirrors the operative twist or "knowing-how" stress that Bacon gives to the ancient conception of Nature as the result of the combination of alphabetical units: the function of the alphabet is expressed in reading *and in writing*, that is, in producing or representing words at will, sometimes even in creating new ones. Likewise, the mastery over the elementary components of Nature "induceth" or leads the knower to the (re)production of natural effects.

But, conversely, to try to know "the form of an oak" (which is a good example of the Aristotelian project of natural science contemporary to Bacon) is something to be despaired of as either impossible or useless: not being an element, an oak cannot be reproduced. Yet to know the Form of such qualities or "natures" as color, density or weight – "upheld by matter" and present in or making up the oak insofar as they separate it out from the other species of trees – falls entirely within the province of Baconian science. As a natural kind, the tree stands textually and functionally on a plane with a metal.

That is why Bacon's pronouncements about gold are so significant historically.[8] No talk of a putative essence or quiddity of that entity is attempted, such as a "substantial form" ultimately but mysteriously accounting for the metal's manifest and occult properties, but what we find defined as gold in the *Novum organum* is a conglomerate of certain qualities that Bacon has already promoted to the rank of "simple natures":

> In gold ... the following properties meet [*haec conveniunt*]. It is yellow in colour; heavy up to a certain weight; malleable or ductile to a certain degree of extension; it is not volatile, and loses none of its substance by the action of fire; it turns into a liquid with a certain degree of fluidity; it is separated and dissolved by particular means; and so on for the other natures which meet [*concurrunt*] in gold (IV, 122; I, 231).

Thus, having offered a list of fundamental properties or "natures" which we are able to tabulate as resulting from our sense perception, the ulterior notion of Form points to that invisible arrangement which can account for them. If there is a given nature which we perceive, then there should be a Form of it which sense cannot attain but whose construal is the work of the intellect governed by true method, that is, by induction. Before alluding to the guiding principle of that process, let us stress the operative component which from the very start is accompanying Bacon's reflections on matter and on the goal of human science, for here we can spot a highly instructive example of the way in which ontology recapitulates epistemology. That is to say: what the world is ultimately composed of is made to depend on or is dictated by the doctrine regarding the kind of goal that a given conception of knowledge postulates as both feasible and desirable. Thus, Bacon adds in one breath in the same aphorism: "For he who knows the forms of yellow, weight, ductility, fixity, fluidity, solution, and so on, and the methods for superinducing them [*modus superinducendi*], and their gradations and modes, will make it his care to have them joined together in some body [*conjungi possint in aliquo corpore*], whence may follow the transformation of that body into gold" (IV, 122; I, 231).

Likewise in the posthumous and highly influential *Sylva Sylvarum*, Bacon confidently asserts that gold

> hath these natures; greatness of weight, closeness of parts, fixation, pliantness or softness, immunity from rust, colour or tincture of yellow. There-

fore, the sure way (though most about) to make gold, is to know the causes of the several natures rehearsed, and the axioms concerning the same. For if a man can make a metal that hath all these properties, let men dispute whether it be gold or no (II, 450).

Now Bacon's train of thought may be satisfactorily reconstructed from these pithy statements. Can an essentialist approach to Nature such as the one proposed by Aristotelian physics, open up the welter of possibilities that this exalted notion of human operation suggests? Clearly not: a substantial form – to mention again the chief parallel Aristotelian doctrine contemporary to Bacon – could be postulated as expressing or codifying that innermost but mysterious cause that accounted for the difference which Nature (or God) has imparted to, say, each kind of metal. (God and perhaps angelic intelligences could have intuitive or direct knowledge of the substantial forms of any lump of matter, or of the immortal soul *qua* substantial form of man, but the concept was wholly opaque to human understanding and, what is most significant in this stance, utterly unsuitable for human operation.) It is noteworthy that the almost universal criticism that the concept of substantial form had to meet in Bacon's age and immediately after was prompted, whether by Descartes, Boyle, Gassendi, or Locke, by the former consideration (i.e., the substantial forms were incomprehensible), but never by the latter, (i.e., no thinker expressly denounced them as sterile *qua* recipes for action or reproduction).[9]

Having thus tacitly disposed of the main rival tool of analysis of physical phenomena, Bacon reveals the full semantics of his own key concept when he proceeds to document its meaning by means of the two further notions of "Latent Process" (IV, 123) and "Latent Configuration" (IV, 124). These concepts reveal what a particulate theory of matter ought to contain if it purports to be scientifically viable: (a) a general commitment to Corpuscularianism, that is, a precise answer to the question about the ultimate composition of matter; and (b) a description of the *modus operandi* of such minimal parts, of their rules of combination or recombination such that the human knower can visualize in his mind though his senses cannot attain it.

The ultimate quiddity of such minimal parts of matter does not appear to have attracted Bacon's attention[10] as perhaps irrelevant to the chief inspiration of his science; but the overall pattern of matter-cum-motion he adopted as an explanation and (ideally at least) as a recipe for the successful reproduction of the "effect" described is made abundantly clear by pronouncements like this: "Seeing that every natural action depends on things infinitely small [*per minima transigatur*] or at least too small to strike the sense, no one can hope to govern or change [*regere aut vertere*] Nature until he has duly comprehended and observed them" (IV, 124; I, 233).[11]

Bacon's steps in the construal of the concept of Form are now very easy to follow. From the canonical division of Aristotelian causes, remembered in the second book of the *Novum organum* (IV, 119–20), he seems to have adopted the notion of an *intrinsic efficient cause* which, by virtue of its being inherent to matter, accounts for its appearance and transformation, and therefore opens the way to man's manipulatory capabilities. On the other hand, the remaining final cause finds no place in the Baconian conception of inquiry and its search is declared a hindrance in the process of knowledge in the *Novum organum* (IV, 120; I, 228). Only simple natures like the ones appearing in the provisional lists of the *De augmentis* (IV, 360–1) are susceptible of being investigated with the aim of discovering their Form. And here enter the most modern-sounding utterances that Bacon has produced concerning his key notion:

I would not be understood to speak of abstract forms and ideas, either not defined in matter at all, or ill defined. For when I speak of Forms, I mean nothing more than those laws [*leges*] and determinations of absolute actuality [*actus puri*], which govern and constitute [*ordinant et constituunt*] any simple nature, as heat, light, weight, in every kind of matter and subject that is susceptible of them. Thus the Form of Heat and the Form of Light is the same thing as the Law of Heat or the Law of Light. (IV, 146; I, 257–8)

Now what is the exact purport of this Baconian law? Its definition is best expressed in Bacon's practical trial at an application of his methodological views. His tentative hypothesis regarding the Form of heat (*Forma caloris*) in the "first vintage" definition or permission awarded to the speculative intellect in the *Novum organum* reads as follows:

Heat [*calor*] *is a motion, expansive, restrained, and acting in its strife upon the smaller particles of bodies. But the expansion is thus modified; while it expands all ways, it has at the same time an inclination upwards. And the struggle in the particles is modified also; it is not sluggish, but hurried and with violence [ut non sit omnino segnis, sed incitatus et cum impetu nonnullo].* (IV, 154–5; I, 266)

It is worth noting here that this definition of heat is but the *analogical* result of reading the evidence accumulated in the repository of instances of various types of heat presented in the preceding tables of absence, presence, and degree (IV, 127–55; I, 236–68). Such an analogical procedure seems to have operated in two ways. First, the postulation of an invisible friction and motion between invisible corpuscles on a par with the ostensive friction occurring in the generation of visible fire or with the motion of visible flame. Second, the adjectives employed ("expansive," "restrained," and the like) are the projection or, in M. Mandelbaum's felicitous term, the "transdiction"¹² of the very same adjectives with which the inquirer has described the phenomena in question. Thus, in order to postulate that the kind of motion heat ultimately amounts to is itself "expansive," Bacon resorts to the appearance of the flame or boiling liquids (IV, 153; I, 265) or to the fact that "all burning acts on minute pores of the body burnt; so that burning undermines, penetrates, pricks and stings the body like the points of an infinite number of needles [*perinde ac si infinitae cuspides acus*]"; and likewise, in order to claim that the invisible motion is not violent but sluggish, Bacon compares "the effects of fire with the effects of time or age. Age or time dries, consumes, undermines and reduces to ashes, no less than fire; indeed with an action far more subtle, but because such motion is very sluggish, and acts on particles very small, the heat is not perceived" (IV, 153–4; I, 265). This is in fact the main reason for Bacon's otherwise fanciful claim, in the absence of any conceivable evidence, that heat "must proceed by particles, minute indeed, yet not the finest of all, but a degree larger [*tamen non ad extremam subtilitatem, sed quasi majusculas*]" (IV, 154; I, 265). No wonder then that Locke, when dealing with scientific method in the *Essay Concerning Human Understanding* (1690) alludes to the "wary reasoning from Analogy" as man's sole and faithful cognitive tool immediately after he has referred to the process of ignition by rubbing two sticks.¹³ Though Locke does not mention Bacon in that passage, his train of thought is so similar to the one expressed in the *Novum organum* (IV, 149–55) that it can be reasonably conjectured that the corresponding aphorisms were not very far from his mind.

Yet, Bacon's exposition of the Form of heat is not exhausted by this purely descriptive or theoretical part. The all-important (from the viewpoint of a good characterization of Bacon's idea of science) addition comes immediately after this, when Bacon presents his Form as a rule of operation: "For the direction is this: *If in any natural body you can excite a dilating or expanding motion, and can so repress this motion and turn it back upon itself, that the dilation shall not proceed equably, but have its way in one part and be counteracted in another, you will undoubtedly generate heat*" (IV, 155).

It is crucial to understand that this is not a purely operative "adjunct." What Bacon has called "Form" is all at once a statement purporting to unveil the quiddity or essence of a phenomenon by redescribing it in a lawlike manner *and a recipe for successful operation or reinstantiation of it on the basis of the pragmatic effectiveness of that law.* The latter part (latter in the order of exposition but not as pertains to its conceptual import) amounts to a built-in guarantee for the former's acceptance. As Bacon states in the preface to the *Novum organum*, "whether or no anything can be known" can "be settled not by arguing, but by trying" (IV, 39), and in *The Advancement of Learning* he declares that "the art of discovery advances with every discovery" (III, 392; cf. IV, 115). In fine, this "trying" or "discovery" of the means of producing an "effect" is the much-sought-for criterion of scientific rationality in these early stages of the history of the *ars inveniendi.* The ultimate criterion of a valid scientific statement appears to be success in operation, and this makes up for the theoretical truth embodied in the "verbal" part of the Baconian Form. For example, it might well be that successive trials make the researcher alter or significantly expand the wake of adjectival modifications appended to his primitive description of that heat-producing motion. This is what Bacon seems to have in mind when he points out that, given the open-ended character of his inquiry, the natural philosopher has to make generous room for the (in Western science) hitherto highly unorthodox notion of "degrees of certainty [*certitudinis gradus*]" (IV, 149; I, 261). Now there can be degrees of certainty in the way we proceed to describe the hidden workings of Nature. There can hardly be when we utilize a given description as a recipe for reproducing a phenomenon, since, however crude it may be in its early stages, the recipe in question has to be conducive to successful operation if it is to be taken as a praxiologically valid statement in the first place. The technical challenge must be met, though the theoretically informed recipe might be refined. Now what sort of gnoseological model was inspiring Bacon's reflection on Forms with its theoretical-cum-practical emphasis?

IV FORMS AND MAKER'S KNOWLEDGE

A tradition which we can trace back to classical Antiquity had identified the human knower as first and foremost a maker or doer (more generally, an agent) and had seen his true character as a knower as wholly or preeminently depending on his credentials as a maker. This tradition has taken firm roots in various fields of Western speculation when trying to account for the phenomenon of knowledge, and the particular history of its unfolding transcends the limits of the present exposition. Suffice it to say, however, that this ideal has been identified as one of the canonical "scientific styles" which Western thought has produced.[14] In Bacon this pattern of reasoning is intimately connected with various cultural *topoi* mirrored by the philosophical import of his concept of Form. One of them is the progressive ground gained by the reflecting "rational artist" of the Renaissance period and probably by the Faustian dreams proper to the alchemical magus. The second and perhaps more prevalently philosophical factor leading to the emergence of this ideal is the radical questioning of the categories wherewith human art and its products can be legitimately perceived, that is, the new "philosophy of technology" which, in stark contrast with the ancient tradition, was being elaborated since at least the fifteenth century in European thought. Let us review these factors in turn.

The notion that true knowledge is to be had only of what is made or can be made (reproduced, modeled, fabricated . . .) has found different expressions in prominent thinkers. This scientific desideratum has been termed the "ergetic ideal" by Amos Funkenstein[15] or the maker's knowledge idea-type, and its hermeneutical identification has been the result of recent research in the field of the history and philosophy of science.[16] As Henri Bergson long ago intimated: *homo sapiens* springs from the reflections of *homo faber* about his own doings.[17] This insight can be seen at work in the realms of mathematics, of craftsmanship, and of theological speculation in various stages, though the full philosophical self-awareness of the ideal had to wait till Giambattista Vico's felicitous formulation of the *verum factum* principle in the early eighteenth century.[18] What is especially noticeable in Bacon's ideal of science as encapsulated in his concept of Form is his epoch-making equation between knowledge and power: seen from the standpoint of the construal of the Form, such equation amounts to the postulation of a hitherto novel criterion of demarcation between true science and pseudoscientific verbiage. In a nutshell: if a scientific statement can lead to the successful (re)production of the phenomenon it purports to describe, however crudely or approximately, then that very statement should be accepted as a full denizen into the realm of practically sanctioned knowledge. No other standard but this seems necessary or forthcoming. Now it is self-evident that, irrespective of the overconfident enthusiasm placed by his author on the notion of Forms as recipes for successful action, Bacon's choice of that specific approach to matter theory can be understood as meaningfully dictated by the operative sterility of alternative doctrines. There is no conceivable way in which the much elaborated theory of the substantial forms as ultimate units of explanation and classification of natural beings could be turned into a praxiologically viable corpus of knowledge.[19] The Aristotelian picture that stood behind such a theory could only appeal to the grasp of a supposedly enlightened beholder, never to the requirements of a prospective manipulator or user. As a point of lexical fact, the latter's activity would fall under the general Aristotelian rubric of *prudentia* (*phronēsis*) rather than under the scope of *scientia* (*epistēmē*), which was no maker's but beholder's knowledge. One should never sufficiently stress that the construction of modern scientific rationality largely consisted in the substitution of one cultural *topos* by the other insofar as the human knower began to engage with Nature in the guise of a self-assured agent and manipulator, an experimenter and theoretically informed technician. In the words of Amos Funkenstein: "The study of Nature in the seventeenth century was neither predominantly idealistic nor empirical. It was first and foremost *constructive*, pragmatic in the radical sense. It would lead to the conviction that only the doable – at least in principle – is also understandable."[20]

Now the economy (and ecology) of scientific proposals would not have let much latitude to the ergetic ideal had a further notion coming from Antiquity not been radically challenged. The maker's knowledge approach to science would have been of little avail as an alternative to Aristotelianism if the age-old consensus about the purported unbridgeable gap between the products of Nature (*naturalia*) and those of human art (*artificialia*) had been maintained. What is the point, gnoseologically speaking, of making or constructing something in order thereby to gain insight into Nature's mysteries if we posit from the very start that no productions of human technology can remotely equal or even approach the essence and subtlety of natural processes? This robust metaphysical presupposition has been aptly termed *le tabou du naturel* by Robert Lenoble, and its deepest roots are to be found not only in Aristotle but appear to be the common verdict of classical and medieval thought.[21] In the oft-quoted terse formula of Cicero: *Nulla ars imitari sollertiam Naturae potest.*[22]

As Aristotle repeatedly asserts,[23] the scope of art is that of imitating Nature, or of bringing about what Nature would in any case produce though in a way more convenient to man's desires or interests, for example, more slowly or swiftly.[24] That art is fundamentally a *mimēsis* of Nature mirrors a corresponding evaluation of the human subject as an "enacter," whenever his technical skills empower him to do so, of models or patterns of things or phenomena that Nature already contains in her all-embracing bosom. This is pithily stressed by Aristotle: "As the man comes from the man by means of his sperm, so the house comes from the house by means of the house-builder."[25] Thus, the scope of inventiveness or of bringing forth a *novum* is resolutely negated. Though technical inventions could sometimes attain surprising heights in Antiquity (e.g., Archytas's legendary dove and Archimedes's war engines), the general slant of classical speculation on these matters tended to explain away or classify such putative innovations as wonderful objects more or less assimilated to inextricably complex toys (*thaumata*). True, they could wake up admiration and prompt encomiastic comparisons with the divine creative intellect (as Cicero does when he mentions Posidonius's construction of an armillary sphere in the *De natura deorum*[26]). However, such technical prowesses in no way affected the overall negative perception of human inventiveness and, being taken as abnormal and exceptional, they did not lead to a

questioning of the old *topos*: art and Nature constituted two recipro-
cally exclusive worlds.[27]

Now, in order to operate with and within the maker's knowledge
ideal in an intellectually unimpeded way, one ought to show that the
dichotomy between natural and artificial objects and operations was
conceptually faulty and (or because) empirically objectionable. In a
word, it had to be stressed that no such chasm existed between
naturalia and *artificialia*. From Nicholas of Cusa in the fifteenth
century or Petrus Ramus in the sixteenth, European thinkers had
tried diverse lines of argumentation and used various strategies in
this process. They had pointed out, for example, that Nature did not
possess archetypes of such simple instruments as spoons – hence no
imitation was feasible – or they had argued that certain man-made
artifacts like mechanical clocks and birds had (even as Nature's own
productions) that inner principle of motion which presumably acted
as an identifying mark of the natural.[28]

V FORMS, NATURE, AND ART

Now Bacon's strategy appears to have abundantly drawn from or
shared into those currents of thought when he extolled the productive power of human agency in the untrammelled and free "generation of Forms" (IV, 155). On the one hand, he expressly denounces
the division between natural and artificial objects as the result of
verbal confusion and faulty reasoning (I, 497, 624; IV, 294, 413; III,
531, 592). On the other hand, he argues that there is no ontological
difference between the spontaneous workings of Nature wherever
she brings about her "effects" and those self-same workings when
directed or manipulated by man's purposive action:

When a man makes the appearence of a rainbow on a wall by the sprinkling
of water, Nature does the work for him, just as much as when the same
effect is produced in the air by a dripping cloud; and on the other hand when
gold is found pure in sands, Nature does the work for herself [*sibi ipsi
ministrat Natura*] just as much as if it were refined by the furnace and
human appliance. Sometimes again the ministering office is by the law of
the universe [*ex lege universi*] deputed to other animals; for honey, which is
made by the industry of the bee, is no less artificial than sugar, which is
made by man . . . Therefore as Nature is one and the same, and her power
extends through all things, nor does she ever forsake herself, these three

things should by all means be set down as alike subordinate only to Nature, namely, the course of Nature; the wanderings of Nature; and art, or Nature with man to help [*ars sive additus rebus homo*]. (V, 507; III, 730–1)

It is noteworthy that in this passage a technical procedure unknown to the ancient world such as the manufacturing of sugar should serve as the signal of an anthropological conception radically different from that bequeathed by classical thought. Human inventiveness serves to qualify the two. The "artificial" has now become the "natural" in man, insofar as man himself is the *inventor* of the technique of sugar production even as the bee is the natural producer of honey: *man's gnoseological nature becomes man's gnoseological history*. Therefore, no fixed boundaries can be drawn as to the potential arts in all kinds of fields that man's historical nature may unveil. Now, since Nature is postulated as always being the same and operating according to the same rules in every instance, there is no need to separate what Nature herself produces of her own accord and what man, as an evolving part of Nature, can bring about in terms of (re)production of Nature's processes or of contrivances which Nature's spontaneous course would not hit upon or manifest.[29] No difference in kind exists between the colors of the rainbow in the sky after the rain and in those contrived by man's manipulation of some drops of water. By the same token, if iron and copper are natural kinds, so is man-made bronze, though it is in man's furnace that Nature normally chooses to produce it. In Bacon's weighty words in the *Novum organum*: "Towards the effecting of works, all that man can do is to put together or put asunder natural bodies. The rest is done by Nature working within [*Ad opera nihil potest homo, quam ut corpora naturalia admoveat et amoveat; reliqua Natura intus transigit*]" (IV, 47; I, 157).

Now it is precisely toward the effecting of such works, that is, *opera*, that the Form, as a key concept in Bacon's train of thought, is ideally intended to provide a practical indication. Bacon emphatically and repeatedly contends that only the inquiry into "the moving principles, whereby, things are produced [*per qua res fiunt*]" is the true aim of science (IV, 67; I, 77): thence the operational doublet that accompanies his investigation into "what Nature does or may be made to do [*quid Natura faciat aut ferat*]" (IV, 127; I, 236). No wonder then if the Baconian Form is colorfully defined as a "source of emanation" and a

"nature-engendering nature [*natura naturans*]" (IV, 119), for this
amounts to stressing its character as a recipe for successful purposive
action over and above its theoretical exactness as a scientific re-
description of the phenomena it purports to explain. That is to say:
contrary to the lexically oriented conceptions of human knowledge
which had monopolized Western speculation, Bacon's idea of science,
as crystallized in his notion of Form, establishes that *to know something (a natural phenomenon) amounts to being able to (re)produce
that very phenomenon on any material substratum susceptible of
manifesting it.* For example, in the case of heat, the Baconian Form is
both an inchoate definition of that invisible sort of motion putatively
accounting for perceptible heat and a practical guide for producing
heat if the knower-agent can manipulate the hypothetical structure
of matter which is being provisorily postulated as really existent (i.e.,
corpuscles in motion). In this sense, the Form is nothing but a "direction" (Bacon's own English in *Valerius Terminus*) for successful manipulation. To quote him again against this background:

> Viewed with reference to operation [*quod vero ad Operativam attined*] it
> is the same thing [*eadem res*]. For the direction [*designatio*] is this: If in
> any natural body you can excite a dilating or expanding motion, and can so
> repress this motion and turn it back upon itself [*reprimere et in se vertere*],
> that the dilation shall not proceed equably, but have its way in one part
> and be counteracted in another, you will undoubtedly generate heat. (IV,
> 155; I, 267)

It is surely undeniable that the pathos conveyed by the newfan-
gled postulation of this standard of truth as maker's knowledge, led
Bacon to conceive chimerical hopes about the reasonable expectations which his project of a purely praxiological science could satisfy. Even his great nineteenth-century admirer William Whewell
was forced to recognize that, as a practical guide, Bacon's inquiry
into the Form of heat amounted to a fiasco. The Form, as a
praeceptum operandi (I, 229) led nowhere: the inquirer "arrives at
nothing but a vague and useless formula."[30] Yet, statements such as
this, even if historically correct, are beside the point if we wish to
reconstruct the philosophical semantics of past concepts of knowledge, of its ideals and of its translations into more recognizable
enterprises. In Bacon's case we are dealing with no less than the
systematic conceptualization of man's material engaging into Na-

ture's processes, which was conducive to far more sober views of experiment and technical know-how.

The Baconian Form had no direct descendents. Though one can generously interpret the concept as "something quite specific: geometrical structure and motion,"[31] the silence of latter-day Baconians about one of the most characteristic notions of their purported master is highly revealing. Perhaps it is the Boylean "texture" that provides the closest parallel to our conception. If this is so, then it should cause no wonder that amongst Boyle's reasons for preferring Corpuscularianism to any alternative matter theory such as the doctrine of the substantial forms, we should find the artificialist twist that inspired so large a part of whole Baconian project. Boyle considers that the possibility of *reproducing* a given effect provides sufficient grounds for accepting this account of Nature:

If then these curious shapes, which are believed to be of the admirablest effects, and of the strongest proof of the *substantial forms*, may be the result of texture; *and if art can produce vitriol itself as well as Nature*, why may we not think that in ordinary phenomena, that have much less wonder, recourse is want to be had to substantial forms without any necessity? (matter and convention of accidents being able to serve the turn without them); *and why should we wilfully exclude those productions of the fire, wherein the chemist is a servant of Nature, from the number of natural bodies?* And indeed: *since there is not certain diagnostic agreed in whereby to discriminate natural and fictitous bodies, and constitute a species of both;* I see not why we may not draw arguments from the qualities and operations of several of those that are called factitous [sic], to shew how much may be ascribed to, and performed by the mechanical characterization and stamp of matter.[32]

And even as was the case with the Baconian Form, the corpuscular texture of matter can be postulated hypothetically insofar as its practical value may be vindicated in view of its fruitfulness in experimentation:

And . . . I will have such kind of superstructure [i.e., hypotheses about the mechanical texture of bodies] looked upon as temporary ones; which though they may be preferred before any others, as being the least imperfect, or, if you please, *the best in their kind we yet have,* yet have they not entirely to be acquiesced in, as absolutely perfect, or incapable of improving alteration.[33]

Which is a clear recognition of the gradual hypothetical inference we spotted above as Bacon's own way of reaching a definition of Form. Yet, even this close resemblance between Bacon's and Boyle's conceptions as regards the subject matter of physical inquiry and the route for achieving its goals, fails to take into account the full import of the cognitive ideal that the Lord Chancellor had so enthusiastically advocated. Boyle may well have believed in the transmutation of metals and petitioned King Charles II to repeal the laws about gold-making,[34] but the Faustian promises of Baconian science about man's unlimited manipulation of the material realm were gradually abandoned and became the appanage of unorthodox, nonscientific speculators – those very occultists and *illuminati* against whom Bacon had reacted. On the other hand, no major figure of European philosophy ever hinted at a conceptual gulf between the triumphant Corpuscularian doctrines of the mid–seventeenth century and the idiosyncratic Baconian Form. The term itself fell into oblivion as perhaps being too close to the substantial forms that the Corpuscularians eventually rejected from the edifice of modern science. But the approach to natural inquiry and the inspiration that stood behind one of Bacon's most characteristic notions was unanimously felt as coterminous with the cognitive interests of the "new philosophy." This is not the only case in which Bacon's reception can be read as a form of unsuspectedly creative misunderstanding. Not only the old *scientia* but also the new had to pay tribute to an established pantheon of real or fictitious authorities.

NOTES

1 Whewell 1967, II, p. 234 (author's italics).
2 Emerton 1984, pp. 66–9.
3 As in *Physics*, I.9.192a.
4 As in *Metaphysics*, VIII.2.1042b.
5 This is the main reason for Mersenne's critique of the Baconian project as expounded in the *Novum organum,* which he discusses in *La vérité des sciences* (1625, Stuttgart-Bad Cannstatt, 1969), pp. 206–18. Cf. Lenoble 1971, pp. 329–31, and Dear 1988, pp. 187f. Gassendi's line of

criticism of Bacon's ideal science is very similar to Mersenne's; cf. Bloch 1971, pp. 5off., and Messeri 1985, pp. 13off.

6 *Metaphysics*, I.4.985b15ff.; *De rerum natura*, I.195–7; IV.688–94.

7 On Bacon's wavering response to atomism, cf. Macciò 1962. On the various versions of Aristotelian matter theory contemporary to Bacon, cf. Emerton 1984, pp. 76–153, especially on minimism pp. 106–25. On the manualists' literature with which Bacon was most probably conversant, cf. Reif 1969.

8 Clericuzio 1984; West 1961; Linden 1974.

9 Emerton 1984, pp. 36, 43f., 60–70. The arguments for the real existence of the substantial forms and their putatively fertile use in scientific inquiries are cogently reviewed by Alexander 1985, pp. 55–9. Cf. also Pérez-Ramos 1988, pp. 63–134, esp. pp. 68–96.

10 Graham Rees has consistently developed the idea that Bacon was ultimately a debtor to a form of Paracelsian cosmology; cf. Rees 1975b, 1977b, 1980, and his Chapter 5. I have examined these claims in Pérez-Ramos 1985.

11 Ellis's translation of *notaverit* as "to observe" is misleading, since it contradicts Bacon's position as expressed in the first sentence. The Latin approaches our sense of "taking cognizance of."

12 Mandelbaum 1964, pp. 61–117. This principle implies the so-called multilevel identity of Nature, that is, the supposition that "the laws of Nature which apply to visible massive bodies also apply to objects which are either too large or too small to be measured or observed," in the words of Laudan 1966. Bacon seems to postulate this principle in the *Novum organum*: the latent process (*latens processus* or innermost workings of the particles in each body) is "a process perfectly continuous [*plane processum continuatum*], which for the most part escapes the sense" (IV, 124; I, 232).

13 "Thus observing that the bare rubbing of two bodies violently upon another produces heat and very often fire itself, we have reason to think that what we call heat and fire consists in a violent agitation of the imperceptible minute parts of the burning matter. This sort of probability, which is the best conduct of rational experiments, and the rise of hypotheses, has also its use and influence; and a wary reasoning from analogy leads us often into the discovery of truths and useful productions which could otherwise be concealed," *Essay*, IV, 16, 12. Also Robert Hooke insists on the value of this type of argument: "The best and utmost we can do . . . is only accurately to observe all those effects . . . which fall within the power of our senses, and comparing them with like effects produced by causes that fall within the reach of own senses, to examine and so from sensibles to argue the similitude of the nature of

causes that are wholly insensible," (*Posthumous Works*, ed. R. Waller, [London, 1705], p. 154). For if I can "comprehend and imagine one local motion that falls under the reach of my senses, I can by similitude comprehend and understand another that is ten thousand degrees below the reach of them," ibid., p. 131. "Similitude" is Bacon's own English: "There is no proceeding in invention of knowledge but by similitude" (III, 218).

14 Crombie 1994, II, pp. 1167–241: "The Analogical Model: Knowing is Making." Cf. also Pérez-Ramos 1988, pp. 48–64, 150–66.

15 Funkenstein 1986, pp. 290–345. For an assessment of Funkenstein's views in relation to this topic, cf. Pérez-Ramos 1990a.

16 Hintikka 1974, esp. pp. 80–97.

17 Bergson 1946, p. 92.

18 Vico's formulation *verum ipsum factum* first appears in *De antiquissima Italorum sapientia*, also called *Liber metaphysicus* (1710). Cf. *Opera*, eds. G. Gentile and F. Nicolini (Bari, 1914–41), I, pp. 23–194. On the sources of that topos cf. Mondolfo 1969.

19 For the tenor of the most evolved versions of this notion, cf. Emerton 1984, pp. 23ff., 48ff., Alexander 1985, pp. 40ff., and Pérez-Ramos 1988, pp. 68ff.

20 Funkenstein 1986, p. L78.

21 Lenoble 1969, pp. 311ff.

22 Cf. *De natura deorum*, II.22, 32, 34, 38, 57.

23 *Physics*, II.8.L99a15–17, L99b30–32; *Metaphysics*, XII.2.1069b19; XII.3. 1070a7.

24 Blumenberg 1957.

25 *Metaphysics*, VII.9.1034a20ff.

26 *De natura deorum*, II.39.

27 For a brief but exhaustively documented study cf. Panofsky 1924. An illustrative collection of loci regarding the Nature–art relationship appears in Close 1969.

28 The example of the spoon is to be found in Nicholas of Cusa's dialogue *Idiota de mente*, in *Philosophisch-Theologische Schriften*, ed. with an introduction by L. Gabriel, trans. D. and W. Dupré [Latin and German], 3 vols. (Vienna 1967), III, pp. 419ff. On Ramus cf. Hooykaas 1958.

29 Cf. *De augmentis*: "But there is likewise another and more subtle error which has crept into the human mind; namely, that of considering art as merely an assistant to Nature [*additamentum quoddam Naturae*], having the power indeed to finish what Nature has begun, to correct her when lapsing into error, or to set her free when in bondage, but by no means to change, transmute, or fundamentally alter Nature [*penitus vertere, transmutare aut in imis concutere*]. And this has bred a prema-

ture despair in human enterprises. Whereas men ought on the contrary to be surely persuaded of this; that the artificial does not differ from the natural in form or essence [*non Forma aut Essentia*], but only in the efficient; in that man has no power over Nature except that of motion; he can put natural bodies together, and he can separate them; and therefore that wherever the case admits of the uniting or disuniting of natural bodies, by joining (as they say) actives with passives, man can do everything [*omnia potest homo*]; where the case does not admit this, he can do nothing" (IV, 294–5; I, 496). The target of the first part of this passage is Aristotle's theory of art; the phrase "joining actives with passives" is of alchemical stock and with it Bacon is pointing to the unsuspected limits of operation which his conception of science entails, that is, the creation of "effects" hitherto unknown. Cf. Primack 1967.

30 Whewell 1831, p. 382. Whewell is reviewing Herschel's *Preliminary Discourse on the Study of Natural Philosophy* (London 1830). On the reasons which led Bacon to illustrate his method with the investigation into the Form of Heat, cf. Millen 1985, esp. pp. 208–11. This student considers heat "the prototype of a manifest quality," p. 210.

31 Crombie 1994, I, p. 630. Other scholars point to different directions. Larsen 1962 emphasizes the Aristotelian heritage he discerns in Bacon's concept of Form; Copenhaver 1988b stresses Bacon's critical links with magical and Neoplatonic currents.

32 *On the Origin of Forms and Qualities, According to the Corpuscular Philosophy . . . Augmented by a Discourse on Subordinate Forms*, in *Works*, ed. Thomas Birch, 5 vols. (London, 1744), II, p. 491, my emphasis. On the concept of "texture," cf. Alexander 1985, pp. 58–61, 74–9.

33 *Works*, I, p. 130, my emphasis. Cf. also IV, p. 232 . Characteristically, Boyle impugns Aristotelianism as "altogether barren for works;" cf. *Works*, III, pp. 5, 8–9, 40–1, 75; V, p. 166 (*Notion of Nature*).

34 Abbri 1984; Clericuzio 1984; Newman 1994; Principe 1994.

5   Bacon's speculative philosophy

Francis Bacon's natural philosophy may be viewed as a single philosophy with two aspects or as two philosophies each with its own peculiar character. Either way it is useful to acknowledge that there is a doubleness to his philosophical enterprise: on the one hand, Bacon's philosophy offers itself to us as a program for constructing a body of scientific knowledge that was supposed to yield immense practical benefits and so release the human race from material privation. On the other hand, it manifests itself as a rather strange corpus of speculative science.

In its first guise Bacon's philosophy shows itself as a set of methodological recommendations together with a bold analysis of their implications for existing attitudes to knowledge and the institutions of knowledge. The object of these recommendations was to establish the "legitimate" science and so supersede the sectarian, sterile bodies of knowledge which had hitherto passed for natural philosophy.

In its second manifestation Bacon's philosophy comprehends a complete but provisional system of speculative science. This system of theories was, to use Bacon's own term, a body of "anticipations"; it was not a product of the "legitimate" method but an elaborate guess at the kind of science the method was expected to create. Bacon hoped to produce a proper account of this philosophy in Part V of the *Instauratio*. This plan was never realized, but contributions to other parts of the *Instauratio* present considerable accumulations of material which enable us to reconstruct the speculative system in detail. Indeed, so far did his thinking about the system stamp itself on his writings that it is very difficult to find one that was not in some way touched by his speculative preoccupations.[1]

The system was eclectic to a fault. Bacon raided disparate natural-philosophical traditions for attractive titbits which he refashioned and spatchcocked together to form a curious hybrid which embodied, even by the standards of the early seventeenth century, some very peculiar alliances of ideas indeed. It developed as a series of responses to the philosophies of the ancients and to the innovators of his own time. The questions he asked may be seen as results of emulative meditation on such things as the atomist and Aristotelian natural philosophies, Copernicanism, Galileian observational astronomy, the work of Paracelsus and the Paracelsians, of William Gilbert, Telesio, Patrizi, and others besides.

The outcome of Bacon's dialogue with past and present was a body of natural philosophy which combined a theory of the physical structure of the universe modeled on the Mosaic cosmogonies of the Paracelsians with ideas about celestial motion derived from the work of an Arab Aristotelian. At its heart was a theory of matter which owed much to the doctrine of the *tria prima* in particular and Renaissance pneumatology in general.[2] The theory of matter was developed so that it reached beyond physical, astronomical and cosmological questions to embrace the domain of living things and mount a challenge to existing medical doctrine. In short, the speculative system grew to a point where it became universal in scope, capable (in principle) of explaining everything in the natural order.

II TELESIO, ALPETRAGIUS, AND CELESTIAL MOTION

In 1592 or thereabouts Bacon endorsed two doctrines which he never thereafter abandoned.[3] The first was concerned with the distribution of matter in the universe, the second with celestial motion. With regard to the first, he claimed that the universe had three distinct zones: the core of the Earth in which solid or tangible matter was concentrated; the heavens which were filled with "spirit"; and a narrow frontier zone between the two in which spirit and solid matter mixed and interacted (III, 97–8; also see III, 773–4). With regard to the second, he espoused certain ideas whose *ultimate* source was a treatise written sometime between 1185 and 1217 by the Moorish astronomer Alpetragius (Al-Bitruji). These ideas and the others in

Bacon's speculative philosophy are as difficult as any in his work, and difficult because they will take on none of the specious gloss of modernity that can be applied to other areas of his work.

Now the two doctrines that I have just mentioned were among the earliest components of Bacon's system and he probably took them from Telesian or deutero-Telesian sources, sources which bulked large in the dialectic of critical emulation that shaped his thought. Taking the doctrine of celestial motion first, in the *De principiis atque originibus* (c. 1612?), Bacon explicitly credited Alpetragian ideas on celestial motion to the Italian anti-Aristotelian Bernardino Telesio (1509–88), though the truth of the matter is that Bacon probably acquired his knowledge of the Moorish astronomer's doctrines from Tommaso Campanella's *Philosophia sensibus demonstrata* (1591).[4] Alpetragius devised the superficially seductive "screw" hypothesis which promised to obviate the poor "fit" between the Ptolemaic geometry used to describe planetary motion and the Aristotelian physical system of spheres used to explain it. The Aristotelian spheres were useless for predicting planetary positions accurately; Ptolemaic geometry yielded adequate predictions but resisted explanation in terms of Aristotelian homocentrics. The Alpetragian program was to close the gap between description and explanation by marrying Aristotelian homocentric spheres to computational devices rivaling Ptolemy's. To achieve this Alpetragius jettisoned epicycles and eccentrics and the received account of periodic motion.[5]

In Ptolemy's astronomy, the planets and stars turn westward about the stationary, central Earth and complete one revolution every sidereal day. However, the periodic motion (motion along the zodiac) of each planet is seen as a much slower motion toward the east and therefore contrary to the diurnal motion. The Alpetragian system recognizes no such contrary motion. Instead, the motion of the heavens was single, simple, and in *one direction*. In fact Alpetragius visualized periodic motion as an *abatement* of diurnal motion, an abatement which arose from the physical behavior of the heavens. A simplified version of the Aristotelian conception, the heavens consist of nine massive homocentric spheres,[6] the lowest of which carries the Moon. The next six carry Mercury, Venus, the Sun, Mars, Jupiter, and Saturn respectively. Saturn's sphere is enclosed in the sphere of the fixed stars which is itself encompassed by the ninth sphere, the first mover or *primum mobile*. The *pri-*

mum mobile completes one revolution from east to west in just under one sidereal day and transmits its motion in an increasingly attenuated form to the spheres beneath it. The stellar sphere therefore lags behind the *primum mobile* and completes its revolution in twenty-four sidereal hours. Each planetary sphere takes slightly longer than the sphere above it to complete one revolution so that the Moon's, the lowest, takes an hour longer than the stellar sphere to complete its much shorter circuit. Thus the lower the sphere the slower it moves and the more it loses ground relative to the *primum mobile*, the lag or progressive loss of ground representing the periodic motion of the planet carried by that sphere.[7] This unidirectional hypothesis is accompanied by another: the lower the planet the more it deviates from perfect circular motion. Alpetragius tried to account for the deviations by substituting a "spiral" for the compounded circles of Ptolemaic astronomy.[8] As to the ways in which Alpetragius attempted to adapt these principles to the observed motions of the planets, they did not detain Bacon so they need not detain us.

Why was Bacon drawn to principles which few other European philosophers took seriously?[9] His adverse reaction to post-Copernican developments in astronomy and cosmology offers the beginnings of an answer. He knew that the Copernican theory was gaining ground at the expense of Ptolemaic celestial geometry and Aristotelian celestial physics. He repudiated the ancient systems but could not bring himself to accept the revolutionary alternative. The Copernican theory offended common sense and was astonishingly arbitrary in that it assigned a central position to the Sun, attributed three motions to the Earth, and, like the Ptolemaic and Tychonic systems, employed compounded perfect circles to account for observed celestial motions (III, 739–41, 742; also see I, 552, 580).

Bacon came to regard the mathematical astronomers as meddlers in philosophical matters that were none of their business. He feared that mathematics, the handmaiden of physics, had come to dominate it. Indeed, he believed that the principal systems of his day were virtually worthless because none represented the actual courses of the heavenly bodies and none could give a decisive answer to the question of the true physical structure of the universe. According to Bacon, the correct geometrical description would emerge only from a correct physical theory. He insisted on the *priority of physics* as an instrument for solving astronomical and cosmological problems, and dismissed the purely descriptive enterprise with its infatuation with compounded circles as a lamentable instance of misapplied effort (I, 553-4, 576-7).[10]

In the *logical* perspective, Bacon's system represents celestial motion as a necessary consequence of its physical structure (III, 773-5). Following the principle of the priority of physics, physical theory yields (in broad terms) the correct geometrical description of celestial motion (I, 201). The idea seems to have been that once the natural philosophers produced a physics giving a general picture of celestial motion, the mathematicians could step in and develop a precise, refined geometrical account of the motions established by the physical model. Yet in the *chronological* perspective, Bacon's adherence to Alpetragian principles preceded his construction of the physical system that was to support them – although he later represented the geometry as a consequence of the physics.

III COSMOLOGY AND THE TWO QUATERNIONS

From about 1612 Bacon began to use Telesio's three-zone conception of the structure of the universe and Alpetragian principles as a framework on which to build a chemical theory of matter. He represented the universe as a finite, geocentric plenum. The central Earth consists almost entirely of dense, passive, *tangible* matter. The rest of the universe is completely filled with weightless, invisible, active, *pneumatic* matter. The distinction between tangible and pneumatic matter is the hinge on which the entire speculative system turns. The interior of the Earth is the abode of pure tangible matter. Above and surrounding this stable core is the Earth's crust which forms part of the frontier zone between the pure pneumatic celestial regions. The frontier zone reaches down a few miles into the Earth's crust, and a few miles up into the air. Only in this zone is pneumatic matter forced to mix with tangible matter; and from this forced association most of the phenomena of the terrestrial realm proceed (III, 756-7, 769).[11]

The pneumatic matter mixed in with tangible matter is called "attached spirit" to distinguish it from the "free spirits" which exist beyond the confines of tangible bodies (III, 769). There are four kinds of free spirit. Two of them, air and terrestrial fire, belong to the

	SULPHUR QUATERNION	MERCURY QUATERNION
Tangible substances	Sulphur (subterranean)	Mercury (subterranean)
(with enclosed spirits)	Oil and oily, inflammable substances (terrestrial)	Water and "crude" noninflammable substances (terrestrial)
Pneumatics substances	Terrestrial fire (sublunar)	Air (sublunar)
	Sidereal fire (matter of the heavenly bodies)	Ether (medium of the heavenly bodies)

The two quaternions.

sublunar region; the other two, ether and sidereal fire, belong to the celestial realm. Ether is the medium in which the planets, globes of sidereal fire, move round the central Earth. The interplanetary ether is, in effect, a very tenuous and pure kind of air; and both air and ether belong to a family of substances which also includes watery, noninflammable bodies, and mercury. This family is the *mercury quaternion*. Terrestrial fire, on the other hand, may be regarded as a feeble, corrupt version of sidereal fire; and the two forms of fire join with oil, oily or inflammable bodies, and sulphur in membership of the *sulphur quaternion* (III, 769–70).[12] The two quaternions express antithetical qualities, so air and ether fight their opposite numbers, fire and sidereal fire. The issue of the struggle depends on distance from the Earth. While all the free pneumatics become purer with distance, air and ether become progressively weaker while terrestrial and sidereal fire become progressively stronger (III, 769–70).

Thus, the heavens can be divided into three regions: the regions where fire or flame is extinguished, concentrated, and dispersed. At or near the surface of the Earth terrestrial fire, surrounded by hostile air at its strongest, cannot last without fuel. It aspires to the globular, concentrated, self-sustaining, mobile nature of sidereal fire, but cannot succeed except briefly in artificial, experimental circumstances (III, 93–4, 745–6, 769–70). Bacon points out that here fire exists only "by succession"; further away from the Earth it almost begins to exist "in identity," that is, as in the "lower comets" where it almost achieves the permanence and constancy of true sidereal fire, the first "rudiment" and last "sediment" of which is the body of the Moon (III, 751–2, 764, 769–70).[13] As we pass from the Moon to the other inferior planets, and then to the Sun and the superior planets, sidereal fire or flame becomes stronger and stronger still, and therefore increasingly capable of resisting the ether and of forming itself into large and independent globes. When we reach the third region, the region of the fixed stars, the ether has become so enfeebled and sidereal fire so dominant that the latter disperses itself through the vanquished ether as a multitude of stars (III, 770–1).

The diurnal motion of the heavens, driven by sympathy or "consent" (consensus), carries the heavenly bodies from east to west about the Earth (III, 773–4). Where the sidereal fire or flame is at its most powerful the motion is swiftest, so the region of the fixed stars completes a revolution in exactly twenty-four hours. But sidereal fire, the very stuff of the planets, becomes weaker with proximity to the Earth; the hostile ether enveloping the planets becomes stronger. A lower planet therefore moves more slowly and erratically than a higher because the condition of its sidereal fire is poorer and more susceptible of interference from the ether. In other words, the lower the planet the more it lags behind the fixed stars and the more erratic and "spiral" does its path become. In short, the nature of the celestial members of the two quaternions is such that motions complying with Alpetragian principles are infallibly generated (III, 774–5).

IV COSMOLOGY: PARACELSIAN ANTECEDENTS

Bacon's theory of the substance and structure of the universe betrays its parentage in the terms sulphur and mercury, for he framed the theory with some of the ideas of the Swiss-German physician, chemist, and philosopher Paracelsus (1493–1541) very much in mind. Put very summarily, Paracelsus taught that the intangible principles sulphur, salt, and mercury, (the *tria prima*) were the active spiritual forces in nature which gave bodies their specific attributes. The principle sulphur bestowed oiliness, inflammability, viscosity, and structure on individual existents; mercury conferred wateriness, "spirit," vapor, and vivifying powers; from the saline principle bodies received their rigidity, solidity, dryness, and earthiness. To a greater or lesser extent, all three principles entered into the particular constitution of every natural thing – including natural sulphur, mercury, and salt.[14] Alongside the idea of the *tria prima* stood the doctrine of the four elements. Paracelsus gave conflicting accounts of the elements, but his followers generally saw them not as simple bodies possessing fixed combinations of qualities but as *matrices* which generated groups of objects each specific to its source. These matrices were composite bodies devoid of qualities; they were "receptacles" in which objects were generated and dwelt. The matrices formed the environments in which the invisible seeds of physical bodies were hatched and endowed with their distinctive qualities by the three principles.[15]

Paracelsus and some of his heirs worked up these doctrines into comprehensive cosmogonies.[16] But it was Joseph Duchesne (Quercetanus) (1544–1609) who elaborated the cosmogony which perhaps most closely resembles the cosmological model offered by Bacon.[17] Duchesne's universe was divided into two regions: the sublunar and celestial; it originated from the Chaos or the abyss of waters which God had created from nothing. The spirit of God moved upon the waters and from the darkness of the waters the Divine Alchemist separated the ethereal heaven, the pure, "spiritual" matter of the celestial region. He then divided the waters themselves. As if by distillation, He separated the subtle, airy, mercurial liquor from the gross, oily, sulphurous liquor, and from the latter He separated a dry, saline residue. In that way He created the three principles informing the physical bodies of the sublunar world. The principles were the active forces in nature, and so were contrasted with the passive element-matrices. Of these only three were sublunary: earth, water, and air. Air was convertible with water; water represented a mean between the rarity of air and the density of earth. Fire was excluded from the company of the sublunar elements altogether because it was not mentioned in the biblical creation story. Following Paracelsus, Duchesne banished true fire to the heavens. Terrestrial fire, weak, corrupt and soon extinguished, was not an element at all; it aspired to the constancy of celestial fire but could never fully resemble it. Terrestrial and celestial fire were coupled with the principle sulphur; water and air with mercury; and earth with salt.[18]

The sublunary elements apparently manifested themselves in a refined form in the celestial realm. The refined elements made up the "quartessence" – so-called to distinguish it from Aristotle's fifth essence. The quartessence was the matrix of celestial manifestations of the three principles. Sulphur was the active principle at work in the celestial fire of the stars and planets; the crystal spheres carrying the heavenly bodies owed their constitution to salt, while the influxes radiating from the heavenly bodies expressed the principle mercury. This state of affairs was paralleled in air, highest of the sublunary elements. The winds were mercurial; the comets sulphurous; thunderbolts, dew, and frost saline. These phenomena differed from celestial ones for the fruits of the principles in the matrix of the air were less constant, pure, and enduring than those of the celestial world.[19]

V PRINCIPLES, ELEMENTS, AND CELESTIAL MOTION

The theory of the two quaternions, the core of Bacon's cosmology, clearly owed a great deal to Paracelsian cosmogony in, for instance, such fundamental features as the association of water and air with mercury, of fire with sulphur, and the extension of those associations in a purer form into the heavens. All the same, Bacon's cosmic chemistry represents a transformation of its sources in three important respects: (1) the nature of various entities invoked in the realm of matter theory; (2) the status of celestial kinematics; and (3) the relationship between Holy Writ and natural philosophy. I shall take these points in order.

Bacon's respect for the *tria prima* was never uncritical (III, 532–3). He dismissed the saline principle as an absurd contrivance got up to bring earthy, dry, and fixed bodies within the scope of Paracelsian doctrine. And, whereas Duchesne had associated salt with the element-matrix earth and the constitution of the crystal spheres,

Bacon, who believed neither in spheres nor matrices, attached no cosmological significance to salt whatever (I, 359; II, 82–3, 459; III, 769–70). Salt certainly cropped up in Bacon's theories about the terrestrial realm (see Section VII), but not in his thinking about the structure of the universe. The banishing of salt, which may owe something to Bacon's preference for dyads rather than triads, left him with a cosmology based on the sulphur and mercury quaternions. But that is not to say that he saw sulphur and mercury as *principles.* He endowed members of the two quaternions with properties which Paracelsians had attributed to sulphur and mercury. Bacon's sulphur, oil, terrestrial, and sidereal fire were all hot, fat, oily, and inflammable; his mercury, water, air, and ether, were cold, crude, watery, and noninflammable. But his sulphur and mercury were no different from tangible brimstone and quicksilver, and in another sense no more than shorthand for the quaternions to which they belonged. There was no sense in which sulphur and mercury could be seen as entities prior to or underlying other members of their respective quaternions; rather, each quaternion was to be seen as a family of substances embodying a particular cluster of "simple natures."[20] Nor were the quaternions like the *tria prima* in another respect; the latter were represented as a key to all phenomena, the former were not. The theory of the quaternions had more to do with cosmological than with most terrestrial phenomena.[21]

Turning now to the elusive Paracelsian distinction between element-matrices and principles, it is clear that it was redundant in Bacon's quaternion theory. Duchesne had associated the elements water and air with mercury, and terrestrial fire with sulphur. Bacon did the same but, in the overall structure of his theory, water and air enjoyed the same status as mercury, and so did terrestrial fire in relation to sulphur. Water, air, and fire were not passive matrices but highly active members of their quaternions. Again, in Bacon's as in Duchesne's system, air and terrestrial fire had relatives in high places. Duchesne's air and fire appeared in a purer, more refined form in the celestial quartessence, and terrestrial fire aspired to the permanence of the true fires of the heavens. Baconian terrestrial fire, surrounded by hostile air and a refugee in an alien environment, also longed for the constancy of sidereal fire, its celestial counterpart (III, 769, 771–2). Sidereal fire was itself immersed in the hostile ethereal medium, and the relations between the two were the same as those between air and fire "but sublimed and rectified" (III, 771–2). The chemical language is unmistakable; in Bacon's system ether and sidereal fire are, so to speak, lighter fractions of the celestial distillation of sublunar air and fire. However, the system had no room for a conceptually indistinct quartessence, celestial manifestations of principles, or, indeed, the manifold ambiguities of Paracelsian cosmogony in general. The quaternion theory streamlined Paracelsian concepts; it gave them a symmetrical structure – at the expense perhaps of their original suggestiveness. It expressed a flexible eclecticism which was able to act on existing bodies of philosophy without conceding too much to their authority.

As for the importance of kinematic principles, Bacon accommodated Paracelsian cosmic chemistry to Alpetragian imperatives; and such a strange conjunction of astronomical and chemical themes occurred nowhere else in seventeenth-century philosophy. Paracelsians would probably have been startled to find that Bacon had devised a Paracelsian-style cosmic chemistry to meet (among other things) the requirements of certain principles concerning the diurnal motion of the heavenly bodies. For Paracelsians mathematical reasoning, however coherent, rested on assumptions that were not borne out by "experience." They tended to equate mathematics with logic, and to damn both as impious instruments of the detested, heathenish philosophers Aristotle and Galen. Paracelsians apparently regarded planetary motion as an expression of the Divine Will and deprecated attempts to reduce it to abstractions.[22] Bacon on the contrary took the Alpetragian abstractions as one of his starting points and later revised Paracelsian chemico-cosmological doctrines to support them. He achieved a marriage of chemistry and kinematics. His bizarre eclecticism set him apart from both the mathematical astronomers and the Paracelsian chemists. Bacon had much in common with the Paracelsians – not least in his view that in theory mathematics and logic had corrupted natural philosophy. Yet he set himself apart from the Paracelsians in the very manner in which he constructed his world system.

VI THEOLOGY AND THE BOUNDARIES OF SCIENCE

Apart from revisions designed to accommodate his kinematic preferences, the most striking feature of Bacon's reworking of Paracelsian cosmogony was his refusal to represent the creation of the universe as a separative process whereby the Divine Alchemist extracted the principles, seeds, and elements of things from Chaos. Bacon stripped Paracelsian materials from their scriptural context,[23] and did not *explicitly* try to legitimize cosmological doctrines by representing them as infallible readings of Genesis. The Paracelsians were wrong when they pretended to find all philosophical truth in the Scriptures and blackguarded all other philosophies as heathenish and profane. There was, Bacon believed, no such enmity between God's word and His works (I, 835).

This is not to say, however, that revealed theology had nothing whatever to do with natural philosophy. Although scientific discourse and revealed theology were apparently different in kind, Bacon seems to have believed that the latter placed limits on choice in the former. Natural philosophy was not to be invaded by revealed theology,[24] but was nevertheless an activity *bounded* by it (III, 218), and any theory that seemed to violate the boundaries were *ipso facto* suspect.

By far the most important boundary condition was the belief that the universe was not eternal. God created Chaos, the makings of the cosmos, in an instant and from nothing; He completed the rest of His work in six days; and at some future date He would liquidate the universe which was, in effect, just a large hiccough in eternity (III, 110–12, 295–6; VII, 221).[25] Now unless that is understood it is difficult to make sense of Bacon's attacks on false principles or his identification of the true. Take, for instance, his critique of classical atomism. He promoted atomism far more for the *values* and *attitudes* it embodied than for its substantive content, and never set out to articulate a system framed in terms of atom and void.[26] He rejected the atomists' positive philosophy because he doubted its adequacy as science, and, whenever he criticized it in detail, he did not appeal to the court of theology but prosecuted his case on physical-rational grounds. Yet at the same time the atomists' positive science was always a nonstarter; it simply did not fit in with Bacon's ideas about the origin and fate of nature. He praised the atomists for asserting the eternity of matter while denying the eternity of the world. In this they came nearer than others to the revealed truth; for Genesis asserted that unformed matter existed before the six days' works (II, 475; III, 110–11, 295, 488; VI, 723, 725; VII, 220–2). Even so the atomists were wrong about the origins of the cosmos. The Democritean fortuitous concourse of atoms, the multiform worlds and essays at worlds could not have made the universe. Faith taught that all such speculations were merely the failed oracles of human sense for the matter and fabric of the universe were both the Creator's work (III, 79–80, 737–8).

Philosophies were to be judged by the extent to which they implied or embodied such truths. If a system of natural philosophy were inconsistent with the theological data it was to be set aside. If, on the other hand, it manifested the lineaments of nature's birth and death then it might be a candidate for serious attention. Bacon evidently framed his own cosmology with such ideas in mind. The *Thema coeli* (1612) opened with the assertion that nature had distributed matter by separating rare bodies from gross; it had assigned the terrestrial globe to the gross, and the rest of the universe to the fine or pneumatic, as to the two primary classes of things. This distinction, between dense or tangible, and rare or pneumatic, was not just fundamental in nature but first in point of time. Bacon did not say that tangible and pneumatic were separated from Chaos by the Divine Distiller, nor did he invoke Genesis. But the thrust of his remarks is quite plain: his conception of the universe implied a beginning of a particular kind, one in which tangible and pneumatic things were still undifferentiated, a chaos (so to speak) from which structure was afterward elicited. Bacon's is a Paracelsian-style reading of Genesis with the religious language cut away. He may have been attracted to Paracelsian cosmogonies precisely because (among other things) they appeared to agree with Holy Writ. He quarreled with the Paracelsians not because they ignored the boundaries set by faith, but because they observed them in the wrong way. To believe that all systems should conform to the theological data was not to believe with the Paracelsians that their proposals *alone* represented the truth of Holy Writ (I, 175–6, 835). To claim conformity with Holy Writ was quite different from claiming that a particular philosophy was the one and only explication of Genesis.

Bacon's own practice conformed to these general precepts. Theological respectability was never enough to persuade him to adopt a theory. Lack of respectability was always sufficient cause for him to reject one. Thus what was fundamental in nature was first in the order of Creation; what was first in the order of Creation was recorded in the Book of Genesis; what Genesis said about the Creation acted as a constraint on natural-philosophical explanation. Bacon's system of the universe began at the junction of cosmogony and ontology, and he believed that all theories about the primary objects of nature had to concur with Holy Writ. For Bacon something with such implicit approval was the doctrine that separation of dense and rare was one of the first and fundamental acts in the making of the natural order.

VII DIURNAL MOTION AND THE TERRESTRIAL WORLD

Bacon's speculative system comprises a version of Paracelsian cosmogony tailored to suit his views about the relationship between revealed knowledge and natural science, and to support the idea that every heavenly body moved, with appropriate lag, westward (and *only* westward) about the static Earth. Now with regard to the diurnal motion, it is important to note that Bacon did not confine it to the heavens alone. Aiming at a unified physics, he broke down the barrier Aristotle had set up between the sub- and superlunar realms and, by a succession of analogical leaps, extended or overextended the explanatory resources of the quaternion theory to take in the motions of wind, tide, and terrestrial verticity.

Two phenomena suggested that the diurnal motion was not confined to the heavens: a general westward revolution of the air, and the cycle of the tides. The general wind, mentioned in passing in the *De fluxu et refluxu maris* (c. 1611), was later given Bacon's full consideration in the *Historia ventorum* (1622). For Bacon this wind had to exist and had to be weak. As a member of the mercury quaternion, air (like celestial ether) could not but take part in the diurnal motion; yet it had to be feeble because the diurnal motion grew weaker as it approached the Earth. In other words the same progressive lag that accounted for planetary periodic motion both predicted and accounted for the existence of a permanent westerly breeze (III, 54–5; II, 26–8).[27]

Compared with the diurnal motion of the heavens the diurnal motion of the air was slow, but the same motion in water, the lowest fluid in the mercury quaternion, was slower still (I, 297). Bacon's most extended account of this motion as it manifested itself in the oceans appeared in the *De fluxu*. Here the chief phenomena are (a) the daily cycle with a twelve-hour interval between each high tide and a six-hour interval between high and low tides and (b) the monthly cycle whereby a given tide in the daily cycle occurs some fifty minutes later on each successive day and so only recurs at the same time of day at monthly intervals. Bacon saw both of these as manifestations of the diurnal motion (III, 47–8).

This belief rested on an argument squaring the diurnal motion with the interval of approximately six hours between ebb and flood in the daily cycle of the tides. The diurnal motion carried the seas westward about the Earth, but their advance was thrown back every twelve hours by the land masses of the Old and New Worlds. Thus in the Atlantic the diurnal motion would cause the waters to pile up on the eastern seaboard of the Americas, and so produce high tides there and low tides on the Atlantic coasts of Europe and Africa. Thrown back by the coasts of the Americas, the seas would then recede and, after six hours, low tide would occur in American waters and a high tide on the western coasts of Europe and Africa. The imbalance would be temporary and the next phase of the daily cycle began as the volume of water accumulated on the coasts of Europe and Africa flowed back westward assisted by the diurnal motion. The time elapsed between ebb and flood would thus be equivalent to just over a quarter of a sidereal day, just over because the daily tidal cycle as a whole represented the diurnal motion in its most attenuated form. The difference between ebb and flood and a quarter of a sidereal day was cumulative and gave rise to the monthly cycle that Bacon mentioned at the start of De fluxu (III, 51–2).

Having dealt with the general westerly breeze and the cycle of the tides, Bacon advanced to one of the most daring and short-lived elaborations of his system. Stretching analogical reasoning to its limits, he argued that verticity, the directional or versorial tendency in the Earth's crust, should be interpreted as the ultimate and most abstruse expression of the cosmic motion. This flight of fancy took off in the De fluxu and reappeared briefly in the Thema, after which it never again recurred in Bacon's writings (III, 58–9, 779–80). Bacon started from the experimental demonstration of verticity by William Gilbert (1544–1603), but saw verticity as a transitional state between the cosmic motion in its rotational form and the absolute stasis of the Earth's interior where no verticity whatever was to be found. The core of the Earth consisted of pure, *passive*, tangible matter, not the pure, *active*, magnetic matter of Gilbert's philosophy. The two philosophers gave very different answers to the question of the sources of activity in the terrestrial realm. For Bacon these sources were not rooted in the entrails of the Earth but beyond them (III, 749–50).[28] The fact that Bacon became interested in verticity at all may mean only that he liked to incorporate new findings and ideas into his theoretical framework – even at the risk of overtaxing its explanatory power. This desire was strong in the presence of data which seemed to tell against the Earth's motion. It was strong too in the period around 1612. At that time, and in the wake of excitement generated by Galileo's telescopic discoveries, Bacon first fleshed out his ideas about cosmic motion by elaborating the quaternion theory, and attempted to forge theoretical links between the motion of the heavens and sublunar phenomena like wind and tide. In these circumstances and given the fact that Bacon was always on the lookout for terrestrial confirmation of the cosmic diurnal motion, the temptation to embody verticity into the framework must have been very strong – even if that meant confining verticity to the Earth's surface to avoid compromising the passive status of the interior.

VIII   THE INTERMEDIATES

In its mature form Bacon's speculative system had two interlocking departments. The first comprised the cosmological phenomena reviewed above; the second dealt with the manifold changes in the animal, vegetable, and mineral kingdoms of the frontier zone between the celestial heavens and the Earth's interior. The second was logically dependent on the first, for the set of explanations applied to the mutable terrestrial domain was systematically integrated with but subordinated to explanations deployed in the cosmological. The first was dominated by the theory of the two quaternions, the second by explanations framed in terms of *intermediates*.[29]

The intermediates combined the qualities of one member of one quaternion with qualities of the corresponding member of the other quaternion. If we recall the table representing the two quaternions, we can adjust it to take account of these important intermediate substances thus: the table displays Bacon's matter theory in its full form. It also exhibits the operation of a characteristic Baconian intel-

	SULPHUR QUATERNION	SALT QUATERNION	MERCURY QUATERNION
Tangible substances	Sulphur (subterranean)	Salt(s) (subterranean and in organic beings)	Mercury (subterranean)
(with attached spirits)	Oil and oily, inflammable substances (terrestrial)	Juices of animals and plants	Water and "crude" noninflammable substances (terrestrial)
Pneumatic substances	Terrestrial fire (sublunar)	Attached animate and inanimate spirits (intangible bodies)	Air (sublunar)
	Sidereal fire (planets)	Heaven of the fixed stars	Ether (interplanetary medium)

lectual reflex, his tendency to assume the existence of in-between states poised between any two antithetical ones.[30] Just as there were four categories in each quaternion so there were four types of intermediate. The highest of these was the heaven of the fixed stars which was in fact a *compound* of sidereal fire and ether, in which the fiery component had the upper hand (III, 770–1, 771–2). The lowest intermediates were those which stood between sulphur and mercury, viz. salts which were nothing other than a "rudiment of life," and quasi–inorganic analogues of the next group of intermediates – the group poised between oil and water (II, 82–3, 543).

The oil–water intermediates were the juices of plants and animals. All plants were commixtures of watery and oily substances finely blended; and all fed to some degree on the salty intermediates (II, 214, 219–26, 303, 476, 485, 520–1, 536, 539–40, 543). The most important intermediates were those of fire and air: the "attached" animate and inanimate spirits. The inanimate spirits were incarcerated in all tangible bodies including living ones, the animate or vital spirits were found in living ones alone, and the behavior of the two kinds of fire–air intermediate accounted for very many of the phenomena of the terrestrial realm (I, 340; II, 214–7, 303, 351–2, 528).

The two kinds were thoroughly corporeal but differed to the extent that in all varieties of inanimate spirit the airy component was dominant whereas in the vital spirits the fiery had the upper hand. The relative "inflammation" of vital spirit gave it powers whose effects were apparent in the behavior of living organisms.[31] Vital spirit was always reluctant to leave the bodies enclosing it for there was nothing in the terrestrial environment similar to it; by contrast, the inanimate spirits always yearned to smash their way out of their tangible prisons for they had an unquenchable longing to unite with the ambient air. Air and spirits conspired to effect the latters' release from tangible matter. But if the spirits were not strong enough to break out, they attacked susceptible parts of their tangible jails and converted them into more spirit. Once enough spirit had been created and the tangible body sufficiently weakened in the process, the spirit escaped into the air. The innate tendency of this restless spirit to undermine tangible substances from within, to convert them into more spirit and to escape into the air lay at the root of many of the most important effects in the terrestrial realm (II, 106, 119–20, 216, 451–2, 556–7).

The distinction between vital and inanimate spirits is crucial to Bacon's philosophy of living beings and above all to his thinking about the prolongation of life. Rejecting earlier theories of aging and death, he staked his claim to originality on a single fundamental assertion: that although living beings were distinctive because they possessed vital spirits, they had to be considered as if they were inorganic things to the extent that their tangible parts were suffused with inanimate spirits. Vital spirits might restrain the impulses of the inanimate, but eventually the latter would prevail and destroy their hosts. Life was in effect a condition of uneasy equilibrium in which the vital spirits temporarily resisted the destructive centrifugal urges of the inanimate spirits lodged in the tissues. Possession of vital spirit entailed constant consumption of the body and therefore the need for nourishment. Other writers on the prolongation of life had mistakenly devoted their attention to the distinctive qualities of living things (II, 106, 119–20, 216, 451–2, 556–7). They had not viewed living bodies as if they were nonliving, as complex arrangements of tangible matter housing the aggressive inanimate spirits. Living organisms had to be considered as cradles of the vital spirit *and* as entities like stones, metals, or gems, that is, as substances subject to the same physical processes of change and decay as lifeless things.

It seems that every terrestrial being can be assigned to one of three categories according to the spirits it possesses: (i) inanimate objects possess only inanimate spirits dispersed in discontinuous portions through their tangible mass; (ii) vegetable bodies have these spirits too but also have vital spirits organized in a network of branching channels; (iii) animals have discontinuous inanimate and branching vital spirits but they differ from plants in that the branching spirits are connected to a cell (*cella*) which is their "senate" or "university." This trichotomy (spirits dispersed, branching, branching with a cell) was the starting point for Bacon's attempt to impose theoretical order on the diversity of living and nonliving forms, and to assimilate a commonplace belief, the notion of the chain of being, to his theory of matter. Ascent of the chain was a matter of increasing vitality, diversity of structure and (in animals) sensory-motor sophistication. Above all, ascent was marked by increasing quantity and "inflammation" of the vital spirit. Living beings constitute a succession of forms in which the higher have vital spirits in greater quantity and more spaciously situated. Every factor governing the position of a species in the chain is secondary to or depends upon the nature of its spirits. Bacon thus effectively annexed an old concept to a new philosophy or, conversely, justified an aspect of his theory of matter in terms of its capacity for explaining the fact of a natural hierarchy (I, 283, 543; II, 208–9, 225, 264, 453, 474, 506–8, 512, 515–16, 529, 531, 547, 557–60, 592–3, 604–7, 630–1, 639).

IX THE NATURE AND POWERS OF THE VITAL SPIRIT

The vital spirits regulate all the vegetative functions of plants and animals. The organs responsible for these functions, for attraction, retention, digestion, assimilation, excretion, and so forth, seem to act by "perception" (*perceptio*) or mere reaction to local stimuli, but these reactions are coordinated and governed by the vital spirit. The higher functions of the spirit manifest themselves only in animals, that is, in beings whose spirit is organized in a branching network and in cells or ventricular concentrations. In these circumstances the vital spirits mediate centrifugal motor functions and centripetal sensory ones. These functions flow from the constitution of the spirit which is an air–flame intermediate. Thus vital spirit has the softness of air to receive impressions and the vigor of fire to propagate its actions. The airy component is the sensory aspect of the spirit; the fiery, the motor aspect (I, 606; II, 215–16, 221, 225).

Death follows from the destruction of the vital spirit, and the spirit lasts only as long as it has suitable motion, coolness, and nourishment. The principal internal organs of the body exist to meet these three needs, so ruination of a vital organ is lethal to the spirit (II, 203, 225). As for coolness, Bacon followed the traditional line that the vital spirit of animals would destroy itself in its own heat if it were not refrigerated by respiration (II, 204–6). Nourishment repairs and restores the parts that sustain the vital spirit, especially the drier, more porous organs most vulnerable to the predatory, desiccating action of the inanimate spirits. However, complete restoration by nourishment or any other means is impossible. Deterioration of vital organs can be delayed but not reversed.[32]

X INANIMATE SPIRIT AND TANGIBLE MATTER

The source of all disintegration in the terrestrial realm is a threefold action of inanimate spirit. The successive stages of this are attenuation, escape, and contraction. Attenuation happens when the spirit attacks the tangible matter imprisoning it and converts some of it into more spirit. This weakens the object's structure and, since the spirit is weightless and tangible matter is not, makes it lighter. Attenuation is followed by the spirit's escape for, once the spirit has increased its volume and weakened the integrity of the matter containing it, it can decamp into the surrounding air. Escape is followed by contraction. A vacuum cannot be created in nature and so, once the spirit has departed, the tangible parts of the body close in to occupy the space vacated by the withdrawing spirit((I, 310–11; II, 213–14).

Flat distribution of spirit is usually found only in man-made objects produced, like brick and tile, by strong, constant heat. Natural bodies are less durable for the extreme variability of the heat of the heavenly bodies renders the distribution of spirit very uneven, and, as Bacon said in the *Historia vitae*, "inequality is the mother of dissolution" (II, 219). The spirit, like a demented prisoner, hurls itself against the walls of its tangible prison and rebounds from them, and slowly but surely breaks them down. This process is aided by the spirit's second impulse – to multiply and thereby conserve itself by converting the susceptible parts of the tangible body into more spirit. The third impulse is to escape and unite with cognate bodies – especially the air. This impulse is a great enemy of durability in inanimate bodies and longevity in living ones.

XI THE PROLONGATION OF LIFE

The aim of prolonging life represented the aims of Bacon's program as a whole. Confident that he lived in an age ordained by Providence for great advances in knowledge, he believed that a reconstructed natural philosophy would improve material conditions and so restore something of the felicity enjoyed by Adam and Eve before the Fall. In several works he marked out the prolongation of life as the first and highest objective of the new philosophy (III, 167, 222).

Bacon knew the writings of many authors on the theme of prolonging life – Aristotle, Galen, Avicenna, Albertus Magnus, Roger Bacon, Arnaldus de Villanova, Ficino, Fernel, Cornaro, Telesio, Paracelsus and the iatrochemists – but set little store by any of them (I, 598; II, 114, 147, 158–9, 174, 199; III, 531–6). The main tradition in this matter stemmed back to Avicenna (980–1037), who developed a theory which was ultimately a refinement of classical Galenic ideas about the nutritive moistures or humors.[33] Food underwent two digestions, one in the stomach, and then another in the liver. The first converted the nutritious part of the food into chyle. Chyle was converted by the second digestion into venous blood. Blood moved from the liver to all the parts of the body where it was assimilated by a third digestion. This was a complex process involving four nutrimental moistures called "secondary humours."[34] Of these the most important was the radical moisture or *gluten* which maintained the continuity and integrity of the parts.[35] This moisture was somehow derived from sperm. It existed in a fixed quantity which determined an individual's life span for, as time passed, it was dried out and consumed by the connatural or innate heat (*calor innatus*) which was the instrument of the soul and source of bodily activity. With age, the heat diminished as it consumed the radical moisture: the older the individuals, the colder and drier their "temperament" or balance of humors. Because of the ever-diminishing heat available for the digestive processes, such restoration as the radical humor received was increasingly imperfect.[36]

Bacon pointed out that the Arabo-Latin theory supposed that aging and death were effects of the ineluctable diminution of "natural heat," and the radical or "primigenial" moisture of the body. The wasting away of the moisture could of course be slowed down but never entirely checked by nutrition. This, according to Bacon, was a deficiency theory of aging and therefore very different from Telesio's "superfluity" theory.[37] According to Telesio's theory, the condition and growth rate of the body varied with the condition of the blood that nourished it. The condition of the blood was governed by the state of the liver and the intensity of the body's heat. Telesio rejected the chilling traditional notion that body heat diminished with age; instead he conceived the cheerful thought that it gradually increased, and slowly but surely baked the liver. The baking did little to increase the liver's efficiency. As time passed, the quality of the blood manufactured by the liver insensibly deteriorated and the blood produced by old men became thick, impure, and increasingly incapable of nourishing the body. Instead of receiving nourishment, the body became encumbered with salty and bilious excrements; death then supervened.[38]

The radical moisture theorists alleged that heat waned with age; Telesio claimed that it increased; Bacon combined the two views: heat increased during infancy and maturity but diminished thereafter. The Italian had at least set out in the right direction, but if he was right about the initial *crescendo*, he failed to notice the subsequent *diminuendo*, and (as the *De viis mortis* [post-1611] has it) mistook a segment of a circle for the circle itself.[39] Bacon's own views were not entirely original,[40] but he certainly departed from the Arabo-Latin consensus in thinking that the processes of aging only took hold once adulthood had begun, and that while a living being was still growing its fabric could be entirely repaired and its parts improved both in quantity and quality. Yet for him, as for Avicenna,

Arnaldus, and Fernel, aging was essentially a process of progressive desiccation which overtook the drier or more porous parts. The drying out of these less reparable parts caused the more reparable to fail. Gradual loss of moisture (humor) from the tissues was accompanied by loss of structural coherence which eventually caused the body to crumble to dust (II, 106–7, 120–1).

To some extent it would not be unfair to identify the juices and moistures of which Bacon speaks with the radical moisture for, while denying the utility of received theories, he often fell back on traditional language and ideas. Such concessions to the past suggest that Bacon was determined to leave no stone unturned in the search for means of prolonging life. They suggest a kind of practical, bet-hedging eclecticism coupled with a certain intellectual "slippage" not unusual in someone struggling to release himself from received ideas. But they do not imply anything like collapse into earlier modes of thought. As we know, he held that the body should be viewed first as an inanimate thing unsupported by aliment and secondly as a living and feeding thing; for the first consideration would provide rules concerning consumption, the second rules concerning repair (II, 184, 189–90, 210–11, 281). This double view owed nothing to the traditions of Bacon's age. No matter what the specific affinities or debts, the geography and disposition of the concepts within Bacon's system of speculative philosophy was not, taken in sum, Galenic, Paracelsian, Telesian, or anything else. The concepts of vital and inanimate spirit were limited or delimited by adjacent concepts within the overall theory of matter which was itself a systematization and transformation of borrowings of an initially eclectic character.

NOTES

1 Rees 1975b, pp. 161–73.
2 Rees 1975a, pp. 92–3.
3 The key ideas appear in a piece called *A Conference of Pleasure*. A manuscript unknown to Spedding is probably the best surviving witness to the text. In this manuscript, now lodged at the Kodama Memorial Library, Meisei University, Tokyo, the two doctrines are outlined on f. 79.
4 *Philosophia sensibus demonstrata* . . . (Naples, 1591), pp. 300–9.
5 Alpetragius, *Al-Bitruji: On the Principles of Astronomy; an Edition of the Arabic and Hebrew Versions with Translation, Analysis, and an*

Arabic–Hebrew–English Glossary, ed. Bernard R. Goldstein, 2 vols., (New Haven and London, 1971), I, pp. 3–5, p. 23, p. 26, pp. 57–9.

6 Ibid., I, p. 57 passim.

7 Ibid., I, pp. 5, 20–1, 63.

8 Ibid., I, pp. 26, 101.

9 See Duhem 1954, III, pp. 243–4, 282–7, 328–9.

10 Also see Rees 1986, pp. 412–77. Bacon was by no means indifferent to the uses of mathematics in natural philosophy: see Rees 1985, pp. 27–48.

11 *De vijs mortis* in *Francis Bacon's Natural Philosophy: a New Source. A Transcription of Manuscript Hardwick 72A with Translation and Commentary*, ed. Graham Rees assisted by Christopher Upton, BSHS Monographs 5 (St. Giles, 1984) f. 23^r, f. 26^r. Also see Rees 1975a, pp. 85–6; idem, 1979, 204.

12 Also see Rees 1975b, p. 86.

13 Francesco Patrizi, *Nova de vniversis philosophia* (Venice, 1593), f. 98^r.

14 Pagel 1958, pp. 87, 101–3.

15 Pagel 1958, p. 82; Debus 1967, p. 129, passim.

16 Gerhard Dorn (fl. 1566–84), Petrus Severinus (1542–1602), Oswald Croll (c. 1560–1609) and Robert Fludd (1574–1637) all attempted something along these lines.

17 On Duchesne and his work, see Pagel 1960, pp. 137–48.

18 *Ad veritatem hermetica medicinae* (Paris, 1604), pp. 162, 167–9, 174–5, 184; *Liber de . . . medicinae materia* (Paris, 1603), p. 20. Also see Pagel 1960, pp. 137–8.

19 *Ad veritatem hermetica medicinae*, pp. 162, 172, 175, 186–7.

20 For simple natures and their place in Bacon's philosophy, see Fattori 1983, pp. 21–34.

21 For doctrines concerning that realm, see below, pp. 134ff.

22 Debus 1973, pp. 5–17; Westman and McGuire, 1977, p. 60.

23 He also stripped them away from other important aspects of the Paracelsian philosophy of nature – in particular those aspects which he judged to be "superstitious," for example, Paracelsian uses of the analogy between macro- and microcosm (III, 340), and teachings concerning the power of the imagination (II, 641).

24 That would expose philosophers to the risk of producing illicit and superstitious mixtures of divine and human knowledge, see I, 197; III, 219.

25 For other aspects of Bacon's doctrine of the Creation, see De Mas 1984, pp. 73–90.

26 See Rees 1980, pp. 549–71.

27 Also see Rees 1975a, pp. 98–9; idem 1975b, pp. 168–71.

28 Rees 1979, pp. 204–5.

29 This topic is considered at greater length in Rees 1977b, pp. 110–25.

30 For instances of mean states, see for example III, 737 (rectilinear motion); I, 636 (the indifferent state between gravity and levity); III, 769–70 (lower comets); II, 529 (coral); I, 310–11 (vivification); III, 57–8 (verticity).

31 See, for instance, *De viis mortis*, ff. 10ᵛ, 11ᵛ, 17ᵛ.

32 *De viis mortis*, f. 22ʳ.

33 Pagel 1967, pp. 257–8; Hall 1971, pp. 4–8; McVaugh 1974, pp. 259–65.

34 So called to distinguish them from the primary humors (blood, phlegm, black and yellow bile).

35 Avicenna, *Liber canonis* (Venice, 1507, [repr. Hildesheim, 1964]), lib. I, fen. 1, doct 4.

36 Ibid., lib. I, fen 1, doct. 3, cap. 3, f. 2ᵛ; lib. I, fen 3, doct. 3, ff. 52ᵛ–53ʳ; lib. IV, fen 1, tract 3, cap. 1, ff. 413ᵛ–414ʳ.

37 *De viis mortis*, ff. 1ᵛ–2ᵛ.

38 Bernardino Telesio, *De rerum natura*, ed. Luigi De Franco, vol. I, (Cosenza, 1965), vol. II, (Cosenza, 1971), vol. III, (Firenze, 1976), II, pp. 540–2.

39 *De viis mortis*, f. 2ᵛ.

40 Hall 1971, p. 15; Gruman 1966, p. 82.

6 Bacon as an advocate for cooperative scientific research

I INTRODUCTION

An important aspect of Bacon's "total reconstruction of sciences, arts, and all human knowledge" (IV, 8) was the organizational and institutional restructuring of natural philosophy. His rhetoric of a revolution in learning was similar to that employed by a number of his near contemporaries, but his vision of how it would be achieved differed. Unlike Descartes, for example, who retained the traditional philosophical emphasis upon the power of individual reasoning, Bacon sought to institute a new method for the investigation of nature, based upon the cooperative efforts of a large workforce.[1]

Bacon's advocacy of cooperative research was in part responsible for his sharp criticism of traditional learning. As he explained, the schools had "usurped a kind of dictatorship in the sciences" (IV, 16), with the consequence that "philosophy and intellectual sciences" had been "fruitful of controversies but barren of works." The "mechanical arts," on the other hand, tended to encourage the collaborative effort of workers and thus they had been "continually growing and becoming more perfect" (IV, 14).[2] Despite the fact that numerous beneficial results had been achieved in the practical arts, however, Bacon believed that they would also require reform before they could be of true service to natural philosophy. Artisans such as chemists, for example, tended to restrict themselves to a few "petty tasks" and "pursued a kind of wandering inquiry, without any regular system of operations" (IV, 17; IV, 80–1). Their results, therefore, had been "produced accidentally" and "not by any art or theory" (IV, 74). The chemists' methods had to be replaced by a more rational approach to the study of nature because their "accidental felicity"

146

did not hold much "chance of success." Rather, "our steps must be guided by a clue, and the whole way from the very first perception of the senses must be laid out upon a sure plan" (IV, 18). Part of Bacon's criticism of the chemists was also directed toward those who either conceived of themselves as solitary magi working in complete secrecy or envisioned collaboration as that which would ensue from the meeting of a few select *illuminati* (V, 191).[3] In the place of such individual or quasi-collaborative efforts, a truly cooperative enterprise had to be instituted that would leave "little to the acuteness and strength of wits" and instead place "all wits and understanding nearly on a level" (IV, 63).

Because Bacon rejected reliance upon "the excellence of wit" or the mere "repetition of chance experiments," his vision of cooperative research represented a radical break with traditional views concerning the way in which knowledge was to be discovered and used (IV, 18). The aim of this chapter is to examine how the idea of cooperation emerged in Bacon's earliest formulation of his reform plans and how his personal background contributed to the suggestions that he offered for the fulfillment of his scheme. This discussion will be followed by a detailed examination of the way in which he incorporated many of his suggestions into his idealized representation of a scientific community in the *New Atlantis*. Finally, the chapter will conclude with a discussion of how Bacon's public pronouncements concerning cooperative research acted as an incentive for the plans of the next generation of natural philosophers in England.

II COOPERATION IN BACONIAN SCIENCE

As early as 1592 Bacon wrote to his uncle, Lord Burghley, that he wished to take "all knowledge for his province," and that a place where one would have "commandment of more wits than of a man's own" was essential for bringing "in industrious observations, grounded conclusions, and profitable inventions and discoveries," that could be used to replace the arid speculations of scholastic philosophy (VIII, 108–9).[4] The idea that a statesman ought to be involved in educational reform was not entirely new. In the generation preceding Bacon, statesmen had called for a restructuring of the universities. In particular, they had advised that more practical subjects ought to be included in the university curriculum. Bacon's innovation came in the way in which he extended the role that government could play in such reforms. He not only called for the addition of new subjects but also insisted that these subjects could be used to transform the content of the traditional philosophical curriculum.[5] In 1594, at a device performed at Gray's Inn for the queen's entertainment, he publicly presented his ideas on some of the ways in which the government could contribute to this reform of learning. He suggested to Elizabeth that she establish four institutions for the advancement of learning that would include: "a most perfect and general library," containing all "books of worth" whether "ancient or modern printed or manuscript, European or of the other parts"; a botanical and zoological garden for the collection of all plants as well as rare beasts and birds; a museum collection of all things that had been produced "by exquisite art or engine"; and a laboratory "furnished with mills, instruments, furnaces and vessels" (VIII, 334–5).[6]

Elizabeth proved unsympathetic to these plans. When James I ascended to the throne in 1603, however, Bacon had reason to believe that there was new hope for his project. Shortly thereafter, he published *The Advancement of Learning* in a renewed attempt to gain government support. He asked the king to consider a reorganization of the universities and particularly favored the establishment of new "foundations and buildings, endowments with revenues, endowments with franchises and privileges, institutions and ordinances for government; all tending to quietness and privateness of life, and discharge of cares and troubles" (III, 323). Once again the theme of cooperation emerged in his call for a "brotherhood of scientists" whereby an exchange of information would take place among all of the scholars of Europe.[7] In a series of unpublished essays dating from the period 1603–8, he also noted that the idea of cooperative learning could be extended to include the work of past scholars. Although he had at first almost completely rejected the usefulness of past learning in the *Temporis partus masculus* in later works such as the *Redargutio philosophiarum* and the *Cogitata et visa* he began to appreciate what he saw as the careful and dynamic style of investigation practiced by the pre-Socratics.[8] In 1609 he published the *De sapientia veterum* and argued that present scholars could gain insight from a critical study of the books of the past.[9] According to Bacon, "the perfection of the sciences is to be looked for not from the swiftness or ability of any one inquirer, but from a succession" of them (VI, 753).

In addition to cooperation among past and present scholars, however, Bacon again stressed the need for cooperation between the liberal and illiberal arts. In *The Advancement of Learning*, he indicated how the knowledge embedded within the practical arts could furnish philosophers with information concerning natural processes. He also noted how two practical achievements, printing and navigation, not only were valuable sources of new information but also provided the means to further cooperation. As he explained, these arts had produced an "openness of the world" and "disclosed multitudes of experiments, and a mass of natural history" (III, 476; cf. IV, 82, 100–1). He argued that this "great storehouse of facts should be accumulated."[10] In turn this experience was to be made "literate" by the compilation of natural histories that could be printed and distributed throughout the learned world and thus foster communication and the free exchange of ideas and information.[11]

The theme of cooperation among all areas of learning became more pronounced in Bacon's published works of the 1620s as he came to appreciate more fully the integral role of natural histories in his plans for reform. Because of the large number and variety of areas that would have to be investigated, the construction of natural histories could not be accomplished by a single individual. As he explained in his *Parasceve*, "the materials on which the intellect has to work are so widely spread that one must employ factors and merchants to go everywhere in search of them and bring them in" (IV, 251–2). At this time he also became more specific about which "mechanical and illiberal" practices ought to be studied. In particular, he noted that the arts most useful for natural philosophy were those in which the material composition of a body is altered, such as "agriculture, cookery, chemistry, dyeing; the manufacture of glass, enamel, sugar, gunpowder, artificial fires, paper, and the like" (IV, 257).

Although Bacon continued to speak of the leveling of wits in these later works and stressed that all could contribute to the advancement of learning, he also developed the idea that within cooperative research a division of labor would be required. His general manifesto of the advancement of learning was meant for "the world" but his more specific plans he decided to circulate among a more restricted audience (X, 87). The role of artisans and mechanics would be limited to the contributions that they could make from their own areas of expertise. Others would be required to compile the information received from these workers and make the experience "literate" through publication. After the practical compilation of such natural histories, a further division of labor would be required at the cognitive level. In his *Parasceve*, Bacon had explained that "all mechanical experiments should be as streams flowing from all sides into the sea of philosophy" (IV, 258). In order to establish "the Foundations of a true and active philosophy," the practical abilities of artisans would have to be augmented by workers with more speculative and rational abilities who would be able to draw axioms and theories from the information contained in the natural histories (IV, 252).¹² Thus, although Bacon's vision of cooperative research was more open and democratic than the approach traditionally followed by scholastic philosophy, his desire for rational order entailed that there would have to be a hierarchical organization by which the efforts of the many workers could be coordinated and directed.

As a statesman, Bacon naturally believed that government institutions would provide the best means for such central control and organization. He also realized that only the state possessed the financial resources that would be required for the completion of his vast project. In *The Advancement of Learning*, he had discussed how large works could only be overcome "by amplitude of reward, by soundness of direction, and by the conjunction of labours" (III, 322). Bacon had called for the cooperation of workers and had supplied them with the methodological directions for their work, but the rewards would have to be provided by the state.¹³ In his *Parasceve* he noted that the construction of a firm factual foundation "is a thing of very great size, and cannot be executed without great labour and expense; requiring as it does many people to help, and being (as I have said elsewhere) a kind of royal work" (IV, 251). His most explicit published appeal for state funding came in his dedication of the *Instauratio magna* to James I. He compared James to Solomon and made "a request no way unworthy of your Majesty" to follow the Hebrew King's "example in taking order for the collecting and perfecting of a Natural and Experimental History, true and severe (unincumbered with literature and book-learning), such as philosophy may be built upon" (IV, 12; XIV, 120, 130).[14]

In order to gain support, Bacon argued that it would be in the best interest of the state to fund his project. In his *Instauratio magna*, he noted that on his plan philosophers would "join in consultation for the common good" and seek truth not "for profit, or fame, or power . . . but for the benefit and use of life" (IV, 21). Beyond the practical benefits that would accrue to the individuals within society, however, he also argued that his new philosophy could help put an end to the religious controversies that were often the cause of civil unrest and thus contribute to the political stability of the commonwealth.[15] In his famous letter to Toby Matthew in 1609, Bacon wrote: "Myself am like the miller of Huntingdon, that was wont to pray for peace amongst the willows; for while the winds blew, the wind-mills wrought, and the water-mill was less customed. So I see that controversies of religion must hinder the advancement of sciences" (XI, 137–8). The focus on charitable works would help to increase religious sentiment, while the reform of philosophy would alleviate some of the tensions that had been created by the incorporation of the "thorny philosophy of Aristotle" into the theological doctrines of the schoolmen (IV, 88). The divided allegiances that were responsible for conflicts within and between states would be replaced by religious toleration. In turn, the orderly and peaceful civil society resulting from such toleration would serve to promote even greater cooperation.

Bacon had a grand vision of how the cooperative labor of many workers dedicated to the pursuit of knowledge would yield innumerable benefits for the commonwealth. Yet he readily conceded that given "the present condition of things" his vision might not "easily be conceived or imagined" (IV, 32). He even pointed out in the preface of the *Instauratio magna* that he "was well aware how solitary an enterprise it is, and how hard a thing" it was "to win faith and credit for" it (IV, 8). But he also told his readers that they should "be of good hope" and not "imagine that this Instauration of mine is a thing infinite and beyond the power of man, when it is in fact the true end and termination of infinite error" (IV, 21). According to Bacon, "by far the greatest obstacle to the progress of science" occurs when "men despair and think things impossible" (IV, 90). In order to combat such despair, he devoted a section of the *Novum organum* to "arguments for hope" (IV, 90–102). He explained that the cooperative nature of his program set it apart from previous styles of philosophy and provided a ground for hope in further progress because

it is not a way over which only one man can pass at a time (as is the case with that of reasoning), but one in which the labours and industries of men (especially as regards the collecting of experience) may with the best effect be first distributed and then combined. For then only will men begin to know their strength, when instead of great numbers doing all the same things, one shall take charge of one thing and another of another. (IV, 102)

III THE *NEW ATLANTIS*

Throughout his works, Bacon made numerous programmatic announcements concerning the possibility of his project and the practical benefits that would be obtained from it. In addition, he wrote the *New Atlantis*, a fable designed to provide his readers with a vivid image of what it would be like to live in a land where his vision of the scientific enterprise provided the overriding structure for society. Because it is a fable, the *New Atlantis* can be analyzed on a number of different levels. It has been frequently interpreted from a literary perspective as part of the popular utopian genre of Bacon's day. It has also been interpreted as a religious allegory, a sociological critique, and a political manifesto designed to support nascent imperialist and capitalist tendencies.[16] In addition, of course, it can be interpreted as a concrete plan for the establishment of a scientific society.[17]

The generation of natural philosophers following Bacon used the *New Atlantis* as just such a plan upon which to base their collaborative efforts. The fable incorporates all of the themes discussed above in connection with how a cooperative research project could be established and the ways in which the health and welfare of citizens would be enhanced by the practical benefits derived from such research.

Bacon's fable resembles the many narratives concerning actual voyages of discovery that had become quite popular in his day. It is composed of a first person account by a Spanish sailor of what happened to him and his fellow sailors when they were thrown off course by strong winds and found themselves "in the midst of the greatest wilderness of waters in the world, without victual" (III, 129). They gave themselves up for lost and had "prepared for death" yet, after having prayed to God, within a day they saw "thick clouds, which did put us in some hope of land" and steering toward the clouds they soon found that "it was a land" and they "entered into a good haven, being the port of a fair city" (III, 129–30). What follows is a detailed "natural history" of the customs, rituals, and culture of the Island of Bensalem.

The first thing readers learn is that the natives of this land are much different from those that had been encountered in real voyages of discovery. Although they were forbidden to land, the sailors met with the leaders of the island on the water and were presented with a scroll signed at the bottom with a cross, written in Hebrew, Greek, Latin, and Spanish, wherein they were advised that "if you want fresh water, or victual, or help for your sick, or that your ship needeth repair, write down your wants, and you shall have that which belongeth to mercy" (III, 130). The sailors were reassured by this display of knowledge, civility, and Christian charity. On the advice of the "Conservator of Health," the islanders had not boarded the sailors' ship, but after this first meeting a notary came on board, carrying an odd scarlet fruit somewhat like an orange that he appeared to use as a "preservative against infection," and told them that on the next day they would be brought on land to stay at the "Strangers' House."

The narrator then relates how, on the way to the house, they were led through "three fair streets" and he described his first impression of the social order exhibited by the citizens of Bensalem:

all the way we went there were gathered some people on both sides standing in a row; but in so civil a fashion, as if it had been not to wonder at us but to welcome us; and divers of them, as we passed by them, put their arms a little abroad; which is their gesture when they bid any welcome. (III, 132–3)

The strangers' house itself was a spacious brick building, prepared with "handsome and cheerful" chambers for the healthy sailors as well as an "infirmary for sick persons" in a "long gallery" with "seventeen cells" set up along one side with "partitions of cedar wood" (III, 133). The narrator was clearly pleased by the accommodations and also by dinner that evening that he described as "better than any collegiate diet that I have known in Europe," which was served with three types of drink "all wholesome and good," including a type of "cider made of a fruit of that country" that was "wonderful pleasing and refreshing." In addition, they were given some of the curious "scarlet oranges for our sick; which (they said) were an assured remedy for sickness taken at sea," and a "box of small grey or whitish pills, which they wished our sick should take" to "hasten their recovery" (III, 134).

The sailors passed the next three days "joyfully and without care" and "every hour" had the "joy of the amendment of our sick; who thought themselves cast into some divine pool of healing, they mended so kindly and so fast" (III, 135). Despite such hospitality, however, the sailors had not been permitted to leave the house. The narrator assumed that the natives were studying them in order to ensure that they were worthy of staying on the island, and he thus advised his men to "behave ourselves as we may be at peace with God, and may find grace in the eyes of this people" (III, 134). On the fourth day the sailors were visited by the "governor of this House of Strangers," a Christian priest "by vocation," who told them that the state had given them "licence to stay on land for the space of six weeks." They were also given the freedom to leave the house, but they were not allowed to go beyond "a *karan* (. . . a mile and an half) from the walls of the city, without especial leave" (III, 135). On the next day the governor again visited the sailors and told them that they would be allowed to ask him any questions that they might have about the island.

The narrator's first question concerned what any reader at this point would like to know. Bacon has set up this island as a Christian society yet, as the narrator points out, it is a remote island "divided by vast and unknown seas, from the land where our Saviour walked on earth" (III, 137). In response, the governor provided a detailed account of how the island came to be Christian in the course of which he made the first reference to "the society of Salomon's House" and described how a fellow of the "college" that "is the very eye of this kingdom" had played an essential role in the island's conversion, thus reinforcing Bacon's contention that science could foster religious sentiment (III, 137). When the governor returned on the following day, the narrator asked him to explain how it was that "we in Europe (notwithstanding all the remote discoveries and navigation of this last age,) never heard any of the least inkling or glimpse of this island," and yet the islanders have knowledge of the languages, books and customs of Europe (III, 139). This question elicited a more extended discussion of the role of Salomon's House in the society, although the governor noted that because of the "laws of secrecy touching strangers" he would have to "reserve some particulars" concerning the knowledge possessed by this kingdom.

First he explained that Bensalem was an ancient civilization that had flourished for over three thousand years. During ancient times the island was known to other nations who freely sailed their ships into its harbors. Such commerce ended, however, when Bensalem alone was saved from a flood that destroyed the other ancient, "mighty and proud kingdoms" (III, 141–2). Because of the destruction of the civilizations that were closest to Bensalem and the decline of navigation in other parts of the world, travel to the island had "long since ceased; except it were by some rare accident, as this of yours" (III, 143). Bensalem had retained its sailing capabilities, however, and in order to explain why the island was not known by "our sailing to other nations," the governor provided an account of King Solamona, "the lawgiver of our nation," who had reigned nineteen hundred years before (III, 144).

Solamona's laws, instituted in order "to make his kingdom and people happy," were responsible both for the lack of European knowledge about Bensalem and for the islanders' knowledge of Europe. The king recognized that the island was self-sufficient and could "maintain itself without any aid at all of the foreigner" and thus "amongst his other fundamental laws of this kingdom, he did ordain the interdicts and prohibitions which we have touching entrance of strangers" (III, 144). Solamona had "preserved all points of humanity," however, and decreed that strangers in distress should be assisted. They were also given the freedom to depart, but if they wished to remain on the island, they would be provided with "very good conditions and means to live from the state" (III, 144–5). During the ensuing centuries, only thirteen strangers had elected to return to their homes, and as the governor surmised, if they had reported about their experience on the island it would have been received by their contemporaries "but for a dream" (III, 145).

In order to explain the superior knowledge of the Bensalemites, the governor then described Solamona's most notable achievement, the "erection and institution of an Order or Society which we call *Salomon's House;* the noblest foundation (as we think) that ever was upon the earth; and the lanthorn of this kingdom." The house, "dedicated to the study of the Works and Creatures of God," was named after "the King of the Hebrews, which is famous with you, and no stranger to us" (III, 145). This is the same king to whom Bacon had compared James I in his dedication of the *Instauratio magna,* and Solamona's reasons for establishing the college were those that Bacon had cited there. The fellows of the order sought to discover "the true nature of all things" so that "God might have the more glory in the workmanship of them, and men the more fruit in the use of them" (III, 146).

Solamona had generally forbidden navigation to foreign lands, yet he allowed that certain members of Salomon's House would be permitted to travel abroad, which explained how the islanders had come to know about Europe. In the governor's words, Solamona had ordained:

That every twelve years there should be set forth out of this kingdom two ships, appointed to several voyages; That in either of these ships there should be a mission of three of the Fellows or Brethren of Salomon's House; whose errand was only to give us knowledge of the affairs and state of those countries to which they were designed, and especially of the sciences, arts, manufactures, and inventions of all the world; and withal to bring unto us books, instruments, and patterns in every kind. (III, 146)

These fellows, later called "merchants of light" (III, 164), fulfilled the function of the "factors and merchants" that Bacon had described in his *Parasceve.* Yet unlike his earlier insistence upon free communication, the excursions of the Bensalemites were described as being cloaked in secrecy. The governor would not reveal any of the details surrounding the voyages and noted that the travelers disguised themselves "under the names of other nations." He emphasized, however, that the purpose of these missions was not for the accumulation of material commodities such as gold or jewels, but "for God's first creature, which was *Light*: to have *light* (I say) of the growth of all parts of the world" (III, 146–7).

The two discussions of Salomon's House up to this point in the narrative have established the central place that this college occupies within the social structure of the island. We have learned that it is a state institution dedicated to scientific endeavors that is apparently responsible not only for practical benefits such as the medicines that cured the sick sailors, but also for the religious, moral, and civic virtues exhibited by Bensalem's inhabitants. The importance of these virtues is reinforced by the expository scheme of the narrative. Instead of moving directly to a more detailed description of Salomon's House, Bacon inserts a lengthy digression concerning a particular social custom of the island called the "Feast of the Family," which is "done at the cost of the state" to honor "any man that shall live to see thirty persons descended of his body alive together, and all above three years old." According to the narrator, this is a "most natural, pious, and reverend custom" that shows Bensalem "to be compounded of all goodness" (III, 147).[18]

The narrator then described his friendship with a Jewish merchant, Joabin, through whom he learned more about the "laws and customs they had concerning marriage" (III, 152). Despite the value placed upon progeny, Joabin says that the island is a "chaste" nation that does not permit a "plurality of wives" and, unlike Europe, they have "no dissolute houses, no courtesans, nor anything of that kind." Indeed, he notes that the Bensalemites "wonder (with detestation) at you in Europe, which permit such things" (III, 152). The introduction of Joabin into the narrative also indicates that the island practices a somewhat high degree of religious toleration, which conforms with Bacon's idea that religious controversy could be kept in check by an enlightened scientific society. The Jews of the island are permitted to follow their own religion, although the narrator notes that this toleration is in part a result of the fact that "they are of a far differing disposition from the Jews in other parts" of the world. Unlike those who "hate the name of Christ," for example, "these . . . give unto our Saviour many high attributes" (III, 151).

Joabin's narration came to an end when a messenger summoned him "away in haste." On the next day Joabin explained that he had learned that "one of the Fathers of Salomon's House" planned a visit to the city, which was a joyful event because "we have seen none of them this dozen years." Although the "cause of his coming" was a "secret," he would come "in state," and Joabin assured the narrator that he would "provide you and your fellows of a good standing to see his entry" (III, 154). Despite the fact that Salomon's House is the guiding institution of the society, we see here that its activities are kept secret from the populace at large and that its members form a privileged social class. According to the narrator, the father was received into the city as royalty. He was elegantly clothed and "carried in a rich chariot . . . of cedar, gilt, and adorned with crystal" as well as "pannels of sapphires, set in borders of gold." In addition to his footmen, he had "before him fifty attendants" and behind him "went all the officers and principals of the Companies of the City" (III, 154–5). Once again, the narrator also commented on the civility of the people, noting that "the street was wonderfully well kept: so that there was never any army had their men stand in better battle-array, than the people stood" (III, 155).

In the course of this fable Bacon has provided rich detail concerning the customs of the island and by the many allusions to the role played by Salomon's House in the life of the society, he has whetted the reader's appetite to learn more about this college. Finally, the narrative turns to such an account when, during a "private conference" arranged by Joabin, the Father tells the narrator that "I will give thee the greatest jewel that I have. For I will impart unto thee, for the love of God and men, a relation of the true state of Salomon's House" (III, 156).

IV SALOMON'S HOUSE

The Father's account began with a brief statement of the "End of the Foundation," which the reader knows by now is "the knowledge of Causes, and secret motions of things; and the enlarging of the bounds of Human Empire, to the effecting of all things possible." He then discussed how this goal is achieved by the "Preparations and Instruments" they have for their works, "the several employments and offices" of the fellows of the society, and the "ordinances and rites" observed by them. The longest section of the narrative concerns the preparations and instruments. Despite its title, however, this discussion provides little description of the actual instruments used and focuses more upon "the riches of Salomon's House," that is, upon the products that are achieved by the use of such instruments (III, 164).

The preparations are first divided into three broad categories that correspond with what Bacon identifies as the three regions of the earth. First there are those that belong to the "Lower Region," such

as "large and deep caves of several depths" that are used for "coagula-
tions, indurations, refrigerations, and conservations of bodies" as
well as for "the imitation of natural mines; and the producing also of
new artificial metals" and "for curing of some diseases, and for prolongation of life in some hermits that choose to live there" (III, 156–
7). In a similar manner, there are instruments designed for the "Upper Region" such as high towers that are used "for insolation, refrig-
eration, conservation; and for the view of divers meteors." Here also
there are "dwellings of hermits, whom we visit sometimes, and
instruct what to observe" (III, 157). Most investigations, however,
are carried on in the middle region, that which is associated with the
surface of the earth, and the rest of this section is devoted to a
discussion of the way in which research is divided in this area.

They have "great lakes both salt and fresh, whereof we have use for
the fish and fowl," as well as some "pools, of which some do strain
fresh water out of salt [water]; and others by art do turn fresh water
into salt" (III, 157).[19] They also have "a number of artificial wells and
fountains, made in imitation of the natural sources and baths" by
which they produce "a water which we call Water of Paradise, being,
by that we do to it, made very sovereign for health, and prolongation
of life" (III, 158). In addition, there are "Chambers of Health, where
we qualify the air as we think good and proper for the cure of divers
diseases, and preservation of health," and "fair and large baths, of
several mixtures, for the cure of diseases" (III, 158). The Bensalemites'
superior medical knowledge had been shown in the earlier section by
their ability to cure the Spanish sailors. At this point in the narrative
we learn that they have acquired this knowledge in part by their
cultivation of the arts of agriculture and husbandry.

The Father provides a lengthy account of the "large and various
orchards and gardens, wherein we do not so much respect beauty, as
variety of ground and soil, proper for divers trees and herbs" (III,
158). They practice "grafting and inoculating" and "by art" are able
to make trees and flowers "come up and bear more speedily than by
their natural course they do," and make "their fruit greater and
sweeter and of differing taste, smell, colour, and figure, from their
nature. And many of them we so order, as they become of medicinal
use" (III, 158). In a similar manner, they practice the art of husbandry
in order to breed "beasts and birds, which we use not only for view
or rareness, but likewise for dissections and trials; that thereby we

may take light what may be wrought upon the body of man" (III, 159). By these trials they "find many strange effects; as continuing life in them, though divers parts, which you account vital, be perished and taken forth," and "resuscitating of some that seem dead in appearance" (III, 159). At the end of this section, the Father stressed that all of these effects are produced not "by chance" but by art and knowledge, thus reinforcing Bacon's notion that experimental productions must be informed by reason (III, 159).[20]

The narrative then proceeds to a discussion of the development of "cookery," which we saw was one of the practical arts that Bacon had recommended for cultivation in his *Parasceve*. The Father explains that they have many "brew-houses, bake-houses, and kitchens, where are made divers drinks, breads, and meats, rare and of special effects" such as drinks that are made "with several fleshes, and white meats; whereof some of the drinks are such, as they are in effect meat and drink both: so that divers, especially in age, do desire to live with them, with little or no meat or bread" (III, 159–60). They also have breads made "of several grains, roots, and kernels: yea and some of flesh and fish dried; with divers kinds of leavenings and seasonings" that "nourish so" that people are able to live on them alone (III, 160). These dietetic and medicinal preparations are made possible by the combined knowledge of the plants and animals used in their production as well as a knowledge of chemistry by which "exquisite distillations and separations" and "exact forms of composition" are achieved (III, 160–1).

So far the division of labor among the islanders has been based primarily upon the standard division of the practical arts. As this section comes to a close, however, a new division, based upon the different human senses is introduced. The Father describes "perspective-houses," for example, devoted to the sense of sight, in which instruments are used to observe "objects afar off; as in the heaven and remote places" as well as "to see small and minute bodies perfectly and distinctly" (III, 161–2).[21] There are also "sound-houses," in which devices are developed such as those to "further the hearing greatly" and "to convey sounds in trunks and pipes, in strange lines and distances" (III, 162–3). There are even "houses of deceits of the senses" where "false apparitions, impostures, and illusions; and their fallacies" are represented. In line with Bacon's injunction against fantastic philosophy, however, the fellows of this house are "forbidden . . . under pain of ignominy and fines" to "shew any natural work or thing, adorned or swelling; but only pure as it is, and without all affectation of strangeness" (III, 164).

In his discussion of the Preparations and Instruments of Salomon's House, Bacon has provided little information about the details of this work, but he has provided an account of how the work proceeds by a practical division of labor. More important, perhaps, in light of his arguments for hope in the *Novum organum*, he has presented a glowing picture of the benefits that would accrue to a nation dedicated to the scientific investigation of nature. Although some of the "riches" described, particularly those designed for overcoming human limitations such as machines for "flying in the air" and "boats for going under water," were somewhat farfetched for Bacon's day, they were not impossible to imagine (III, 163). Other productions, such as "papers, linen, silks, tissues," and "excellent dyes" were quite common and only entailed a greater perfection of extant mechanical arts (III, 161).

It would appear that a large percentage of the island's population is involved in the nation's scientific research. When the Father of Salomon's House next turns to a discussion of "the several employments and offices of our fellows," however, we learn that they are actually few in number. Aside from twelve "Merchants of Light" who "sail into foreign countries," there are eight other categories of employment each of which is composed of three fellows. These thirty-six fellows are those who oversee the tasks performed by the much larger workforce of practical laborers and closely represent the division of cognitive labor discussed in Bacon's methodological works. In addition, there is a hierarchy within Salomon's House itself. At the lowest level are those fellows who are in charge of gathering information. The Merchants of Light belong to this class, as do those called Depredators who "collect the experiments which are in all books"; the Mystery-men who "collect the experiments of all mechanical arts; and also of liberal sciences; and also of practices which are not brought into arts"; and the Pioneers or Miners who "try new experiments, such as themselves think good" (III, 164). This class is followed by the Compilers who "draw the experiments of the former four into titles and tables, to give the better light for the drawing of observations and axioms out of them" (III, 164–5).

At the next highest cognitive level are the Dowry-men or Benefactors who build upon the experience compiled above. Their exercise of "learned experience" is seen in the way in which they "bend themselves, looking into the experiments of their fellows, and cast about how to draw out of them things of use and practice for man's life, and knowledge as well for works as for plain demonstration of causes, means of natural divinations [predictions], and the easy and clear discovery of the virtues and parts of bodies" (III, 165). The Dowry-men are primarily in charge of deriving the practical benefits and theoretical knowledge from the compilations of experiments. Given the centrality of this goal to the work of Salomon's House, however, the Father notes that they also hold "divers meetings and consults of our whole number, to consider of the former labours and collections" (III, 165). After this general consultation, the next highest division takes over. These are the Lamps who "direct new experiments, of a higher light, more penetrating into nature than the former," and the Inoculators who "execute the experiments so directed, and report them" (III, 165). Finally, at the top of the hierarchy are the Interpreters of Nature who "raise the former discoveries by experiments into greater observations, axioms, and aphorisms" (III, 165).

Although the fellows are few in number, they employ many "novices and apprentices," so that "the succession of the former employed men do not fail," as well as "a great number of servants and attendants, men and women" (III, 165). It is clear that the fellows comprise a powerful and privileged social class. They decide in "consultations" among themselves "which of the inventions and experiences which we have discovered shall be published, and which not; and take all an oath of secrecy, for the concealing of those which we think fit to keep secret" (III, 165). In the Father's discussion of the "ordinances and rites" that govern Salomon's House, we also learn that the fellows are generously compensated for their work. In one of "two very long and fair galleries" there are statues in honor "of all principal inventors" of the past and every time an "invention of value" is produced by one of their own members, "we erect a statua to the inventor, and give him a liberal and honourable reward" (III, 165–6).[22]

At the end of the discussion of these ordinances and rites, Bacon returned once again to the themes of religious sentiment and charity. The narrator is told that the fellows hold daily services in which

they thank "God for his marvellous works" and ask for his continued "aid and blessing for the illumination of our labours, and the
turning of them into good and holy uses" (III, 166). In addition, the
fellows visit the "principal cities of the kingdom" in order to "publish such new profitable inventions as we think good" and to an-
nounce impending "diseases, plagues, swarms of hurtful creatures,
scarcity, tempests, earthquakes, great inundations, comets, temperature of the year, and divers other things; and we give counsel thereupon what the people shall do for the prevention and remedy of
them" (III, 166).[23] The Father concludes his relation of Salomon's
House by giving the narrator "leave to publish it for the good of
other nations" (III, 166). At this point the fable of the *New Atlantis*
also comes to an end.

Bacon never completed this work. According to his assistant, William Rawley, Bacon had originally intended to finish his story of
Bensalem with an account of the civil laws of the land, but he felt
that the scope of such a project would divert his attention from his
primary interest, which was the completion of his natural histories.[24] From the standpoint of Bacon's reform of natural philosophy,
the fable could be considered complete because in it he did manage
to provide his readers with a vivid image of how his notion of cooperative research based upon a rational division of labor would
result in a great society dedicated to enhancing the lives of its members. Even in this context, however, there are inherent tensions in
Bacon's writings.

In his *Instauratio magna* and elsewhere, Bacon had called for an
open, democratic approach to the study of nature whereby the
knowledge produced by all members of society would be freely communicated for the benefit of all. In contrast, secrecy is a pervasive
theme of the *New Atlantis*. Information is not only kept from the
strangers to the island. The fellows of Salomon's House withhold
information from the public at large and from the government itself
(III, 165).[25] The social structure of the island also appears to be one
based upon an elitist meritocracy. The Father of Salomon's House
was treated as royalty upon his entrance into the city. It could be
assumed that the other fellows would be treated in much the same
way. At the top of the social hierarchy, they are the ones who give
direction to the large servile labor force and the ones who have the
power over the dissemination of knowledge.[26] The tensions between

openness and secrecy, democracy and meritocracy, need not be attributed to a failure by Bacon to exhibit his vision accurately in his fabled society, however. As a brief look at how the future generation in England attempted to model their new science upon Bacon's precepts will show, such tensions are an inherent part of cooperative research.

V THE LEGACY OF SALOMON'S HOUSE

Bacon never received state or popular support for his program during his lifetime but his writings strongly influenced the next generation of natural philosophers. In the two decades after Bacon's death a general reform of learning had taken place throughout Europe. Largely through the efforts of such seminal thinkers as René Descartes, Galileo, and William Harvey, the traditional scholastic philosophy was being gradually replaced by newer mechanical accounts of nature. In England this reform was accompanied by an emphasis upon the practical implications of the new learning and the ways in which knowledge could be used for charitable purposes. Bacon's writings would play a central role in the programmatic works of these English reformers.

One of the first systematic attempts to bring to fruition Bacon's vision of cooperative scientific research was that which occurred in London during the 1640s under the guiding force of Samuel Hartlib, a Prussian émigré and educational theorist. Hartlib envisioned a new educational system that would replace traditional studies in divinity, law, and logic with more practical subjects such as glassmaking and metalworking. He also sought to make learning more encyclopedic by encouraging the free communication of information on every subject, and the compilation of such knowledge by vast research institutions that would in turn apply it to concerns for human welfare.[27] Through his correspondence he linked together a number of European intellectuals, and in London he brought together such diverse thinkers as the evangelist John Dury, the poet and educational reformer John Milton, and the mechanical philosopher and chemist Kenelm Digby. Hartlib's circle also encouraged the efforts of its younger members, such as the anatomist William Petty and the chemist Frederick Clod, and sought to instill in them an attitude of public spiritedness. Hartlib discussed how Digby and Clod, for example, had set about to establish a "universal laboratory, to be erected after such a manner as may redound, not only to the good of this island, but also to the health and wealth of all mankind."[28]

According to Robert Boyle, one of the younger members of this circle who would become the most vocal proponent of Baconian methods, Hartlib had established a "new philosophical college, that values no knowledge, but as it hath a tendency to use."[29] Elsewhere Boyle emphasized the charitable intent of this useful knowledge when he wrote of the Hartlib circle that they "endeavour to put narrow-mindedness out of countenance, by the practice of so extensive a charity . . . And indeed they are so apprehensive of the want of good employment, that they take the whole body of mankind for their care."[30] Although Hartlib received a small pension from the parliamentary regime that subsidized his efforts, some of his more ambitious schemes such as the building that he hoped to have constructed at Lambeth Marsh "designed for the execution of my Lord Verulam's New Atlantis," were never realized.[31]

The members of Hartlib's circle appreciated the need for social stability, particularly since they often found their efforts stymied by the controversies and intrigues that occurred during this revolutionary period in England. Hartlib and Dury sought to establish unity among the numerous religious factions that had sprung up, and advocated a reliance upon Bacon's conception that true natural philosophy and the charitable use of its products would lead to religious enlightenment. Boyle wrote to Dury that he found his "pious endeavours of twisting our forward parties into a moderate and satisfactory reconcilement" to be "prudent and unwearied."[32] He also praised Hartlib's attempts at unity and made an explicit appeal to Bacon's link between religious and social stability, when he added that "taking notice of, and countenancing men of rare industry and publick spirit, is a piece of policy as vastly advantageous to all states, as it is ruinously neglected by the most."[33]

During this same period another group, not as public as Hartlib's circle and composed primarily of mathematicians, astronomers, and medical doctors, had formed in London. According to John Wallis, a member of the group, they met weekly at various members' lodgings in order to "discourse and consider of philosophical inquiries, and such as related thereunto, as physic, anatomy, geometry, astronomy, navigation, statics, magnetics, chemics, mechanics, and natural experiments, with the state of these studies, as then cultivated at home and abroad."[34] John Wilkins, another member of the group, was appointed by Cromwell as warden of Wadham College, Oxford, in the late 1640s and shortly thereafter other members joined him at the university. They continued to meet weekly to discuss philosophical topics and gradually incorporated new participants, in particular two of the younger members of Hartlib's circle, Boyle and Petty. In a letter to Hartlib, Boyle described this group as "ingenious and free philosophers, who I can assure you not only admit and entertain real learning but cherish and improve it."[35]

Members of the Oxford group shared a number of similarities with Hartlib's circle. They advocated charitable works and religious toleration, and believed that the development of natural philosophy could help to put an end to sectarian controversy. Their experimental agenda was much more organized and sophisticated than that of the London group, however. The members often worked together to improve experiments in chemistry, physiology, and pneumatics. They made detailed telescopic and microscopic observations, pioneered new techniques for anatomical dissections, and developed new instruments, such as the air pump constructed by Boyle and Robert Hooke that was used to determine the weight and pressure of the air.[36] By the early 1660s members of the Oxford group had begun to publish reports of their results and to achieve an international reputation for careful research.

The restoration of the English monarchy in 1660 provided the catalyst for members of both the London and Oxford groups to suggest the establishment of a truly national research institution. In 1662 Charles II officially recognized their efforts by giving a charter to the new Royal Society of London, which had been purposefully modeled after Bacon's New Atlantis. As Joseph Glanvil described it, Salomon's House had provided the "Prophetick Scheam of the ROYAL SOCIETY."[37] Their plans were ambitious. Aside from public meetings to discuss developments in natural philosophy, Henry Oldenburg, the first secretary of the society, described how they sought state funding to construct a "college" within the society "where we may meet, prepare and make our Experiments and Observations, lodge our Curators and Operators, have our Laboratory, Observatory and Operatory all together."[38]

The founding members of the Royal Society were frequently disappointed. They received little funding from the king and even less ambitious plans often failed. Periodically, for example, the attempt was made to divide their labors by setting up specialized committees to consider particular areas of investigation. Even when such committees were instituted, however, they did not remain in place for long and they failed to produce any significant results.[39] There were also disagreements among the members about the true aim of the society. Some believed that it should be devoted to the development of theoretical knowledge as Bacon had advised in his *Novum organum*, while others felt that most effort should be given to the construction of natural histories on the model of Bacon's *Sylva Sylvarum*.[40] Despite these failings and disagreements, there was at least one resounding success. Under the careful editorial guidance of Oldenburg, the *Philosophical Transactions* of the Royal Society was established as an international journal that carried news about the society's endeavors as well as information and critical papers from philosophical correspondents on the Continent.[41]

With the official constitution of a society for the advancement of learning, the tensions inherent within cooperative research became all the more apparent. In 1667 Thomas Sprat wrote a history of the Royal Society, the intent of which was to present an account of a unified society dedicated to the disinterested pursuit of knowledge. He stressed the role played by "plain, diligent, and laborious observers" in the activity of the society and how the work of all classes would ultimately result in the civil stability and economic advantages that had been so glowingly described by Bacon.[42] Despite Sprat's polemics, the society was neither as unified nor as democratic as he claimed. The lower classes, to which tradesmen and some merchants belonged, were not widely represented among the society's ranks, and some members believed that membership ought to be more selective and restricted to those who made actual contributions to the society's work.[43]

Members of the Royal Society also disagreed about the extent to which knowledge should be freely communicated to the public. Because the society aimed at improving human welfare, it could be argued that they had a duty to restrict the dissemination of knowledge that would have a deleterious effect. Because the new experimental learning was concerned with the production of practical techniques and processes, it could also be argued that secrecy was necessary since inventors have the right to profit from their innovations. Tradesmen and artisans, for example, would be reluctant to share the secrets of their processes with the fellows of the Royal Society unless they had the assurance that these would not in turn become public knowledge. In addition, Robert Hooke argued that in order to make membership in the society meaningful, access to its archives should be denied to nonmembers. In effect, he maintained that the knowledge produced by the society ought to be the sole property of its members.[44]

Bacon's advocacy of cooperative scientific research was an influential source for the development of a more open and democratic approach to the study of nature than that which had been practiced in the earlier scholastic philosophical tradition. The very nature of large scale research, however, entails that there must be a division of labor, which in turn implies the need for a hierarchy of managers to direct the work, and the need for an adequate reward structure by which those responsible for innovation are recognized. In addition, as scientific research advances, knowledge becomes more and more esoteric and only a limited number of specialists in a given field will have the expertise required for further progress. Bacon's works are significant not only for the way in which they popularized the ideal of cooperative research, but also for the way in which they foreshadowed the tensions inherent in the project.

NOTES

1 See, for example, René Descartes, Discourse on the Method, part 2, in The Philosophical Writings of Descartes, John Cottingham, Robert Stoothoff, and Dugald Murdoch (eds.), (Cambridge, 1985), I, p. 116. See also Clarke 1992, pp. 271–83; Garber 1992, pp. 30–62; McMullin 1992, p. 13; and Vickers 1987, p. 4. Box 1989b, p. 3, argues that Bacon's appeal to cooperative research indicates that he was not doing philosophy.

2 In the Redargutio philosophiarum Bacon noted that in the mechanical arts "the wits of individuals mingle," Farrington 1964, p. 126.

3 See Rossi 1968, p. 27. Bacon also criticized the chemists in his Sylva Sylvarum (II, 448). Despite such criticism, however, he was strongly influenced by the chemists' accomplishments. See Briggs 1989, p. 148; and McMullin 1992, p. 14.

4 See Farrington 1964, p. 13; Rossi 1968, p. 23.

5 See Martin 1992 for a detailed discussion of the history of educational reform in England and how Bacon's plans fit within the movement.

6 See Rossi 1968, pp. 23–4; Farrington 1964, p. 15; Davis 1981, pp. 122–3, for discussions concerning the Gray's Inn entertainment. See Martin 1992, pp. 69–71; and Farrington 1964, p. 31, for how Bacon believed that the institutional advancement of knowledge could be used to promote social and political ends.

7 See in general, III, 322–5; XI, 65–7. Rossi 1968, p. 24.

8 *Cogitata et visa*, in Farrington 1964, pp. 75, 84–7.

9 See Farrington 1964, pp. 48–50, for a discussion of Bacon's views on past learning.

10 Farrington 1964, p. 99.

11 Farrington 1964, p. 119. See Jardine 1990, pp. 51, 56–7; Rossi 1968, pp. 154–6; and Farrington 1964, pp. 43–4, for more detailed discussions concerning Bacon's concept of *"experientia literata."*

12 See Davis 1981, p. 128; Farrington 1964, pp. 118–19; and Martin 1992, pp. 64, 144–6, 163, for more discussion on the hierarchical nature of Bacon's project.

13 In his *Novum organum*, he noted that "it is enough to check the growth of science, that efforts and labours in this field go unrewarded" (IV, 90).

14 See Rossi 1968, p. 23; and Martin 1992, p. 146, for the unsuccessfulness of Bacon's appeals to James I. Part of Bacon's lack of success could be attributed to James's apparent favor of the work of the alchemist Robert Fludd who was pursuing the type of project that Bacon had criticized above. See Huffman 1988.

15 See Hunter 1981; van den Daele 1977; and Webster 1975, for accounts of the religious controversies of the time. See Box 1989b, p. 125, for his discussion of Bacon's Christian conservatism. See Martin 1992, pp. 43–5, for a discussion of how knowledge and peace were linked together in Bacon's programmatic statements.

16 See, for example, Achinstein 1988; Albanese 1990; Martin 1992; Wheeler 1990; Whitney 1986, 1990; and Weinberger 1976. Peltonen 1992, has argued against the political interpretation of the *New Atlantis*.

17 Briggs 1989; and McMullin 1992, discuss the fable from this perspective. McMullin, p. 15, aptly describes the *New Atlantis* as an "object of hope."

18 The narrator describes the ceremony in great detail, III, 147–51.

19 The development of a process by which salt water could be made potable was of extreme importance in Bacon's day because of the need for a large supply of fresh water for long voyages at sea. In the next generation Robert Boyle would attempt to develop such a process. See Boyle's "Ob-

servations and Experiments about the Saltiness of the Sea," in *The Works of the Honourable Robert Boyle*, ed. Thomas Birch, 6 vols. (London, 1772), III, pp. 764–81.

20 Bacon noted, for example, that new kinds of animals were produced by "commixtures and copulations of different kinds" by knowing "beforehand of what matter and commixtures what kind of those creatures will arise" (III, 159).

21 Telescopes and microscopes were already in use during Bacon's time. For a history of the development of such instruments see van Helden 1983.

22 Statues were erected to Columbus and the "monk that was the inventor of ordnance and gunpowder" (Roger Bacon), as well as to the inventors of music, letters, printing, glass, silk, wine, corn, bread, and sugar.

23 In the *Historia ventorum*, Bacon noted that such a history could be helpful for discovering ways by which to foretell the successfulness of harvests and the occurrence of epidemics, V, 199.

24 Albanese 1990, p. 509; and Whitney 1986, pp. 189–91, maintain that the incomplete structure of the *New Atlantis* reflects the dynamic, open-ended nature of Bacon's project. Box 1989b, p. 125, on the other hand, characterizes the work as "timeless."

25 For discussions of the secretive elements in the *New Atlantis*, see Achinstein 1988, p. 252; Box 1989b, p. 133; Briggs 1989, p. 170; Martin 1992, p. 139; and McMullin 1992, p. 14.

26 For discussions of the elitist tendencies in the *New Atlantis*, see Achinstein 1988, p. 250; Martin 1992, p. 163; Wheeler 1990, pp. 299–300; and Whitney 1990, p. 259.

27 For more detail on the Hartlib group see Hunter 1981, pp. 24–5; Rattansi 1968, pp. 130–7; Vickers 1987, p. 5; and Webster 1970, 1975. Shapiro 1991, p. 49, discusses how the emphasis upon charity can also be traced to sixteenth-century humanism.

28 Samuel Hartlib to Robert Boyle, 8 May 1654, in Boyle, *Works*, VI, p. 86. See Rattansi 1968, p. 130, for an account of Petty's proposal to Hartlib for the establishment of a great institution where skilled artisans would work out technical problems.

29 Boyle to Isaac Marcombes, 22 October 1646, in Boyle, *Works*, I, p. xxxiv.

30 Boyle to Francis Tallents, 20 February 1646, in Boyle, *Works*, I, pp. xxxiv–v.

31 Hartlib to Boyle, 8 May 1656, in Boyle, *Works*, VI, p. 88.

32 Boyle to John Dury, 3 May 1647, in Boyle, *Works*, I, p. xl.

33 Boyle to Hartlib, 8 May 1647, in Boyle, *Works*, I, p. xl. See also, Hunter 1981, pp. 27–9; and Rattansi 1968, p. 136.

34 As quoted by Thomas Birch in the introduction to Boyle, *Works*, I, p. xlii.
35 Boyle to Hartlib, 14 September 1655, quoted in Maddison 1969, p. 85.
36 For more detail on the activities of the Oxford group see Frank 1980; Hunter 1981; and Maddison 1969. Vickers 1987, p. 5, also notes that some members of the College of Physicians in London likened their organization to Salomon's House.
37 Joseph Glanvil, *Scepsis Scientifica* (London, 1665), [p. 22].
38 Hunter 1981, p. 39.
39 Hunter 1981, pp. 92–4; Hunter and Wood 1986, pp. 51–9.
40 Hunter and Wood 1986, pp. 65–7.
41 See Hunter 1988, pp. 168–70, for a fuller account of Oldenburg's editorial efforts.
42 Hunter 1981, pp. 29–31, from Thomas Sprat, *The History of the Royal Society of London* (London, 1667).
43 Hunter 1981, pp. 59–86; Hunter and Wood 1986, p. 74.
44 Hunter and Wood 1986, p. 74. See McMullin 1985, pp. 19–22, for how Bacon's conception of practical knowledge turned it into a product that could be patented and thus increased the need for secrecy. Boyle, in his "Proëmial Essay" to *Certain Physiological Essays*, in Boyle, *Works*, I, p. 315, noted that he would not disclose practices of tradesmen when their "livelihood" depended upon them. The idea that members of the Royal Society had a responsibility not to disseminate knowledge that could be harmful to the public was expressed by Isaac Newton in a letter to Henry Oldenburg, 26 April 1676, in Boyle, *Works*, VI, p. 286.

7 Bacon's science and religion

We must make therefore a complete solution and separation of
nature, not indeed by fire, but by the mind, as if by a divine fire
[*tamquam ignem divinum*]. (IV, 145; I, 257)[1]

[It is an age] wherein, if science be increased, conscience is
rather decayed; and if men's wits be great, their wills be more
great . . . . (VII, 315)

I THE SEPARATION OF SCIENCE AND RELIGION

A longstanding commonplace in Bacon scholarship has been the
notion that the Baconian advancement of learning depends upon a
strict separation of divinity and natural philosophy.[2] In a number of
memorable passages Bacon indeed warns his readers of the dire consequences of confusing divinity with natural science: to combine
them, he says, is to confound them. This is supposedly what Plato
and the scholastics did, and what Bacon explicitly designs the new
learning to overcome. Even the acceptable hybrid "divine philosophy," when it is "commixed together" with natural philosophy,
leads to "an heretical religion, and an imaginary and fabulous philosophy" (III, 350). According to this emphatic strand of Baconian
doctrine, religion that joins with the study of nature is in danger of
becoming atheistic, or an enthusiastic rival of the true church. Natural philosophy that traffics unwisely with divinity collapses into
idolatry or fakery.

Bacon's exemplum of these abuses in a modern proto-science is
the divine philosophy of the Paracelsian school, which seeks "the
truth of all natural philosophy in the Scriptures." The Paracelsians

mirror and reverse the heresies of pagan pantheism by seeking what is "dead" (mortal or natural) from among the "living" (eternal) truths of divinity, when "the scope or purpose of the Spirit of God is not to express matters of nature in the Scriptures, otherwise than in passage, and for application to man's capacity and to matters moral or divine" (III, 485–6). If we take Thomas Sprat at his word, the Royal Society was founded on generally similar principles. The first corruption of knowledge, he argues, resulted from the Egyptians' concealment of wisdom "as sacred Mysteries." The current age of inquiry benefitted from "the dissolution of the *Abbyes*, whereby their Libraries came forth into the light, and fell into industrious Mens hands." Surrounded by the warring forces of contrary religions (the society's rooms at Gresham College, London, were occupied by soldiers in 1658), the founders of the Royal Society – according to Sprat's account – were "invincibly arm'd" not only against scholastic Catholicism, but against the "inchantments of *Enthusiasm*" and "spiritual Frensies" that sometimes characterized the Protestant revolutionaries.[3]

In Bacon's project, there is an explicit, delineated role for the study of divinity, which he carefully separates from his own work. Reason is at work "in the conception and apprehension of the mysteries of God to us revealed" and in "the inferring and deriving of doctrine and direction thereupon" (III, 479). In the first instance reason stirs itself only to grasp and illustrate revelation; it does not inquire. This is the foundation of Bacon's distinction between true natural philosophy, which inquires into the world as God's manifestation of his *glory* or power, and true theology, which piously interprets the scripturally revealed meaning of God's inscrutable *will*. The natural world declares God's glory but not his will (III, 478). Reason's power in theology therefore "consisteth of probation and argument." It formulates doctrine only insofar as God's revelation, largely or wholly through Scripture, makes it possible. The Lord "doth grift [graft] his revelations and holy doctrine upon the notions of our reason, and applieth his inspirations to open our understanding" (III, 480).

These axioms, all drawn from *The Advancement of Learning*, support Bacon's defense of the new sciences as nonthreatening complements to established principles of Divinity.[4] But their significance is influenced by their participation in *The Advancement of Learning*,

which is Bacon's most public and self-consciously introductory dis-
quisition on the nature of the new sciences. Bacon lets it be known
elliptically that he writes "not in hand with true measure, but with
popular estimation and conceit." It is "not amiss" to write askant of
"true measure" in order to cope with popular misconceptions of
scientific learning. Bacon is particularly concerned about resisting
the opinion that scientific learning places more importance upon
"second causes" than upon God. His fundamental opponent is the
notion that scientific learning is necessarily a breeding ground for
heresy, even for atheism (III, 274).[5]

Bacon uses various forms of indirection, including blunt statements and covert argumentation in dispersed passages, to avoid and
overcome popular misunderstandings that threaten his project.
When he elaborates upon the meaning of the separation of Divinity
and natural philosophy, his discourse is often complex:

[L]et no man, upon a weak conceit of sobriety or an ill-applied moderation,
think or maintain that a man can search too far or be too well studied in the
book of God's word or in the book of God's works; divinity or philosophy;
but rather let men endeavour an endless progress or proficience in both;
only let men beware that they apply both to charity, and not to swelling; to
use, and not to ostentation; and again, that they do not unwisely mingle or
confound these learnings together. (III, 268)

Here the surprise for modern readers is that Bacon's familiar insistence upon the separation of Divinity and natural science is incorporated within a strategy for inquiring energetically into Scripture as
well as into nature. The repressive enthusiasm of schismatics has
come to block true inquiry into Scripture, just as it has inquiry into
the world of God's works (III, 481). Bacon wrote to the earl of Rutland in the mid 1590s that without knowledge "there can be no true
religion, all other devotion being but blind zeal, which is as strong in
heresy as in truth" (IX, 11).

Without assuming that Sprat's history of the Royal Society gives us
the final word on Bacon's legacy, it is evident that Sprat's own treatment of religion's relation to science is, like Bacon's, more complex
than his emphatic doctrine of separation. Sprat endorses the ancient
view that the most learned philosophers are "skill'd in all *Divine* and
human things."[6] On his roster of the founders of the Royal Society, he
first lists "the present Bishop of Exeter,"[7] and cites the protection

afforded to the Society by churchmen who "have shewn that in our *veneration of Gods almighty power*, we ought to imitate the manner of our respect to *Earthly Kings.*"[8] To match John Wallis's contention that the Society was "an invisible college" whose business excluded "matters of theology," we have Boyle's dedication of his doings to the glory of God and the charitable treatment of mankind.[9] Sprat's *History* includes Abraham Cowley's famous poem likening Bacon to Moses. The metaphor ostensibly emphasizes Bacon's freeing of the intellect from its pharaoh-like schoolmasters, and yet Cowley's enthusiasm leads him to invest Bacon with something of the archaic power of the biblical lawgiver.

Another surprise awaits the reader who comes upon Bacon's condemnation of Paracelsians who arrogantly search the Scriptures for all the truths of natural philosophy. In fact, says Bacon, "they set the rest of natural philosophy at war with Scripture": "there is no such enmity between God's word and his works" if they are approached more temperately (III, 486). Properly conceived, the new sciences provide a possible opening to the understanding of God's will by means of a new method. One key to Bacon's understanding of this relation lies in his strangely pervasive, largely biblical definition of wisdom, sometimes called Sapience (IV, 337), a term he uses to describe *"Philosophia prima."* In *Philosophia prima*, divine, natural, and human philosophy meet "in one stem" (III, 346). With uncommon consistency, Bacon uses *wisdom* to invoke this extraordinary idea in numerous passages. In the section just quoted, Bacon's use of "unwisely" suggests that divinity and nature (he means divine philosophy and natural philosophy) can indeed be mixed if mixed *wisely.*

One way Bacon justifies mixing divinity and philosophy is to define Christianity as a mean between purer yet ultimately inferior treatments of religion by the ancients and by believers in Islam. Heathenism depends entirely upon argument and so dismisses belief; Islam "interdicts argument altogether" (V, 113). In keeping with Bacon's early writings on religious moderation, *Philosophia prima* offers a way of mixing divinity and natural philosophy moderately so as to escape pagan unbelief and religious zealotry. Is Bacon merely making the conventional argument that Christianity permits reason to mix with true doctrine, or is he saying something more particular and daring about the way in which divinity and natural philosophy can combine within the new sciences?

II THE RESTORATION OF PARADISE

In the *Novum organum*, we see more of Bacon's willingness to allude to what this mixture of divinity and natural philosophy might be. Commentators have often remarked upon the religious cast of the work's diction. Bacon proceeds with "religious care" (IV, 105). He expresses a desire to become a conduit of God, Son, and Holy Ghost so that "they will vouchsafe through my hands to endow the human family with new mercies" (IV, 20). It appears that the method of becoming that channel for mercy must be a sort of scientific religion, not just Christian observance. The new science is "a certain course and way" (IV, 32), accompanied by "divine assistance" that helps bring about a "true and legitimate humiliation of the human spirit" (IV, 19–20). Entrance into the new sciences depends upon their followers' imitating the little children favored by Christ, children whose lack of vanity gives them privileged access to the kingdom of heaven (IV, 69).

With these preparations, Bacon asks that God "graciously grant to us to write an apocalypse or true vision of the footsteps of the Creator imprinted on his creatures" (IV, 33). In the created world there are traces and signatures of the divine mind – of the supposedly inscrutable divine will. The fulfillment of Daniel's unlikely prophecy that seafarers will discover new lands is a sign that the advancement of the sciences is "destined by" Providence (IV, 91–2). The human race can legitimately seek its "right over nature which belongs to it by divine bequest" (IV, 115). The Fall was the result of a flaw in man's moral knowledge, not his capacity to know nature (III, 264, 296–7), and now his very labor – the curse that he work by the sweat of his brow – seems capable of reversing nature's rebellion from man, as God has intended (IV, 247–8, 33).

In this context, Bacon's religious metaphors seem to be more than casual exploitations of the familiar religious vernacular. Imitating Solomon, Bacon is intent upon "laying a foundation in the human understanding for a holy temple after the model of the world" (IV, 107). The new natural philosophy is connected to religion as a subordinate yet powerfully complementary instrument. It is "after the word of God[,] at once the surest medicine against superstition, and the most approved nourishment for faith, and therefore she is rightly given to religion as her most faithful handmaid" (IV, 89). The goal of that handmaid is nothing less than to reverse a major consequence of the Fall: to restore man's mastery over nature to "its perfect and original condition," or if that proves impossible, to improve the human condition radically by means of scientific charity (IV, 7, 20). The new sciences aspire to remake an Eden for human knowledge in tandem with Divinity's repair of man's moral condition.

The *Novum organum* distinguishes itself from *The Advancement of Learning* by using religious language to focus on the "total reconstruction" of learning (IV, 8). It suggests that the new sciences might be involved in adapting or even renovating the religion to which they are handmaids. The *Novum organum*'s most explicit teaching in this regard is as emphatic as it is opaque: "Only let the human race recover that right over nature which belongs to it by divine bequest, and let power be given it; the exercise thereof will be governed by sound reason and true religion" (IV, 115). Faith will presumably repair the fall from innocence, and science will restore dominion over nature (IV, 248). But the conjunction of the activities of science and faith in renewing the Edenic life raises the question of what the new sciences might do to religion, or what they might do with religion as their instrument, to ensure that the new sciences will prosper.

It is worth remembering that Prometheus is Bacon's image of Providence, whose "peculiar work . . . was the creation and constitution of Man." Man, Bacon explains, "may be regarded as the centre of the world," for "the whole world" including the stars "works together in the service of man" (VI, 746–7). Man's dominion over what he can use, as long as it is providentially available for his use, opens the door to a mastery of nature that is limited only by God's will, which itself might be glimpsed in apocalyptic signs.

III IDOLS AND SUPERSTITION, INDUCTION AND SOLOMONIC DISCOURSE

The *Novum organum* contains Bacon's famous analysis of the enemies of the new learning, which he calls the Four Idols. Permeating his discussion is the notion that opposition or resistance to the new sciences is really a form of heresy – if not an explicit religious heresy, at least one that profoundly corrupts and indicts the inner being of those who embrace it. Idolatrous heresies need to be smashed, or neutralized by those who have shattered idolatrous tendencies in themselves. Legacies of the Fall, such heresies are forms of superstition or innate error that hold the mind enthralled. Bacon argues that superstition's power is especially great (greater than atheism's [III, 349]) because it imitates the power of true religion, making effects that pass as miraculous or magical even though they create dangerous enchantments and controversies. In the form of "the blind immoderate zeal of religion," superstition disrupts the peace that is the precondition and goal of the new sciences (IV, 87–8). It threatens to displace even true religion, "the thing which has most power over men's minds" (IV, 87–9).[10]

As perverse religion, superstition has a commensurate power to tempt the faithful by presenting them with misleading auguries (IV, 76–7) and other instruments of exaggeration that make for vain wonder. It manipulates admiration for knowledge so that men are satisfied with what is inadequate or incomplete (IV, 85). It is bound up with the enchanting power of "fables and superstitions and follies which nurses instil into children" (IV, 30). Hence Bacon's deep distrust of poetry, which in the wrong hands produces "enchantments" of such influence over men's powers "that they have been made impotent (like persons bewitched) to accompany with the nature of things" (IV, 82).

The fact that idolatry can be manipulated by spell makers[11] suggests that some people might be able to transcend superstition. Bacon lets it be known in the De augmentis that he has a great appreciation for the power of certain enchantments if they are "well directed." Particularly in the theater, enlightened spells can be used against benighted ones, for it is "one of the great secrets of nature, that the minds of men are more open to impressions and affections when many are gathered together than when they are alone" (IV, 316). A scientifically pious mastery of enchantment, however, is not possible unless idols can be "marked and reproved." And that accomplishment is not practical, it seems, without its being laid down "once for all as a fixed and established maxim, that the intellect is not qualified to judge except by means of induction, and induction in its legitimate form" (IV, 27). Wise inquirers know that ordinary induction is not enough. Overcoming idolatry requires, at a minimum, an inductive discipline of such strictness and significance that it resembles religious self-denial and purgation, even exorcism (IV, 30).

Along with the new induction goes a new discourse that enforces the experience of arduous, self-denying interpretation. "[B]orrowing the term from the sacred ceremonies," Bacon distinguishes "initiative" from "magistral" discourse. The former can break away from the false authority of idolatrous transmission of knowledge because it reenacts (and requires its reader, or perhaps only its wise reader, to reenact) the difficult inductive method by which the knowledge it communicates has been invented. Initiative discourse creates purgative rituals that resemble the few ceremonies of religion that Bacon is willing to call "things real." Religious fastings and other "humiliations of the body," Bacon argues, destroy idolatry by taking into "consideration" – literally, by commemorating, enacting, and resisting – the mind's profound dependence upon the wayward body (III, 369). The initiative ceremonies of science are supposedly the experiments by which idolatries are experienced reductively yet nobly, like the baths and fires of an enlightened alchemical manufacture of gold.

Probably the most suggestive site of this struggle is the Solomonic aphorism, which Bacon imitates in the *Novum organum*. The sacred aphorisms break knowledge into bits from which a deeper wisdom can emerge if the reader could resist being satisfied with the superficial, merely proverbial wisdom of Solomon's teachings. For Bacon, it is the ordeal of reading Solomonic discourse, refraining from giving one's inner being to desirable (hence wayward or premature) conclusions, which prepares one for a new synthesis of fragments. By similar means, Solomon is presumed to have written the natural history of Lebanon (thought to be lost, but now available in the New Atlantis if one get access to them). Even though his great achievements and possessions would have corrupted almost any king, Solomon was somehow able to impose upon himself the ordeal of studying the least of things. Thus he combined an enlightened, scientific monasticism with a wise epicureanism. He showed himself capable of taking immense pleasure in the power and luxuries that accrued to his prosperous reign, and yet he somehow made sure, Bacon insists, that idolatrous passions did not come rest in his heart or soul (IV, 114).

Bacon's second model of the initiatory man of science is, according to his own testimony, King James I, to whom he dedicates *The Advancement of Learning*. There Bacon explicitly compares James to Solomon (III, 262), specifically praising him for his Solomonic power to see into the great and the small, the divine and the human (III, 263). He is "almost a miracle" because he combines the divine with the human, even though "it should seem an impossibility in nature for the same instrument to make itself fit for great and small works" (III, 262). Most notably, James is praised for his inquiries into witchcraft. He is Solomonic because he can immerse himself in worldly, even corrupt and threatening phenomena while inquiring into the laws and forms of things. He can interrogate what he considers to be the dangerous, misguided science of witchcraft, while keeping his kingship pure.

In his inquiry into witchcraft, James has dared to write the sort of natural history that true initiates must scrutinize, experience, and ponder. Looking ahead, Bacon calls for an even more comprehensive and "severe collection" of things in nature that have undergone "digression and deflexion from the ordinary course" (III, 330–1). James's work contributes to the "superstitious" natural history Bacon wants to see expanded to include witchcraft, dreams, and divination:

... it is not yet known in what cases, and how far, effects attributed to superstition do participate of natural causes; and therefore howsoever the practice of such things is to be condemned, yet from the speculation and consideration of them light may be taken, not only for the discerning of the offences, but for the further disclosing of nature. (III, 331)

Superstition, which mixes heresy with grotesquery and silliness, is an ideal subject for the new sciences because it requires its enlightened students to undergo a Solomonic initiation:

Neither ought a man to make scruple of entering into these things for inquisition of truth, as your Majesty hath shewed in your own example; who with two clear eyes of religion and natural philosophy have looked deeply and wisely into these shadows, and yet proved yourself to be of the nature of the sun, which passeth through pollutions and itself remains as pure as before. (III, 331)

What makes the danger endurable? James, like Solomon, is protected by the eye of religion, for him the foundation of a king's divine right. King Solomon petitioned for, and received from God, a "grant donative" which enabled him to write the aphorisms of the wisdom literature and natural history as God's favorite (III, 298). The assurance of divine favor made him capable of extraordinary self-assurance and prodigious restraint: he made "no claim to any of those glories" even though (or because) he was God's favorite (III, 299, 220). For understandable reasons, Bacon scrupulously avoids referring to James's shortcomings; neither does he mention Solomon's succumbing to idolatrous lust – and his fall from divine favor. But in the end he does not need to avoid the story of Solomon's fall because Sapience according to Bacon's definition is recoverable if it is wisely discovered and interpreted by means of the new sciences' collective machinery, which is supposed to possess an unwavering power to test inquirers and their findings.

The initiatory function of the new machine is perhaps what Bacon had in mind when he formulated his famous proverb that nature, to be mastered, must be obeyed. Power cannot come but through submission; and yet submission, particularly when it is undergone by a group of wise inquirers, promises empire. How then can the Solomonic researcher proceed so as not to unleash the lusts that brought down his Solomonic precursor? The fact that the new sciences depend upon cooperation and disinterested validation is not in itself an assurance that the entire enterprise will not go the way of a corrupt king.

IV HUMILITY, CHARITY, AND SABBATH

In Bacon's scheme of things, the truth of scientific works is measured according to their lack of vanity. Those works must not come from vain imaginations, from a desire for power or fame, or from the wish for comfort (IV, 21, 73). They must and can be the works of charity, "the virtue most communicative of good" (IV, 338). True knowledge is dedicated to "the benefit and use of life"; it must be actively charitable (III, 218, 221–2; V, 9). But benefit and use are not enough. The new sons of science must follow the Apostle Paul's example of humility in 1 Corinthians: they must strive to endure all things, even as their obedience to nature brings ever greater control and comfort (III, 265–6). Without self-denying, perfective suffering, the new learning's revelation that knowledge is power threatens to plunge its practitioners into perdition, as did the proud knowledge that cast down Lucifer and Adam (IV, 21; V, 132; VII, 222, 243). And if they are successful in experiencing wisely scientific suffering, can they undergo the experience without creating a self-ingratiating idolatry of humility?

The end of the new sciences, as Bacon says in the *Novum organum*, is a "sabbath" attained not by scientific labor alone, but by that labor for the sake of providing mankind with rest from hardship (IV, 33). Scientific charity must therefore be a labor for the sake of an extraordinary release from labor, presumably to be enjoyed mostly by the masses. But those masses, according to Bacon, not only do not know the ways of science; they do not know how to escape the new idolatries that are bound to arise from the pleasures that charitable science bequeaths them. For the sake of combatting idolatry, the enlightened makers of those pleasures must therefore rule. Can they take on this responsibility without taking ever greater pleasure in their radical superiority, or despising their vulgar beneficiaries, or yielding to the growing temptation to let the recipients of their charity worship those who seem to give them their happiness? And what besides corrupting pleasures can prevent the beneficiaries of the new sciences from becoming resentful slaves?

Given the new sciences' problematic dependence upon (and resemblance to) Christianity, what then keeps Bacon's advancement of learning from becoming a powerful heresy? Bacon supplies two apparently contradictory methods of protecting the new sons of science from apostasy. First, he surprisingly reminds his readers that contemplation takes precedence over the active life. In his well-known aphorism equating knowledge and power, his emphasis is on the practical precedence of contemplation over "operation" as well as use. Nature must be studied and "obeyed" before its laws can be exercised: "Human knowledge and human power meet in one; for where the cause is not known the effect cannot be produced. Nature to be commanded must be obeyed; and that which in contemplation is as the cause is in operation as the rule" (IV, 47). Bacon praises Solomon most for his detection of concealed laws of nature, not for the fruits he brought forth with them (IV, 114). Moreover, he insists that "works themselves are of greater value as pledges of truth than as contributing to the comforts of life" (IV, 110).

Bacon's second defense, however, casts doubt on the first. The faith of the sons of science, he argues, will ultimately be justified by the *fruits* of their intellectual labors. Such fruits are much more than benefits because they are supposed to exhibit the benefactor's faith:

"Wherefore, as in religion we are warned to show our faith by works, so in philosophy by the same rule the system should be judged of by its fruits" (IV, 74). Elsewhere Bacon explains that the charitable deeds of the new sciences serve as "the seal which prints and determines the contemplative counterpart" (IV, 121). This means that even though contemplation precedes the work in terms of significance and time (as it does in Genesis 4.125), the work that science does is somehow equivalent to – and generative of – scientific contemplation. The practical applications of knowledge not only reveal the laws of natural operation; works justify and determine wisdom. This paradoxical relationship between contemplation and action must be embraced faithfully so that it does not cultivate new forms of vanity.[12] "[M]an is a god to man" when he provides charitable inventions (IV, 114). Man's scientific works are "blessings" superior to any conquest over men because they apparently "confer benefits without causing harm or sorrow to any" (IV, 113). But if "[h]uman knowledge and human power meet in one," can human beings fuse these things without reducing knowledge to power, wisdom to willful force?

Bacon's earliest explicit formulation of the idea that "knowledge is power" is instructive because it occurs in an explicitly religious context: the *Meditationes sacrae*. There he refers only to the knowledge and power of God, intimating that their convergence is beyond human understanding (VII, 253). Two decades later this formulation becomes, in the *Novum organum*, the famous and problematic justification for human beings to equate knowledge with power (IV, 32). It is problematic because, by Bacon's own standards, charitable acts performed by the new sciences are eminently susceptible to imitations performed by charlatans. The trademarks of the false, idolatrous sciences such as traditional alchemy and astrology are fantastic promises of what the new sciences would routinely offer: power to change metals and history at will.

Perhaps the most powerful temptation facing the scientific charitable impulse has to do with the huge gap between Solomonic science and common ignorance.[13] Both the old and the new sciences are irrevocably conditioned by common ignorance: Bacon speaks with contempt of the inevitable vulgarization of sciences in the public, political sphere: "there is but one form of polity in the sciences; and that always has been and always will be popular." For Bacon, what is popular is generally bad because the superstitious masses embrace pseudoscientific doctrines that are either "contentious and pugnacious" or "specious and empty" (IV, 15). In the *Novum organum* he goes so far as to argue that the new sciences "cannot be brought down to common apprehension, save by effects and works only" (IV, 113). Effects indeed reveal the laws of their causes, but only to those who wisely endure a proper initiation and the proper experimental procedures. Vulgar recipients of the sciences' largesse will not only be ignorant of the laws of nature and the sources of the technology that governs the sciences' gifts to them. They will not be equipped to know what might be the deeper purposes of those gifts if the givers' charitable intentions are not pure and obvious.

Whatever then might be the charitable sciences' appearance of harmlessness and philanthropy, they will be cryptic. Bacon observes that the new sciences, like religion, are "adverse to common sense" (III, 503). They must arise from an initiatory ordeal and a Solomonic sanction that most of the beneficiaries of their gifts neither know nor experience. Given the idolatrous corruption of men's minds, the new sciences must transcend vulgar popularity by developing their own polity of kingly charity: they must undergo and exploit the discipline of living magnanimously, splendidly, and secretly – as Bacon praises the Solomonic James for doing. The virtues and grace that are the source of the scientific king's charity are "sequestered" within "the strangeness and darkness of this tabernacle of the body" (III, 262). For Bacon, good scientific government is therefore hidden government, though he assumes that the good governor will have a visible prominence in human affairs. The scientific king rules very much as the heavens declare the glory of God, but not God's divine will (III, 478). Of course, the king ought to be in communication with the common people: "all things ought, as far as the frailty of man permitteth, to be manifest and revealed" (III, 474). But his communication is cryptic in its imitation of God's occultation of the laws that govern nature. These laws, though they are hidden in order to be discovered, are profoundly remote from the masses who know them only by their superficial effects. Their source in the king's will is beyond any commoner's inquiry.

Scientific principles do come to light as technologies are exposed to public view; but in the Baconian world, scientific innovation inevitably runs ahead of public perception, along trails that are only selectively open to scrutiny. The premium that Bacon puts on intelligent and full disclosure, sincere revelation of sharable doctrines, and charitable applications must be understood in the light of his interest in spying and encryption, whose business is to protect from disclosure the most important activities of the king and the sons of science.

V SCIENCE, NATURE, AND THE DIVINE CODE

The quasi-religious importance of the principle of encryption in the new sciences is evident in Bacon's theory of codes. Whereas ordinary induction and inference are capable of making only accidental inferences, Baconian induction deciphers nature's code not just by thwarting the common love of making analogies, but by gathering interpretations from "very various and widely dispersed facts," materials so divergent from one another that they "seem harsh and out of tune; much as the mysteries of faith do" (IV, 52). This is Bacon's heuristic for reading prophecy, the wisdom of the ancients, and the wisdom of Solomon's aphorisms. Solomon's and Bacon's discourses present themselves as accessible – in fact highly appealing – forms of edification. But they offer more cryptic, quasi-religious readings when their wise interpreters read them dispersedly, by experiencing the harsh juxtaposition of the common with the adverse and the remote. The best natural history is therefore one of "digression and deflexion from the ordinary course." Collecting curiosities is not sufficient. There must be "a substantial and severe collection" (III, 331), one that requires "trials and vexations" so that nature and inquirer are "crossed" just as the prophet Proteus was when Menelaus captured him for his secrets (III, 333).

The best code hides something valuable in something mean or opposite. Thus we have gunpowder and the compass, discoveries from easily ignored, lowly sources. Such breakthroughs evoke wonder because they confound expectations. Yet their apparent indispensability tends to reduce them to ordinary things. Bacon observes that codes, once they are broken, become all too obvious and expected. Heroic decipherment changes the Sphinx-like mystery of science into a public carcass (VI, 757), and so risks creating new idolatries when the vulgar classes believe that they have mastered science, or that they should be entertained or awed by the unexpected.

Science can retain its true nature as a deciphering ordeal only by keeping its most important secrets. But does this then mean that the difficulty of the new sciences determines their truth? Is scientific decipherment merely (or perhaps impossibly) a process of searching for what one is least capable and least expectant of finding? Basing the advancement of learning on radical encryptions and decipherments, which change enigmas into revelations and seem capable of transforming everything into everything else, seems to encourage lassitude and recklessness as much as ingenuity and wise prudence.[14]

Bacon is of course acutely aware of this possibility, since he finds it typical of the pedantry and idolatry of the old learning. Whether he is a new man of science or an idolater, man's mind is an enchanted glass. Even his machines, which expand his vision of some things, tend to reflect his self-deluding image. There would seem to be no escape from idolatry, were it not for the mind's being a God-given thing. Despite its love of vain imaginings, the enchanted glass is "capable of the image of the universal world" (III, 220). To Job and Solomon, it intimates visions of divine motions (III, 222, 298–9). "[T]here seemeth to be a liberty granted, as far forth as the polishing of this glass." The mind might indeed afford a person "some moderate explication," an illumination of the "enigma" that is the anagogical meaning of the Scriptures (III, 485).

What then is "moderate explication" of such important matters? When Bacon sets to work translating and revising *The Advancement of Learning*, he retains his discussion of scriptural illumination, but omits the emphatic warning against overreaching (V, 117–9). He defines correct explication by modifying and in some instances omitting strategic sentences. In the first version, for example, he identifies four prohibitions on the aspirations of the sciences. The inspired author of the Scripture knew four things, Bacon argues, "which no man attains to know": "the mysteries of the kingdom of glory; the perfection of the laws of nature; the secrets of the heart of man; and the future succession of all ages" (III, 485). But Bacon's later, Latin translation leaves out the first two proscriptions, and goes on to emphasize the second pair: "there are two things which are known to God the author of the Scriptures, but unknown to man; namely, the secrets of the heart, and the successions of time" (V, 117). Why these changes?

Bacon's Latin protects two possibilities: that man might "attain" to knowledge of the kingdom of glory and that he might gain the "perfection" or full knowledge of the natural laws. The mind that sees through a glass darkly can see more than we think when the new sciences polish it. When Bacon describes the true scientific induction that is made "as if by divine fire [*tamquam ignem divinum*]" (IV, 145; I, 257), he could mean that reason is quasi-divine in the ancient sense (open to inspiration), or assisted by revelation, or capable of directing fiery scourges that have the sanction of religion. The *De augmentis* does maintain two prohibitions on scientific activity: the bans against inquiry into the succession of the ages and against inquiry into the secrets of men's hearts. Yet these rules are severely tested by the new sciences. Bacon's writings are full of speculation about divine motive and the shape of history, and the shadowy character of kingly and courtly intentions. From the time of his earliest publication – the 1597 *Essays* – he moves toward a social science dedicated to decoding and working the minds of men, despite (or rather, because of) his warning against the manipulation of souls. Minds and natural matter become remarkably similar objects of scientific study, both revealing themselves most tellingly under the pressures of extreme circumstances.

Paradoxically, Bacon introduces a form of inquiry into men's minds that is all the more permissible because it is supposedly separate from inquiry into the heart of men's faith. No one but God, Bacon assumes, can know the truth of a soul's piety. Yet declaring the spiritual soul beyond the reach of the new sciences frees the investigator to inquire into and test men's spirits as though he could do the soul no harm. Again, Sprat's clumsier formulation sheds light on Bacon's sophisticated one. Advocating the scientific study of "spirits" and "blood," Sprat looks forward to a time when investigators can make "neer ghesses . . . even at the more *exalted*, and *immediate* Actions of the *Soul*; and that too, without destroying its *Spiritual* and *Immortal* Being."[15]

The scientific freedom that results from putting the soul and divine intention off limits has an effect on what the new scientists can say about Providence. A probing scientific interpretation of the history of prophecy is permissible precisely because it does not presume to prognosticate about what is inscrutable (III, 341–2). If it is known that Providence works its radical opposite, the sons of science have at their disposal a ready means of knowing the unimaginable without seeming to anticipate what that pattern is. If they accept the paradox, they can know and remain ignorant at the same time. This seems to be the tenor of Bacon's reference to a Providence that "contrives out of subjects peculiarly empty and destitute of providence, and as it were blind, to educe by a fatal and necessary law all the order and beauty of the universe" (VI, 731). Strangely, interpretation draws tremendous power from the assumption that the created world is inscrutable.

Respect for religion in this sense licenses the new sciences' radical inquiries not only into the affairs of the created world but into Divinity itself. Thomas Sprat's account of the origins of the Royal Society in the ebb tide of civil war sheds light upon the next generation's willingness to open new frontiers of inquiry in the name of pious restraint:

... I should not doubt (if it were not somewhat improper to the present discourse) to prove, that even in Divinity itself they [the nonscientific writers of the past] are not so necessary, as they are reputed to be: and that all or most of our Religious controversies, may be as well decided, by plain reason, and by considerations, which may be fetch'd from the *Religion of mankind*, the Nature of *Government*, and *human Society*, and *Scripture* itself, as by the multitudes of Authorities, and subtleties of disputes, which have been heretofore in use.[16]

Rather than simply make science religious, Sprat is confident that scientific inquiry will help save religion from controversies that have defined religious outlooks for generations. Sprat's daring claim is not too far from the point of Bacon's editorializing translation of the Ninetieth Psalm, a prayer by Moses, which hints at God's offer of natural as well as divine wisdom through "holy lore" that might be disclosed to initiates. The Baconian version tells of the punishment that awaits idolaters who presume to find lore in dreams devoid of religion:

> Both death and life obey thy holy lore,
> . . .
> Thou carriest man away as with a tide:
> Then down swim all his thoughts that mounted high:
> Much like a mocking dream, that will not bide,
> But flies before the sight of waking eye . . . (VII, 279)

In the King James Version, which is closer to the Vulgate, the passage conveys neither Bacon's explicit promise of knowledge nor his mocking of vain dreamers:

> Thou turnest man to destruction; and sayest, Return ye children of men.
> . . .
> Thou carriest them away as with a flood;
> they are as a sleep . . .

Elsewhere Bacon reminds his readers that Orpheus is a pious poet, and that myth as well as Scripture can extend scientific wisdom into divine lore – but only if the investigator is appropriately prepared and proceeds with the proper method. Poetry "was ever thought to have some participation of divineness" (III, 343). In the preface to the *De sapientia veterum*, Bacon contends that ancient myths are a "method of teaching" that is "sometimes indispensable" to the sciences. Using a phrase that he repeats in the *Novum organum*, he argues that "religion delights in such veils and shadows, and to take them away would be almost to interdict all communion between divinity and humanity" (VI, 696). Although the ancient and prehistoric poets knew not what they did, their works encode subtexts perhaps more venerable than the canonical Bible. In their radical ambiguity, fables resemble nature itself. In them idolatry and a kind of revelation intermix (VI, 712), for like the nature-god Pan, the created world is "in truth biformed and made up of a higher species and a lower" (VI, 711). Fables combine or mix the lowest world and the highest – the trivial with the profound – much as Providence did when Joseph was sold into Egypt for the sake of his later mastery of the Egyptian world (VI, 711). Properly initiated readers might interpret the fables for what they reveal about the world as "the great proclaimer of the divine wisdom and goodness," even though "the more secret judgments of God, sound somewhat harsh and untunable" (VI, 712–3).

God has made available in myth as well as nature "the true signatures and marks" that he has set upon creation (IV, 51). The person who becomes the true, chosen inquirer is like the untunable myth: he somehow manages to appear on the scene even though he is the unlikeliest prospect as a seer. In Bacon's mythography, Oedipus succeeds as such a hero because he hobbles, rather than rushes, toward the Sphinx which Bacon calls Science. The hero has been prepared for the ordeal by a combination of election and perdition: the kingly wrath of his father, whose fatherhood made him the blood heir of Thebes, has bound Oedipus's ankles and cast him out to die (VI, 755–8). By the time the unlikely hero grows old enough to approach the Sphinx, he has therefore been mortified yet saved by his childhood. His paradigmatic mastery of science by enduring a "painful and cruel" method of approaching it exposes a disturbing, deeper meaning in Bacon's principle that the true sciences must resemble "the kingdom of heaven, whereinto none may enter except as a little child" (IV, 69).

Bacon's mythography indicates that in order to decipher the mingled code of the created world, the direct approach is almost as fatal as seeing God through a glass clearly. The vain scholastics, who presume without special preparation to engage the Sphinx, die in its claws. Pentheus, who climbs a tree to witness strange revels and so "penetrate the divine mysteries," is torn to pieces (VI, 720). Orpheus, who finds his yearning embodied in Eurydice, loses her when he turns to face her beauty, making himself vulnerable to the wrath of idolatrous enthusiasts. Conversely, when Diomedes (for Bacon, the embodiment of religious zeal) dares to overcome Venus by pursuing and wounding her, his own fervor makes him vulnerable to the rage of other zealots, who turn against Venus's pursuer when they think he has brought them misfortune (VI, 732–4).

In the pantheon of Bacon's *De sapientia veterum*, the inventive Prometheus is an overreacher who becomes a hero of the new sciences by indirect means. The reputation he makes for himself in direct action is ambiguous. He makes false sacrifices to the gods, along with true ones. He is both an idolater and an admirable figure: a type for "the truly religious man and the hypocrite" (VI, 750). Having formed man out of the elements and then journeyed to heaven to find fire for him, Prometheus aspires to win the praise of the human being he has made; but he fails. Mankind is not grateful. The gods become angry. Prometheus's ascent to the heavens for fire provokes their wrath, and they accuse him of assaulting Minerva ("divine wisdom" [6.752]). For his crimes he is bound to a rock where he suffers daily torture. Nevertheless, Bacon argues, it is good that Prometheus suffers. He needs more than his own heroic deeds. His shortcomings also reveal that human beings are dissatisfied with mere pleasure. Their ingratitude masks their reverence for the "divine nature, with the perfection of which they almost presume to compare." Without the ingratitude that Prometheus stimulates, there would be no drive for perfection in the invention of "new discoveries" of useful things (VI, 748–9).

To gain the freedom that will release the inventive powers of man, Prometheus must undergo punishment for presuming to know divine wisdom. But that ordeal occurs in such a way that he receives a kind of liberatory grace that changes his irreverence into inventive power. The divine sanction is a training in wisdom. A savior breaks his bonds: the mighty Hercules, who sails to his rescue in a delicate cup given by the Sun. The hero's power to escape his torment is neither wholly religious nor wholly scientific. It

was not natural to Prometheus, but adventitious, and came by help from without; for it is not a thing which any inborn and natural fortitude can attain to; it comes from beyond the ocean, it is received and brought to us from the Sun; for it comes of Wisdom, which is as the Sun, and of meditation upon the inconstancy and fluctuations of human life. (VI, 752)

Although Bacon does not speculate further about the religious ramifications of the myth, he cannot refrain from intimating that "there are not a few things beneath" the fable "which have a wonderful correspondency with the mysteries of the Christian faith" (VI, 753).

Is it grace, then, that finally enables Prometheus to transcend idolatrous vanity, and so to become one of the greatest founding heroes of the new sciences? Bacon seems to bow to this conclusion in the last paragraphs of his mythography, where he says that the superior means of overcoming the Sirens, whose fatal temptations distract and stymie the advancement of learning, is "religion" manifested in the praises that Orpheus sings to God (VI, 763–4). But if Orpheus is a more complete example of the religious scientic hero, his history is more problematic. Orpheus uses his song to spare the Argonauts from the fatal sounds of the Sirens' calls. In pious song, he faces the danger without mechanical aid (VI, 763) and so seems superior to the Promethean Ulysses who must be tied to a mast. But by drowning out the sounds of temptation, he undermines the Argonauts' scientific virtue as explorers of the unknown. The religious devotion of Orpheus's singing removes his friends from the ordeal of temptation which, elsewhere in Bacon's works, defines scientific virtue. Eventually Orpheus himself will succumb to temptation when he turns toward Eurydice. Religious poetry does not save him from what Bacon calls idolatry. Is the ordeal of the Baconian hero then simply too dependent upon religion or too arduous, his receipt of grace too arbitrary or "adventitious" for true science to be methodically pursued?

VI RELIGION IN THE *NEW ATLANTIS*

To explore the extent of Bacon's thinking about these matters, it is worth going to the *New Atlantis*. For it is in his account of Bensalem, the visionary island upon which science grows from archaic roots and modern prophecy, that we see Bacon most fully permitting himself to indulge and explore the notion that a kind of religious devotion is the gate and the problematic end of the new sciences.

Bensalem is a kind of heaven, and the almost broken seafarers who stumble upon it are happy to be its prisoners rather than commercial adventurers who have learned that their desire for mere profit has made them eminently vulnerable to death. The island society seems "a picture of our salvation in heaven" after the rescue. The hoped for (yet unlooked for) harbor is an entrance into a "happy and holy ground" that offers them "nothing but consolations" (III, 136). Almost all of Bensalem's attention seems to be given to performing charitable works (III, 156, 166). The lost sailors think they have entered a "divine pool of healing" that is later called "Water of Paradise" (III, 135, 158). Calling Bensalem "a land of angels," they bow before their governor, who seems to have power to extend their lives as well as to deny them treatment.

King Solamona, "the lawgiver of our nation," seems to have embodied this principle in his kingdom when he exercised his "large heart" – his desire to make everyone "happy" – and barred almost all strangers from the island (III, 144). In closing Bensalem to almost all outsiders, he wished to avoid the fate of China, whose open door to strangers made that country superstitious, and whose subsequent prohibition against all outsiders was an act of fear. Bensalem's apparently more moderate policy toward strangers now exerts a power which Bacon's narrator calls "divine." To avoid China's double excess of permitting all strangers or welcoming none, Solamona promoted enlightened sciences in a house of se-

crets and instituted comprehensive surveillance of the rest of the
world for the sake of Bensalemites' happiness. The regime thereby
took on a kind of divinity, charitably revealing some of its work
while concealing the most important powers that made it possible.
It seems impossible that Bensalem could gather such extraordinary
intelligence without showing itself to that world, or compromising
its own institutions. As the house's governor concedes, a place so
open to the outside yet immune to scrutiny seems to operate with
occult power: it is "supernatural" (III, 145).[17] The things it does
reveal, in the form of artifices that provide health, power, wealth,
and convenience, are easily (if not accurately) taken to be angelic or
magical manifestations of deep natural laws – as though the Bensalemites' wonderful conversion of effects into causes were telegraph-
ing, by means of their inventions, the notion that nature is an
encoded communication between God-given nature and man.[18]

Long ago, when the Scriptures appeared to the people of the island
under a pillar of light, a Bensalemite scientist was able to approach
the holy book and certify that it was indeed miraculous (III, 137–
8).[19] It is difficult to determine whether his interpretation was a
pious reflection on his previous knowledge of the book of God's
works, or a wise appropriation of religion into science. Bensalemite
science precedes the arrival of Christianity on the island, and so it
might not need orthodox religion except as a cover for its work.
When the narrator himself says "It is a kind of miracle [that] hath
brought us hither" (III, 134), he is being faithful to the experience of
being saved by charitable souls from near death at sea. But when we
later hear that the Bensalemite researchers have mastered the winds,
the possibility arises that the sailors were first brought near death,
and then saved, by means of a preternatural force that was engi-
neered inside the College of the Six Days' Works.

Like Orpheus, Bensalem's men of science sing hymns daily to
ward off the furies that tempt the users of power (III, 166). The
Bensalemite scientists observe an oath of secrecy, and supposedly
adhere to strict rules against using scientific knowledge merely to
make strange effects (III, 164). However, the scientific and political
workings of Bensalem's strange polity, unlike the workings of
More's *Utopia*, remain almost entirely cryptic. The government of
the island, particularly the relationship between the researchers and
the rulers, is undisclosed. More's *Utopia* is literally a "nowhere,"

dependent upon the obviously implausible abolition of private property. By contrast, Bacon's island gives the impression that it has been on earth for some time. Its fusion of faith with the practical power of the new scientific engineering is presented as though it were eminently reasonable, though its rational and political foundations are remarkably obscure. A profound doubleness is built into Bensalem's political and scientific constitution.[20]

The great miracle, or near miracle, of Bensalemite science is the prolongation of life, including resuscitation of things that "seem dead" (III, 159). Bacon warns in the *Historia vitae et mortis* against the idolatrous love of long life for its own sake (V, 266). But he focuses on extending life without being too much concerned about its natural limits. More than the mere eradication of disease, his goal is the extension of life. Given this priority, the sons of science might profitably turn their interest toward the vivifying powers of superstition: Bacon notes that philosophies that "have some touch of superstition" are conducive to longevity (V, 263).

Christianity is itself the religion of the physician, since Christ's miracles most resemble the workings of medicine, whose chief function is "prolongation of life" (III, 377, 373). The lengthening of life is "of earthly gifts perhaps the greatest – of which, next to God, they [physicians] may become the dispensers and administrators." Their gift is as a "divine grace" (IV, 390), even though they prolong lives that are not assumed thereby to be divinely distinguished. Long life is supposedly not in itself the result of "grace or holy line," but longevity does provide the means to prolong the exercise of charity. Bacon is careful to note that this was the case with "the beloved disciple," John, who outlived the rest (V, 243, 306, 217). Does this highest Baconian endeavor – the prolongation of life – arise from and perhaps extend the reach of religion and charity, or is it more simply a useful, perhaps debased, secular adaptation of religious concerns and doctrines of salvation?

VII EPILOGUE: THE SONS OF SCIENCE

Bacon's new sciences are supposed to do their highest, vivifying work upon the "spirit." Bacon usually maintains that the spirit of all tangible bodies, including human beings, is fundamentally distinct from the rational soul that is the subject of religious ministrations.

Yet he observes that the spirit is "the organ of the reasonable soul" (V, 335). In the last entry of the *Sylva Sylvarum*, he looks ahead to a science of spiritual influence: mastery of the distance-defying, crowd-animating influences that are exerted by sympathy, envy, admiration, ambition, and perhaps more ethereal functions of the reasonable soul. Such a science would be eminently qualified to mix science with religion, for it seems "as if all spirits and souls of men came forth out of one divine limbus" (II, 672).

What is most disturbing about this exhilarating prospect (as D. P. Walker has observed) is that Bacon almost entirely avoids discussing the higher soul that was traditionally understood to shape and interpret these influences. He relegates the study and care of that soul entirely to Divinity, while developing the idea of an invisible, bodily spirit that behaves much like the spirit of alcohol.[21] The *Essays*, which counsel the political, ethical, and religious concerns of the reasonable soul, are most essentially collections of advice about wise technique. Their moral and political instruction is an encoded version of Bacon's inquiries into motion, power, and antithetical wisdom.[22] The poverty of the explicit Baconian doctrine of the soul is symptomatic of what Laurence Berns has called Bacon's "failure to develop the expected human philosophy" that would help modern science avoid becoming a philosophy of sheer power.[23]

Inheritors of Bacon's legacy of divinity-purged yet strangely pious science face the challenge of considering how to order their moral and political lives, along with their understanding and use of science, on the basis of what is known about nature and human nature, and the possible existence of something higher. What sort of guidance do Bacon's paradoxes offer for thinking about human conduct and human aspirations, once their covering of conventional religion dissipates or is taken for granted? The new Baconian sciences depend upon faith in the existence of the maker's code; but in discovering that cipher, they deny in principle the possibility of truthful, ordinary trust in the visible world.[24] Depending upon the charitable good sense of scientific practitioners, the new sciences offer vast new powers that tempt the sons of science to rule absolutely under a cover of benevolence. Finally, they cultivate a high-mindedness that stimulates an iconoclastic contempt for motives that are not purely altruistic.

While the new Baconian sciences amplify the importance of religion as a counterweight to their tyrannical possibilities, one continues to be struck by the depth of Bacon's systematic antagonism toward idolatrous, false religion. Paradoxically, his attack on idolatry in the very bones of individual believers, peoples, and institutions – and in the language of the marketplace of ideas – makes it increasingly difficult to distinguish between his opinion of traditional Christianity and his view of heresy, particularly when he promotes the enlightened manipulation of superstition for the sake of scientific ends. Science and false religion, liberation and domination, threaten to become the same thing. In the last words of the *Sylva Sylvarum*, Bacon himself warns against a "depraved" ambition for innovation that is "an affectation of tyranny over the understandings and beliefs of men" (II, 672). What now distinguishes the new sciences' rule from that kind of tyranny?

Students of Bacon have often concluded that the case is moot: the new sciences are either too clearly charitable, too disinterested, to be tyrannical; or they are too bound up in the rhetoric of conquest not to domineer over the mass of humanity as they do nature. Religion is either an accidental, though perhaps welcome, contributor to the new sciences' enlightened power, or it is one of the sources of ecological and social degradation.[25] But these positions do not do justice to the complexity of Bacon's debt to, and use of, religion. They do not adequately account for the tension between Bacon's solemnity, which moderns tend to underestimate, and the nearly grotesque, perhaps deeply subversive pretension of the New Atlantis's appropriation of religion for the sake of the new sciences.

We are the trustees of sciences that Bacon helped to make. With increasing powers, new sciences offer us the grace of longevity, and the challenge of finding meaning in long life. They give us tantalizing, often horrifying glimpses of more wondrous powers that might be within our ken. Too great a willingness to attribute power to these sciences, or to believe that they have vanquished religion, or that religion is immune to their claims, ignores our freedom to inquire into the limits of the new sciences as well as their reach. One of the outgrowths of the Baconian revolution is the encouragement to look into smaller things as well as *philosophia prima*, not to be transfixed by Baconian paradoxes which have a way of becoming idols that are as misleading as the four that Bacon analyzed. Baconian science works upon individual human beings, whom we still think of as being capable of inquiry, of making political, ethical, and spiritual choices, whether or not they are sons of science. It is an open question whether the Baconian innovation and the great machine of modern science control those decision, assist them, or have some other effect. They at least have failed, so far, to dominate the freedom of Bacon's trustees to worship, inquire, and choose.

NOTES

1 This translation of *tamquam ignem divinum* ("as if by divine fire") suggests that a kind of divine quality or agent might be needed in the process of the solution and separation. The English of Spedding's edition is less precise: the process is effected "by the mind, *which is a kind of divine fire*." For drawing my attention to this anomaly, I am grateful to Berns 1978, p. 6.

2 Consensus over Bacon's religious affiliations, if any, is more elusive. Macaulay called him a theologian, and Aubrey wrote that he was a "sincere believer" in Christianity, *Brief Lives and Other Selected Writings* (New York, 1949), p. 118. Rawley concluded "This lord was religious" (I, 14). Bacon dedicated his translation of the Psalms to George Herbert, and a treatise on holy wars to Lancelot Andrews (VII, 11–15). His mother, it is well known, was a reformist Protestant. She criticized him, in a letter to his brother, for being "too negligent" about his prayers (VIII, 113); but this advice is better evidence of her almost meddling concern for his spiritual life, which was at least outwardly conventional. For an excellent, broadly based introduction to the larger question of how religion and science interact in Bacon's work, see Brooke 1991, especially pp. 52–81.

3 Thomas Sprat, *History of the Royal Society*, ed. Jackson I. Cope and H. W. Jones (St. Louis, 1958 [first published 1667]), pp. 5, 23, 57, 53–4.

4 For an elaboration of this reading of Bacon, see Kelly 1965.

5 See the extensive contemporary controversy over this issue in George Hakewill's *An Apologie of the Power and Providence of God in the Government of the World, Vindicating of God's glory, the advancement of learning, and the honour of the Christian and reformed religion* (Oxford, 1627), which is an essentially Baconian reply to Goodman's *The Fall of Man or the Corruption of Nature Proved by the light of our Naturall Reason* (1616, 1618, 1629).

6 Sprat, *History*, p. 72.

7 Sprat, *History*, p. 55.

8 Sprat, *History*, p. 132.

9 See Klaaven 1977, pp. 103–4.

10 See the essay "Of Superstition," Bacon's criticism of vulgar heresy in his reply to the Marprelate controversialists (VIII, 74–9), and the addendum to his copy of Camden's *Annales*, in which he refers to the 1591 conspiracy of one Hacket, "a man newborn from the vilest dregs of the Anabaptists" (VI, 356).

11 For an example of how one idolatry can be used against another, see II, 634.

12 For a penetrating exploration of this ambiguity in Bacon's stress on charitable works, see Berns 1978, p. 4.

13 Thomas Sprat argues that Solomon's histories were exceedingly unusual because the Jews did not pursue natural philosophy; *History*, p. 15.

14 See Briggs 1989, pp. 15–24, 32–40, 142–3, and passim. To describe the power of turning everything into everything else, Bacon uses the phrase *omnia per omnia*. It is quite possible that he took the expression from the Apostle Paul's letters in the Vulgate Bible (1 Corinthians 9.20). There Paul describes how he undergoes the rigors of protean disguise, seeming to be a Jew to the Jews while seeking to convert them. It is Paul's orthodox and rigorous charity (in his words, the endurance of all things) that is supposed to justify his protean disguise and his decipherment of the resistances of the unconverted. The relationship between Bacon's employment of these principles and Paul's use of them is a subject worthy of further study.

15 Sprat, *History*, p. 33.

16 Sprat, *History*, p. 22.

17 A provocative discussion of these matters can be found in Renaker 1990.

18 See Melzer 1993, p. 294.

19 The ark came to Bensalem by natural as well as divine means: warned by an angel, the apostle Bartholomew had committed the book to the sea before it arrived in Bensalem. According to Eusebius's *Ecclesiastical History* (v. x.), it was indeed Bartholomew who first brought parts of the gospel to India (the Book of Matthew written in Hebrew). Bartholomew's *Questions* and *Book of the Resurrection of Christ*, apocryphal works mentioned by Jerome and Bede, consist of inquiries into the secrets of the virgin birth, the devil, and the resurrection – secrets that at first are said to be closed to inquiry because of their mortal danger to those who search them out. But Bartholomew and the other apostles succeed in hearing these secrets after they prostrate themselves and persist in begging to hear them, whatever the consequences. See *The Apocryphal New Testament*, trans. Montague Rhodes James (Oxford, 1953), pp. 166–86. It is not known whether or not Bacon had access to the Greek and Latin manuscripts of Bartholomew's books; but in choosing that apostle to be an agent of Bensalem's conversion, he selected a

shadowy biblical figure who was associated in some traditions with gnostic lore.

20 Given the highly controlled nature of island life, it is remarkable that Chaldeans, Jews, Arabs, Indians, and Persians are residents of Bensalem. But Bacon explains how the Jews manage to live there, believing in the Virgin Birth and God's elevation of Christ to rule over the angels (III, 151). Their faith in the coming of their own Messiah is, says Bacon, a "dream." Still, he calls his Jewish informant, Joabin, "a wise man, and learned, and of great policy, and excellently seen in the laws and customs of that nation" (III, 151). Joabin's role as a social scientist, a master of the law, and a counselor to the great makes him a type for Bacon himself. When King David came to power in the vacuum left by the death of Saul's heirs, Joab became one of his chief counselors and champions (2 Sam. xix. 1-8; 1 Chron. xi. 4–9). King James resembles David not only in the circumstances of his accession, but in his putative role as the designer of a new Solomonic Temple. Perhaps the key to Bacon's ambiguous treatment of Joabin is Bacon's own scientific interest in the secrets of Solomonic wisdom. His narrator skeptically but carefully reports, without explicitly certifying its truth, that the Bensalemite Jews believe in a "secret cabala" from Moses, which sets down their laws.

21 Walker 1972, p. 125.

22 See Briggs 1989, pp. 215–48 and passim.

23 Berns 1978, pp. 17, 1–26, passim. See also Weinberger 1985, Westfall 1958, Kocher 1953.

24 Charles Whitney has suggested that Bacon combines religion and science into a radically negative theology; see Whitney 1984.

25 For a wide-ranging and provocative discussion of these issues and a host of secondary references, see Melzer 1993 and other contributions in the same volume.

8 Bacon and rhetoric

I INTRODUCTION

Given the important place occupied by rhetoric in Bacon's career, one might imagine that by this late date an abundance of serviceable studies would exist. But, perhaps as another proof of his observation that "the opinion of plenty is amongst the causes of want" (III, 327–8), such is not the case. There are three book-length studies frequently cited: Karl R. Wallace's pioneering study, *Francis Bacon on Communication and Rhetoric*, Lisa Jardine's revised Cambridge dissertation, *Francis Bacon: Discovery and the Art of Discourse*, and the overall history by W. S. Howell, Jr., *Logic and Rhetoric in England, 1500–1700*. There are also some shorter essays, of varying value.[1] But it is not being unkind to say that none of these offers a satisfactory account of either Bacon's theory or practice of rhetoric. In some cases major emphases in Bacon's theory have simply not been registered, or were misunderstood. In others, the writers' evaluation of Bacon was adversely affected by their general conception of rhetoric, and the place it held in European intellectual life.

Karl Wallace, to begin with, organized his pioneering study mainly around the five processes of rhetorical composition, *inventio, dispositio, elocutio, memoria,* and *pronuntiatio* or gesture – *actio*, as it was sometimes called. While obviously making sense from a rhetorician's point of view, this scheme arouses expectations that Bacon had something significant to say on each of these topics. He was certainly familiar with this five-part scheme, but he never gave a systematic account of rhetoric as a whole. Indeed, he declares rhetoric to be "a science excellent, and excellently well laboured" (III,

409), and not therefore needing detailed treatment. Wallace does not recognize the partial, occasional nature of Bacon's utterances on rhetoric, which he seldom treats on its own, but usually in relation to some other issue.

W. S. Howell was another pioneer, the first to provide a detailed history of English logic and rhetoric between 1500 and 1700. Unfortunately, Howell's work was vitiated by a number of faults.[2] His claim that Bacon held a purely cognitive concept of rhetoric as against its emotional and persuasive function[3] is completely false to Bacon's text. According to Bacon himself, "the duty and office of Rhetoric is to apply Reason to Imagination for the better moving of the will" (III, 409). Equally misleading is Howell's other claim that Bacon believed that "the tropes and figures, as a great system of violations of normal ways of speaking, were not an acceptable imperative for learned discussions."[4] Any detailed study of Bacon's writings, in English or Latin, will show that he used the figures and tropes of rhetoric fluently and imaginatively, throughout his career.[5]

Lisa Jardine's study of Bacon in the context of sixteenth-century dialectic teaching is much more scholarly, and has a far greater historical consciousness, but it also yields a seriously distorted account of Bacon's views on rhetoric. Her enthusiastic advocacy of Renaissance dialectic results in a dismissive attitude towards rhetoric, a polarization that no Renaissance scholar, always aware of the complementarity of the two arts, would ever have indulged in. Her account of the sixteenth-century Cambridge curricula[6] overvalues the status of dialectic, claiming that it occupied the "central position" in the arts course,[7] and virtually excludes rhetoric from consideration. She refers briefly to the logical textbooks recommended in university and college reading lists, but never at all to those in rhetoric. This ignoring of a major subject would be unwise at any time, but is especially strange for a historian of the sixteenth century, given that the humanist reform of dialectic widened the subject's scope by including much material previously treated in the rhetoric handbooks, achieving in the process what has been called a "rhetoricization of logic."[8]

Jardine's advocacy of dialectic makes her appropriate for it many functions actually given to rhetoric in the Renaissance, and to trivialize rhetoric itself, a bias which inevitably distorts her view of Bacon. She claims that "method" in dialectic covered "the *art of discourse*," and that "the principles of composition" in the sixteenth-century universities were "taught first and foremost from the 'new look' dialectic handbook."[9] Jardine seems to have misunderstood the division of labor between the two arts, logic being an *ars disserendi* which taught "discourse" in the sense of rational argument, as in the common Renaissance phrase for thinking, "discourse of reason" (Thomas Wilson's logic book is called *The Rule of Reason*), while the *ars bene loquendi* put thought into the most effective structure and form of argument, according to the audience addressed and the speaker's or writer's intent. Jardine's over-elevation of dialectic makes her blot out rhetoric from serious consideration. According to her reconstruction of sixteenth-century attitudes, dialectic was "able to account for all but the most ornamental techniques of oratory":[10] so why did people then continue to spend so much time studying rhetoric? William Holdsworth, a Cambridge don (subsequently master of Emmanuel College), writing in about 1645, held that rhetoric was the most important subject of all, to which an undergraduate should devote every afternoon for four years, and without which "all other learning, though never so eminent, is in a manner void and useless."[11]

Jardine projects her own biased evaluation on to Bacon, claiming that he "subordinates rhetoric to dialectic, and characterises rhetoric as something overlaid upon discourse composed according to dialectical rules."[12] But there is no evidence in his writings for any such subordination: on the contrary, as we shall see, Bacon always sees the two arts as complementary. Furthermore, she writes that "Bacon, like other educational reformers, chooses to reserve the term *rhetoric* for 'the doctrine concerning the Illustration of Discourse' [IV, 454], or ornamentation. The end of rhetoric is 'to fill the imagination with observations and images', so that by embellishment and illustration the author's views are made appealing to his audience, *without the use of formal argument* [IV, 456]."[13] This is doubly misleading. Jardine has not only misunderstood the meaning of "illustration," by equating it with "ornamentation" and "embellishment," she has failed to quote the whole of Bacon's sentence (in the slightly expanded discussion in the *De augmentis*), and has given it a completely unjustified gloss, in the words that I have italicized. Bacon's actual sentence reads: "For the end of logic is to teach a form of argument to secure reason, and not to entrap it; . . . the end of rhetoric is to fill the imagination with observations and images, to second reason, and not to oppress it" (IV, 455–6). The operative word there is "to second" or support, in what Bacon evidently conceived as a joint operation between logic and rhetoric. Here, as throughout her book, Jardine tries to appropriate reason wholly for logic (or dialectic), and to reduce rhetoric to ornament, or purely sensory appeal. Her subsequent discussion argues that for Bacon rhetoric "exploits the image-making capacity of the mind, just as logic does its ratiocinative capacity":[14] this exclusive opposition would deny rationality to rhetoric, evidently an absurd position. But in attempting to drive a wedge between the two arts Jardine not only commits a historical anachronism, she also ignores Bacon's definition of the "duty and office" of rhetoric as being "to apply Reason to the Imagination for the better moving of the Will" – where, I think, we can now understand "better" as meaning not just "more effectively" but "to better ends."

As for Bacon's account of the persuasive effect of rhetoric, directed toward the appetite and will, Jardine at least (unlike Howell) discusses his use of faculty psychology.[15] But she curiously fails to comment on its relevance to his treatment of rhetoric. Instead, she claims that Bacon "emphasise[s] the mechanical effect of [rhetorical] figures at the expense of the traditional claim for the imitative and natural emotive force of rhetoric," and that Bacon's belief in "the persuasive effectiveness of figures of rhetoric" is "the direct result of the way in which the senses are stimulated," that is, by arousing "a purely auditory stimulus" through "direct sensory stimulation."[16]

It would be very odd, to start with, given Bacon's frequently expressed scorn for those who value words more than matter, if he had then held a purely sensory theory of persuasion, detached from all considerations of meaning: but of course he did not. Jardine quotes, but misunderstands, that passage (she quotes it from *Valerius Terminus*, III, 230: the more familiar, and more accessible version is in *The Advancement of Learning*, III, 348–9) in which Bacon makes a suggestive comparison between the working of figures in language and similar devices in music:

The repetitions and traductions in speech and the reports and hauntings of sounds in music are the very same things. . . . Now in music it is one of the ordinariest flowers to fall from a discord or hard tune upon a sweet accord. The figure that Cicero and the rest commend as one of the best points of elegancy, which is the fine checking of expectation, is no less well known to the musicians . . . [in an interrupted cadence].

Jardine identifies this figure as *aposiopesis*, which she imperfectly defines as "the natural breaking off of speech through shame, fear or anger . . .," citing[17] Henry Peacham's definition in *The Garden of Eloquence* (1577, 1593). However, Peacham, at least, grasped the essential point of the figure, which is that it is when the orator is overcome by passion that he "breaketh off his speech before it be all ended. *Virgil*. 'How doth the childe Ascanius, whom tymely *Troy* to thee – ' breaking off by the interruption of sorrow." The whole point of *aposiopesis* is that such speeches are incomplete from a semantic point of view, the speaker being unable to finish a sense-unit due to an emotional disturbance. Thus there is nothing in the theory or practical application of this figure to suggest that Bacon believed that such effects worked by "a purely auditory stimulus." And in any case Jardine misidentifies the trope concerned, which was properly indicated by Aldis Wright in his edition of *The Advancement of Learning* over a century ago by the page references he gave to Cicero and Quintilian, namely the trope *aprosdoketon*, a form of verbal wit which consists in "cheating expectations by taking words in a different sense from what was intended."[18] Since the whole point of this trope consists in ambiguity concerning meaning, Jardine's claim that Bacon believed the persuasive effectiveness of rhetorical figures to derive from simple "sensory stimulation" is completely false.

This brief review of the best-known, and most frequently cited modern studies of Bacon's rhetoric can serve a cautionary function, reminding us to trust the author rather than his interpreters. In order to give a truer account I shall first discuss what rhetoric texts Bacon knew, and when he first studied them. I shall then outline his theory of rhetoric, paying particular attention to its links with psychology and ethics. Finally I shall discuss Bacon's criticisms of rhetoric, the limitations he attached to it within his general theory of language, and then as relating to science.

II RHETORIC IN BACON'S CAREER

Bacon must have been introduced to rhetoric at an early age, born as he was into one of the leading humanist families in England. George Puttenham, author of one of the most humane Renaissance works in rhetoric and poetics, arguing that "our writing and speaches publike ought to be figurative," instanced as examples of public speakers who had mastered "the use of rhetorical figures" and could therefore speak "cunningly and eloquently" both Bacon's father "Sir *Nicholas Bacon* Lord Keeper of the great Seale" and his uncle (Lord Burghley) "the now Lord Treasurer of England . . . From whose lippes I have seen to proceede more grave and naturall eloquence, than from all the Oratours of Oxford and Cambridge . . . " Puttenham records that "I have come to the Lord Keeper Sir *Nicholas Bacon*, & found him sitting in his gallery alone with the works of *Quintilian* before him, in deede he was a most eloquent man, and of rare learning and wisedome as ever I knew England to breed . . ."[19] The precision of Puttenham's testimony as to the book being read, coupled with its vagueness about the time and place of occurrence, may put this anecdote in the category of the mythical rather than the historical, but its collocation of rhetoric and Tudor humanism is undoubtedly accurate.

Bacon's mother, Lady Ann Bacon (1528–1610), was one of the five remarkable daughters of Sir Anthony Cooke, an eminent classicist who gave his daughters the standard humanist education. Lady Ann was also one of the small and select band of English women who published books, first a translation of some sermons by Bernardino Ochino, then the work for which she was celebrated, the authorized English version of John Jewel's *Apologia ecclesiae anglicanae* (1562).[20] She played the leading role in appointing a tutor for her two sons by Sir Nicholas, Anthony (1558–1601) and Francis (1561–1626). As recorded by a grateful acknowledgment in one of his sermons, John Walsall, newly graduated from Christ Church, Oxford, acted as their tutor certainly from 1566 (when Anthony was eight years old, Francis five) to 1569, and perhaps afterward.[21]

In the seven to eight years education that the boys received until they went up to Trinity College, Cambridge, in April 1573, they would have gone through the whole of the normal primary and grammar-school curriculum. From the exhaustive reconstruction of such curricula by T. W. Baldwin,[22] it is clear that they would have progressed from elementary texts such as Cato's *Distichs* and Aesop to more advanced authors, including Ovid, Horace, and Virgil, learning to construe and translate these texts, identifying historical allusions and mythological figures. They would also have received a first introduction to rhetoric, either from the standard classical texts, Cicero's *De inventione* and the *Rhetorica ad Herennium*, or through one of the popular Renaissance syntheses, such as those by Melanchthon or Erasmus. Like all their contemporaries, they would have learned up to a hundred rhetorical figures and tropes, identified such devices by marginal notes in the books that they read, and reused them in their own (Latin) compositions, prose and verse.

When Anthony and Francis went up to Cambridge in 1573, we know from the accounts kept by their tutor, John Whitgift (master of Trinity, later Archbishop of Canterbury), that he bought for their use the major classical texts and commentaries, including "2 aristotells" (i.e., 2 copies), for which he paid 36 shillings (the price suggests a substantial edition); two copies of Plato for 24s.; "tullies workes" (probably Cicero's philosophical writings, and perhaps his letters) for 30s., and a separate edition of "ciceronis rheto." (the rhetorical works, probably including the *Rhetorica ad Herennium*), 4s. Other books on rhetoric that he bought for their studies included "one commentarie of tullis orations," 13s., the *Orations* of Demosthenes, 1s., and "hermogenes in greke and laten" (various treatises forming his *Ars rhetorica*), 7s.6d. Historical works included the *Commentarii* of Julius Caesar (2s.), "one salust," 1s.4d. and "one zenophon gre. and latin," 18s. Whitgift also expended, "for a latin bible for antho[ny]," 7s.[23] This triple emphasis, on philosophy, rhetoric, and history, was a typical feature of Renaissance humanism, especially for anyone entering public life, where ability in speaking was vital.

Bacon's knowledge of rhetoric was not, of course, limited to his preuniversity schooling and his time at Cambridge. Having spent two and a half years in France in the train of the English ambassador Bacon returned to England after his father's sudden death in February 1579, being left without the expected inheritance and forced to occupy a much less glamorous level in the *vita activa* by becoming a law student at Gray's Inn. From the meager documentation concerning the curricula of the Inns of Court, together with what can be reconstructed of their practical training, we can surmise that rhetoric played some part in the training exercises. To a certain extent the "moot" and the "bolt" (which consisted of arguments *pro* and *contra*), and the surviving "Readings" or formal lectures (including Bacon's) were organized according to the principles of rhetoric.[24] As Bacon wrote in 1603, "we see orators have their declamations, lawyers have their moots, logicians have their sophems . . ." (X, 120).

Increasingly in this period students entering the Inns of Court had had a grammar-school and university education, with a thorough grounding in rhetoric, and as future lawyers they were keenly aware of the prestige of legal oratory as exemplified by Demosthenes and Cicero. Bacon must have continued to study rhetoric throughout his life, for we find references to such classical texts as Aristotle's *Rhetoric* and Cicero's *De oratore* in many of his written works from the 1580s to the 1620s.

Rhetoric meant different things to Bacon at different periods of his life. Arguably the most important function it had, early and late, was as a practical guide for those occasions when he had to speak in a face-to-face context with other speakers on matters of public interest. Spedding's seven volumes of *Letters and Life of Francis Bacon including all his Occasional Works* contain many letters of advice to the two sovereigns whom he served so loyally, and to so little effect, treatises expressing his own considered opinions on matters of current national importance. He was also regularly employed in writing quasi-official defenses of his country's political actions, to counter critics at home and abroad. Even after his fall from grace in 1621 Bacon identified himself with Demosthenes, who had also been exiled on a charge of corruption, but had still been politically active, as Bacon was for the remaining four years of his life, drafting political utterances *pro bono publico*.[25]

Most important, he uttered his opinions *in propria persona* in England's highest political councils – the two Houses of Parliament – throughout his life from the age of twenty (1581) to that of sixty (1621). In his contributions to parliamentary debate he demonstrated that the *philanthropia* which he ascribed to himself in the famous letter to Burghley of 1592 (VIII, 109), and which animated the whole of his life-long attempt to renew natural philosophy for the benefit of mankind, was neither a covert desire to gain political power or flatter King James, nor an empty profession (as some cynical modern biographers suggest), but a coherent part of his life and work. As for the form of his speeches, rhetorical techniques (especially the conscious use of *partitio* or division) provide the structure, and a full examination of them (yet to be performed) would show that their texture is given clarity and emotional power by a skillful use of rhetorical figures and tropes.[26]

III RHETORIC AND LOGIC

Turning now to Bacon's theory of rhetoric and its place in the human sciences, we can note to begin with that he regularly bracketed it with logic, recognizing their complementary roles within the *trivium*, which was still the basis for education in the Renaissance, as in antiquity. The elementary course began with grammar, a subject which Bacon described as "the harbinger of other sciences," and to which he attached more than usual importance (III, 400–1; IV, 440–2). At the primary and secondary levels of education students mastered grammar and rhetoric, and would have acquired much practical familiarity with rhetorical terms and methods by the time they left school. At the tertiary, university level, the first year of the arts course concentrated on rhetoric, developing and extending their knowledge before moving on to two years' study of dialectic, a subject which would be new to them. For Bacon, as for all his contemporaries, it was axiomatic that these two arts, rhetoric and logic, constituted a dual training for the mind and a preparation for the intellectual confrontations of real life. As the conclusion to his Essay "Of Studies" (1597) puts it, "Histories make men wise, Poets wittie: the Mathematickes subtle, naturall Phylosophie deepe: Morall grave, Logicke and Rhetoricke able to contend" (VI, 525).

Their joint importance in the formation of Renaissance man meant that special care needed to be given to their teaching, and to their place within university curricula. In Book Two of *The Advancement of Learning* Bacon diagnosed as "an error"[27] the fact

that scholars in universities come too soon and too unripe to logic and rhetoric; arts fitter for graduates than children and novices: for these two, rightly taken, are the gravest of sciences; being the arts of arts, the one for judgment, the other for ornament; and they be the rules and directions how to set forth and dispose matter; and therefore for minds empty and unfraught with matter, and which have not gathered that which Cicero called *sylva* and *supellex*, stuff and variety, to begin with those arts, (as if one should learn to weigh or to measure or to paint the wind,) doth work but this effect, that the wisdom of those arts, which is great and universal, is almost made contemptible, and is degenerate into childish sophistry and ridiculous affectation. (III, 326)

By describing logic and rhetoric jointly as "the arts of arts" Bacon may have been deliberately challenging Melanchthon, who (following the thirteenth-century logician Peter of Spain) had defined dialectic alone as "the art of arts, the science of sciences."[28] All the more reason, then, to avoid premature exposure to these arts, which would only produce "superficial and unprofitable" results. The proper sequence of study, he advised Sir Henry Savile in "A Letter and Discourse touching helps for the intellectual powers" (c. 1602), was that "Logic and Rhetoric should be used to be read after Poesy, History, and Philosophy" (VII, 103).

Logic and rhetoric were complementary, but they had distinct fields of operation, depending on both subject-matter and the audience addressed. As Bacon expounded their traditional relationship,

It appeareth also that Logic differeth from Rhetoric, not only as the fist from the palm, the one close, the other at large; but much more in this, that Logic handleth reason exact and in truth, and Rhetoric handleth it as it is planted in popular opinions and manners. And therefore Aristotle doth wisely place Rhetoric as between Logic on the one side and moral or civil knowledge on the other, as participating of both: for the proofs and demonstrations of Logic are toward all men indifferent and the same; but the proofs and persuasions of Rhetoric ought to differ according to the auditors. . . . (III, 411)

If logic and rhetoric constituted a joint training in thinking, arguing, and expressing arguments in persuasive form, any attempt to keep them separate while treating the whole spectrum of human communication would be doomed to failure. Bacon classifies the "Rational Knowledges," those "keys of all other arts," which not only "direct, but likewise confirm and strengthen the operations of the mind," in best Aristotelian fashion,

according to the ends whereunto they are referred: for man's labour is to *invent* that which is *sought* or *propounded*; or to *judge* that which is *invented*; or to *retain* that which is *judged*; or to *deliver over* that which is *retained*. So as the arts must be four; Art of Inquiry or Invention; Art of Examination or Judgment; Art of Custody or Memory; and Art of Elocution or Tradition. (III, 383–4)

Bacon includes within this scheme material deriving from logic and rhetoric, poetics, grammar, linguistics and pedagogy, an original (if inevitably untidy) attempt to redefine and interrelate all the arts of language. The first category, the "Art of Inquiry or Invention," includes both logical and rhetorical invention (III, 389). The second category, the "Art of Examination or Judgment" (III, 392–7), includes logical processes involving "proofs and demonstrations," namely syllogism; elenches; fallacies innate to the human mind (a first version of the "Idols"); and analogy. The third category, the "Art of Custody or Memory" (III, 397–9), deals with writing (including the keeping of commonplace books), and the art of memory as found in classical rhetoric. The fourth category, the "Art of Eloquence or Tradition" (III, 399–417), deals with all of what Bacon calls the "transitive" arts, governing "the expressing or transferring our knowledge to others." It includes a discussion of rhetoric (III, 409–17), considering its links with philosophy, ethics, and psychology. Bacon also discusses its provision of aids to argument, which are deemed to be deficient (the "Colours of Good and Evil," the "Antitheses of Things," and "Formulae"), concluding with two appendices, on textual criticism and pedagogy.

Bacon's classification of the rational arts, combining faculty psychology on one plane with the conventional curriculum subjects on another, then adding a series of genres or procedures (aphorisms, ciphers) which belong to neither, is a hybrid and certainly original, as we can see from his concluding self-defensive comment: "if I have made the divisions other than those that are received, yet would I not be thought to disallow all those divisions which I do not use" (III, 417). Logic and rhetoric, far from being clearly separated (let alone opposed), appear in one form or another in every section, a realistic recognition of the artificiality of attempts to separate these two complementary arts.

IV THE USES OF RHETORIC

From Bacon's placing of rhetoric within his overall scheme it is obvious that he conceives of it as effective, persuasive discourse, capable of having a decisive effect on human affairs. Indeed, his discussion of rhetoric begins by locating it firmly in the Florentine humanist tradition, with its high valuation of language within the *vita activa*.[29] Moving on to "the Illustration of Tradition" Bacon describes rhetoric as "a science excellent":

For although in true value it is inferior to wisdom, . . . yet with people it is the more mighty, for so Salomon saith . . . ["the wise in heart shall be called prudent, but he that is sweet of speech shall compass greater things"]; signifying that profoundness of wisdom will help a man to a name or admiration, but that it is eloquence that prevaileth in an active life. (III, 409)

This sociopolitical conception of rhetoric's role in the *vita activa* is seen in many places, such as Bacon's recommendation of Demosthenes as the best orator to imitate, "both for the argument he handles, and for that his eloquence is more proper for a statesman than Cicero's" (IX, 25; III, 274). In his early device *Of Tribute* the speaker praising Fortitude celebrates Julius Caesar as combining all the civic virtues:

the bravest soldier, a man of the greatest honour, and one that had the most real and effectual eloquence that ever man had; not a sounding and delightful eloquence, for a continuate speech, but an eloquence of action, an eloquence of affairs, an eloquence that had suppressed a great mutiny by the only word 'Quirites', an eloquence to imprint and work upon any to whom he spake.[30]

It is completely typical of the increasingly great importance attached in the sixteenth and seventeenth centuries[31] to *elocutio*, and above all to the orator's power of *movere*, moving the auditor's feelings, that Bacon should emphasize the unequaled power of Caesar's "real and effectual eloquence" to "imprint and work upon any to whom he spake."

As these passages show, Bacon sometimes used the traditional conception of rhetoric achieving its effect by overpowering the emotions, not considering any other intellectual faculties. Although Plato had developed a three-part model of the soul, other philosophical traditions, especially those invoked by rhetoric, were content to work with the two basic components of the human psyche, reason and the passions. When he uses this two-part model, Bacon shows what might be called ethical realism, readily conceding that an unscrupulous orator can abuse his persuasive skills to evil ends. In the *Colours of Good and Evil* he had frankly acknowledged the adversarial nature of rhetoric, so strongly emphasized in Roman (predominantly legal) rhetoric, as a battle between opposed advocates, declaring that "the persuader's labour is to make things appear good or evil, and that in higher or lower degree" (VII, 77). In that long sequence of *The Advancement of Learning* discussing the passions, when Bacon considers *De cultura animi* and the various ways of "medicining the mind," he holds it essential to know the diseases and infirmities of the mind, which are no other than the perturbations and distempers of the affections. For as the ancient politiques [politicians] in popular estates were wont to compare the people to the sea and the orators to the winds,[32] because as the sea would of itself be calm and quiet if the winds did not move and trouble it, so the people would be peaceable and tractable if the seditious orators did not set them in working and agitation; so it may be fitly said, that the mind in the nature thereof would be temperate and stayed, if the affections, as winds, did not put it into tumult and perturbation. (III, 437; V, 23)

Yet, if rhetoric can be misapplied by "seditious orators," Bacon is quite clear that it can also be used to create or reinforce social harmony. This was a long-established *topos* in the *laus rhetoricae* tradition from Isocrates to the Renaissance and after.[33] One of Bacon's favorite images for his ideal of social harmony was the ancient myth (regularly found in these praises of rhetoric) of Orpheus,[34] taming the beasts with his music. It recurs in *The Advancement of Learning* in a context which significantly links music and rhetoric as typifying the power of knowledge to turn human conflict into concord. Rhetoric, Bacon argues, is a valuable tool for social harmony (as even Plato, otherwise the arch-enemy of rhetoric, conceded in his late work, the *Laws*), but it can also be misused (III, 302).

Bacon's realistic awareness that rhetoric can be used for both good or evil purposes aligns him with Aristotle, who in his *Rhetoric*[35] answered the charges made by Plato in the *Gorgias* that rhetoric was an inherently immoral art, a form of flattery or pandering to the audience's appetites that put it in the same category as cooking.[36] Aristotle's reply was to assert not only that "rhetoric is useful" in everyday life but that it had in fact a positive ethical role, "because things that are true and things that are just have a natural tendency to prevail over their opposites . . ."[37] Similar assertions of the ethical nature of rhetoric can be found throughout the *laus rhetoricae* tradition, its most famous formulation being the elder Cato's definition of the *rhetor* as "vir bonus peritus dicendi," which Quintilian elevated to a quite unreal corollary, that only good men can speak well.[38] (This unfounded idealism can be found in the Renaissance, notably in Thomas Wilson's *Art of Rhetoric* [1553, 1560], in a more extreme form.)[39] Bacon's conception avoids such naïveté, but he agrees with Aristotle in seeing rhetoric as not just neutral but fundamentally ethical. The key element in his discussion, however, is not ethics but psychology. Here again he aligns himself with Aristotle, who discusses ethics in his major work on psychology, the *De anima*. I shall argue that Bacon owes a lot to this book, but that like most Renaissance writers he synthesized classical and postclassical doctrine.

V RHETORIC AND PSYCHOLOGY

De anima, which was required reading for the B.A. course in most universities, is a dense and complex work, from which we only need consider those key passages which, I think, influenced Bacon. In Book 3 Aristotle discusses the "two distinctive peculiarities" of the human soul: "(1) local movement and (2) thinking, understanding, and perceiving."[40] Starting with the intellectual processes, Aristotle attributes to the imagination a status that will surprise anyone who only knows the largely negative view of it found in the Renaissance.[41] Imagination "is that in virtue of which an image arises for us," the primacy of a visual element being justified on etymological grounds: "as sight is the most highly developed sense, the name *phantasia* (imagination) has been formed from *phaos* (light) because it is not possible to see without light."[42] Imagination is, however, an integral part of thought processes, indeed thinking is defined as being "in part imagination, in part judgment," both also depending on sensation.[43] In brief, "the soul never thinks without an image," and imagination exists alongside our "primary thoughts," which "necessarily involve images."[44]

When he takes up the second faculty peculiar to the soul, that of "originating local movement,"[45] Aristotle moves from psychology not to physiology, as one might expect, but to ethics. Such movement, he argues, "is always for an end and is accompanied either by imagination or by appetite."[46] The mode of thought involved in local movement is defined as that "which calculates means to an end, i.e., practical thought,"[47] but it is intimately linked with appetite, for appetite – what we would call desire – like imagination, provides the original stimulus to approach the desired goal. But since "appetite and imagination may be either right or wrong," the object of appetite originating movement "may be either the real or the apparent good."[48] What matters to the appetite, however, is that the good must be one "that can be brought into being by action."[49] Yet precisely here conflicts occur, in human beings, who alone have both a concept of time and a sense of right and wrong:

Since appetites run counter to one another, which happens when a principle of reason and a desire are contrary and is possible only in beings with a sense of time (for while thought bids us hold back because of what is future, desire is influenced by what is just at hand: a pleasant object which is just at hand presents itself as both pleasant and good . . . because of want of foresight into what is farther away in time),

– then appetite, the source of movement, is single, while the forms it takes are many.[50]

Aristotle's discussion of the soul moves freely between psychology and ethics, linking those subjects in a way that was to be followed throughout the Renaissance. But the relative clarity of his exposition became overlaid in time with many other philosophical, medical, and theological traditions.[51] One particularly important influence was from medicine, which frequently claimed Galen as its founder, although the real development of these ideas took place in the medieval Latin tradition, both Arabic and European.[52] This tradition classified three mental faculties, *cogitatio, phantasia* (or *imaginatio*), and *memoria*, locating each in a separate ventricle within the brain, and assigning to each a relative autonomy within its space. This theory was widely disseminated throughout Renaissance psychology, and it figures strongly in Pierre Charron, whose book Bacon certainly knew. Charron grants the imagination both autonomy and an initiating power in a formulation that may have stimulated Bacon:

The imagination is active and stirring, it is it that undertaketh all, and sets all the rest a worke. . . . The imagination first gathereth the kinds and figures of things . . . afterwards it presenteth them, if it will, to the understanding, which considereth of them, examineth, ruminateth, and judgeth; afterwards it puts them to the safe custodie of the memorie . . . .[53]

VI RHETORIC, REASON, AND IMAGINATION

That briefest outline of Aristotelian and faculty psychology was intended to provide the basic background to Bacon. He used psychological models of the mind in order to describe both the way in which rhetoric functions and its fundamentally ethical nature. Particularly well known is Bacon's use of faculty psychology (memory, imagination, and reason) as the basis of his classification of knowledge (III, 329). When he reaches that part of his plan devoted to the knowledge respecting "the Faculties of the Mind of man," Bacon divides it into two kinds; "the one respecting his Understanding and Reason, and the other his Will, Appetite, and Affection; whereof the former produceth Position or Decree, the later Action or Execution" (III, 382). There Bacon clearly distinguishes between the "judicial" process, rational analysis leading to decisions ("Position or decree"), and the "ministerial" process, involving the will. In Renaissance ethics the latter becomes the foundation of moral philosophy, since it controls the process of putting rational decisions into action. Bacon's division leaves imagination in a middle state, able to move in either direction, as required:

It is true that the Imagination is an agent or nuncius [messenger] in both provinces, both the judicial and the ministerial. For Sense sendeth over to Imagination before Reason have judged: and Reason sendeth over to Imagination before the Decree can be acted; for Imagination ever precedeth Voluntary Motion: saving that this Janus of Imagination hath differing faces; for the face towards Reason hath the print of Truth, but the face towards Action hath the print of Good; which nevertheless are . . . [sister-faces]. Neither is the Imagination simply and only a messenger; but is invested with or at leastwise usurpeth no small authority in itself, besides the duty of the message. (III, 382)

That formulation, in which imagination has the crucial pivotal role, owes something to both faculty psychology and to Aristotle. Bacon's category of "Voluntary Motion" – that is, movement governed by the will – grafts a post-Aristotelian concept (credit for the first clear recognition of the will as an autonomous process being given sometimes to St. Augustine, sometimes to Petrarch) onto Aristotle's discussion of "local movement," where, as in Bacon, imagination (and appetite) precede movement.

But Bacon not only individualizes imagination as an autonomous faculty preceding action, he attributes to it from the outset a beneficent capacity. As he writes, "in all persuasions that are wrought by eloquence and other impressions of like nature, which do paint and disguise the true appearance of things, the chief recommendation unto Reason is from the Imagination" (III, 382). While that remark might seem to give imagination an amoral role, as in Aristotle's caveat that the imagination "may be either right or wrong," and so its goals may be either "the real or the apparent [but mistaken] good," for Bacon the two faces of the imagination are both right: that toward Reason is called "Truth," that toward Action is "Good." This beneficent conception of the imagination pervades the whole of Bacon's subsequent discussion of rhetoric, where ethics and psychology again merge:

The duty and office of Rhetoric is *to apply Reason to Imagination* for the better moving of the will. For we see Reason is disturbed in the administration thereof by three means; by Illaqueation or Sophism, which pertains to Logic; by Imagination or Impression, which pertains to Rhetoric; and by Passion or Affection, which pertains to Morality [moral philosophy]. (III, 409)

Most definitions of rhetoric describe the art in general terms, as an *ars bene loquendi*, or – in Melanchthon's formulation – *Eloquentia facultas est sapienter et ornate dicendi*. But Bacon attempts from the outset to describe how rhetoric works. And whereas the standard conception of persuasion as "arousing" or "overcoming" the hearer's passions is all too vague, Bacon's account is much more precise. His definition addresses not only the psychological operation, by which reason is applied to imagination in order to move the will, but also, from the beginning, insists on its ethical nature. Although a more elaborate conception than Aristotle's, Bacon expresses the same realistic acknowledgment that rhetoric, like other good things in life, may be misused. Indeed, by immediately describing the nonfunctioning of the reason when disturbed by the misuse of logic, rhetoric, and moral philosophy, and by conceding, further, that rational purposes can be undermined both externally, "in negotiation with others," and internally, in "negotiation with ourselves," Bacon achieves a tactical victory: For by simply conceding the point that "those powers and arts . . . have force to disturb reason," he at once draws the enemy's fire. Yet if that is the case, then they also possess the opposite, beneficial powers, namely "to establish and advance" reason:

for the end of Logic is to teach a form of argument to secure reason, and not to entrap it; the end of Morality is to procure the affections to obey reason, and not to invade it; the end of Rhetoric is to fill the imagination to second reason, and not to oppress it: for these abuses of arts come in but *ex obliquo*, for caution. (III, 409–10)

That is, he has given an account of "these abuses" obliquely, as cautionary tales.

Bacon's strategy of first conceding the negative point so as to affirm the positive gives him an added impetus with which to defend rhetoric by attacking Plato: "And therefore it was great injustice in Plato . . . to esteem of Rhetoric but as a voluptuary art, resembling it to cookery, that did mar wholesome meats, and help unwholesome by variety of sauces to the pleasure of the taste" (III, 410). Bacon's reply, like Aristotle's, is to embrace a form of ethical optimism by affirming that "speech is much more conversant in adorning that which is good than in colouring that which is evil; for there is no man but speaketh more honestly than he can do or think: and . . . no man can speak fair of courses sordid and base" (III, 410). Where a Quintilian or a Thomas Wilson would make their ethical affirmations categorically, on a yes/no basis (Wilson ends his work with the pious maxim that "the good will not speak evill: and the wicked can not speake wel"), Bacon's more/less model is more cautious, not challenging credibility head-on. Then, turning the tables on Plato by quoting a famous sentence from the *Phaedrus*[54] – a sentence which, in Renaissance Latin editions, is often printed in capital letters, for greater emphasis – Bacon aligns rhetoric squarely with virtue:

And therefore as Plato said elegantly, *That virtue, if she could be seen, would move great love and affection*; so seeing that she cannot be shewed to the Sense by corporal shape, the next degree is to shew her to the Imagination in lively representation: for to shew her to Reason only in subtilty of argument, was a thing ever derided in Chrysippus and many of the Stoics; who thought to thrust virtue upon men by sharp disputations and conclusions, which have no sympathy with the will of man. (III, 410)

Such a use of "sharp disputations," he says in the next paragraph, confuses the procedures of logic, which "handleth reason exact and in truth," with those of rhetoric, which "handleth it as it is planted in popular opinions and manners" (III, 411). This is to reuse Aristotle's distinction, in the *Rhetoric*, between arts that deal with "such things as come . . . within the general ken of all men and belong to no definite science,"[55] and scientific reasoning, a more rigorous process which aims at universal and necessary conclusions. Only where Aristotle had bracketed rhetoric and dialectic together as popular arts, based on *doxa*, as opposed to scientific reasoning, based on *episteme*, by the mid–sixteenth century logic had come to occupy the "scientific category."

This whole discussion is based on a realist acceptance of human nature. If we all naturally practiced rational choice, maximizing the benefits accruing from any course of action by distinguishing real from apparent goods, there would be no need for rhetoric or any other form of persuasion to good ends. But the reason and the will are weak, and both respond to sympathetic treatment better than to mercilessly logical analysis. Here the beneficent role that Bacon ascribes to the imagination is crucial, for it is given the task of censoring out images of vice, selecting only images of virtue, and conveying them in a "lively" – vivid, attractive – representation.

Another part of the human *psyche* that, according to Bacon, needs help from rhetoric is the passions, for

if the affections in themselves were pliant and obedient to reason, it were true there should be no great use of persuasions and insinuations to the will, more than of naked propositions and proofs; but in regard of the continual mutinies and seditions of the affections, –

> Video meliora, proboque;

> Deteriora sequor: –

reason would become captive and servile, if Eloquence of Persuasions did not practise and win the Imagination from the Affection's part, and contract a confederacy between the Reason and Imagination against the Affections. For the affections themselves carry ever an appetite to good, as reason doth; the difference is, *that the affection beholdeth merely the present; reason beholdeth the future and sum of Time;* and therefore the present filling the imagination more, reason is commonly vanquished; but after that force of eloquence and persuasion hath made things future and remote appear as present, then upon the revolt of the imagination reason prevaileth. (III, 410–1)

And so, Bacon concludes his defense of rhetoric from Plato's attacks, "Rhetoric can be no more charged with the colouring of the worse part, than Logic with Sophistry, or Morality with Vice" (III, 411).

In that coherent and vividly imagined sequence it is particularly striking how Bacon uses the autonomous categories of faculty psychology but involves them in constantly shifting interrelationships, according to the emphases of his argument. In the standard traditional inventory of the psychic faculties, above all in the Christian Latin tradition, *ratio* has the supremacy, exercising its powers in a hegemony that alone derives credit for success, blame for failure, in its struggle against the flesh and the passions. In Bacon's account reason is at the mercy of the affections unless other faculties, and – more importantly – the human sciences come to its aid. The "end" or *telos* of the three arts which Bacon evoked, logic, moral philosophy, and rhetoric, the goal which (as Aristotle so often taught) determines their whole mode of existence, is that of aiding reason. Collectively they must exert themselves "to secure reason, and not to entrap it," persuading the affections "to obey reason, and not to invade it," filling the imagination with images of good things so as "to second reason, and not to oppress it." Each of these arts must counter the enemies that reason alone would be powerless to withstand: logic must attack sophism or "Illaqueation" (ensnaring the mind); rhetoric must defend reason from "Imagination or Impression," that is, those images which, without the necessary censorship, can be forcibly "impressed" or imprinted on the mind; while moral philosophy must preserve it from the passions by inculcating the virtues of fortitude, temperance, justice, and prudence. If reason has an unstable role, autonomous but not self-sufficing, imagination's role is also fluid. At one level it is a messenger in both the "judicial" and the "ministerial" provinces, acting as an essential medium between sense-perception and reason on the receptive or epistemological side, and playing an equally vital role in the related outgoing side, the executive process involving reason and the will. Imagination is not just a messenger either, "but is invested or at least usurpeth no small authority in itself," either being given power or seizing it for itself:

For it was well said by Aristotle [*Politics*, I.5; freely adapted], *That the mind hath over the body that commandment, which the lord hath over a bondman; but that reason hath over the imagination that commandment which a magistrate hath over a free citizen;* who may come also to rule in his turn. For we see that in matters of Faith and Religion we raise our Imagination above our Reason; which is the cause why Religion sought ever access to the mind by similitudes, types, parables, visions, dreams. (III, 382)

Yet, although the imagination has this domain of independence and supremacy, and although it is essentially oriented toward both truth and goodness, it, too, would be liable to be overcome by "the continual mutinies and seditions of the affections," if it were not for rhetoric. Reason, Bacon believes, would become a slave to the passions "if

Eloquence of Persuasions did not practise" – by repeated attempts – "and win the Imagination" away from the passions. So this triad of the faculties is in a continuously fluctuating relationship, the key, anchor role being played by rhetoric, for it alone can contract "a confederacy between the Reason and the Imagination against the Affections."

Bacon's account of rhetoric's functioning, then, uses both Aristotelian and faculty psychology in a typically fluid way, moving from one register to another to create a more plausible, precise, and above all dramatic model of the way in which persuasion functions, involved in a constant *psychomachia*, both overt and covert, against the passions. In his theory of rhetoric Bacon is making the best of his privileged position, writing at a time when the medieval model of faculty psychology still had enough general currency and vitality to be viable, yet not forced to accept the frequent corollaries in medieval thought, the imagination's negative value and the depravity of man. Well aware elsewhere of the consequences of the fall of Adam and Eve, Bacon here presents the human psyche in an essentially positive light, untouched by human misery. For not only does he align the imagination with truth and goodness, but the other parts of his fluctuating triad are also beneficent, "for the affections themselves carry ever an appetite to good, as reason doth." That benign conception evidently implies a Renaissance emphasis on the dignity rather than the depravity of man, and we can say of it, as of Bacon's model of rhetoric as a whole, that it could not have been written much before the sixteenth century.

Bacon writes from a privileged position in another sense, for his century was the first that had both the knowledge and the evaluative skills needed to be able to distinguish the genuine work of Aristotle from its postclassical overlay.[56] At several points, I have suggested, Bacon's discussion is truer to Aristotle's *Rhetoric* than to any other source in the rhetorical tradition. But he also knew the *De anima*, and it is significant that when Bacon comes to describe the reason's vulnerability to the assault of the passions he should quote the anguished utterance of Ovid's Medea, "I see the better course, and approve it; I follow the worse."[57] While quoting that celebrated tag he also seems to be recalling Aristotle's account of the two mainsprings of human movement toward a desired object, "appetite and thought (if one may venture to regard imagination as

a kind of thinking; *for many men follow their imagination contrary to knowledge . . .*)," unable to distinguish a real from an apparent good.⁵⁸ *De anima* is certainly in Bacon's mind in the next
sentence, for he quotes it in arguing that while the reason and the
affections both "carry ever an appetite to good" the difference is,
"that *the affection beholdeth merely the present; reason beholdeth
the future and sum of time;* and therefore the present filling the
imagination more, reason is commonly vanquished . . . ." Although
editors dutifully repeat the italicization of that passage, no one
seems to have recognized it as a quotation from this same sequence
in *De anima*, where the conflict within the appetites and between
"a principle of reason and a desire," is said to be only possible in
human beings, who possess "a sense of time (for while thought bids
us hold back because of what is future, desire is influenced by what
is just at hand)."⁵⁹

Bacon exactly follows Aristotle's argument, but with one great difference. Aristotle sees reason as vulnerable to the assaults of desire,
which makes "a pleasant object . . . just at hand" seem good now, only
because desire lacks "foresight into what is farther away in time" –
when, presumably, the difference between real and apparent good will
become tangible, not without pain. In this process reason is alone, and
stands or falls accordingly: but in Bacon rhetoric comes to the rescue.
Its role being, as he put it earlier, to "fill the imagination to second
reason," in this inverted state of affairs, with "the present" – that is,
immediate sense-gratification – "filling the imagination, reason is
commonly vanquished . . . ." But "after that force of eloquence and
persuasion hath made things future and remote" – that is, the real
good which desire, lacking foresight, does not know – "appear as present, then upon the revolt [turning around] of the imagination reason
prevaileth."

In this way Bacon's description of rhetoric fuses ethics and psychology, the Aristotelian and the Galenic traditions, into a triumphant
unity, a model of persuasion that has considerable explanatory power.
And far from Bacon conceiving rhetoric as having simply a cognitive
function (as Howell claimed), or a purely ornamental function, with
logic governing the mind's "ratiocinative capacity" (as Jardine
claimed), reason plays a major role throughout, aided and supported
by the force of "Eloquence of Persuasions," that art best able to insinuate into the will of man a preference for real, not apparent, goods. As

Bacon describes it in another striking phrase, "the subject of Rhetoric" is "Imaginative or Insinuative Reason" (III, 383).

VII *RES* AND *VERBA*

Bacon's involvement with rhetoric is part of a larger concern with language, which takes several forms. One of these derives from Roman rhetoric, the tendency to divide all human utterance into the two categories of *res* (subject matter) and *verba* (language or style), with the almost invariable emphasis on the primacy of *res*. Although classical and Renaissance rhetoricians spent most of their time theorizing about or dealing in *verba*, they would almost all accept the injunction of the elder Cato, *rem tene, verba sequentur* ("Look after the subject-matter and the words will look after themselves").[60] That is, writers ought to achieve a functional balance between argument and its verbal form, above all not allowing words to proliferate at the expense of sense. Bacon expressed this caveat many times, as in his laconic observation that "words and discourse aboundeth most where there is idleness and want" (III, 451). In particular, it explains his desire that all the "partitions of knowledge" he had suggested should be "accepted rather for lines and veins, than for sections and separations," lest one should destroy "the continuance and entireness of knowledge," that "common fountain" from which all are "nourished and maintained." Failure to preserve these links "hath made particular sciences to become barren, shallow, and erroneous," as "Cicero the orator complained of Socrates and his school, that he was the first that separated philosophy and rhetoric; whereupon rhetoric became an empty and verbal art" (III, 366–7; III, 228). A similar split between subject matter and style provoked Bacon's devastating account, in *The Advancement of Learning*, of the perversion of discourse brought about in sixteenth-century Latin writings by the cult of Ciceronianism. (Bacon is not attacking humanism, as some scholars think.[61]) In this period admirers of Cicero, who reached the sycophantic excess of only ever using words and word forms authenticated by the master, developed an obsessive concern for eloquence and copiousness, which

grew speedily to an excess; for men began to hunt more after words than matter; and more after the choiceness of the phrase, and the round and clean compositon of the sentence, and the sweet falling of the clauses, and the varying and illustration of their works with tropes and figures, than after the weight of matter, worth of subject, soundness of argument, life of invention, or depth of judgment. (III, 283)

Those five concluding clauses not only sum up Bacon's view of a writer's proper priorities, but by their pithiness of expression enact a reproach to the inflated style of the first half of the sentence. The priority of *res* over *verba* was an unshakeable principle for Bacon: "substance of matter is better than beauty of words" (III, 285), so that it is a true

distemper [disorder] of learning, when men study words and not matter . . . It seems to me that Pygmalion's frenzy is a good emblem or portraiture of this vanity; for words are but the images of matter; and except they have life of reason and invention, to fall in love with them is all one as to fall in love with a picture. (III, 284)

Rawley, his chaplain and secretary, recorded that Bacon "would often ask if the meaning were expressed plainly enough, as being one that accounted words to be but subservient or ministerial to matter" (I, 11). As he himself wrote in 1596, "the true end of knowledge is clearness and strength of judgment, and not ostentation or ability to discourse . . ." (IX, 14).

Since the distinction between *res* and *verba* could be made so clearly, for Bacon it was axiomatic that in some situations subject matter should be transmitted without any attention to words – at least not in the rhetorical sense of skillfully arranging them for persuasive effects. In his *Parasceve* or "Preliminary ritual" to a *Description of a Natural and Experimental History, such as may serve for the foundation of a true philosophy* (IV, 251), Bacon outlined this important branch of his project for the renewal of science, which would consist of direct observations of the natural world, set down without any art. He advised future writers of natural history "not to consult the pleasure of the reader, no nor even that utility which may be derived immediately from their narrations; but to seek out and gather together such store and variety of things as may suffice for the formation of true axioms" (IV,254). They must take their material from direct observation, not from ancient authors, nor get involved in controversies over textual readings or anything purely philological.

And for all that concerns ornaments of speech, similitudes, treasury of eloquence, and such like emptinesses, let it be utterly dismissed. Also let all those things which are admitted be themselves set down briefly and concisely, so that they may be nothing less than words. For no man who is collecting and storing up materials for ship-building or the like, thinks of arranging them elegantly, as in a shop, and displaying them so as to please the eye; all his care is that they be sound and good, and that they be so arranged as to take up as little room as possible in the warehouse. (IV, 254–5)

Some commentators on Bacon have misunderstood this passage as proof that he rejected rhetoric, but of course he did not, nor did the many scientists later in the seventeenth century who were inspired by his call for reform.[62] In fact, his remarks in the *Parasceve* conform exactly to one of the basic principles in rhetoric, decorum, the need for an appropriate adjustment of utterance to subject matter.

We must be quite clear what Bacon is saying here. He is not affirming that natural philosophy, or any other kind, should never use rhetoric. Indeed, he explicitly says the opposite: "it is a thing not hastily to be condemned, to clothe and adorn the obscurity even of philosophy itself with sensible and plausible elocution. For hereof we have great examples in Xenophon, Cicero, Seneca, Plutarch, and of Plato also in some degree . . ." (III, 284). Beyond a certain point, though, eloquence can be "some hinderance" to "the severe inquisition of truth, and the deep progress into philosophy . . . because it is too early satisfactory to the mind of man, and quencheth the desire of farther search. . . ." In such cases progress is more likely to be made by using aphorisms and axioms, discrete observations which can be submitted to enquiry in a properly worked-out induction. Rhetoric as a whole has its limits, then. But one procedure within rhetoric has a larger and fundamental application within all the sciences, namely analogical reasoning, which can open up parts that other approaches cannot reach.[63] As Bacon puts it in *The Advancement of Learning*, "it is a rule, *That whatsoever science is not consonant to presuppositions, must pray in aid of similitudes*" (III, 407, 218).

Like all rhetoricians, Bacon takes it for granted that the same idea can be expressed in many different ways. The flexibility and, as far as we know, infinite malleability of language carries with it, however, certain potential disadvantages for philosophers and scientists wishing to describe the real world. This problem, so familiar in twentieth-century philosophy, was addressed by Plato long ago, in the *Cratylus*, where Socrates establishes the primacy of physical reality over language, mocking anyone "who follows names in the search after things,"[64] and asserting the crucial principle "that the knowledge of things is not to be derived from names. No, they must be studied and investigated in themselves."[65] The conclusion is decisive: "no man of sense will like to put himself or the education of his mind in the power of names. Neither will he so far trust names or the givers of names as to be confident in any knowledge which condemns himself and other existences to an unhealthy state of unreality . . . ."[66] The fruits of the *Cratylus*, that subtle and much misinterpreted dialogue, were culled by Aristotle in *De interpretatione*,[67] and Bacon partially quotes Aristotle's formulation in *The Advancement of Learning*: "for Aristotle saith well, 'Words are the images of cogitations, and letters are the images of words' " (III, 399). Bacon's awareness that language and reality exist on independent planes made him particularly conscious of the possible inadequacies of language. Although we have no hard evidence that he had read the *Cratylus* (but equally, none to the contrary), a Socratic skepticism about language as a reliable medium for the knowledge of reality pervades many of his critical remarks on the deficiency of natural philosophy as commonly practiced. Scholastic logic, for instance, so dependent on the syllogism, is a fundamentally unsuitable instrument of enquiry. Of its many unsatisfactory features, the most serious is its reliance on purely verbal procedures. These may satisfy "sciences popular," or even provide a "satisfactory reason" in natural philosophy – "satisfactory" in the ironic sense that Bacon often gives it, as "satisfying to superficial enquirers" – "but the subtilty of nature and operations will not be enchained in those bonds: for Arguments consist of Propositions, and Propositions of Words; and Words are but the current tokens or marks of Popular Notions of things; which notions, if they be grossly and variably [crudely and unsystematically] collected out of particulars," no amount of verbal enquiry can ever correct such basic errors (III, 388; IV, 411; IV, 24, 49). In that critique, one might say, Bacon uses Aristotelian linguistic categories to make a Platonic warning about the inadequacies of a science supposedly of reality but actually deriving from language.

From this perspective, which puts physical reality on the primary, language on the secondary level, the limitations of rhetoric for the goals of natural pilosophy are evident. Although Bacon shows great respect for *inventio*, the initial process in rhetorical composition, allotting it the most space in his account of rhetorical theory,[68] when he comes to discuss the "Art of Inquiry or Invention" he dismisses it as irrelevant:

Invention is of two kinds, much differing; the one, of Arts and Sciences; and the other, of Speech and Arguments. The former of these I do report deficient; which seemeth to me to be such a deficience as if in the making of an inventory touching the estate of a defunct it should be set down *that there is no ready money*. For as money will fetch all other commodities, so this knowledge is that which should purchase all the rest. (III, 384)

An important part of Bacon's methodological reforms was designed to remedy this lack of any "invention of sciences." As to rhetorical *inventio*, it taught how to find appropriate arguments for the case at issue, but was unable to discover new knowledge.

Bacon's skepticism about language as an adequate medium for the apprehension of reality may derive, as I have suggested, from Plato, who of course expressed more fundamental doubts about the value of visible phenomena as against the realm of forms. But Bacon may have also known the more systematic skepticism of Sextus Empiricus, whose *Outlines of Pyrrhonism* was introduced to the Renaissance in 1562, through the Latin translation by Henry Estienne.[69] Bacon's own warnings about the unreliability of language in philosophy reached their most powerful formulation in his doctrine of the *eidola* (delusions, fallacies) to which the human intellect is naturally subject. In his first published account, in *The Advancement of Learning*, they are three in number, the third (subsequently called "the Idols of the Market-place") including

the false appearances that are imposed upon us by words, which are framed and applied according to the conceit and capacities of the vulgar sort: and although we think we govern our words, . . . yet certain it is that words, as a Tartar's bow, do shoot back upon the understanding of the wisest, and mightily entangle and pervert the judgment; so as it is almost necessary in all controversies and disputations to imitate the wisdom of the Mathematicians, in setting down in the very beginning the definitions of our words and terms, that others may know how we accept and understand them, and whether they concur with us or no. For it cometh to pass for want of this, that we are sure to end there where we ought to have begun, which is in questions and differences about words. (III, 396–7; also IV, 433–4, expanded)

Sensible though that remedy may appear, Bacon came to see that it merely perpetuated the disease. In the *Novum organum*, published some fifteen years later, he added: "Yet even definitions cannot cure this evil in dealing with natural and material things; since the definitions themselves consist of words, and those words beget others: so that it is necessary to recur to individual instances, and those in due series and order" (IV, 61).

It is significant that on the numerous occasions when Bacon described the final perfection of his scheme of natural philosophy, at some far-off future time, he regularly used the metaphor of a marriage to symbolize the establishing of a lasting new arrangement. But he never looked forward to the marriage of words and things. Rather, at this millennial point, the mind of man should be able to commune directly with those "natural and material things." As he wrote in the "Plan of the Work," prefixed to the torso of his *Great Instauration* (1620),

the true relation between the nature of things and the nature of the mind, is as the strewing and decoration of the bridal chamber of the Mind and the Universe, the Divine Goodness assisting; out of which marriage let us hope (and be this the prayer of the bridal song) there may spring helps to man, and a line and race of inventions that may in some degree subdue and overcome the necessities and miseries of humanity. (IV, 27)

For all the importance he attached to rhetoric in the active life, and for all the enormous impact that he had on succeeding ages, due in great part to his mastery of language, in the last resort Bacon did not place his greatest hope in words.

NOTES

1 See McNamee 1950, Harrison 1957, Cogan 1981.
2 Vickers 1981, Vickers 1991b.
3 Howell 1956, pp. 371–5.
4 Howell 1956, pp. 385–8.
5 See, e.g., Vickers 1968b, chs. 4 and 7, "Syntactical Symmetry," and "Literary Revisions."
6 See also Jardine 1974b, which gives more detail of recommended texts in logic and rhetoric, partly from statutes and partly from surviving booklists. Jardine, however, used this material to reiterate her valuation of dialectic over and against rhetoric, commenting on "the frequency with

which dialectic manuals (and not rhetoric manuals) occur" in these lists (p. 46). A footnote qualifies this absolute negation, recording that the lists she has looked at contain "five times as many dialectic handbooks as rhetoric handbooks" (p. 46 n.38). Yet, as is well known, students had studied rhetoric at school, but were approaching dialectic for the first time at university, and therefore needed more help. Not surprisingly, the lists that Jardine quotes include many of the standard works on rhetoric by Cicero, Aphthonius, Erasmus, Mosellanus, etc. At all events, it seems unhistorical to try to over-value logic at the expense of rhetoric.

7 Jardine 1974a, pp. 13, 25–6, 73, 262.

8 See, e.g., Vasoli 1968, Heath 1971.

9 Jardine 1974a, pp. 2, 12.

10 Jardine 1974a, p. 27.

11 Holdsworth, "Directions for a Student in the Universitie," cited in Curtis 1959, p. 110. For a complete transcript of Holdsworth's work, and for the best study of the Cambridge curriculum so far (unaccountably ignored by Jardine) see Fletcher 1956 II, with the "Directions" printed as an appendix, pp. 623ff.

12 Jardine 1974a, p. 14.

13 Jardine 1974a, p. 216; my italics.

14 Jardine 1974a, p. 219.

15 Jardine 1974a, pp. 88–96.

16 Jardine 1974a, pp 218 n., 216, 218.

17 Jardine 1974a, pp. 217–18.

18 *The Advancement of Learning*, ed. W. Aldis Wright (2nd ed., Oxford, 1880), p. 294, citing Cicero, *De oratore*, II.lxiii.255, and Quintilian, *Institutio oratoria*, VI.iii.24. Cicero classified this effect as one of the forms taken by verbal wit, "exemplified when we are expecting to hear a particular phrase, and something different is uttered." The correct name for this device is *para prosodokian*, as Anton Leeman and Harm Pinkster point out in their commentary (*De oratore libri III*, [Heidelberg, 1989], III, pp. 273–4), noting that Cicero uses it here as an example of ambiguity caused by misplaced sense order, and that he subsequently repeats his praise of it as a source of laughter: "of all these devices nothing causes more amusement than an unexpected turn" (II.lxiii.284), for "what excites laughter is disappointing expectations" (II.lxiii.289).

19 *The Arte of English Poesie*, ed. D. Willcock and A. Walker (Cambridge, 1936, 1970), pp. 139–40. First printed in 1592, this treatise evidently dates from 10 to 15 years earlier. I have regularized spelling throughout for the long 's', u/v.

20 See the *Dictionary of National Biography*, I, pp. 795–6; also McIntosh 1975, Tittler 1976.

21 See Heltzel 1948. Martin 1992, not knowing Heltzel's article, declares that "we know almost no details of the schooling [Bacon] received in his father's house. . . . He learned Latin grammar . . . and other primary school accomplishments. . . . Who tutored him is uncertain. . . ." But if he went up to Cambridge this meant that he had already received the equivalent of a grammar-school education from his tutors, as did other contemporaries, such as Donne. The context of Bacon's education has been recreated with a superior grasp of historical detail by Levine 1987, pp. 123–54.

22 Baldwin 1944.

23 Whitgift's accounts were first printed by Maitland 1847/1848, listing Anthony and Francis Bacon's expenses between 5 April 1573 and Christmas 1575. W. Aldis Wright cited these documents in his edition of *The Advancement of Learning* (2nd ed., Oxford, 1880, pp. iv–v), but they escaped the attention of most Bacon scholars till now, including Martin 1992. Lisa Jardine refers to them in Jardine 1974b, pp. 44–5 and note 34, quoting the titles on dialectic, but silently ignoring those on rhetoric. For a more accessible edition see now Gaskell 1979.

24 See, e.g., Vickers 1968b, pp. 39–46, 271–3; Schoeck 1953. Sir Thomas Elyot, writing in 1531, pointed out that ". . . in the lernyng of the lawes of this realme, there is at this daye an exercise, wherin is a maner, a shadowe, or figure of the auncient rhetorike. I meane the pleadyng used in courts and Chauncery called motes; where fyrst a case is appoynted to be moted by certayne yonge men, contaynyng some doubtefull controversie, which is in stede of the heed of a declamation called *thema*. The case beinge knowen, they whiche be appoynted to mote, do examine the case, and investigate what they therin can espie, which may make a contention, wherof may ryse a question to be argued . . . ," *The Governor*, ed. H. H. S. Croft, 2 vols. (London, 1883), I, 148–9.

25 See the Letter to Lancelot Andrewes (XIV, 371–4), included, with commentary, in Brian Vickers (ed.), *Francis Bacon*, in the "Oxford Authors" series (Oxford, 1996).

26 On their rhetorical structure see Vickers 1968b, pp. 46–51. Other studies of Bacon's speeches include Hannah 1926, Wallace 1957, and Wallace 1971.

27 Bacon shared this opinion with other Renaissance humanists, notably Vives, see Vives, *De ratione dicendi* [1533], *Praefatio*, in *Opera omnia*, ed. G. M. y Siscar, 8 vols. (Valencia, 1782–90; repr. London, 1964), II, pp. 91–2; tr. J. F. Cooney, "*De Ratione Dicendi*: A Treatise on Rhetoric by Juan Luis Vives," Ph.D. Diss., Ohio State University, 1966, p. 24; *John Rainolds's Oxford Lectures on Aristotle's "Rhetoric"*, ed. L. D. Green (Newark, 1986), pp. 98–9.

28 Monfasani 1988, p. 201. It is hard to see how, after this, Jardine can state that, for Bacon, "dialectic and rhetoric are both social, conventional arts, and in the last resort parasitic activities" (Jardine 1974a, p. 170).

29 See Garin 1965, Gray 1963, Monfasani 1988, Vickers 1988a. For a discussion of Bacon's fusion of the Christian concept of charity with the classical ethos of the *vita activa* see Vickers, 1984b.

30 Quoted from the newly edited text in Brian Vickers (ed.), *Francis Bacon* (Oxford, 1996). For the significance of Caesar's use of the word *Quirites* see Bacon's fuller account in *The Advancement of Learning* (III, 312).

31 Cf. Vickers 1988a, pp. 279–86, 345–7, 356–9, 368–72.

32 Cicero, *Pro Cluentio*, 49.

33 *Pro Cluentio*, 9–11, 155–9.

34 Cf. Vickers 1971, at pp. 215–16.

35 Vickers 1988a, pp. 160–3.

36 Vickers 1988a, pp. 84–120.

37 Aristotle, *Rhetoric*, 1355a 21ff. All quotations from Aristotle are from *The Complete Works of Aristotle. The Revised Oxford Translation*, ed. Jonathan Barnes, 2 vols. (Princeton, 1984).

38 *Institutes of Oratory*, Book 12.

39 Cf. Vickers 1983.

40 *De anima*, 427c17ff.

41 See, e.g., Pico della Mirandola, *On the Imagination*, ed. H. Caplan (New Haven, Conn., 1930), especially ch. 7, "On the numerous Evils which come from the Imagination"; Rossky 1958.

42 *De anima*, 428a1, 429a3.

43 Ibid., 427b15, 28.

44 Ibid., 432a10ff.

45 Ibid., 432a15ff.

46 Ibid., 432b15f.

47 Ibid., 432b13f.

48 Ibid., 432b26ff.

49 Ibid., 432b28ff.

50 Ibid., 433b5–12.

51 For a valuable up-to-date survey of this vast tradition see Park and Kessler 1988, Kessler 1988, Park 1988.

52 See, e.g., Harvey 1975, pp. 35–6 (Galen), 10–12 (Razes), 15–19 (Haly Abbas), 22–7 (Avicenna). Despite its title, this work has very little on the Renaissance. See also Klibansky, Panofsky, and Saxl 1964, pp. 66–7, on the dissemination of the triple categorization of mental faculties (imagination, reason, memory) in the Middle Ages, and p. 67 n.5 on its ultimate source (if undeveloped) in Galen. A thorough recent study by Grazia Tonelli Olivieri (1991) has shown Bacon's general debt to both

the Aristotelian psychological tradition and to the medical tradition deriving from Galen and his fourth-century commentator, Nemesius Emesenus. However, she has failed to find any direct source for Bacon's classification, concluding that "Bacon was the first author ever to group the arts and sciences according to the three faculties of the soul," p. 71.

53 Pierre Charron, *De la sagesse*, 1601, English trans. S. Lennard (London, n.d.; before 1612), p. 50. In *The Advancement of Learning* Bacon quotes from Charron in discussing the wisdom of the serpent (III, 430–1).

54 *Phaedrus*, 265C. All quotations from Plato are from *Plato. The Collected Dialogues*, trans. Benjamin Jowett, ed. E. Hamilton and H. Cairns (rev. ed. N.Y., 1963).

55 Aristotle, *Rhetoric*, 1354a1ff.

56 Cf. Park and Kessler 1988, pp. 460, 479, 516–17.

57 *Metamorphoses*, vii.20.

58 *De anima*, 433a9ff., my italics; 433a26ff.

59 Ibid., 433b5ff.

60 Cf. Howell 1946.

61 This error has been made by Bush 1962, p. 276; Webster 1975, p. 105; Quinton 1980, pp. 13, 23, among others.

62 See Vickers 1985, at pp. 26–41.

63 Cf. Pérez-Ramos 1988, pp. 259–62, 292–3. On this outstanding study see my essay, Vickers 1992, pp. 501, 507–8, 510–18.

64 *Cratylus*, 438B-C.

65 Ibid., 438E-439B.

66 Ibid., 440D.

67 *De interpretatione*, 1–2.16a2–28.

68 Wallace 1943, pp. 51–85, 176–7, 180–1, 205–7.

69 See Grendler 1988, pp. 38–9; Copenhaver 1988a, p. 80; Kristeller 1988, p. 120; Park and Kessler 1988, p. 460; Popkin 1988, pp. 679–84. Commenting on Book 1 of *The Advancement of Learning* (III, 292) Wolff denied that Bacon knew Sextus (Wolff 1910, I, pp. 243–4). Commenting on later passages in Book 2, however (III, 387, 388), Michèle Le Doeuff affirmed the contrary (Le Doeuff 1991, p. 340).

9   Bacon and history[1]

I INTRODUCTION

In the *De augmentis*, Bacon divides the kinds of learning into three primary categories – history, poetry, and philosophy – which correspond to the three faculties of the rational soul – memory, imagination, and reason. He then divides history into two kinds – civil and natural – each of which is further subdivided into subcategories (IV, 292–300). History is not only given a very wide domain in Bacon's division of knowledges, but because he identifies *historia* with *experientia*, its role in his inductive philosophy is also fundamental: of the reconstruction of the sciences, he claims, "the foundation must be laid in natural history" (IV, 28). As for civil history, Bacon claims that its "dignity and authority are pre-eminent among human writings. For to its fidelity are entrusted the examples of our ancestors, the vicissitudes of things, the foundations of civil policy, and the name and reputation of men" (IV, 302).

I shall be primarily concerned with Bacon's theory and practice of civil history. His theory of history is presented in *The Advancement of Learning* and the *De augmentis*, and he also wrote, or started to write, a number of historical works, the most important of which, because it is the only extended history that he completed, is his *History of the Reign of King Henry VII*. I shall argue that this history needs to be understood in the context of the classical and Renaissance understanding of history as a rhetorical genre.[2] Within this context, I shall argue that Bacon is conventionally humanist in his approach to the writing of history, except that, like other later humanists, such as Guicciardini, he tends to shift his emphasis from a praise of virtue to a more acute awareness of the vicissitudes of

232

fortune. My argument thus stands in contrast to scholars such as Fussner, who argues that "Bacon's programme represented a radical break from both the humanistic and scholastic traditions," and Dean, who argues that "Bacon is in sympathy with Machiavelli and his classical models – Tacitus, Polybius, and Thucydides – and is like them opposed to the rhetorical and moralistic conception of history writing."[3] Sympathy with Machiavelli or Tacitus would not make Bacon either antirhetorical or antihumanist. The humanists of the Renaissance, according to Kristeller, were students or teachers of the humanities – history, rhetoric, poetry, grammar, and moral/ political philosophy – which they modeled on the texts of classical rhetorical culture.[4] Tacitus, one of the foremost orators of his day, was an obvious rhetorical model for the humanists; and Machiavelli, the Florentine poet, historian, and moral/political philosopher who exhorted his contemporaries to study the examples of the ancients, was a classic humanist. In what follows, I shall begin by describing briefly Bacon's theory of the divisions and uses of history, and I shall then locate his practice of writing history beside some important approaches to history writing that were current in the late Renaissance.

II BACON'S GENRES OF HISTORY

Bacon's theory of civil history consists largely of a division and subdivision of genres. In *The Advancement of Learning*, he dealt only with a relatively narrow definition of civil history, but in the *De augmentis*, while he retained his original discussion under the title of civil history proper, he expanded the general category of civil history to include ecclesiastical history and a new proposal for a history of learning. The history of learning, which strongly resembles the history of arts that he proposed as one of the subdivisions of natural history, is his most novel contribution: it would examine the antiquity, progress, and migration of different kinds of learning, and the conditions under which they flourish and decline (IV, 300–1). As for ecclesiastical history, Bacon's brief discussion consists of a further subdivision into ecclesiastical history proper, which "describes the times of the Church Militant," and in which he finds "no deficiency, but rather superfluities"; the history of prophecy, in which "every prophecy of Scripture [ought to] be sorted with the event fulfilling the same"; and the history of providence, which records the manifest fulfillments of God's will, especially in recent judgments and deliverances (IV, 312–13).

Bacon's discussion of civil history proper is more elaborate. He first divides it into memorials (which are bare records of persons and acts), perfect history, and antiquities (which consist of the laborious recovery of lost fragments of the past). Bacon dismisses memorials and antiquities quickly, in order to turn his attention to perfect history, which he subdivides into chronicles (which are histories of times), lives (which are of single persons), and relations (which are narratives of particular actions). He claims that there is a deficiency of all three forms of perfect history dealing with British affairs. In *The Advancement of Learning* and again in the *De augmentis*, he presents a brief sketch of English history from the Union of the Roses to illustrate how valuable a particular history of times dealing specifically with England would be (IV, 304–8; III, 336).

In general, however, Bacon is critical of history of times, and claims that while lives excel "in profit and examples" and relations excel "in verity and sincerity," chronicles of times excel only "in estimation and glory" (IV, 304). He further subdivides histories of times into universal and particular, and into annals and journals. He is particularly critical of universal histories (which record "the history of the world from the beginning") because of their necessary inattention to detail, and somewhat less censorious of journals, which indiscriminately record every passing detail. By implication, his preference is for an annalistic narrative of a particular time – one that "contains the deeds of some kingdom, commonwealth, or people" – such as his proposed history of England from the Union of the Roses (IV, 308–10).

There is very little that is original in this discussion of civil history proper: Bacon's examples are all classical and his main contribution lies in his advocacy of a history of recent English affairs. He does, however, add two codas that reflect more recent developments. In the first, he distinguishes pure from mixed histories, of which he gives two instances: "ruminated history," which contains disconnected narratives accompanied by politic observations (the reference to Machiavelli is unstated but unmistakable); and history of cosmography, which must have been inspired by recent voyages of discovery. In the second, he distinguishes the history of men's actions from the recording of their words, which consist of orations, letters, and apothegms (IV, 310–14). He places particular emphasis on the value of letters in a way that reflects the priorities of the humanists, who were primarily letter writers.[5]

Bacon's own earliest writing in the field of civil history is probably his fragmentary *History of the Reign of K. Henry the Eighth, K. Edward, Q. Mary, and Part of the Reign of Q. Elizabeth*, which appears to date from Elizabeth's own reign, though it may also be related to a project to honor her memory that he proposed around 1605 (VI, 17–22).[6] Despite its title, it contains only an introduction and a preliminary sketch of Henry VII. Bacon later honored Elizabeth's memory with a much shorter historical memorial of the queen which dates from around 1608 (VI, 283–318). This memorial appears to be the first historical work that he actually completed. Meanwhile, in *The Advancement of Learning* of 1605, he presented his sketch for what he claimed was a much-needed history of England "from the Uniting of the Roses to the Uniting of the Kingdoms" (III, 336) – a history that would begin with James's ancestor, Henry VII, rather than with Elizabeth's father. By 1610 Bacon had sent the opening pages of just such a *History of Great Britain* to the king, though in fact they contain little more than a prefatory discussion of James's succession (VI, 273–9).

But Bacon did not forget the project. After his fall from political power, the first work he completed was a *History of the Reign of King Henry VII*, a fair copy of which was sent to James before the end of 1621. It was printed early the following year with a dedicatory epistle to Prince Charles. At Charles's request, Bacon also started work on a history of Henry VIII, which would have followed his original plan to write the history of Britain down to James's reign, but he only managed to complete a brief introduction (VI, 269–70).

Bacon's *History of Henry VII*, his major completed history, is particularly interesting in the context of his theory of the genres of history because it does not conform exclusively to any of his categories. His proposal for a history of England was an example of a particular history of times, but rather than write it as a continuous history of "some kingdom, Commonwealth, or people," he turned to a life of Henry VII from the time of his accession, and started work on the life of his successor. Furthermore, though he apparently set out to write his history in the framework of an annal, proceeding year by year through Henry's reign, this framework was confused by his tendency to arrange the history around a series of major events in the reign, as though it were also to some extent a connected string of relations of particular actions. His history is therefore a kind of hybrid combination of a history of times, a life, and a collection of relations. What ties the whole work together, however, is Bacon's focus on Henry himself in the circumstances of his fortune. As Bacon observes in his dedicatory epistle, he has "endeavoured to do honour to the memory of the last King of England that was ancestor to the King your father and yourself" (VI, 25). The history is above all a memorial life of the king himself, which is necessarily combined with a history of his times and a relation of the major events of his reign.

III   THE USES OF HISTORY

Apart from distinguishing the genres of history, Bacon, like other humanists of the Renaissance, was most insistent that history should be useful.[7] When he observes that to civil history are entrusted "the examples of our ancestors, the vicissitudes of things, the foundations of civil policy, and the name and reputation of men," he appears to envisage three main uses of history. The first, and one of the most common functions of history for the humanists, was to provide a storehouse of examples that could be used in argument as models for imitation or avoidance. As a practical politician, Bacon regularly used "the examples of our ancestors" to support arguments and even to provide consolation, in a way that had been familiar in humanist writings since Petrarch. In his speech for general naturalization, for instance, he raises examples to support his case with the argument that "the time past is a pattern of the time to come" (X, 311; cf. X, 319; VII, 407); in his speech on taking his seat in chancery, he alludes wryly to his predecessor "of whom I learn much to imitate, and somewhat to avoid" (XIII, 189); and in a letter to Lancelot Andrewes, he observes that "amongst consolation, it is not the least to represent to a man's self like examples of calamity in others. For examples give a quicker impression than arguments" (XIV, 371).

In the *De augmentis*, however, Bacon distinguishes between two ways of using examples, and is relatively critical of "examples alleged for the sake of the discourse, [which] are cited succinctly and without particularity, and like slaves only wait upon the demands of discourse." By contrast, "when the example is laid down as the ground of the discourse, it is set down with all the attendant circumstances, which may sometimes correct the discourse thereupon made, and sometimes supply it, as a very pattern for imitation and practice." He takes the opportunity to praise Machiavelli for the way he bases his observations upon history, rather than merely cite examples to prove a point (V, 56). This is the second use of history, not simply as a storehouse of argumentative examples, but as a ground for inductive discourse. As with his natural philosophy, however, Bacon insists on separating history itself from the discourse based upon it: Machiavelli's discourses upon history are distinguished from "perfect history" in which, "though every wise history is pregnant (as it were) with political precepts and warnings, yet the writer himself should not play the midwife" (IV, 311).

In Bacon's philosophy, natural history has two uses, "either for the sake of the knowledge of the things themselves that are committed to the history, or as the primary matter of philosophy." Its second use makes it "the stuff and material of a solid and lawful Induction, and may be called the nursing-mother of philosophy" (IV, 298). He also argues that the usefulness of a history of learning would be that it would "very greatly assist the wisdom and skill of learned men in the use and administration of learning; that it would exhibit the movements and perturbations, the virtues and vices, which take place no less in intellectual than in civil matters; and that from the observation of these the best system of government might be derived and established" (IV, 301). By analogy, it would appear that Bacon should also view civil history as the foundation of civil philosophy.[8] He divides civil knowledge into conversation, negotiation, and government, and further subdivides negotiation into the doctrines concerning scattered occasions and advancement in life. Machiavelli's discourses on history are presented as an exemplary model of the use of history for the doctrines of scattered occasions (V, 56). As for the grander subject of government, Bacon, loyal servant to the crown that he was, tactfully remained silent about its divisions (V, 31–2, 78). Both history's record of the "vicissitudes of things" and its "foundations of civil policy," therefore, appear to be used more as material for scattered precepts than as the ground for a systematic political philosophy.

There is little doubt that Bacon wrote his history of Henry's reign in such a way that scattered observations about the nature of politics in general – and about James's reign in particular – could easily be induced from it. In his essay "Of nobility," for instance, Bacon observes that "for their nobles, . . . to depress them, may make a king more absolute, but less safe . . . I have noted it in my History of King Henry the Seventh of England, who depressed his nobility; whereupon it came to pass that his times were full of difficulties and troubles" (VI, 422).

Even more pointed is the emphasis he gives to the issue of succession. To write a history of Henry VII was in itself to draw attention to the ancestry that legitimated James's succession, and this may be the reason why he did not proceed with his history of Henry VIII, despite promptings from Charles: it could only obscure, rather than highlight, the title of the king whose favor he wanted to regain. But there was also a parallel between James and Henry VII: both were kings who interrupted the line of straight succession. Of his early draft of a *History of Great Britain*, Bacon only managed to complete a preface which gathers together as many arguments as Bacon could find for the legitimacy of James's succession (VI, 275–9). It is therefore striking that, at the beginning of his *History of Henry VII*, the first "point of great difficulty and knotty to solve" that confronts the king is that "there were fallen to his lot, and concurrent in his person, three several titles to the imperial crown." Henry resolves to rely on only one of these titles (the claim of the House of Lancaster), and Bacon notes that this decision "did spin him a thread of many seditions and troubles" (VI, 29–31). The lesson for James and his son is clear, that they should take equal advantage of all the titles to the crown that they could lay claim to – titles which Bacon had enumerated earlier in his draft of the *History of Great Britain*.

One of the uses of civil history, then, which is analogous to one of the uses of natural history, is to serve as material from which can be induced the precepts of civil knowledge. For this function, history needs to be both detailed and accurate. Bacon's main criticisms of the history of times are that it "omits and covers up in silence the smaller passages and motions of men and manners," and that it "is sure to meet with many gaps in the records, and to contain empty spaces which must be filled up and supplied at pleasure by wit and conjecture." By comparison, lives "contain a more lively and faithful representation of things," and relations of actions "cannot but be more purely and exactly true" than histories of times (IV, 304–5). Since detail and accuracy are also crucial for natural history (IV, 26, 109, 297), Bacon's criteria for both natural and civil history are to some extent parallel.

The model of Bacon's natural history is important in this regard because he was surprisingly inexplicit about the relationship between civil history and civil philosophy. In the case of natural history, he makes the same argument over and again that natural history is the foundation of natural philosophy. But in the case of civil history, while he does observe, for instance, that "Histories of Times are the best ground for . . . discourse upon governments" (V, 56), he nevertheless does not spell out his inductive method with any of the labored explicitness that he lavishes on natural history. It may be that he thought the point was too conventional and obvious to warrant a long discussion. Rhetoric had been particularly associated with induction, and with the inductive use of historical exempla, at least since John of Salisbury in the twelfth century.[9] As rhetoricians, the humanists placed an emphasis on the writing of history, and on the study of the past for the direction of the future, that contrasts strongly with the dialectical culture of scholasticism. But it is also possible that Bacon's omission reflects a cautious, or even skeptical, attitude toward the early humanists' enthusiastic commitment to the usefulness of historical study for moral and political philosophy.

There is a third use of civil history, however, which is in practice the use that Bacon refers to most frequently and explicitly. This use is to some extent parallel to the first use of natural history, "for the sake of the knowledge of the things themselves." It is, simply, that history is entrusted with "the name and reputation of men." In the dedicatory epistle to his *History of Henry VII*, he emphasizes his intention "to do honour to the memory" of the king; his early historical sketch of Elizabeth is entitled *In felicem memoriam Elizabethae*; and in his discussion of lives in the *De augmentis* he concludes that "in that style or form of words which is well apportioned to the dead – (of happy memory, of pious memory, of blessed memory), – we seem to acknowledge that which Cicero says (having borrowed it from Demosthenes), 'That good fame is the only possession a dead man has' " (IV, 308). It is important that Bacon decided to recast his history of England in the form of lives of the monarchs. Lives are memorials, rather like funeral eulogies, which preserve the fame and reputation of men. He does claim of such memorials that "you may more safely and happily take [them] for example in another case" than histories of times, but his main focus is on the honoring of the "many worth personages . . . that deserve better than dispersed report or dry and barren eulogy." He recounts the fable of the swans that pick only a few names out of Lethe and preserve them for posterity (IV, 307). If such a purely memorial function appears to minimize history's practical usefulness, this may again reflect Bacon's skepticism about the early humanists' exaggerated respect for the past – a respect of which he was particularly critical in his attacks on received natural history and philosophy.

IV HISTORY AND RHETORIC

If Bacon was critical of some humanist faiths, however, he was also deeply imbued with their classicist and rhetorical assumptions. Roman authors interpreted history as a species of rhetoric. Since Aristotle, rhetoric had been divided into three genres – judicial, deliberative, and demonstrative – corresponding to the three main settings in which oratory was practiced – the law courts, political (deliberative) assemblies, and ceremonial occasions such as funerals.[10] History was a species of the demonstrative genre.[11] Its function, like the funeral oration, was to memorialize, and to bestow praise and blame. As we have seen, Bacon understood history in very much these terms. It is true that, in his discussion of the history of arts in the *De augmentis*, he argued against "wasting time, after the manner of critics, in praise and blame, but simply narrating the fact historically, with but slight intermixture of private judgement" (IV, 301). But in a letter to James accompanying the early draft of his *History of Great Britain*, he refers more candidly to "the law of an history, which doth not clutter together praises upon the first mention of a name, but rather disperseth and weaveth them through the whole narrative" (VI, 274). He does not reject the demonstrative project of praise, but insists that it should emerge from the narrative itself, rather than be imposed upon it.

Part of the reason for avoiding a "clutter" of praise was to avoid the suspicion of partisanship. Whereas the judicial and deliberative genres were forms of debate, and dealt with controversial or doubtful subjects, the demonstrative genre, according to Cicero, "does not establish propositions that are doubtful but amplifies statements that are certain, or advanced as being certain."[12] Obviously partisan praise in demonstrative history would introduce an element of controversy into what was supposed to be a nonargumentative genre. History was about the uncontroversial, about facts. "Who does not know," Cicero asked, "history's first law to be that an author must not dare to tell anything but the truth? And its second that he must make bold to tell the whole truth? That there must be no suggestion of partiality anywhere in his writings?"[13] Thomas More reiterated the truism, tongue in cheek, when he referred in a defense of his *Utopia* to the "historian's devotion to fact."[14]

Bacon's emphasis on the veracity of history – "simply narrating the fact" – is therefore entirely consistent with the classical and Renaissance rhetorical theory of history writing. Modern history is also explicitly dominated by a concern with faithfulness to the facts. But it is instructive to observe that the major difference between classicist and modern academic approaches to history lies in the unproblematic attitude toward historical truth displayed by the former, and the skeptical attitude displayed by the latter. Classicist rhetoricians viewed historical narratives as uncontroversial, and were accordingly content to accept the version of the past that their audience *regarded* as true – the received narrative. It has been the distinction of modern "accurate" historians to introduce skepticism about received narratives, a critical attitude toward sources, and a willingness to dispute facts. In brief, they have made history into a controversial genre. To be more precise, historiography has tended to shift from the demonstrative genre to the judicial.[15] The significance of modern history in this context is that it echoes Bacon's own innovations in the field of natural history and philosophy, which are marked by criticism of the "idols" of observation, and by a skeptical attitude toward received knowledge. The question that is naturally raised is whether Bacon's civil history is characterized by the same level of skepticism and critical concern for accuracy that he advocated in natural history – and, by consequence, whether he is as much the father of modern critical history as he is often said to be the father of modern empirical science.

I shall argue that the answer to this question is disappointing. We might think of modern accurate history as Baconian in its skepticism and in its empirical rigor, but Bacon did not practice it, even though its methods were pioneered in the Renaissance, and he was fully aware of them.[16] Arnaldo Momigliano claims that the method of accurate modern history grew in part out of antiquarianism, which Bacon mentions as one of the forms of civil history.[17] An Antiquarians' Society had been founded in London as early as the 1580s.[18] One of the leading lights of that Society, William Camden, published the first edition of his antiquarian *Britannia* in 1586, and Bacon himself added corrections to Camden's *Annals of Queen Elizabeth*. But Bacon's remarks about antiquities in the *De augmentis* are at best condescending: "In these kinds of Imperfect History I think no deficiency is to be assigned; for they are things, as it were, imperfectly compounded, and therefore any deficiency in them is but their nature" (IV, 304). He makes it very clear that his preference is for "perfect history," which he separates from antiquities without any suggestion that perfect historians might be able to learn from the researches of antiquarians. In fact, Bacon regards the study of antiquities as the work of closet scholars who devote themselves to "things which few people concern themselves about" (IV, 304). By contrast with such mere scholars, Bacon insists in his memorial to Elizabeth that "monks or closet penmen . . . are no faithful witnesses as to the real passages of business. It is for ministers and great officers to judge of these things" (VI, 305). Bacon's remarks allude to a traditional tendency of humanist men of affairs to despise closet scholars:[19] it is Bacon's experience in high affairs that gives him insight as a historian; he has no need to become an antiquarian scholar. He thus did not make effective use of original documents that were available to him while writing his *History of Henry VII,*[20] and he reproduced in it an interpretation of Henry's character that he had already formulated in his fragmentary *History of the Reign of K. Henry the Eighth . . .* , written years before he began his actual research.

There was, however, a second kind of accurate history that was pioneered in the Renaissance, which Bacon might have been expected to find more conducive. This was a form of philological scholarship that had its roots in the rhetoric of judicial argument, and which has bequeathed many of its terms and procedures to modern historians.

In Aristotle's division of the rhetorical genres, each is assigned a different time: deliberative oratory concerns the future (advice about what is to be done), demonstrative concerns the present (celebration of the values of the community), and judicial concerns the past (judgment on what has been done).[21] From a modern perspective, the judicial genre was always the logical option for history. Judicial argument gathers witnesses and testimony, and subjects sources and documents to criticism, in an effort to get at the truth of what happened. What is more, this critical, judicial approach to history dates back at least to the fifteenth century (and even earlier, to the late Middle Ages, according to Kelley[22]). Valla's philological declamation on the *Donation of Constantine* is particularly celebrated among modern scholars because it is regarded as a landmark in the development of accurate, critical historical scholarship. It is also a formal classical oration of the judicial genre. To be more precise, it is of the species of judicial oratory known as "conjectural" – a term that philology borrowed from law – which was the kind of judicial oration designed to search out arguments in order to establish a matter of fact.[23]

It is important to note that modern historiography is still rhetorical. What has tended to change is the genre of its rhetoric. The significance of this lies not in its style[24] but in its invention (*inventio*), which was the first of the five classical "offices" of rhetoric. *Inventio* meant, literally, "finding." The theory of invention consisted largely of "topics" (Greek *topoi*, Latin *loci*) – literally "places" where the orator "found" the lines of arguments for a speech. The way in which the three genres of oratory were distinguished was according to their different "special" or particular topics, for the simple reason that different contexts and kinds of discourse demanded different lines of argument. For instance, the conjectural issue employed such topics as motive, subsequent events, "signs" (time, place, occasion, and so forth),[25] most of which are still entirely familiar from the burdens of proof of modern detective work. Their relevance for modern historians, whom R. G. Collingwood compared to detectives, should be obvious.[26]

It will be noticed here that while invention refers to lines of *argument* and belongs to the *art* of rhetoric, it is not the mere manipulation of language that is now so often associated with rhetoric: a judicial trial can only take place if there is some doubt as to what really happened, and the topics direct the orator what questions to ask and where to look for arguments and evidence that may establish probability. In part, these artistic topics directed the orator where to look for *in*artistic proofs – material evidence, relevant testimony, and so forth. Bacon was fully aware of this inventional lore. He was not only a lawyer, but he observed in the *De augmentis* that "I for my part receive particular Topics (that is places of invention and inquiry appropriated to particular subjects and sciences) as things of prime use," and adds that a topic serves not only "to prompt and suggest what we should affirm and assert, but also what we should enquire or ask. For a faculty of wise interrogating is half a knowledge" (IV, 423–4). Bacon's defense of special topics is particularly striking in its historical context, because they had already been noisily rejected in Ramus's influential theory of rhetoric and dialectic.[27] By contrast, Bacon claimed that "so much importance do I attribute to Particular Topics, that I design to construct a special work concerning them" (IV, 427).

Furthermore, Bacon did employ the particular topics of conjectural argument, probably derived from *Rhetorica ad Herennium*, in his *History of Henry VII*.[28] In the second year of Henry's reign, an imposter named Lambert Simnell, apparently trained by the priest Richard Simon, impersonated Edward Plantagenet. But Bacon is skeptical about the traditional story. He opens his enquiry (which is at VI, 45–7) by observing

that which hath no appearance; that this priest, being utterly unacquainted with the true person according to whose pattern he should shape his counterfeit, should think it possible for him to instruct his player . . . any ways to come near the resemblance of him whom he was to represent. . . . So that it cannot be, but that some great person, that knew particularly and familiarly Edward Plantagenet, had a hand in the business.

This is the conventional conjectural argument of hope of success (*spes perficiendi*): the priest, who was not familiar with the royal family, could not have hoped to train the imposter to impersonate a member of royalty. Bacon later adds the conjectural topic of comparison, by which it is asked whether anyone other than the accused had a better motive, or means, or opportunity. He uses the topic to focus suspicion on the Queen Dowager: "None could hold the book so well to prompt and instruct this stageplay, as she could."

Having cast doubt on the traditional story, Bacon begins his conjectural reconstruction on the conventional ground of *probabile*, under its two headings of life (*vita*) and motive (*causa*): "That which is most *probable*," Bacon writes, using the formal judicial term for this kind of proof,

out of the precedent and subsequent acts, is, that it was the Queen Dowager from whom this action had the principal source and motion. For certain it is, she was a busy negotiating woman, and in her withdrawing-chamber had the fortunate conspiracy for the King against King Richard the Third been hatched; . . . and was at this time extremely discontent with the King, thinking her daughter (as the King handled the matter) not advanced but depressed [my emphasis].

In other words, she was the sort of woman who would commit this crime, she had been engaged in similar conspiracies before, and she had a motive (of revenge and family advancement). Finally he adds the conjectural proof of *argumentum*, which is highly circumstantial and by which, according to *Herennium*, "guilt is demonstrated by means of [prior or subsequent] indications that increase and strengthen suspicion."[29] Bacon adduces two such indications from subsequent events, which he acknowledges only "fortify" suspicion: first, "that which doth chiefly fortify this *conjecture* is, that as soon as the matter brake forth in any strength, it was one of the King's first acts to cloister the Queen Dowager;" and second, "it is likewise no small *argument* . . . that the priest Simon himself after he was taken was never brought to execution" (my emphases).

What this episode reveals is that Bacon was fully aware of the possibilities of conjectural argument for skeptical historical enquiry, and that he was capable of a critical and argumentative approach toward the establishment of events in the past. But his argument is not particularly satisfactory. The problem is not that it is rhetorical and conjectural, but that it is incomplete and perfunctory. For instance, it is clear from the perspective of the conjectural topics themselves that Bacon has relied on the most speculative arguments – probability, comparison, and argument – and has failed to adduce a single scrap of solid evidence for the "signs" of guilt – place, time, duration of time, occasion. Bacon argues that the queen trained Simnell, but provides no inartificial evidence whatsoever that she did in fact train him, nor when, where, or for how long this training could have been undertaken. His argument is plausibly presented, but an enquiry conducted by the conjectural topics themselves quickly reveals its weakness.

The conjectural proof in his *History of Henry VII* is also disappointing from the point of view of Bacon's own theory of natural history. He claims that the past has bequeathed a confused mass of fact, fiction, and misguidedly hasty theory about nature (IV, 229). He deplores the fact that people are "occupied with unsound doctrines and beset on all sides by vain imaginations." The corrective to this will be a program not only of careful observation but also of systematic criticism and checking. In this context, what is disappointing about his approach to civil history is that he does not subject his historical conjecture to the kind of skeptical enquiry into material evidence and counterevidence that he recommends in natural history. Neither the suspicion that he harbored about received wisdom in natural history, nor therefore the emphasis he placed on checking facts and theories, is carried over into his civil historiographical practice.

The fact of the matter is that Bacon was hostile to both antiquarianism and conjectural controversy, which were the two means of accurate historical enquiry developed in the Renaissance: "First then, away with antiquities, and citations of authors," he writes in *Parasceve*, "also with disputes and controversies and differing opinions; everything in short which is philological. Never cite an author except in a matter of doubtful credit: never introduce a controversy unless in a matter of great moment" (IV, 254). These remarks would make no sense if he were not fully aware of the work of philologists and antiquarians – and actively hostile to it. Conjectural arguments such as the one surrounding Simnell thus appear only at isolated moments in his history. For the most part, he avoids argument and critical enquiry in favor of the uncontroversial, demonstrative project of presenting a vivid narrative and amplifying "statements that are certain, or advanced as being certain." To understand his overall procedure, therefore, we should turn to the conventions of the demonstrative genre.

VI HUMANIST HISTORY AND DEMONSTRATIVE RHETORIC

The demonstrative genre had three main topics – spirit (*animus*), body (*corpus*), and external circumstances (*res externae*). The topic of *animus* consisted entirely of the virtues – the four cardinals and their numerous subdivisions – and Cicero also refers to this topic simply as *virtus*.[30] By contrast, *corpus* and *res externae* were regarded as gifts of fortune (*fortuna*). There was therefore a fundamental division in the demonstrative genre between *virtus* or moral character on the one side, and *fortuna* – everything that depends on chance and is in some way external to spirit – on the other. These two demonstrative themes, which are most familiar to us from Machiavelli's adoption of them,[31] were seen as inextricably interwoven: praise was awarded to *virtus* by observing how the subject had conducted himself in relation to the circumstances of fortune. The assumption here is that, while *virtus* can only be assessed in relation to *fortuna*, nevertheless only *virtus* is really praiseworthy: "It is foolish," Cicero said, "to praise one's good fortune and arrogant to censure it, but praise of a man's *animus* is honourable and censure of it very effective."[32]

The classical rhetoricians outlined two alternative modes of arrangement (*dispositio*) for a demonstrative oration. It could be arranged by topic, "dealing separately with the various virtues, fortitude, self-control and the rest of them and assigning to each virtue the deeds performed under its influence"; or it could "set forth the things we intend to praise or censure; then recount the events, observing their precise sequence and chronology, so that one may understand what the person under discussion did and with what prudence and caution."[33] Bacon clearly thought of history as conforming to these two demonstrative arrangements, though he conventionally preferred the chronological approach: "When I read in

Tacitus the actions of Nero or Claudius, with circumstances of times, inducements, and occasions, I find them not so strange; but when I read them in Suetonius Tranquillus gathered into titles and bundles, and not in order of time, they seem more monstrous and incredible" (III, 365–6). But he actually wrote histories in both kinds of arrangement. His *History of Henry VII* is chronological, but his memorial to Queen Elizabeth, probably his first completed historical work, is topical in arrangement.

Bacon begins his early memorial by announcing the two conventional topics of the demonstrative genre: "Elizabeth both in her *nature* and her *fortune* was a wonderful person among women, a memorable person among princes" (my emphasis). What is unconventional in his memorial is that he claims he will concentrate on only one of these topics: "Of . . . [her] felicity I propose to say something; without wandering into praises; for praise is the tribute of men, felicity the gift of God" (VI, 305). Praise (according to Cicero) is reserved for virtue, while felicity is good luck, the product of fortune. Bacon gathers his material, not in chronological order, but under such topics as the queen's birth and parentage, her health, the people she ruled, her reputation in and activities concerning other countries, the "nature of her times," her failure to marry, her lack of children, her physical appearance, the manner of her death, and finally the "posthumous felicities" of a good successor and a lasting fame. These are all conventional *topoi* of *fortuna*, which Bacon attributes to providence because, as Cicero put it, "it is proper to panegyric [i.e., demonstrative oratory] to attribute what is merely good fortune to the verdict of divine wisdom" – that is, to providence.[34] (Bacon reproduced this argument in his discussion of the rhetorical colors of good and evil [IV, 469].) What is unconventional is Bacon's announced focus on *fortuna* rather than *virtus*.

Bacon was aware of his break with convention and, in the event, he could not carry it through to the end. Having completed the praise of Elizabeth's felicity that he announced at the outset, he added a whole new section to the end of the memorial, with a prefatory apology:

And if any man shall say in answer, as was said to Caesar, "Here is much indeed to admire and wonder at, but what is there to praise?" surely I account true wonder and admiration as a kind of excess of praise. Nor can so happy a fortune as I have described fall to the lot of any, but such as besides being singularly sustained and nourished by the divine favour, are also in some measure by their own virtue the makers of such fortune for themselves. And yet I think good to add some few remarks upon her moral character; confining myself however to those points which seem most to give opening and supply fuel to the speeches of traducers. (VI, 312)

Another strategy of demonstrative oratory, beside attributing good fortune to divine wisdom, was to attribute it to moral purpose: according to Aristotle, the orator "must assume that accidents and strokes of good fortune are due to moral purpose; for if a number of similar examples can be adduced, they will be thought to be signs of virtue and moral purpose."[35] Bacon has it both ways, attributing Elizabeth's felicity both to providence and to her "own virtue." The reason for his doing so appears to be his awareness of rhetorical expectation: he feels compelled to cover the two conventional topics of *virtus* and *fortuna*.

In the previously unannounced second part of his memorial, Bacon presents the argument that "in religion Elizabeth was pious and moderate, and constant, and adverse to innovation" (VI, 312). In Roman rhetoric, piety was a subtopic of justice, moderation was a major topic, and constancy (perseverance and patience) was a subtopic of courage.[36] Resistance to innovation is not a standard topic, but could be considered a subtopic of prudence. In other words, Bacon tacks onto the end of his memorial the praise of Elizabeth's virtues that his classically trained contemporaries would expect of a demonstrative oration. What is significant for our purposes is, first, the extent to which he arranges his historical memorial in terms of the standard demonstrative topics; and second, his *un*conventional move of privileging *fortuna* over *virtus*.

There are several possible reasons for Bacon's unconventional move, and all of them could be operative at the same time. First, he could have been squeamish about attributing *virtus* to a woman. Second, his memorial appears to be a specifically religious defense of Elizabeth against sectarian criticism, in which context his emphasis on providence and divine favor had a special relevance. Third, it is possible that Bacon in general tended to place more emphasis on fortune than on virtue. It is the third possibility that I wish to explore further.

VII BACON AND *FORTUNA*

The topics of the demonstrative genre were peculiarly important for Renaissance humanism as a cultural and intellectual movement. For the humanists, Greece and especially Rome were exemplars of virtue. As Bacon himself put it with humanist zeal, "it hath pleased God to ordain and illustrate two exemplar states of the world, for arms, learning, moral virtue, policy, and laws; the state of Graecia, and the state of Rome" (III, 335). By contrast, the "dark ages" that separated the humanists from their admired model were dominated by *fortuna*. Petrarch, at the beginning of the humanist movement, complained that the recently famous victories of certain medieval princes "occurred because of good fortune . . . so that the success was not at all a question of military valor or true glory."[37] The Middle Ages were not only imaged as "dark,"[38] but above all as chaotic, disorderly, at the mercy of capricious fortune. The humanists' program was to dispel the rule of *fortuna* by reviving classical *virtus* in arms, learning, and moral virtue.

However, *virtus* and *fortuna* were rhetorical topics that could be, and were, related to each other in various ways. Questions such as whether *virtus* or *fortuna* is the more powerful, and how they are related, were among the most conventional problems addressed by the Roman tradition of demonstrative history. In his *Bellum Iugurthinum*, for instance, Sallust repeatedly observes that Marius owed his successes to fortune rather than to ability, and at one point in his *Catilina* he remarks that "beyond question Fortune holds sway everywhere." But he was not consistent about this: he remarks of Sulla that "many have hesitated to say whether his bravery or his good luck was the greater," and claims that success depends on a mixture of fortune and virtue.[39]

Among the humanists of the Renaissance, it was Machiavelli who produced the most celebrated and flexible meditations on the relationship between virtue and fortune. It is important to observe that Machiavelli kept shifting the relationship between virtue and fortune: in the space of a couple of pages in *The Prince* he talks of affairs being "governed" by fortune and of the inability of men to "correct" fortune, he calls for virtue to "resist" fortune, and then to "adapt" to fortune, and then to avoid acting in a way "out of harmony" with fortune, and then of fortune being "in harmony" with men's actions, and finally of men "holding down" fortune, "battering" and "push-ing" her, of fortune being "vanquished" and of men "commanding" her.[40] There is here a constant shifting of the verbs used to articulate the relationship between *virtus* and *fortuna* that is characteristic of Machiavelli's thought. One of Machiavelli's great political and his-torical insights, after all, is into the radical instability of the relation-ship between virtue and fortune. In rhetorical terms, this is expressed as a protean, constantly shifting rearticulation of the relationship between the two demonstrative topics. Thus, for instance, Machia-velli accorded high praise to *virtù*, but paradoxically this also led him to place tremendous emphasis on *fortuna*: the *virtuoso* prince must adapt to fortune, and perhaps even imitate it. In practice, Machiavelli adds, "no man can be found so prudent that he knows how to accom-modate himself to this."[41]

Bacon often paraphrases Machiavelli's observations: "Nothing is more politic than to make the wheels of the mind concentric and voluble with the wheels of fortune," he writes, "for nothing hinders men's actions or fortunes so much as . . . for men to be as they were, and follow their own nature, when occasions change . . . . But this viscous and knotty temper which is so averse to change is nature in some; in others it is the result of habit" (V, 71).[42] He was usually optimistic about the power of virtue, observing in his essay "Of Fortune" that "the mould of a man's fortune is in his own hands" (VI, 472), and envisaging a department of civil knowledge entitled "architecture of fortune." But he also debated the question whether virtue or good fortune is preferable (IV, 469–70), and observed that "great and truly wise men have thought it right to ascribe their successes to their fortune, and not to their skill or energy" (IV, 58).

Perhaps to an even greater extent than Machiavelli, Bacon insists that the architecture of fortune depends on the habit of observing fortune and making the best of whatever happens: "We must strive with all possible endeavour to render the mind obedient to occasions and opportunities, and to be noways obstinate and refractory. . . . For nothing is more impolitic than to be entirely bent on one action. He that is so loses an infinite number of occasions, which indirectly fall out by the way" (V, 70–1, 74). In brief, success depends not on per-sonal greatness, but on habits of observing fortune and framing ac-tions that will fit the accidents that arise. What is implied by all of this is that the most important function of civil history will not be to describe exemplary men who were remarkable for one or another virtue, but to provide a kind of vicarious experience in the observation and understanding of the accidents of fortune.

Many of Bacon's remarks about observing accidents could easily be transferred from his project of experimental natural history. "Simple experience," according to Bacon, "if taken as it comes, is called accident [*casus*], if sought for, experiment" (IV, 81; I, 189). Experiment is, therefore, an orderly way of seeking out accidents and observing what happens. In a sense, Bacon's idea of experiment is a controlled way of speeding up time in order to force the kinds of occurrences that happen only rarely and accidentally in nature. But in his essay "Of Innovations," Bacon insisted that "it is good also not to try experiments in states" (VI, 433). If civil history is to imitate natural experimental history, it must find subjects that happen to offer a peculiar concentration of the strange and the accidental. This is exactly what he claims in the *De augmentis* for the importance of recent English history, that "there has been a greater variety of strange events than in like number of successions of any hereditary monarchy has ever been known" (IV, 306). This focus on rare historical accident is quite insistent in Bacon's writing. In his unfinished history from Henry VIII to Elizabeth, he highlights the "new and rare variety of accidents and alterations," and the "accidents memorable" of the period:

There have not wanted examples within the compass of the same times neither of an usurpation, nor of rebellions under heads of greatness, nor of commotions merely popular, nor of sundry desperate conspiracies, . . . nor of foreign wars of all sorts; invasive, repulsive of invasion, open and declared, covert and underhand, by sea, by land, Scottish, French, Spanish, succors, protections, new and extraordinary kinds of confederacies with subjects. (VI, 19–20)

In short, the period is a collection of wonders, a kind of historical laboratory.[43]

In his *History of Henry VII*, we find a similar emphasis on wonders. The history begins as Henry, "when the kingdom was cast into his arms, met with a point of great difficulty and knotty to solve, able to trouble and confound the wisest King in the newness of his estate" (VI, 29). After Henry has weathered this novelty, Bacon turns to a new wonder: "There followed this year, being the second of the

King's reign, a strange accident of state, whereof the relations which we have are so naked, as they leave it scarce credible" (VI, 44). A few pages later he turns aside from his narrative to give a short biography of the Queen Dowager because "this lady was amongst the examples of great variety of fortune" (VI, 50).

Bacon is not merely being a sensationalist. What interests him are variety, accidents, historical rarities – the footsteps of *fortuna*. The point of recording a great man's life, for most humanists, was to present a notable exemplar of virtue or of vice that could serve as a model for the reader's imitation or avoidance. By contrast, Bacon's interest is focused primarily on fortune (or providence) rather than *animus*. This focus may help to explain the emphases in his history of Henry VII.

Bacon conceives his *History of Henry VII* in terms of the conventional demonstrative topics: "He had parts (both in his *virtues* and his *fortune*) not so fit for a common-place as for observation" (VI, 238, my emphases). Henry's virtues, summarized at the end of the history (VI, 238–45), are fairly conventional: he was religious and a good lawmaker (the virtue of justice), "valiant" and "of a high mind" (the virtue of courage), and known for his prudence. His defects are more interesting. "Of nature," Bacon tells us, ". . . he coveted to accumulate treasure; and was a little poor in admiring riches" (VI, 239). In terms of the classical virtues, Henry's greed suggests a lack of moderation. In conventional humanist fashion, the virtues and vices summarized in the conclusion of the history have been demonstrated in the chronological narrative of the circumstances of fortune that makes up the body of the text. But the quality in Henry that Bacon most emphasizes, and which is most ambiguously treated, is his suspiciousness. Bacon not only emphasizes that Henry was "full of apprehensions and suspicions" (VI, 243), he also focuses on events in his reign – such as Simnell's conspiracy – in which appearance is deceptive. His whole history might be summarized by his observation that Henry "were a dark prince, and infinitely suspicious, and his times full of secret conspiracies and troubles" (VI, 242).

But what is unclear is whether Henry's suspiciousness is a virtue or a defect. Suspicion is often a laudatory term in Bacon's vocabulary. The "wonder" of his *Instauratio magna* is that "such great *suspicions* concerning matters long established, should have come into any man's mind" (IV, 11, my emphasis). Henry's suspiciousness makes him into a kind of Baconian model of scrupulous enquiry and diligent collection of information: "He was careful and liberal to obtain good intelligence . . . his instructions [to ambassadors] were ever extreme curious and articulate; and in them more articles touching inquisition than touching negotiation: requiring likewise from his ambassadors an answer, in particular distinct articles, respectively to his questions"; he employed "secret spials" both at home and abroad; he was "sad, serious, and full of thoughts and secret observations; and full of notes and memorials of his own hand, especially touching persons" (VI, 241, 243). But the result of Henry's suspicions and his diligent collections of information is that "his thoughts were so many, as they could not well always stand together; but that which did good one way, did hurt another" (VI, 243). And for all his caution and suspiciousness, "the sight of his mind was like some sight of eyes; rather strong at hand than to carry afar off. For his wit increased upon the occasion; and so much the more if the occasion were sharpened by danger" (VI, 244).

Bacon repeatedly notes that Henry lacked great foresight, which was one of the subtopics of prudence.[44] Henry was, he says, "in his nature and constitution of mind not very apprehensive or forecasting of future events afar off, but an entertainer of fortune by the day" (VI, 31). Henry appears constantly to react to circumstances (and profit by them if possible), rather than really forecasting and controlling his fortune. In fact, Bacon takes some trouble to reattribute Henry's reputation for foresight to his fortune: "The King by this time was grown to such a height of reputation for cunning and policy, that every accident and event that went well was laid and imputed to his foresight, as if he had set it before" (VI, 156). Bacon's prose is detached and ironic as he deflates Henry's reputation for foresight and expresses his own skepticism about the pretensions of prudence: what we attribute to human foresight is merely accident.

Bacon's portrait is oddly contradictory: on the one hand, he emphasizes Henry's cautious collection of information and his suspicion, yet on the other he goes out of his way to reject the common opinion of Henry's foresight, claiming that, despite his efforts, he could really only see things close at hand, was not effective in planning ahead, and acted most effectively "upon the occasion," on the spur of the moment and "so much the more if the occasion were sharpened by danger" (VI, 244). In the way Bacon constructs his portrait of Henry, the king's great care of collecting information – his spies, his suspicions, his inquisitions, his memoranda – are oddly gratuitous and even grimly comic, for they "troubled himself more than others" (VI, 243). Bacon presents the ironic picture of a man deceived by his own suspicious fears of deception.

   This portrait has the effect of underlining the limitations of prudence in politics. Henry's reign is driven by *fortuna*, and for all the king's "thoughts and secret observations," Bacon continues to emphasize accident: "In this fourteenth year also, by God's wonderful providence, that boweth things unto his will, and hangeth great weights upon small wires, there fell out a trifling and untoward accident, that drew on great and happy effects" (VI, 198–9). It is not Henry, with all his spials, who draws on "great and happy effects," but a "trifling and untoward accident." Bacon's own minute observation of the trifling and accidental, which is consistent with his ideas about detailed observation in natural history, underlines the inadequacy of conventional political wisdom in civil affairs: "great affairs," he observes, "are commonly too rough and stubborn to be wrought upon by the finer edges or points of wit" (VI, 74). In civil affairs, *fortuna* takes the lead. What appears most valuable in this context is not Henry's quasi-scientific obsession with collecting information, but his openness to the accidents that come to meet him. Civil history is the realm of the accidental – such appears to be the message of Bacon's *History of Henry VII* – and success depends on making the most of it. Bacon's recent fall from power may have made him particularly sensitive to the power of *fortuna*, but his attitude toward it is not necessarily negative. Where classical and humanist writers had commonly seen fortune as hostile and dangerous, Bacon often regards accident more positively. He refers to England under his patron, King James, as "such a kingdom as mought . . . *enable* a king by variety of accidents" (VI, 276, my emphasis).

   There is a parallel between Bacon's natural history and his civil history in that both emphasize the detailed observation of variety and accident. The difference is that the art of scientific experiment can order accident and chain nature, but the accidents of fortune in civil affairs remain unpredictable, even for such a scrupulous observer as Henry. Perhaps this is why Bacon was not among the pioneers of modern, accurate historiography: a scrupulous checking of the facts of the past would serve little purpose since history would continue to be accidental and unpredictable. Humanist history always had a lesson, but the lesson of Bacon's *History of Henry VII* is not so much that any particular virtue should be cultivated, as that a ruler must remain open to accident and ready to seize its opportunities.

In the context of humanist historiography, therefore, Bacon is unconventional in emphasis, rather than pioneering in method. Humanists – even Machiavelli – characteristically placed their emphasis on virtue – especially prudence. Bacon still operates within the relationship between virtue and fortune that shaped classical and humanist history, but he highlights fortune. Bacon's particular focus gives his prose, in turn, a peculiarly ironic and detached tone: for all the effort of human virtue and planning, effects are caused by accident, by "God's wonderful providence, that boweth things unto his will, and hangeth great weights upon small wires." Bacon's portrait of Henry is explicitly laudatory, but he records even the end of his reign with an emphasis on chance that approaches satire: "Now there was nothing to be added to this great King's felicity . . . but an opportune death, to withdraw him from any future blow of fortune" (VI, 237).

Bacon's ironic tone is not novel so much as an expression of contradictions that had emerged in the later Renaissance within humanism.[45] Machiavelli had already defined *virtù* in terms of such immense powers of prudence and adaptability that it had become a practical impossibility. His younger contemporary, Francesco Guicciardini, was more skeptical about the practical efficacy of prudence: "It sometimes happens," he observed, "that fools do greater things than wise men. The reason is that wise men, unless forced to do otherwise, will rely a great deal on reason, and little on fortune; whereas the fool does just the opposite."[46] (Erasmus had made a similar claim in his *Praise of Folly*.[47]) Guicciardini's emphasis on minute observation, which prefigures Bacon's, led him to strike at the very roots of the humanists' justification of history as philosophy teaching by examples:[48] "To judge by example is very misleading. Unless they are similar in every respect, examples are useless, since every tiny difference in the case may be a cause of great variation in the effects."[49] And for exactly the same reason that examples from the past are useless, foresight into the future is impossible: "Every tiny, particular circumstance that changes is apt to alter a conclusion. The affairs of this world, therefore, cannot be judged afar but must be judged and resolved day by day."[50] It will be noticed that some of Bacon's comments about Henry closely parallel Guicciardini's observation.

In Cicero's threefold division of prudence into past, present, and future – memory, intelligence, and foresight – Guicciardini preserves only intelligence and the mutable present.[51] But the humanists defended history precisely on the ground that it cultivated the prudence of memory and foresight: it presented lessons from the past to the present for the guidance of the future. By cutting memory and foresight away from prudence, Guicciardini, closely followed by Bacon, thus cut the function of humanist history from under its form. And yet both Guicciardini and Bacon still turned to formal humanist topics and to humanism's own faith in the usefulness of history, which they had rejected, in order to justify the writing of history. Guicciardini says of his *History of Italy* that "numerous examples will make it plainly evident how mutable are human affairs,"[52] but it is this very mutability that makes historical examples useless for the guidance of the present. When Bacon insists that Henry was "not so fit for a common-place as for observation" (VI, 238), he also implies that the king's life does not provide maxims directly applicable to the present, so much as an opportunity to observe the power of accident and fortune. This exactly reverses the humanists' focus on *virtus* triumphant over accident, and it is the source of Bacon's irony, which is sometimes mistaken for realism: he uses the methods of humanist history, but he reverses its cherished faith in exemplary virtue and its depreciation of accident.

There is the basis here for a radical new interpretation of history, which does not see the past in relation to the present and future, providing models for imitation, but sees history as a series of mutations from one set of present accidents to the next. The accidents of the past had causes (according to Bacon), but those causes belonged to the present of that time, not to this. Nevertheless, this new view is not the product of a pioneering new method of historiography, so much as it depends on subverting the faiths of the old humanist history from within its own methods. The modernity of Bacon's civil history – or rather, its postmodernity – lies more in the insights provided by this ironic subversion from within of the old humanism than in the pioneering of a new method.

Bacon's detached observation of historical accident is in harmony with his approach to natural history. It does not, however, produce the kind of modern historiography, judicial or "scientific" in method, that we might expect from him. The modernity of his *History of Henry VII* lies, rather, in the ironic insights produced by his rearrangement of conventional humanist topics. At least in his civil historiography, Bacon is more an ironic late humanist than a scientific progressivist.

NOTES

1 The author wishes to thank Michael Witmore for sharing his stimulating work on Bacon's philosophy.
    Classical texts are cited from the editions in the Loeb Classical Library, published at Cambridge, by Harvard University Press.
2 Cf. Tinkler 1987.
3 Fussner 1962, p. 263; Dean 1941, p. 176; cf. Berry 1971.
4 Kristeller 1979, p. 22.
5 Kristeller 1979, p. 24; Witt 1982. On the role of rhetoric in humanist education, see especially Baldwin 1944, Grendler 1989.
6 See Levy 1972, pp. 251–2.
7 Gilmore 1963.
8 Nadel 1966 and Morrison 1977, pp. 595–7 place more emphasis on the relationship between history and psychology or ethics in Bacon's thought.
9 John of Salisbury, *Metalogicon*, trans. Daniel D. McGarry (Berkeley, 1955), pp. 102, 192–3.
10 Aristotle, *Rhetoric*, I.3.
11 Tinkler 1988a.
12 Cicero, *De partitione oratoria*, xxi.71.
13 Cicero, *De oratore*, II.xv.62.
14 Thomas More, *Utopia: A Norton Critical Edition*, ed. and trans. Robert M. Adams, 2nd ed. (New York, 1992) 124–5.
15 Tinkler 1988c.
16 Cf. Woolf 1987.
17 Momigliano 1966, pp. 1–39.
18 On the English Antiquarian enterprise, see Levine 1987, pp. 73–106.
19 On this tension, see O'Malley 1988.
20 According to Busch 1895, pp. 416–23, though Woolf 1984 has to some extent revised Busch's criticisms.
21 *Rhetoric*, I.3.

22 Kelley 1974.
23 De Caprio 1978.
24 As in White 1978.
25 *Rhetorica ad Herennium*, II.3–9.
26 Collingwood 1949, p. 270; cf. Davis 1988, p. 575.
27 See Peter Ramus, *Arguments in Rhetoric against Quintilian*, trans. Carole Newlands (Dekalb, 1986), pp. 110–13.
28 *Rhetorica ad Herennium*, II.3–9.
29 *Rhetorica ad Herennium*, II.8.
30 Cicero, *De inventione*, II.lix.177.
31 Tinkler 1988b.
32 *De inventione*, II.lix.178.
33 Quntilian, *Institutio oratoria*, III.vii.15; *Rhetorica ad Herennium*, III.vii.13.
34 *De oratore*, II.lxxxv.347.
35 *Rhetoric*, I.9.
36 *De inventione*, II.159–64.
37 Kohl 1974, p. 139.
38 Mommsen 1942.
39 *Bellum Iugurthinum*, XCII.7, XCII.4; *Bellum Catilinae*, VIII.1; *Bellum Iugurthinum*, XCIII.4; *Bellum Catilinae*, I.5–7.
40 Niccolò Machiavelli, *Il principe e discorsi*, ed. Sergio Bertelli (Milan, 1960), pp. 98–101.
41 *Il principe*, p. 100.
42 Cf. *Il principe*, p. 100.
43 Another list of the "variety of strange events" in the same period appears in the *De augmentis* (IV, 306).
44 *De inventione*, II.liii.160.
45 On this tendency, see Bouwsma 1976.
46 Francesco Guicciardini, *Maxims and Reflections*, trans. Mario Domandi (Philadelphia, 1965) p. 75.
47 Desiderius Erasmus, *The Praise of Folly and Other Writings: A Norton Critical Edition*, ed. and trans. Robert M. Adams (New York, 1989), pp. 27, 73.
48 Cf. Gilmore 1963.
49 Guicciardini, *Maxims*, p. 21.
50 Guicciardini, *Maxims*, p. 70.
51 *De inventione*, II.liii.160.
52 Francesco Guicciardini, *The History of Italy*, trans. Sidney Alexander (New York, 1969) p. 3.

10 Bacon's moral philosophy

I INTRODUCTION

The first thing that needs to be said about Bacon's ideas on morality and moral knowledge is that they do not constitute a systematic moral philosophy. Primarily, this is because the project of initiating a great Instauration of learning represented for Bacon not a new philosophy but a new task: "a work to be done," as he put it, "not an opinion to be held" (IV, 21). Such an opposition of works to words, of action to contemplation, entails a dismissal of all that is merely philosophy on the grounds that the relief of man's estate depends less on philosophical belief than on rigorous investigation. Only in the sweat of our brow could we reap the fruits of science.

Apart from this general suspicion of philosophy as promoting the speculative or contemplative attitude over the active, Bacon also held traditional moral philosophy responsible for diverting attention from the more fruitful investigation of nature to the necessarily disputatious study of ethics. In his view, the Socratic turn in philosophy from nature to man encouraged a type of inquiry that is "fruitful of controversies but barren of works" (IV, 14). The result has been a proliferation of philosophical systems all clamoring for assent but none sufficiently grounded in the empirical data of natural history to warrant it. It is precisely such philosophical systems or idols of the theatre, as Bacon described them, that need to be put aside before the task of rebuilding the temple of knowledge can begin. Using modern language one might say that the "idols" represented by traditional philosophy constitute an "ideological" barrier to the more fruitful and truthful investigation of nature.[1]

We have touched on two reasons for Bacon's discomfort with

moral philosophy: one, his suspicion of all that is purely theoretical; the other, his view that the Socratic interest in man has led to an impoverished knowledge of nature. There is, however, a third reason why the label of moral philosophy does not easily fit Bacon's work and this has to do with the fragmentary nature of his scientific writings. Of the projected six parts of the Instauration only the first, a general summary of existing knowledge, could be considered complete. As for the rest, the second part on method, represented by the *Novum organum*, was left incomplete when Bacon turned his attention to the natural histories belonging to the third part. These are also unfinished and there remain only scattered prefaces to represent the remaining parts of the Instauration.[2]

While this formal incompleteness helps to explain the absence of a systematic body of philosophy in Bacon's work, its real significance lies in calling attention to the necessarily unfinished quality of his project of scientific reform. The scientific writings are designed to spur industry in others, to rally support for a collective undertaking by promoting the value of scientific knowledge and explaining how best to proceed with our investigation of nature. In this respect, the fragmentary character of the individual works reflects what Charles Whitney has called Bacon's "compulsion not to finish,"[3] a compulsion which is in keeping with the ongoing character of the Instauration itself. Far from being advanced, the collective project Bacon envisaged is actually hindered by presenting a body of work that gives the appearance of methodical completeness. To put it another way, if the task of interpretation is at hand, its successful completion requires the combined efforts of all those who appreciate how much remains to be done. By contrast, the development of a systematic body of philosophy would tend to discourage the very kind of ongoing investigation Bacon was proposing.

The unfinished quality of Bacon's project helps to explain his tendency to continually revise and expand works like the *Essays*, to compile lists of histories yet to be written and investigations yet to be undertaken, and to prescribe rules for experiments not yet performed. It also accounts for the tentativeness of his conclusions, all of which suggest work in progress rather than philosophical system. And since Bacon's intention was not to teach a system but to initiate investigation, he favored an aphoristic style over one that was magisterial and methodical. As he explained in the *De augmentis*: "aphorisms, representing only portions and as it were fragments of knowledge, invite others to contribute and add something in their turn; whereas methodical delivery, carrying the show of a total, makes men careless, as if they were already at the end" (IV, 451).

Although Bacon's work does not contain a systematic moral philosophy, it has an important ethical dimension. For one thing, moral knowledge is one of the branches of science surveyed in the first part of the Great Instauration and Bacon makes a number of important recommendations designed to place it on a more empirical footing. He divides ethics into two parts, one concerned with the ends of ethical conduct which he calls the "exemplar or platform of good," and the other with the means to approach these ends, termed "the regiment or culture of the mind" (V, 5). This second part of moral philosophy is said to be deficient, in part because of the traditional philosophic disregard of such common matters as the practical improvement of conduct.

Although the treatment of moral knowledge in the De augmentis amounts to no more than thirty pages, similar concerns are addressed, albeit from a more pragmatic perspective, in Bacon's literary and professional writings. It isn't surprising that on matters pertaining to practical conduct Bacon's scientific, professional, and literary interests overlapped. He was, after all, among the most public of philosophers; his circuitous "rising to great place" combined with his precipitous fall lending a very personal quality to his views on public life. This is particularly true of the last English edition of the Essays which, written after his impeachment, draws upon his own experiences and observations to flesh out the more academic observations of the scientific writings. The work reflects the same hierarchy of values that places action higher than contemplation and public life above private life. It also offers an analysis of passions and dispositions, and observations on moral culture corresponding in large measure to that second part of moral knowledge described in the De augmentis.[4] In considering the two parts of Bacon's ethical theory, therefore, we draw upon both scientific and literary sources.

The final part of this chapter turns from the treatment of ethical concerns in the scientific and literary works to consider the larger issue of the moral underpinnings of the Instauration itself. The project of advancing our knowledge of and power over nature was presented as an essentially moral undertaking justified by appeals to several of the principles advanced in the scientific and literary works. At the same time, to the extent that it combines elements of public service and Christian charity, the Instauration highlights what at times seem to be the competing demands of Bacon's Christian and civic values.

II THE NATURE OF THE GOOD

The *De augmentis* presents a complex scheme for organizing the various branches of knowledge. Within this structure, moral knowledge appears with logic as part of a more inclusive "philosophy of humanity" concerned with the operation of the faculties of the human soul. Where logic examines the functioning of the understanding and reason, moral knowledge deals with the workings of will, the appetites, and affections. The other components of the larger philosophy of humanity are medicine and those related arts concerned with the health of the body, and a philosophy concerned with the nature and faculties of the soul itself.

Although the divisions of inquiry appear to be quite rigid, as is the case with the rest of the Instauration, Bacon advises that they be used "rather for lines to mark or distinguish, than sections to divide and separate them" (IV, 373). Using more organic imagery he likens the divisions of knowledge to "branches of a tree that meet in one stem" (IV, 337). So, for example, logic and ethics "are, as it were twins by birth" (IV, 405) with the proper end of both being to uphold the "government of reason" in human life. Where logic secures reason against fallacious arguments and rhetoric supports reason through appeals to the imagination, the end of moral philosophy is "to procure the affections to fight on the side of reason, and not to invade it" (IV, 456). This similarity between the ends of morality and logic suggests something of the moral implications of Bacon's reformed logic, a point we shall return to below.

The close connection between logic and ethics is not extended to civil or political philosophy and in fact Bacon claims to depart from the traditional view by separating moral from civil knowledge. The traditional Aristotelian view was that as sciences concerned with the practical knowledge of human conduct, ethics and politics, though not identical, were necessarily interconnected. Aristotle's

Ethics begins and ends with a discussion of politics and his *Politics* makes clear that the political association exists not for the sake of mere life but for the good life. Bacon departs from this view, at least formally, by emancipating civil knowledge "into an entire doctrine by itself" (IV, 405). The crux of his distinction is between those sciences such as medicine, logic, and ethics which consider man "segregate" and civil philosophy which treat individuals "congregate and in society" (IV, 373).

On the face of it this distinction seems problematic. How can moral conduct be examined outside a social context? Bacon attempts to clarify his position by explaining that moral obligations involve the "regimen and government of every man over himself, and not over others" (V, 15). Such a regimen is designed to predispose the individual to fulfill his various obligations, both public and domestic. In this sense the end of moral philosophy is "to imbue and endow the mind with internal goodness" (V, 32), fostering in the individual a due appreciation of the responsibilities associated with family life, profession, rank, and citizenship. At the same time, to be effective such instruction must have an effect on conduct: to some degree internal goodness must carry over into an external goodness. The earlier *Advancement of Learning* acknowledged this link between inner disposition and public conduct pointing out that "neither can a man understand Virtue without some relation to society, nor Duty without an inward disposition." Yet for reasons most likely having to do with the statesman's reluctance to subject political conduct to moral scrutiny, the later Latin version of *The Advancement of Learning* omits these provisos, insisting only on a strict separation of moral and civil philosophy.⁵

The importance of bending the will and directing the affections toward the acceptance of public and domestic responsibilities gives an indication of the moral value Bacon placed on service to others, a value that is made explicit in the analysis of the "Exemplar and Platform of Good." In examining this first part of moral philosophy he begins by dismissing "those infinite disputations and speculations" of philosophers on the degrees of goodness (V, 5), pointing out how Christianity settles the question of the greatest good for an individual by associating it with a hope resting on faith. This same faith is used to support the priority of what is called the "Good of Communion" over individual and self-good. As natural law dictates that bodies gravitate to the earth, so Christianity reinforces this natural predilection, teaching that love of others should prevail over love of self and by extension that public good is higher than private. More than any philosophy or sect does Christianity "exalt the good which is communicative, and depress the good which is private and particular" (V, 7).

This survey of the nature of good relies on Christian teaching to buttress the central claims that action is higher than contemplation and that service to others is higher than service to self. Christianity settles the question of the superiority of action to contemplation on the grounds that contemplation is a private good while action has a closer affinity to public good. "Men must know that in this theatre of man's life it is reserved only for God and Angels to be lookers on" (V, 8). In making this claim, Bacon explicitly takes aim at those Greek philosophical schools which counseled various forms of withdrawal from public life. The Epicureans who placed felicity in individual pleasure or in the "serenity of a mind free from perturbation" (V, 9), the skeptical followers of Pyrrho of Elis who admitted "no fixed and consistent nature of good and evil" (V, 9), and the later Stoic, Epictetus, are all censured for undervaluing involvement in public affairs, and elevating the felicity associated with private repose and an imperturbable soul. This critique also reflects Bacon's more general complaint that philosophers are by profession "men dedicated to a private life, free from business and from the necessity of applying themselves to other duties" (V, 14). A truer appreciation of the relative merits of the active and contemplative life is likely to proceed from men like Bacon who have experienced both: "for the writing of speculative men on active matter for the most part seems to men of experience . . . to be but dreams and dotage" (V, 15).

The insistence that public life is morally superior to private life is drawn partly from Christian doctrine on the preeminence of charity over other virtues and partly on Bacon's acceptance of that long tradition of associating virtue with citizenship that extends back at least to Aristotle and which is most fully developed in Cicero. The value of the *vita activa* is one of the key pillars of Bacon's platform of good.[6] These civic values are reinforced by the claim that public life is more active than private and that nature accords greater value to action than to repose. This last point appears in the precedence accorded to active individual or self-good over passive good. "Enterprises, pursuits and purposes of life" even if they are of a purely private nature have a higher standing than simple self-preservation, for as in nature where propagation is a stronger and more worthy appetite than preservation, so in human life "much pleasanter is it to be doing than to be enjoying" (V, 11, 12).

The values of action and public service, central to the exemplar of the good, are carried over into Bacon's literary works, particularly in the later essays of 1625. Developing the theme that public life is superior to private life, the *Essays* also suggest something of the tension between the civic values of the *vita activa* and the central tenets of Christian morality. So for example, the essay "Of Goodness and Goodness of Nature" begins by affirming that Christian charity is the highest moral good without which "man is a busy, mischievous, wretched thing; no better than a kind of vermin" (VI, 403). But it goes on to suggest that these "*misanthropi*," "the very errors of human nature," are nonetheless "the fittest timber to make great politiques of" (VI, 404–5). This point that political life requires qualities that are often at odds with conventional Christian morality is reinforced by other essays. There are occasions, for instance, when "active men are of more use than virtuous" (VI, 495). The essay "Of Revenge" contends that while loving one's enemies may hold in private life, "public revenges are for the most part fortunate; as that for the death of Caesar" (VI, 385). The same holds true for the vice of envy which despite being "the vilest affection, and the most depraved" (VI, 397), may yet serve a useful public function by bridling those popular figures whose power has become excessive.

If vice can be useful in public life, it is also true that virtue can be dangerous. This theme is developed in the essay "Of Love" where no mention is made of the description of charity in the *De augmentis* as "the bond of Perfection" (V, 29). Instead, we read that "it is impossible to love and to be wise" and "that great spirits and great business do keep out this weak passion" (VI, 398, 397). Though love be a cardinal private virtue, it has little public value. On the other hand, vanity, though sinful, is often publicly useful. In fact, the ambition to distinguish oneself in honor and reputation is a prerequisite for public service: "in militar commanders and soldiers, vain-glory is an essential point; for as iron sharpens iron, so by glory one courage sharpeneth another" (VI, 504). Some desire for public recognition is essential in one dedicated to public service because "dispositions that have in them some vanity are readier to undertake the care of the commonwealth" (IV, 480).

These various examples lend support to the view that in the *Essays*, Bacon examined private morality from a civil perspective, demonstrating that even apparently immoral dispositions may have a "right use" in public life.[7] However, it would be a mistake to conclude that Bacon's ethical pronouncements are crudely Machiavellian, subordinating morality to immediate considerations of power politics. Rather, as previously discussed, political life itself takes on a moral aspect in Bacon's writings as it does in Machiavelli's. If there is a Machiavellian quality to the later essays, it rests in this commitment to public service and to the vitality of a public life. In fact the subordination of private to public concerns in the *Essays* is quite similar to the case made for civic values over private morality in the *Prince*. Machiavelli argues that while everyone would acknowledge the value of compassion, honesty, generosity, piety, and related virtues, there are occasions in public life when these can only be practiced at one's peril. To maintain his rule, a Prince "is frequently obliged to behave in opposition to good faith, to charity, to humanity and to religion."[8] Moreover, such is the nature of public life that the practice of private virtues in public life often has consequences other than those intended. Taking as his examples the virtues of generosity and compassion, Machiavelli argues that a prince genuinely concerned for the prosperity and security of his state cannot flinch from being miserly with public funds or ruthless toward the few who might threaten public peace. To act otherwise is to invite public unrest. The essential thing is to avoid the hatred and contempt of the people and this can be accomplished by keeping the public satisfied, securing their goods while projecting an image of decisive, if at times ruthless, leadership.

Bacon's subordination of private to public morality in the *Essays* is reminiscent of this argument. In the same way as the *Prince* contrasts public and private virtues, the *Essays* point to occasions when the exercise of private vice may be a public virtue. Simulation and dissimulation, envy, vanity, revenge, and ambition are frequently necessary to further the public good and are justified by this higher principle. While this may give the appearance of political opportunism and expediency, the principle at stake is less individual gain than the moral value of public life. The argument does not suggest that morality must be sacrificed in the name of advancement in life; instead, it develops the claim made in the Instauration that public life has a higher value than private life and that "it is a poor centre of a man's actions, himself" (VI, 432).

This priority of public to private life also helps to explain the critique of what might be called domestic values in the Essays and several other of Bacon's literary works. In the Essays, for example, wife and children are described as "impediments to great enterprises, either of virtue or mischief" (VI, 391). Possibly thinking of his own contributions to the public weal, the childless elder statesman goes on to say that "Certainly the best works, and of greatest merit for the public, have proceeded from the unmarried or childless men" (VI, 391). The reason why domesticity detracts from public service is explained in the interpretation of the Orpheus fable offered in the De sapientia veterum. There, public action is said to arise from a desire for recognition which in turn stems from a keen awareness of one's own mortality. Memento mori prompts one to public service in the expectation that one's name and reputation will outlive one's body: "For true it is that the clearer recognition of the inevitable necessity of death sets men upon seeking immortality by merit and renown" (VI, 722). By contrast, family life seems to offer a kind of surrogate immortality: "the sweets of marriage and the dearness of children commonly draw men away from performing great and lofty services to the commonwealth; being content to be perpetuated in their race and stock, and not in their deeds" (VI, 722). In short, because they "mitigate the remembrance of death," children tend to dampen one's enthusiasm for that public recognition which is the spur to political action. This is the chief reason why Bacon, at least in the Essays, shows so little regard for domestic life and the values associated with it.

There is a heroic dimension to this morality of public action which is evident in several essays. "Of Adversity" claims that the goods associated with adversity are higher than those of prosperity, on the grounds that while prosperity may encourage the practice of temperance, adversity presents obstacles to the attainment of our ends that offer an opportunity for the nobler virtue of fortitude. Heroic themes also appear in Bacon's interpretation of the fable of Ulysses's and Orpheus's encounter with the Sirens, in the De sapientia veterum. According to the fable, where Ulysses "caused the ears of his crew to be stopped with wax" so that the songs of the Sirens would have no effect (VI, 762), Orpheus chose to resist their entreaties by raising his own songs of praise to the gods. The fable is seen as describing two possible methods of resisting the temptations of pernicious pleasures. "The first method of escape is to resist the beginnings, and sedulously to avoid all occasions which may tempt and solicit the mind" (VI, 764). Such is "the waxing up of the ears, and for minds of ordinary and plebeian cast – such as the crew of Ulysses – is the only remedy" (VI, 764). The second method suits "minds of a loftier order, [who] if they fortify themselves with constancy of resolution, can venture into the midst of pleasures; nay and they take delight in thus putting their virtue to a more exquisite proof" (VI, 764).

The opposition of ordinary and lofty minds, of plebeian and noble characters, shows Bacon's sympathy for those heroic and aristocratic values associated with a life of public action, as well as his contempt for a life occupied with merely private or domestic concerns. The long essay "Of the True Greatness of Kingdoms and Estates" reflects these views. Although it appears in the *De augmentis* as an example of a treatise on one of the arts of government, the essay expresses Bacon's long-held conviction that a truly healthy people is one engaged in public action even to the point of war: "For in a slothful peace, both courages will effeminate and manners corrupt" (VI, 450). The odd foreign war by contrast encourages those martial virtues of courage and fortitude as well as a willingness to sacrifice self for country that Bacon so much admires.[9]

With its intermingling of ethical and political concerns, the very title, *Essays: Civil and Moral*, illustrates the difficulty of following the injunction in the *De augmentis* to separate civil and moral inquiry. Further, with its subordination of Christian moral precepts to the traditional civic virtues of the *vita activa*, the work also demonstrates the difficulty of reconciling these two strands of Bacon's exemplar of the good. The values espoused in the *Essays* are more martial than pacific with civic greatness and individual recognition counting for more than domestic harmony and Christian charity. In this respect the work not only represents a counterpoint to the peaceful, Christian society of science described in the *New Atlantis*, it also calls attention to Bacon's own divided loyalties. As a statesman, he sought "to extend the power of . . . [his] country and its dominion among men" but as a proponent of a great Instauration of learning he envisaged a more innocent "empire of man over things" (IV, 114). We will return to this problem in the final section of the chapter.

III THE GEORGICS OF THE MIND

In introducing his scientific discussion of moral knowledge, Bacon claims that his intention is not to belabor the philosophical analysis of good, virtue, duty, and felicity but to indicate "how a man may best take his aim at them" (V, 3). Consistent with the practical intention of the Instauration he recommends that more attention be paid to the culture of the mind and to the empirical knowledge on which it rests and less to philosophical speculation on the nature of the good.

The first point to note about this proposed moral culture is that it is a program of limited moral reform and Bacon draws on Christian teaching to reinforce this impression. Unlike the heathen who "imagined a higher elevation of man's nature than it is really capable of," "we, instructed by the Christian faith, must all acknowledge our minority, and content ourselves with that felicity which rests in hope" (V, 5). Christians are called to a perfection which is unobtainable by their own efforts and recognition of this fact should serve to temper our expectation for any definitive science of human improvement.

The claim that Bacon's expectations for the science of moral reform were more modest than his hopes for the science of nature is reinforced by the imagery used to describe it. As several recent critics have explained, the use of medical and agricultural analogies, as evident for instance in the description of the new moral regimen as a "georgics" of the mind, is particularly apt for representing a moral philosophy constrained by faith to strive for improvement through gradual modification, rather than perfection through definitive knowledge.[10]

The significance of the agricultural/medical imagery in moderating the claims for moral reform is evident in the following passage from The Advancement of Learning: "The husbandman cannot command neither the nature of the earth nor the seasons of the weather; no more can the physician the constitution of the patient nor the variety of accidents. So in the culture and cure of the mind of man, two things are without our command; points of nature, and points of fortune" (III, 433). The role of the physician is to care for the sick in the hopes of restoring the patient to health. He is not in a position to eradicate the causes of illness or to change the constitution of the patient. Similarly agriculture, far from overcoming nature, is only successful when it is responsive to nature's rhythms. Therefore the moral reform envisaged in the Instauration aims less to transform human nature than to make practical use of our knowledge of it. Using somewhat less pastoral imagery, Bacon described moral reform as an attempt "to set affection against affection, and to master one by another; even as we use to hunt beast with beast" (III, 438). The affections are not erased, but they are used against themselves. Only this type of modest reform escapes the religious condemnation of moral philosophy as a sinful attempt to replace divine authority over moral conduct by critical reason, in the vain hope of acquiring knowledge of and power over human nature.

The limited and pragmatic objectives of moral culture recast moral philosophy into a kind of therapeutic psychology.[11] Where medicine relies on prior knowledge of the "constitution of the sick man" and his afflictions, the preconditions of moral therapy are knowledge of "the different characters of disposition, the affections, and the remedies" (V, 20). The similarity between ethics and medicine is also reflected in the fact that both are sciences of man "segregate." Where one strives to heal the body, the other treats the mind, but neither can claim definitive knowledge or prevent the inevitable deterioration of body and mind.

Where medicine relies on empirical knowledge of the body and of the diseases to which it is subject, moral therapy relies on the knowledge of characters and affections derived from natural and civil histories. These are provided by "the wiser sort of historian" (V, 21) among whom Bacon mentions Livy, Tacitus, and Guicciardini. As with the earlier discussion of the platform of the good, there are some interesting differences between the treatment of this part of moral culture in *The Advancement of Learning* and the *De augmentis*. In particular, the earlier version has a list of natural dispositions that are supposedly beyond our control, including a natural malignity or benignity, an aptitude for weighty matters or trivia, and a narrow or broadmindedness. This is omitted in the later version and the only examples of characters or disposition mentioned are those arising from

certain innate conditions like age, health, and beauty and those produced by fortune such as prosperity, adversity, or obscure birth. The
effect of deleting examples of so-called natural dispositions is to
strengthen the link between character and circumstance. This is the
very stuff of the historical narratives Bacon recommends. In any
event, moral philosophy is to make use of the individual portraits
provided by historians as the basis on which to develop "a scientific
and accurate dissection of minds and characters" (V, 22).

The historians together with the poets are also seen as a source for
knowledge of "the affections and perturbations," how they work,
how they are "kindled and excited, and how pacified and restrained"
(V, 23). The importance Bacon paid to the development of such histories is evident from its inclusion in the *Catalogue of Particular
Histories* to be carried out as part of the work of the Instauration. In
addition, the *Novum organum* mentions the need to develop "a
history and tables of discovery for anger, fear, shame and the like"
(IV, 112).

The resulting combination of civil and natural histories provides
empirical information concerning characters and passions that will
provide the "groundwork of the doctrine of remedies" (V, 20) in
much the same way that knowledge of the body and its diseases
serves as the basis for medical treatment. As for therapies, Bacon
recommends careful inquiry into the power of circumstance in effecting an improvement in our moral health mentioning in particular "custom, exercise, habit, education, fame, studies, praise" and
the like.

In the same way that the literary works develop the ethical principles of the *De augmentis*, so do they contribute to the part of moral
philosophy concerned with moral culture. Although the *Essays* of
1597 and 1612 may be said to reflect Bacon's own narrow preoccupations with personal advancement, by 1625 he was not writing from
the standpoint of an ambitious suitor but rather as a former statesman concerned with more enduring issues of morality and policy.[12]
Among other things, this change of interest from career advancement to larger issues involving the role of private character in public
life helps to explain the inclusion of a number of new essays in the
1625 edition. Essays on Revenge, Adversity, Envy, Boldness, Anger,
and Simulation and Dissimulation, analyse character traits and dispositions, the circumstances that produce them, and their role in

public affairs. In this sense they take up the suggestion made in the *De augmentis* for an analysis of the effects of innate and external conditions like health, property, and wealth on individual character. In addition, the later versions of the *Essays* make better use of historical evidence and other illustrative material than do the earlier ones. Recalling the comment that the poets and historians are "the best doctors of the affections," it isn't surprising that in these studies of affections and perturbations, historical and mythological examples are more evident in the 1625 edition than in either the editions of 1597 or 1612.

As mentioned, an important feature of the later *Essays* which contributes to the view of moral philosophy as a kind of husbandry of the affections, is the tendency to assign the causes of conduct to circumstance and custom more than to nature. The 1625 version of the essay "Of Nature in Men" adds a new conclusion that exemplifies this georgic idea of moral culture: "A man's nature runs either to herbs or weeds; therefore let him seasonably water the one, and destroy the other" (VI, 470). Though the seeds of character may be planted by nature, they are nourished by circumstance and "there is no trusting to the force of nature nor to the bravery of words, except it be corroborate by custom" (VI, 470). This recognition of the influence of custom and circumstance on character directs the analysis away from gross generalizations about human nature and toward more particular diagnoses of individual conduct and character. This is consistent with the georgic idea of moral philosophy as a kind of moral husbandry. It also explains why one can read through all the essays describing individual characteristics, dispositions, virtues, and vices without being able to draw any general conclusions about human nature. Observation and evidence, whether historical or contemporary, directs the investigation away from generalizations about an abstraction like human nature and toward more particular determinants of character.

While they offer few general truths about human nature, neither do the essays merely confirm the commonplace judgment that people are different. Instead, the essays on deformity, travel, marriage, studies, and so on attempt to establish specific causal connections between circumstance and disposition. Thinking of his cousin, Robert Cecil, the earl of Salisbury, for example, Bacon wrote that "all deformed persons are extreme bold" (VI, 480), the public scorn they suffer often stirring them to great industry. In this instance as in others, character and disposition are confirmed by circumstance. The essay "Of Studies" uses agricultural imagery to make a similar point. Studies "perfect nature, and are perfected by experience: for natural abilities are like natural plants, that need pruning by study" (VI, 497). Specifically, "Reading maketh a full man; conference a ready man; and writing an exact man" (VI, 498). Marriage, about which Bacon was ambivalent to say the least, is also examined from the perspective of its effect on individual character. Because it serves as a kind of discipline, marriage is said to soften an otherwise cruel disposition. So, for example, among the Turks it is their "despising of marriage" that "maketh the vulgar soldier more base" (VI, 392). More generally, because single men lack the responsibility of wife and children, and "though they may be many times more charitable, because their means are less exhaust, yet, on the other side, they are more cruel and hardhearted" (VI, 392).

Such examples suggest Bacon's resistance to generalization in matters of character. Habit, custom, and circumstance, rather than human nature in the abstract, determine the variety of human types and conditions. If one asks why some men are more steadfast than others, the answer probably lies in their different situations. Recalling an example mentioned earlier, since fortitude is a virtue associated with adversity, it is less likely to be found in those accustomed to prosperity. In this respect the various essays correspond, at least in part, to that moral husbandry described in the *De augmentis* as requiring an improved knowledge of the effects of innate and external conditions on character. Such investigations lay the groundwork for a mental therapy that relies on the power of custom, habit and the like "to affect and influence the will and appetite" (V, 24).

Traditional moral philosophy appears in the Instauration as an obstacle to scientific progress, promoting words at the expense of works and distracting attention away from the investigation of nature. Bacon sought an end to fruitless philosophic debates over the nature of the good, content to accept an uneasy alliance of Christian charity and public service as principles on which to base conduct. As we shall see, he also used these same principles to support his own project of social reform through science. Beyond this, however, he hoped to redirect moral inquiry from philosophy to therapy by developing more empirical analyses of affections and characters in order to encourage a georgics or husbandry of the mind. The *Essays* contribute something to this effort and, to an extent that is seldom appreciated, so does the work of the Instauration.

IV THE MORALITY OF THE INSTAURATION

Although ethical concerns are explicitly addressed in the scientific and literary works, they also play an important role in the larger project of scientific and social reform represented by the Instauration. The same appeals to Christian charity and the values of the *vita activa* underpin both the larger undertaking and the *Essays*. For one thing, because it appears as a work to be done rather than an opinion to be held, the Instauration enjoys that superior moral standing accorded to works over words in Bacon's exemplar of the good. In the new natural philosophy the test of truth becomes practice and a theory is said to be true not in the sense that it represents reality, but to the degree that it allows for successful "intervention" into nature.[13] The knowledge of causes results in the production of effects and on the ladder of any genuine natural philosophy the investigator is always "ascending from experiments to axioms, and descending from axioms to the invention of new experiments" (IV, 343). In other words there can be no formal separation between the speculative and operative aspects of Baconian science.

The Instauration not only reflects the moral superiority of action to contemplation, it also conforms to the superior value of public action over private. The work of advancing knowledge is not seen as an individual undertaking but as a collective one. For instance, although the job of interpretation may require special skills and abilities, even those of meanest capacities have an important role to play in compiling the data supplied by natural history.[14] In fact, Bacon complained at being required to "spend my own time in a matter which is open to almost every man's industry" (IV, 252).

In this respect, science is a form of public action both in terms of its objectives and organization. The politicization of knowledge which subordinates inquiry to "the benefit and use of life" (IV, 21) has its counterpart in the political organization of investigation. Bacon's own role in such an exercise was to sound the trumpet in order to rally our collective forces not against one another, but "against the Nature of Things" so as to "extend the bounds of human empire" (IV, 373).

As with any other form of public service, there are rewards for those who further the common good. In the *New Atlantis* for instance, the glory formerly associated with heroic men of action also accrues to inventors: "for upon every invention of value, we erect a statua to the inventor, and give him a liberal and honourable reward" (III, 166). Furthermore, the important political powers exercised by the Fathers of Salomon's House suggest the degree to which the new natural philosophy has become a political program. And as in political life, the spur to scientific activity is said to be adversity not prosperity: "opinion of store is one of the chief causes of want" (IV, 13). The adversity described in the *Essays* as encouraging the virtue of fortitude will, in the Instauration, arise from dissatisfaction with the impoverished state of our collective knowledge of and control over nature. Far from being content with our lot, we will learn to acknowledge the meagerness of our knowledge and strive to increase it. Finally, since hope for the future prompts political action in the present, it becomes a key virtue in Bacon's scientific program: "by far the greatest obstacle to the progress of science" being "that men despair and think things impossible" (IV, 90).[15] As in political life, hope becomes the great spur to that collective scientific activity which promises glory to the participants and material benefits to the society.

Although the advancement of knowledge reflects moral values and disciplines similar to those of Bacon's political and literary writings, there remain some important differences. In particular, it would be a mistake to think that Bacon sees in the conquest of nature that ultimate foreign war that would somehow bring honor and glory only to Englishmen.[16] Because the new science reflects a Christian love for humanity more than a strictly civic concern for one's fellow citizens, it is difficult to link it to any narrowly political or imperialistic ends. So too, the Machiavellian morality associated in the *Essays* with war, military prowess, civic greatness, and individual recognition is not easily applied to a conquest of nature carried out in the name of peaceful cooperation, *philanthropia*, and Christian charity. In short, Bacon's primary moral defense of the Instauration was not that it would benefit the state, but that it would save humanity and this ethical principle reflects a Christian preoccupation more than any purely secular concerns. The development of science is the primary way to demonstrate our Christian love for others, since it is the means by which we are able to develop those technologies and practices that improve the quality of human life.

We have seen that there are both civic and Christian underpinnings to the Instauration. Although it was Bacon's intention to combine these, in practice the one representation constantly threatened to overwhelm the other. This is apparent, for instance, in the way that political descriptions of the Instauration in terms of power and conquest over nature invariably confront its Christian representation as the innocent realization of man's love for his fellows and the reestablishment of some original state of innocence.[17] The *Novum organum* for example associates private, political, and scientific activity with three grades of ambition: the concern for personal advancement arising from the degenerate ambition for personal power, political activity from the more honorable ambition to enhance the power of one's country, and science from the wholesome and noble ambition to "extend the power and dominion of the human race itself over the universe" (IV, 114). But Bacon questions whether the desire to empower humanity can be properly understood in the political language of ambition at all. It becomes apparent here that the vocabulary of power and ambition is inadequate to describe the Instauration, for the simple reason that in any Christian representation of the will to know, science is not a manifestation of ambition for power, but of a Christian obligation to seek truth and to demonstrate love for one's neighbor.

Another example of this strain between Christian and civic values is the conflict between domestic and military virtue in Bacon's writings. Life in Bacon's scientific utopia, the *New Atlantis*, for instance, is the epitome of that peaceful domesticity criticized so roundly in the *Essays* and *De sapientia veterum*. The citizens of Bensalem, unlike those of the *Essays*, have lived in peace for almost two thousand years. Internally, the city suffers from none of those divisions of sects and religions described in the essay "Of the Vicissitudes of Things." Jew and Christian live peaceably together and the whole society seems to the travelers as a "land of Angels." In sharp contrast to the *Essays*, marriage and domesticity are held in such high esteem that an official celebration known as the Feast of the Family is held to honor any man with thirty living descendants over the age of three (III, 149). In short, it appears as though that "perpetuity by generation" described in the *Essays* as "common to beasts" but not proper to men, is as honorable in the society of science as the contributions of the statesman or inventor (VI, 390). And in sharp contrast to the characters that populate the *Essays*, the citizens of Bensalem are, without exception, humane, tolerant and charitable, with the whole society being "unique for the chaste minds of . . . [its] people" (III, 152).

The envy, ambition, and pride described in the *Essays* seems a far cry from this peaceful scientific utopia. Yet rather than abandon the Machiavellian morality of the *Essays* for the Christian charity of the *New Atlantis*, Bacon's scientific program draws on elements of both. As a result, the Instauration appeals to aspects of reformation theology and the values of Christian charity, as well as to an ethic of public service and individual recognition associated with the much less harmonious world of political action.

V   CONCLUSION

Bacon's moral views are best summarized in the following passage from the essay "Of Regiment of Health": "In sickness, respect health principally; and in health, action" (VI, 453). The Instauration redirects moral inquiry from philosophy to a psychological therapy intended to promote mental health for the sake of the active life of public service. The later *Essays* reflect these themes: elevating action over contemplation and public over private life, and offering a diagnosis of the effects of circumstance on character traits and dispositions.

In the view of the *Essays*, public service has a moral status because it furthers a collective good and provides an opportunity for the display of those virtues of courage, self-sacrifice, and fortitude associated with the *vita activa*. Where the *Essays* and other more political writings develop this civil dimension of Bacon's ethical views, his project for advancing knowledge attempts to combine this with the more Christian and humanitarian principles of the *New Atlantis*. As we have seen, the Instauration appeals to that most public of goods, the good of humanity. In so doing it transcends the lesser values of private recognition and public glory, substituting for the greatness of this or that society, the greatness of humanity. But it is difficult to combine the political principles of the *Essays* with the more Christian ethics of the *New Atlantis*. The collective goods of peace and prosperity achieved by the new science of the *New Atlantis* look very much like those domestic values that Bacon condemned so roundly in the *Essays*. Equally problematic is the attempt to transfer those individual qualities associated with public action to the scientific activity envisaged by the Instauration. The ideal Baconian scientist is too much moved by Christian pity and charity to display much of that heroic virtue associated with Machiavellian morality. And as a cooperative public undertaking, the new science has little room for the ambitious struggle for recognition that characterizes political life.

Although it is not easy to reconcile the values supporting the Instauration, it should be remembered that Bacon was less concerned with developing a consistent set of moral principles than with improving the culture of the mind. He argued that traditional moral philosophy was deficient in developing an empirical body of knowledge on which to base an effective moral culture. While the Instauration reflects various aspects of the platform of the good, it can also be said to contribute something toward this second aspect of moral knowledge. As a work to be done, not an opinion to be held, the task of improving and extending knowledge exerts on its practitioners a discipline that is as moral as it is methodological.

The best example of the moral effects of the new science is found in the *Novum organum*, which offers a series of prescriptions for curbing our natural dispositions and for treating those idols of the mind that interfere with the acquisition of true knowledge. Such idols, as the *De augmentis* explains, are associated with a kind of moral and mental illness: "a corrupt and ill-ordered predisposition of mind, which as it were perverts and infects all the anticipations of the intellect" (IV, 431). This sort of medical imagery serves more than a rhetorical purpose, for it suggests that the scientific program is nothing less than an attempt to heal the human condition and that it accomplishes this not only through specific discoveries and inventions, but also through the very process of investigation itself. By nature, it seems, we prefer the vacuous generalizations offered by grand theories to the fragmentary knowledge of natural history. We tend to "anticipate" more than we "investigate," seizing upon evidence that confirms our preconceptions while disregarding contrary instances. Such deficiencies really amount to moral failings more than methodological errors. It is our native indolence that stands in the way of scientific progress and this can only be overcome through the rigorous discipline of the new logic. In this respect, the methodological directives prescribed in the *Novum organum* are not only rules to guide investigation, but serve equally as a moral and intellectual discipline, a kind of "mental hygiene" for the diseased mind.[18]

In its therapeutic capacity, the new science starts by identifying deficiencies of will, and proceeds to establish a method for strengthening our resolve, supplying us with the instruments necessary for the acquisition of genuine and useful knowledge. This is at least one of the effects of those elaborate procedures of investigation described in Book II of the *Novum organum*. The tabulation of various kinds of instances serves to discipline our otherwise lazy disposition, arming our faculties with helps for the understanding that might overcome our natural frailties. Their purpose is to strengthen our resolve to perform the arduous tasks of investigation. For example, a genuinely fruitful and illuminating natural philosophy requires that the investigator suspend judgment and inquire into nature with a doubting faith, avoiding both skepticism and dogmatism on the grounds that each refuses to accept a disciplined form of investigation. The initial task of inquiry, therefore, is to resist the temptation of easy assertions, either that nothing can be known or that nothing worthwhile is left to know.

This notion that science is a moral undertaking not only from the vantage point of its objectives, but in so far as it serves as a kind of moral culture, is made explicit in the passage cited above from the essay "Of Studies." To recall, studies "perfect nature, and are perfected by experience: for natural abilities are like natural plants, that need pruning by study" (VI, 497). In a similar way, the studies outlined in the *Novum organum* not only facilitate the acquisition of knowledge, they exert a moral discipline, promoting the difficult work of diligent and patient inquiry over facile generalizations, and encouraging industry over idle speculation. Being less concerned with speculation than with cultivating qualities of industry and perseverance in the individual, the new science itself becomes a corrective for the mental diseases of dogmatism and skepticism, instilling hope in place of despair, substituting illumination for error and confusion, and encouraging a commitment to a life of collective action devoted to the "relief of man's estate," that most complex and universal of public goods.

NOTES

1 For a recent discussion of the various senses of *idolum* in Bacon's work, see Whitney 1986, pp. 37–9.
2 See Bacon's "Plan of the Work" (IV, 22–33); R. L. Ellis's "Preface to the *Novum organum*" (I, 71–7); and the discussion in Whitney 1986, pp. 189–93.
3 Whitney 1986, p. 189.
4 Compare for example, the topics addressed in the *Essays* with the following suggestion from the *De augmentis*: "And not only should the characters of dispositions which are impressed by nature be received into this treatise, but those also which are imposed on the mind by sex, by age, by region, by health and sickness, by beauty and deformity, and the like; and again, those which are caused by fortune, as sovereignty, nobility, obscure birth, riches, want, magistracy, privateness, prosperity, adversity, and the like" (V, 22). The classic treatment of the argument that the *Essays* were intended to contribute to Bacon's scientific program is Crane 1923, pp. 272–92.
5 There are a number of differences in the treatment of moral knowledge in *The Advancement of Learning* and the *De augmentis*. On the issue of social obligations considered as part of moral, rather than civil philosophy, the later work omits two passages that originally suggested an overlap between the two sciences; cf. III, 428 and V, 15.
6 The best discussion of Bacon's acceptance of the traditional values of the *vita activa* is Vickers 1984b. However, in identifying the classical virtues of citizenship with the "philanthropia" of the Baconian scientist, he seems to overlook the differences between the particular loyalties of the one and the universal concerns of the other.
7 Kiernan 1985, p. xx.
8 Niccolò Machiavelli, *The Prince*, edited and translated by James B. Atkinson (Indianapolis, 1976), p. 283.
9 Bacon's advocacy of martial values is evident in a number of his professional writings and public speeches. As early as 1592–3 he wrote in a pamphlet that "it is a better condition of an inward peace to be accompanied with some exercise of no dangerous war in foreign parts, than to be utterly without apprentisage of war, whereby people grow effeminate and unpractised when occasion shall be" (VIII, 174). Similar sentiments were expressed in a speech to the Commons in February 1606–7 in which he

rebuked the Members for thinking more of "utility and wealth" and "reckonings and audits" than "greatness and power" (X, 324).

10 See for example Le Doeuff 1990b, pp. 119–38 and Low 1983, pp. 231–59. For the contrary view that Bacon's georgics of the mind reflects a modern will to power over human nature, see Briggs 1989, especially pp. 35–40.

11 Nadel 1966, argues that Bacon turned to civil history from traditional moral philosophy in order to develop "something like a scientific corpus of behavioural knowledge."

12 There is a good discussion of the link between Bacon's personal circumstances and the subject matter of the various editions of the *Essays* in Marwil 1976.

13 On this distinction between a science that aims to represent the world and one that intervenes in it, see Hacking 1983.

14 Bacon argued that the interpretation of nature "is not a way over which only one man can pass at a time (as is the case with that of reasoning), but one in which the labours and industries of men (especially as regards the collecting of experience) may with the best effect be first distributed and then combined" (IV, 102).

15 As explained in Le Doeuff 1990a, pp. 9–24, "hope" was, for Bacon, the chief corrective for both the closed life and the closed mind.

16 For the view that Bacon's scientific proposals served certain imperialistic political ends, see Martin 1992, esp. ch. 6.

17 Charles Whitney asks: "to what degree does Bacon's appropriation of a rhetoric of political domination in his use of *instauratio* compromise his philanthropic and pragmatic science?" in Whitney 1989, p. 372.

18 The term is used in Minogue 1983. Blumenberg 1983 points out that for Bacon "failure to progress is due to man's indolence"; see p. 383. Indolence is a moral failing, not an intellectual one.

11 Bacon's political philosophy

I INTRODUCTION

Francis Bacon was a politician and a statesman for most of his life. He received an education designed to train him for an active life and he sat in the House of Commons for the first time at the tender age of 20. He considered himself first a *"bonus civis"* – which amounted to being "a good and true servant to the Queen" – and only after a *"bonus vir,* that is an honest man" (IX, 132, 190–1). Up to the time of his unexpected fall in 1621, Bacon was actively involved in high politics at the court of James, and he never abandoned hope of a political comeback. A month after his impeachment he was already planning to offer instruction in politics (XIV, 285), and his *History of Henry VII,* written in 1621 and published in March 1622, was partly intended to show his abilities as a counselor. At the same time he planned to ask the king to employ him again "publicly upon the stage" and, in 1624, he declared himself ready to travel to the Continent to negotiate a league with France (XIV, 349, 443–4). Although Bacon confessed to Lancelot Andrewes that *"my Instauration"* was the work he most esteemed, he also asserted that he could not "desert the civil person that I have borne" (XIV, 373; VII, 13–4; V, 79).

Bacon was thoroughly convinced that statesmen, above all others, should think and write about politics. He never tired of ridiculing the fruitless attempts of lawyers and philosophers to make sense of political issues. Whereas lawyers could never broaden their horizons beyond the particular laws of the country they happened to inhabit, philosophers lacked any practical experience, so that their writings were nothing "but dreams and dotage" (III, 270, 428–9). It should, therefore, come as no surprise that Bacon considered himself, espe-

283

cially in later life, to be particularly well equipped to express his opinion about political issues. In the *De augmentis* he pointed out with studied moderation that he was not "entirely unqualified to handle" the doctrine of "Civil Government [*Doctrina de Republica Administranda*]" (I, 792; V, 78–9). And, as the political situation grew more tense, Bacon felt that his skills would be in great demand. "My good Lord," he wrote to the marquis of Buckingham in 1623, "somewhat I have been, and much have I read; so that few things which concern states or greatness, are new cases unto me" (XIV, 424). In 1624, he ventured to advise Prince Charles to go to a war with Spain, because, as he explained, he had a "long-continued experience in business of estate and much conversation in books of policy and history" (XIV, 469).

The aim of what follows is to analyze the fruit of Bacon's confidence in his own ability to write about politics. I shall begin by discussing Bacon's career as James I's counselor, and his statements about the constitutional issues of the day. I shall then move to the question of the place of politics in Bacon's program for the advancement of learning. The two final sections of the essay will be devoted to Bacon's relation to the classical humanist tradition in general and to his views about two central issues of this tradition in particular: citizenship and civic greatness.

II   THE KING AND THE ANCIENT CONSTITUTION

Perhaps the most obvious question of Bacon's political philosophy was his career as James's counselor. In his official roles as Solicitor General (1607), Attorney General (1613), Lord Keeper (1617), and Lord Chancellor (1618), Bacon saw himself as the king's man and presented himself accordingly. After the death of the king's counselor and his own cousin, the earl of Salisbury, in 1612, Bacon not only censured Salisbury's competence as a politician, but recommended himself as an able successor. As the most pressing matter was, according to Bacon, "the consideration of a Parliament," he stressed his "little skill in that region," but to avoid any misunderstanding, added that he was "a perfect and peremptory royalist" (XI, 280). In 1613 Bacon recommended himself to the place of Attorney General on the grounds that he would be able "to recover that strength to the King's prerogative which it hath had in times past, and which is due unto it" (XI, 381). The chief aim of the Chancery, Bacon explained to James in 1616, was the "strengthening of your prerogative according to the true rules of monarchy" (XII, 252).

An important way in which Bacon attempted to defend the king's position was to employ "a rhetoric of reconciliation." In order to hide their ideological differences, both absolutists and their opponents often appealed to the idea of balance, emphasizing the particularly close connection, often described as a marriage, between the king's prerogative and the subject's liberty.[1] "The King's Sovereignty and the Liberty of Parliament," Bacon told the Commons in 1610, "are as the two elements and principles of this estate . . . [which] do not cross or destroy the one the other, but they strengthen and maintain the one the other" (XI, 177). He explained to George Villiers that the common laws of England gave the king "the justest Prerogative, and the People the best liberty" (XIII, 18). Matters of state belonged to the king, and parliament "was only to meddle with *meum et tuum*" (XI, 183). Bacon acknowledged that there were those who feared that the king's prerogative was growing and that "the balance might go too much on that side," but he attempted to convince the Commons that this was not the case (XII, 38) and advised James to emphasize the same point (XII, 29).

Although Bacon employed the idea of a balanced constitution in a run-of-the-mill manner, his exposition was underlain by astute calculation. His advocacy of a balanced constitution went hand in hand with a reluctance to get involved in ideological disputes, such as the controversy spawned by the oath of allegiance imposed upon Catholics in 1606. The Catholics argued that the king received his authority from an act of transference from the people. His authority was thus limited, and the people might legitimately resist a king who exceeded his powers. James and his supporters countered by arguing that the royal power was derived from God alone.[2] Although Bacon did not contribute any substantial treatise to this discussion, he was involved in two legal cases against Catholics. But rather than developing any theoretical reply to the Catholic theorists, he was content to shower abuse on them, describing Francisco Suárez as "A fellow that thinks with his magistrality and goose quill to give laws and manages to crowns and scepters" (XII, 9). As to their arguments, he specifically said he would not "argue the subtlety of a question: it is rather to be spoken to by way of accusation of the opinion as impious, than by way of dispute as of a thing doubtful." Because their opinions required rather "detestation than contestation," Bacon argued "as a man bred in civil life" and not as "a divine or scholar." For him, the whole question was an issue of politics rather than ideology. Those who wrote in favor of resistance or regicide deserved "rather some holy league amongst all Christian Princes of either religion, Papists and Protestants, for the extirping and razing of this opinion and the authors thereof from the face of the earth, as the common enemies of mankind, than the stile of pen or speech" (XII, 165, 154).

Another and even more important context in which Bacon tried to avoid theoretical debate was Parliament. He wanted to give the impression that the failures in Parliaments of 1610 and 1614 could be explained by political intrigues and faction and that there was thus no need for explanations based on a deep ideological division. He told the king in 1613 that "[t]he opposite party" of 1610 "is now dissolved and broken," and suggested that some courses should be taken to avoid a packed house and "to make men perceive that it is not safe [to] combine and make parties in Parliament, but that men be left to their consciences and free votes" (XI, 365, 367–8, 370; XII, 179, 181–2). Even more importantly, the council should never appear divided in Parliament (XIII, 171).

The most crucial thing for a successful Parliament was, however, the king's own behavior. Bacon told the king in 1613 "that above all things your Majesty should not descend below yourself; and that those tragical arguments and (as the schoolmen call them) ultimities of persuasions which were used last Parliament should for ever be abolished." Instead, the king should act "in a more familiar, but yet a more princely manner" (XI, 371). This amounted to an avoidance of "the language of a Merchant" as well as that of "a Tyrant." The king should not act as a merchant "crying of his royalties to sale" (XII, 26). But neither should he act as a tyrant, telling the MPs that "he most set upon the tenters his laws and prerogatives, if they will not supply him" (XII, 26).[3] If the king should thus keep away from airing absolutist principles, the MPs should no less forbear from using ideological arguments. They were not summoned "to make long and eloquent orations, but to give counsel and consent." They should not change their attire of "counsellors" to that of "merchants or scholars" (XII, 24). Bacon seemed to believe that the grave prob-

lems which surfaced in Parliaments could be avoided as long as men
set their ideological arguments aside. Politicians should act as politicians and not as scholars; they should see everything as an issue of
practicality rather than theory.

Nonetheless, since Bacon was engaged in defending the king and
his prerogatives, he could hardly avoid altogether the employment
of absolutist principles. The earliest traces of his acquaintance with
these arguments come from his writings for the Christmas revels in
1594. These took the form of various speeches for counselors which
advised the prince to follow different courses of action. The fourth
counselor, advising the king about "Absoluteness of State and Treasure," argued that the prince should "conquer . . . the overgrowing of
your grandees in faction, and too great liberties of your people." He
should likewise conquer "the great reverence and formalities given
to your laws and customs, in derogation of your absolute prerogatives." The consummate counselor would be he who could "make
you the only proprietor of all the lands and wealth of your subjects"
(VIII, 338).

Bacon often spoke about the king's inherent prerogatives (X, 268,
270), but what exactly he meant by this notion becomes clear in his
1607 memorandum to the Jurisdiction of the Provincial Council of
the Marches. Although it was argued by some that the king's prerogatives were given to him by the common law, Bacon replied with a
staple absolutist argument that the king held some of his prerogatives "mediately from the law, but immediately from God." Some of
his prerogatives were indeed of such nature that they could be disputed "in his ordinary courts of Justice." But "his sovereign power"
could not be censured by any judge. Because the king's sovereign
power was a "matter of government and not of law," it was beyond
ordinary jurisdiction. God had entrusted the king with the government of the realm, and the king could hardly be said to cope with
this formidable task without being able to use his discretionary authority. Because "the end of all government" was the "preservation
of the public," it was "necessary" that the king could flout the law.
As soon as "prerogatives are made envious or subject to the construc-
tions of laws," a monarchy, Bacon argued, would degenerate into an
aristocracy or oligarchy (X, 371–3), and "further way may be opened
to Parliament or lawyers to dispute more liberties" (X, 380). But the
consequences could be much worse than that. Bacon warned that

those who wanted to limit prerogatives by "subjects' birthrights and laws" were perhaps opening "a gap unto new Barons' wars" (X, 371–2). A good king did indeed govern by the law. Had not James himself admitted that "God forbid . . . that we should be governed by men's discretions and not by the law?" But this did not entail the limitation of the royal power by the law, for the king was accountable to God alone.

In 1608, Bacon argued in Calvin's case, trying to demonstrate that Scots born after James's accession to the English throne were born English subjects. In order to prove his case, Bacon drew arguments from existing absolutist ideas. Like Lord Chancellor Ellesmere,[4] Bacon based his argument on the nature of kingship. Other forms of government were so complicated that they "of necessity do presuppose a law precedent." But in hereditary monarchies "the submission" of the people was "more natural and simple" (VII, 643–4). Monarchies were based on three different kinds of "platforms" or "patterns": father, shepherd, and God. Monarchies, unlike other forms of government, were thus both sacred and natural (VII, 644–5). In addition, the relationship between the king and his subjects was based on four different kinds of "submissions," all of which were natural and thus "more ancient than law": patriarchy, admiration of virtue, conduct in war, and conquest. According to Bacon, these natural submissions explained the ways in which monarchies had been founded (VII, 645–6, 666). Monarchies were older than any law, and the people owed their allegiance directly to the king and not to the law. It followed that since the king of Scotland and England was the same person, the subjects of the king of Scotland were at the same time subjects of the king of England, and therefore naturalized subjects in England (VII, 671).

But these arguments by themselves said little if anything about the extent of the king's power and authority. In Calvin's case, Bacon did not, in other words, follow his argument that the king's power was derived from God alone to the absolutist conclusion that the king could flout the law. On the contrary, having established that monarchy was the primitive form of society, Bacon went on to argue that the law limits the power of the king. "[A]lthough the king, in his person, be *solutus legibus*, yet his acts and grants are limited by law, and we argue them every day" (VII, 646–7). Subjection was owed to the person of the king, but it did not follow that the king's power was "infinite" (VII, 670).⁵

Bacon argued consistently throughout his career that the common law defined the king's authority and prerogative. In 1587, he asserted that "the Law is the most highest inheritance that the King hath; for by the law both the King and all his subjects are ruled and directed" (VII, 509). The king's prerogatives, he argued several times, were given to him by the common law (VII, 632, 420–1, 689; XI, 165). Accordingly, "the King's prerogative and the law are not two things; but the King's prerogative is law, and the principal part of the law" (XIII, 203). When Bacon was defending the king's right of impositions in Parliament in 1610, he aimed at proving the proposition that "the King by the fundamental laws of this kingdom hath a power to impose upon merchandise and commodities both native and foreign" (XI, 191–2). Indeed, Bacon explicitly denied the absolutist claim that the king's absolute power was beyond the law. He told the Commons that "where the King's acts have been indeed against the law, the course of law hath run and the Judges have worthily done their duty" (XI, 192).

Sometimes, to be sure, Bacon said that the common law endowed "the King or Sovereign with more prerogatives or privileges" than any other law (VII, 420–1). But his general argument – that the common law decided the extent of royal authority – was in many respects closer to the antiabsolutists' than absolutists' arguments. He pointed out that "the ancient laws and customs of this kingdom" had been "practised long before the Conquest" (VII, 749) and held that the common law decided the sphere of Chancery (VII, 415, 410–11, 760). In 1587, Bacon went so far as to assert that "the ancient Maxims, Customs, and Statutes of this land" directed the king. It followed that "if any Charter be granted by a King the which is repugnant to the Maxims, Customs, or Statutes of the Realm; then is the Charter void" (VII, 509–10). It had indeed been alleged that "a prince's power is not bounded by rules or limits of the law," but the main thrust of Bacon's argument was directed at refuting this claim. He even noted that neither the king nor even an act of Parliament could "change any one point contained in" Magna Charta (VII, 513).

Bacon did not believe that "the supreme power resides with the people," but "in the case where defects in governments regarding the safety of the people have completely prevailed" it followed that "the people may rightly deprive the government of the power they have given it, and take it upon themselves." According to him, it was a "solid, politic and true" opinion that "a most cruel and evil tyranny was worse than sedition and civil war." Bacon was, in other words, subscribing to resistance theory.[6]

It is thus arguable that although Bacon defended the king's prerogative in general and his right of impositions in particular, and although he sometimes employed absolutist arguments, he cannot be classified as an absolutist. The king's power was derived from the common law, which set limits on its use. Every time he defined sovereignty as law-making authority, he attached it to Parliament.[7] Furthermore, advising James about Parliament, Bacon always stressed its prime importance. "Parliament," he told the king in 1613, "hath been the ordinary remedy to supply the King's wants," and he repeated the same point after the unsuccessful Parliament of 1614 (XI, 365; XII, 176). James should do everything possible to refute the rumor "which is sometime muttered, That his Majesty will call no more Parliaments" (XII, 85; XI, 371).

III POLITICS AND SCIENCE

Some of the best scholarship on Bacon's political philosophy has seen the relation between Bacon's political theory and his program for the advancement of science as its main problem. This is so not merely because Bacon included civil knowledge in *The Advancement of Learning*, but also and perhaps mainly because they had obvious similarities. If the ideal statesman combined learning and practical experience, the ideal scientist combined, *mutatis mutandis*, rational and empirical knowledge (e.g., IV, 92–3). Advising the king about his finances, Bacon wrote that "your Majesty's recovery must be by the medicines of the Galenists and Arabians, and not of the Chemists or Paracelsians" (XI, 312).

The question of the relation between politics and the Baconian science has two closely related but distinct aspects of great importance. First, did Bacon think that one political system was more conducive to the advancement of learning than another? Second, did his suggestions for a political science live up to the standards of his more general theory of science?

Although Bacon did not provide a straightforward answer to the first question, there are shorter passages in his writings which suggest the direction of his thinking. Listing the different impediments to the advancement of sciences in 1603, Bacon noted that "there is no composition of estate or society . . . which have not some point of contrariety towards true knowledge." According to him, "monarchies incline wits to profit and pleasure" (III, 252). In addition, all governments in general but monarchies in particular opposed all changes and alterations whether political or otherwise (IV, 89, 63; III, 597). By implication, Bacon was suggesting that monarchies would not be particularly favorable for advancing sciences. On the other hand, he insisted that it was of great importance to secure decent working conditions for scientists, in order for learning to advance. Scientists needed to be able to devote their time to learning without any disturbance from outside. They must, in other words, be given freedom to lead a life without any civic commitments (IV, 78; III, 595). But republics inclined men "to glory and vanity" (III, 252). By implication, a strong monarchy would be the most conducive form of government for the advancement of learning.

Because of this ambiguity, scholars have been most eager to seize upon Bacon's *De augmentis*, where he said that "if my leisure time shall here after produce anything concerning political knowledge, the work will perchance be either abortive or posthumous" (V, 79). Although there are several pieces which conform with these descriptions, scholars have taken the *New Atlantis* to be the writing which Bacon had in mind. Evidence to corroborate this conjecture is provided by Bacon's literary secretary's remark that it had been Bacon's original plan to include a description of "the best state or mould of a commonwealth" in the *New Atlantis* (III, 127). Scholars have drawn the conclusion that the unfinished tract must, at the very least, contain hints of what Bacon's ideal commonwealth would have looked like, had he had the time to finish it. For some scholars, these traces point to a strong monarchy sustained by a ubiquitous bureaucracy.[8] Other interpreters of Bacon, while acknowledging the *prima facie* conservatism of Bensalem, the society of the *New Atlantis*, have emphasized its curiously apolitical character.[9] Finally, some students have detected a less conservative undercurrent in the politics of Bensalem. The story invests authority in science and its representatives. The role of political power, as exercised by the king, is peculiarly marginalized and monarchy is described as an antiquarian concern.[10]

Bacon emphasized both the cooperative nature of science and the importance of political support for the advancement of learning, but, apart from a few general remarks, there is little in his writings to suggest that a particular political system would be more favorable to the advancement of science than another.

The more important question is whether Baconian civil knowledge could live up to the standards of his general theory of science. On the surface, it seems that this question can be answered in the affirmative. Civil knowledge formed an integral part of Bacon's classification of sciences, and some of his methodological remarks emphasized unity rather than diversity. In a well-known passage in the *Novum organum*, he wrote:

It may also be asked ... whether I speak of natural philosophy only, or whether I mean that the other sciences, logic, ethics, and politics, should be carried on by this method. Now I certainly mean what I have said to be understood of them all; and as the common logic, which governs by the syllogism, extends not only to natural but to all sciences; so does mine also, which proceeds by induction, embrace everything. (IV, 112)

If natural history formed the basis of natural philosophy, it was civil history which provided the empirical basis for civil knowledge. In his *Parasceve ad historiam naturalem et experimentalem* (1620) Bacon discussed natural history alone, but in the catalog of particular histories he listed under histories of man such things as "History of Pleasure and Pain," "History of Affections," "History of the Intellectual Faculties," and "History of the Art of War." These, if completed, would have formed the foundation for morality and civil knowledge (IV, 269–70). Given the crucial importance of history for Baconian civil knowledge, it is easy to see why he thought that the passage of time had made political philosophy possible. Where "the wisdom of the more ancient times" had to rely on fables, Bacon's own times "abound with history," which provided the necessary material for political philosophy (III, 453).

Nevertheless, there are several serious problems with a demonstrative civil science. The most obvious was the delicate nature of its subject matter. In both *The Advancement of Learning* and the *De augmentis* Bacon was reticent when considering the art of government. The details of this knowledge were simply not "fit to utter" (III, 473–4). Since every innovation constituted an impending danger in politics, and since "a change even for the better is distrusted," it followed that matters of state were not to be studied openly (III, 597; IV, 89). And since a major aim of Baconian science was, of course, to improve the human condition, it is difficult to see how this lofty aim could be reconciled with the fear of political changes.

Moreover, Bacon emphasized that fortune played a prominent part in politics: the politician "hath no particular acts demonstrative of his ability" and is therefore "judged most by the event." It was impossible to say, "if a state be preserved or ruined, whether it be art or accident" (III, 371; IV, 380–1). The secretive nature of politics was due not merely to its moral and theological difficulty but also to its feasibility: human behavior was much more complex than natural phenomena, and civil knowledge was simply "hard to know" (III, 474). The subject matter of civil knowledge was "of all others . . . most immersed in matter, and hardliest reduced to axiom" (III, 445, 406; V, 32).

When Bacon discussed in detail the methods of acquiring civil knowledge and when he gave his concrete examples of this knowledge, his discussions were dominated by conventional modes. He confessed that the nature of the subject matter had led many to skepticism. More to the point, he ranked politics, morality, and law as "popular sciences," which used the traditional methodology of syllogism (III, 388, 607; IV, 411–12). Indeed, political matters rested on "authority, assent, reputation and opinion" rather than on "demonstration and truth" (III, 597; IV, 89). It was, as Bacon pointed out in the *De augmentis*, "eloquence which prevails most in action and common life" (IV, 455). Bacon's civil knowledge had much in common with the classical Ciceronian conception of a *scientia civilis*.[11] In his interpretation of the Orpheus fable, Bacon echoed the opening passages of Cicero's *De inventione* and wrote that civil philosophy applies "her powers of persuasion and eloquence to insinuate into men's minds the love of virtue and equity and peace, teaches the peoples to assemble and unite and take upon them the yoke of laws and submit to authority, and forget their ungoverned appetites, in listening and conforming to precepts and discipline" (VI, 722).

Writing to the earl of Rutland on behalf of the earl of Essex in the mid 1590s, Bacon presented an entirely traditional view of "civil knowledge," as he already called it. This knowledge, he assured the earl of Rutland, was completely based on learning in "the liberal arts." Books of history were especially useful, since they would instruct "in matter moral, military, and politic." Furthermore, Bacon marked a strong contrast between civil knowledge and "all flourishing states" on the one hand and "artes luxuriae" and long periods of peace (which in his philosophical works are regarded as a necessary requirement for the advancment of sciences) on the other (IX, 11–13).

Later in life Bacon made no drastic changes in this concept of civil knowledge. Not only did he recommend Machiavelli's methods in both The Advancement of Learning and the De augmentis, noting in the latter that "the form of writing, which of all others is fittest for such variable argument as that of negotiation and scattered occasions, is that which Machiavelli most wisely and aptly chose for government; namely, Observations or Discourses upon Histories and Examples" (V, 56). Bacon's own examples of civil knowledge were dominated by traditional techniques for deriving useful precepts by generalization and argument by analogy.[12]

Despite his claims of the universality of his new induction and of his hope to unite theoretical (contemplative) and practical (operative) parts of sciences, Bacon's civil knowledge lacks the theoretical part. In natural philosophy the operative element was termed natural prudence or wisdom, but in civil knowledge Bacon called every single part "wisdom." There was no theoretical part of civil philosophy, no "civil science" and consequently no "inquisition of causes" in civil knowledge. Even though Bacon emphasized that the theoretical and active parts of science were inseparable, it seems as if the idea of a theoretical part of civil philosophy did not even occur to him. In The Advancement of Learning, to be sure, he noted that "in civil matters there is a wisdom of discourse and a wisdom of direction" (III, 351), but in the De augmentis this remark is withdrawn. There is not a single clue as to what this theoretical part of civil knowledge would have looked like.[13]

Until recently scholars have tended to see Bacon's Essays as an account of his civil knowledge.[14] Of late, however, the best scholarship has questioned this conclusion. Despite his pronounced confidence in his own ability to offer sound counsel, Bacon seems to have later become less sanguine, if not wholly skeptical, about the possibility of political science. According to this account, the final edition of the *Essays* (1625), while treating the moral and political topics listed in *The Advancement of Learning* as demanding fuller treatment, stresses the contingency and instability of political affairs, which hardly conform to the requirements of a demonstrative science.[15] Indeed, by 1622 Bacon counted his *Essays* "but as recreation of my other studies" (XIV, 374; VII, 14–15), and in 1625 he noted that his writings on ethics and politics (including the *History of Henry VII* and the *De sapientia veterum*) formed no part of his "Instauration" (XIV, 531).

IV THE CITIZEN AND THE COMMONWEALTH

If Bacon's remarks about civil knowledge in general and about its methods in particular were traditional in character, so, too, was his account of the content of civil knowledge. In order to understand what Bacon may have been doing in his writings on civil knowledge, we must have a brief look at the development of classical humanist political thought in the sixteenth century.

It is a well-known fact that early humanist political discourse had been dominated by Ciceronianism, either in its monarchical form – a prince exhibiting cardinal virtues and thereby safeguarding the good of his subjects – or in its republican form – the citizen leading a virtuous civic life for the good of his commonwealth. It has often been pointed out that, toward the end of the sixteenth century, the predominance of Ciceronian humanism was seriously challenged by a new kind of humanism, where the leading ancient guide was Tacitus, and where politics was seen more as an interplay of interests, as an exercise of the principles of reason of state rather than civic virtues. The venerable Ciceronian idea of the virtuous *vita activa* in the service of one's commonwealth was challenged, and a new emphasis placed on moral skepticism and self-interest, self-preservation, and constancy: one should remain steadfast in the face of abrupt changes of fortune, keep aloof from public life, and attempt to enter a state of apathy. Another reaction was to apply the principles of reason of state to one's private life and to focus on the ruthless advancement of one's career.[16] Although this new kind of humanism has sometimes been seen as completely replacing the older Ciceronian humanism, it is arguable that there was less a comprehensive replacement than a partial transformation of the humanist political vocabulary. Tacitism introduced new elements into the tradition of classical humanism, but the older values of Ciceronian humanism not only survived, but merged with the newer strand. Bacon is a case in point.

Some of the features of this new kind of humanism are present in Bacon's writings. He argued, to begin with, that in history Tacitus was "simply the best" and that even in ethics he offered "livelier observations of morality" than Plato or Aristotle (IX, 25; III, 538). The Tacitean values of constancy play a prominent part in Bacon's interpretation of the Prometheus fable (VI, 752).

A more important way in which Bacon's writings incorporated this new kind of humanism was his assessment of civil knowledge. First, as we have seen, there was a skeptical tinge in Bacon's concept of civil knowledge, while his work on history was strongly Guicciardinian.[17] Second, Bacon divided civil knowledge into three different disciplines: the wisdom of conversation, the wisdom of negotiation or business, and the wisdom of government. The wisdom of conversation concerned itself mostly with outward behavior in social intercourse, and Bacon did not enlarge on the subject. In The Advancement of Learning he devoted most of the space to the second, the wisdom of negotiation or business, which was meant to offer counsel in all kinds of private and public business. The most important part of this discipline was devoted to what Bacon called the "architecture of fortune." Its chief doctrine was "to teach men how to raise and make their fortune" (III, 456). Fortune could have an exceptionally great power in human affairs, but the first lesson of Bacon's architecture of fortune was that fortune could be won and that a man was the maker of his own fortune (III, 454–5; VI, 472; VII, 98–9). In order to accomplish this, one should not only seize every available opportunity, he should also create them (III, 465; VI, 427–8). "A wise man will make more opportunities than he finds" (VI, 501).

Running alongside this enjoinder to seize every occasion is an argument about the importance of deceit and dissimulation. Bacon could claim that his precepts were those of "good arts" as against those of "evil arts," which he ascribed to Machiavelli (III, 471). Nevertheless, he agreed with Justus Lipsius that, while an excessive use of dissimulation was imprudent, it was prudent to have "dissimulation in seasonable use; and a power to feign, if there be no remedy"

(VI, 389).[18] The reason was not far to seek. In places where flattery and baseness loomed large, there was no need for traditional virtues (VI, 728). Princes' courts answered this description, for those who were "brought up from their infancy in the courts of kings and affairs of state scarce ever attain to a deep and sincere honesty of manners" (V, 27).

As early as 1596 Bacon had put these precepts into practice in advising the earl of Essex to use dissimulation: "It [the earl's martial greatness] is a thing that of all things I would have you retain, the times considered, and the necessity of the service; for other reason I know none. But I say, keep it in substance, but abolish it in shows to the Queen. For her Majesty loveth peace." Bacon went on about the earl's popularity: "The only way is to quench it *verbis* and not *rebus*. And therefore to take all occasions, to the Queen, to speak against popularity and popular courses vehemently; and to tax it in all others: but nevertheless to go on in your honourable commonwealth courses as you do" (IX, 43, 44).

All this should not prompt us to the overhasty conclusion that Bacon abandoned the traditional classical humanism for the new kind of Tacitism. His whole discussion of the nature of the moral good was presented as a critical commentary on the central principles of Tacitean humanism: skepticism, self-preservation, and apathy.[19]

Bacon readily admitted that the "architecture of fortune" was "an inferior work," because "no man's fortune can be an end worthy of his being"; it should be nothing but "an organ of virtue and merit" (III, 456). When George Villiers was created Viscount in 1616, Bacon wrote to him: "I do not see but you may think your private fortunes established; and therefore it is now time that you should refer your actions chiefly to the good of your sovereign and your country," because "men are born . . . not to cram in their fortunes, but to exercise their virtues." For Bacon, this meant a "dedication of yourself to the public," and the Viscount was advised to "countenance, and encourage, and advance able men and virtuous men and meriting men" (XIII, 6).

Whereas in the "architecture of fortune" Bacon argued that one should be "beware of being carried by an excess of magnanimity" and that one must not "row against the stream" (V, 73), in defending the civic life he asserted that the only means to nip corruption in the bud was to "row against the stream and inclination of time," by "industry, virtue, and policy" (X, 105). It was an obvious indication of self-love that a man wanted to avoid appearing "in public" or engaging "in civil business" and to live a "solitary and private" life (VI, 705).

Given Bacon's strong commitment to the ideals of a virtuous civic life, it is hardly surprising that in his political writings he set great store by those who were engaged in this mode of life. The best way to win honor and praise, since they were nothing but "the reflexion of virtue," was to embrace virtue itself (VI, 501). The promotion of the common good brought such an everlasting glory to a man that he could claim to have "the character of the Deity" (VI, 403). The proper goal for a man's life was therefore to perform "great and lofty services to the commonwealth" and to seek "immortality by merit and renown" (VI, 722).

In defending *negotium*, Bacon invoked the venerable image of counselor. A consummate counselor's vital qualities included, of course, experience and learning. This prompted Bacon to stress the role of education. He wanted to found a college where "such as were so disposed might give themselves to histories, modern languages, books of policy and civil discourse, and other the like enablements unto service of estate" (III, 323–4). Bacon regarded "the colleges of the Jesuits" – bastions of humanist education – as places to be imitated (III, 276–7).[20] An accomplished counselor also had to master the intricacies of rhetoric. Although a counselor was able to offer sensible advice, he failed to persuade if he was unable to use the powers of eloquence (VI, 701–2). But the most important condition of counseling was freedom of speech. Commending the ideal consultation of the commission for the Anglo-Scottish union in 1604, Bacon described it in the following manner: "there was never in any consultation greater plainness and liberty of speech, argument and debate, replying, contradicting, recalling any thing spoken where causes was, expounding any matter ambiguous or mistaken, and all other points of free and friendly interlocution and conference, without cavillations, advantages, or overtakings" (X, 244).

It was these standards of the public good that Bacon wanted Parliament to meet. Identifying himself with Demosthenes (and contradicting his own usage of the rhetoric of reconciliation), he requested MPs to "raise their thoughts, and lay aside those considerations which their private vocations and degrees mought minister and present unto them, and . . . take upon them cogitations and minds agreeable to the dignity and honour of the estate. For certainly," Bacon went on, "Mr. Speaker, if a man shall be only or chiefly sensible of those respects which his particular vocation and degree shall suggest and infuse into him, and not enter into true and worthy considerations of estate, he shall never be able aright to give counsel or take counsel in this matter" (X, 308).

The importance Bacon attached to counselors is shown by his claim that if the princes "be not tossed upon the arguments of counsel, they will be tossed upon the waves of fortune" (VI, 423). In his essay on civic greatness Bacon wrote that it was mainly the business of "counsellors and statesmen" to "make a small state great" (VI, 444).

If Bacon's idea of public life "had more of a republican than a princely spirit to it," as one scholar has recently put it,[21] so, too, did the far from ideal picture of kingship which emerged from some of his writings. Although kings were in great need of sage advice and often consulted with their councils, they wanted, Bacon believed, to appear to make the decisions themselves, and even more importantly wanted "the world [to] think that the decision comes out of their own head, that is out of their proper wisdom and judgment" (VI, 761–2). Princes were cautious and prone to suspicion, with the consequence that they liked favorites who had "a quiet and complying disposition" and who displayed "simple obedience rather than fine observation" (VII, 717–18).

But the good of the commonwealth, Bacon held, ultimately hinged more on the counselors than on the prince. In *The Advancement of Learning* he asserted that "the governments of princes in minority (notwithstanding the infinite disadvantage of that kind of state) have nevertheless excelled the government of princes of mature age," because learned counselors had an exceptionally prominent place during a prince's minority (III, 270). According to Bacon, a prince became a tyrant as soon as he took "all into his own hands" and did not care "for the consent of his nobles and senate [*ordinum et senatus*]," but administered "the government by his own arbitrary and absolute authority" (VI, 702–3).

Bacon's republican inclinations emerge most clearly, however, in the sincere, albeit restricted, respect which he showed for republican and aristocratic forms of government. In 1608 he reminded himself

of the "Bookes in commendac[ion] of Mon[archy] mix[ed] or Aristoc-
[racy]" (XI, 73). As early as 1584 he had written in favor of a league
with Venice (VIII, 55),²² and in 1589 he readily acknowledged that
"[i]t may be, in civil states, a republic is a better policy than a
kingdom," although he added "that God forbid lawful kingdoms"
would be altered (VIII, 85). Writing to James in 1617, he named "the
senate of Venice" as "the wisest state of Europe" (XIII, 246). When
Bacon wrote in *The Advancement of Learning* (and repeated in the
De augmentis) that "it was ever holden that honours in free monarchies and commonwealths had a sweetness more than in tyrannies"
(III, 316; I, 481), he scarcely used the term "free monarchies" in the
same sense as James I. For Bacon, a free monarchy was something
akin to a republic.²³

In the essay "Of nobility" he lauded the republican form of government in even bolder terms. Because republics selected the counselors on the basis of their merits rather than their birth, it followed
that the commonwealth flourished: "men's eyes are upon the business, and not upon the persons; or if upon the persons, it is for the
business sake, as fittest, and not for flags and pedigree." Contemporary republics were a testament to his view. Despite the diversity of
its religion, Switzerland thrived, since "utility is their bond, and not
respects." Similarly, "the Low Countries in their government excell;
for where there is an equality, the consultations are more indifferent,
and the payments and tribute more cheerful" (VI, 405).

V CIVIC GREATNESS

If the wisdom of business filled most of the space reserved for civil
knowledge in *The Advancement of Learning*, Bacon was more reticent about the wisdom of government, which constituted "secret
and retired" knowledge (III, 473–4). He imposed a similar silence on
himself in the *De augmentis* (V, 78), although he gave an important
example of a central branch of this knowledge: a treatise on the
extension of empire. By 1623, civic greatness was no new thing in
Bacon's political vocabulary. On the contrary, it had been one of its
most central notions since the beginning of James's reign. He had
first discussed it in connection with the Anglo-Scottish union project, when he wrote the unfinished tract "Of the true greatness of the
kingdom of Britain." In his second edition of the *Essays* in 1612,

Bacon published an essay "Of the greatness of kingdoms." This essay formed the basis of the treatise in the *De augmentis*, which was,
in turn, translated into English and published as "Of the true greatness of kingdoms and estates" in the third and final edition of the
Essays in 1625. There were thus two distinctive periods when Bacon
was preoccupied with the theme of civic greatness: the beginning
and the end of James's reign. If in the first case Bacon's writings were
intended for the Anglo-Scottish union project, his writings on civic
greatness in the early 1620s can be read as comments on a critical
period of English foreign policy.

   The political contexts of Bacon's writings provide an insight into
their polemical intentions, but it is equally important to recall the
earlier development of the idea of civic greatness, which set the
terms for Bacon's own account of the theme. Many Italian republican humanists of the fifteenth and sixteenth centuries, most conspicuously Machiavelli, had argued that a commonwealth attained
grandezza through certain moral and political values. Most important among these was liberty, which was upheld by the civic virtues
of the people and a mixed constitution. Together these guaranteed
the degree of virtue in the population at large and thereby the liberty
of both the citizen and the whole community. Toward the end of the
sixteenth century this traditional view of civic greatness came under
fierce attack from the same quarters that had called the old Ciceronian ideal of the virtuous *vita activa* into question. The new,
competitive ideal of civic greatness was most clearly set forth by the
Dutchman Justus Lipsius and the Piedmontese Giovanni Botero.

   Machiavelli, Lipsius, and Botero agreed on such central points as
the importance of military strength and a large population, but there
were marked differences in their treatments of these issues. Whereas
Machiavelli argued for a citizen militia, Lipsius and Botero supported a standing army, which they thought would improve military
discipline and provisionals.[24] Lipsius wrote that a standing army
consisted of soldiers "who make dayly profession of armes, as their
proper function and vocation" and published an entire treatise on
armaments and military equipments.[25]

   But Lipsius and Botero's most radical departure from the Machiavellian idea of *grandezza* was their preoccupation with the economic factors which underlay civic greatness. Without sufficient
wealth there was no way to attain civic greatness. Lipsius argued

that "[m]oney was the very sinewes of a state" and devoted the whole second book of the *Admiranda, siue, de magnitudine Romana* to the economy of imperial Rome in general and to its system of taxation in particular.[26] Botero argued that money and wealth, industry and trade were the most important elements to support civic greatness. According to him, "the power of a state is today judged as much by its wealth in money as by its size." But the prince could not gather wealth and money without industrious people. "Nothing is of greater importance for increasing the power of a state and gaining for it more inhabitants and wealth of every kind than the industry of its people and the number of crafts they exercise."[27]

Lipsius's *Politicorum* and Botero's *Relationi universali* and his tract on the greatness of cities were translated into English, and captured the attention of Englishmen like Matthew Sutcliffe. Sutcliffe followed in the new line by supporting the idea of a well-disciplined standing army and discussing its economic foundations in *The Practice, Proceedings, and Lawes of Armes* published in 1593.[28]

It is possible to discern some of these themes in Bacon's writings. But, on the whole, his treatises on civic greatness should be understood as a highly critical reaction to these accounts. When Bacon penned "Of the true greatness of the kingdom of Britain," he began "by confuting the errors or rather correcting the excesses of certain immoderate opinions, which ascribe too much to some points of greatness which are not so essential, and by reducing those points to a true value and estimation" (VII, 48).

According to Bacon, one's judgments about civic greatness should be "grounded upon reason of estate"; it was pointless to speak "of mathematical principles" when "[t]he reason of state is evident" (VII, 50, 51). Expounding his theory of civic greatness to his colleagues in the House of Commons, Bacon advised them to look "into the principles of estate" and to "true reason of estate" (X, 312, 314). In presenting his argument in these terms, Bacon was following the new trends of humanist political parlance, which almost invariably couched political arguments in terms of interests and reason of state.[29] Furthermore, he admitted the occasional need to override conventional morality, asserting that "a just fear" was "a just cause of a preventive war" (XIV, 476–7). There was only "one true and proper pledge of faith" in negotiations and treatises of princes, and this was "not any celestial divinity" but "Necessity" (VI, 706–7). It was a rule in "state-prudence [*prudentia civilis*]" "to distrust, and to take the less favourable view of human affairs" (IV, 91; III, 302). Bacon once pointed out in parliament that "[w]e live not in Plato his Commonwealth, but in times wherein abuses have got the upper hand" (XII, 52).

Another and even more important way in which Bacon showed his close allegiance to this new school of civic greatness was with his argument that the most important characteristic of a truly great state was "martial virtue and discipline"; civic greatness, he argued with distinctive Lipsian resonances, consisted "in the valour and military disposition of the people it breedeth: and that . . . they make profession of arms" (VII, 48). "But above all," he wrote, "for empire and greatness, it importeth most, that a nation do profess arms as their principal honour, study, and occupation" (VI, 449). Amongst modern states only Spain had followed this rule: "the strength of a veteran army . . . always on foot, is that which commonly giveth the law . . . as may well be seen in Spain" (VI, 451).

There is a further sense in which Bacon seems to follow Lipsius and Botero as he turns to insist that, in addition to military discipline, a large population was indispensable for civic greatness. Instead of referring to Lipsius or Botero, however, Bacon chose to invoke Machiavelli, who had put forward a similar argument. "So likewise," Bacon wrote in defense of the Anglo-Scottish union in 1603, "the authority of Nicholas Machiavel seemeth not to be contemned; who enquiring the causes of the growth of the Roman empire, doth give judgement, there was not one greater than this, that the state did so easily compound and incorporate with strangers" (X, 96). Those states which were conducive to empire "have been ever liberal in point of naturalization." And since England was a "magnanimous nation," the law of England should "open her lap to receive in people to be naturalized" (VII, 664–5; VI, 447–8).

Having thus far followed the new account of civic greatness, Bacon suddenly parted company with it and adhered to the Machiavellian theory, which he used to launch a scathing attack on the new theory. Where Lipsius, for example, had given a strong emphasis to arms, equipments, and victuals, Bacon contrasted these issues with military virtue. "Walled towns, stored arsenals and armories, goodly races of horse, chariots of war, elephants, ordnance, artillery, and the like";

Bacon wrote, "all this is but a sheep in a lion's skin, except the breed and disposition of the people be stout and warlike" (VI, 445). There could hardly be a more emphatic refutation of Lipsius's argument.

But Bacon's repudiation of the new theory of civic greatness turned into derision when he began to explore the central doctrine underlying this new theory – the treasure of the state and its economic structure. These considerations received nothing short of ridicule from Bacon. He opened his discussion by emphasizing that money was negligible in war. "Neither," Bacon told the House of Commons in 1607, "is the authority of Machiavel to be despised, who scorneth the proverb of estate taken first from a speech of Mucianus, that Moneys are the sinews of wars; and saith there are no true sinews of wars but the very sinews of the arms of valiant men" (X, 323–4). Elsewhere Bacon added that "the records of all times that do concur to falsify that conceit, that wars are decided not by the sharpest sword but by the greatest purse" (VII, 55–6).[30] Bacon remarked that it might be easy to measure certain arbitrary features of a state, such as "[t]he greatness of an estate in bulk and territory" and "the greatness of finances and revenew," but "the right valuation and true judgment concerning the power and forces of an estate" was an exceedingly difficult task (VI, 445). The conclusion was, of course, that neither the greatness of territory nor a great revenue had anything to do with the true principles of civic greatness. It is not difficult to see Bacon refuting Botero's central claim that civic greatness should be estimated by money and territorial size.

Bacon conceded that in certain circumstances riches could increase civic greatness (VII, 58–61), but, on the whole, his account is organized around the traditional humanist polarity between virtue and riches. Civic greatness might require some material qualities, but in the last resort it was a question of public morality. In the "popular discourse," which he wanted to refute, "too much [was] ascribed to treasure or riches" (VII, 48). When he enlarged on this principle, he argued that "no man can be ignorant of the idolatry that is generally committed in these degenerate times to money, as if it could do all things public and private" (VII, 55). Contrasting "effeminate" and "merchant-like" states with "magnanimous" states, he argued in a court case that, since the laws of England "looketh to the greatness of the kingdom," England was not a "merchant-like" state, and did not waste much time pondering on "husbandlike considerations of profit" (VII, 548). Referring to Guicciardini, Bacon told James in 1617 that "prosperity" made states "secure and underweighers of peril" (XIII, 246). Furthermore, a central mistake in popular theories of civic greatness was that too much was "ascribed to the fruitfulness of the soil, or affluence of commodities" (VII, 48). Sharpening the contrast between the fashionable but popular account and his own estimation, Bacon claimed that civic greatness always rose from poverty and barren soil (X, 324; VII, 55–7, 59).[31] All those states which had attained civic greatness, he added provocatively, had "no other wealth but their adventures, nor no other title but their swords, nor no other press but their poverty" (VII, 57).

If Bacon's adherence to the Machiavellian theory of civic greatness emerges in his assessment of the negligible roles of opulence, trade, and the affluence of commodities, it arises even more clearly in his discussion of the more general conditions which he found indispensable for a great state. Bacon stressed "that every common subject by the poll be fit to make a soldier, and not only certain conditions or degrees of men" (VII, 48–9). It was thus the classical idea of the armed citizen which underlay Bacon's conception of civic greatness. He admired the veteran Spanish army and could demand that the people ought to "make profession of arms," but he also claimed that people should not become "professed soldiers" (VI, 449) and was emphatic that mercenaries should be avoided at all cost (VI, 446). A central part of the active role of the people was their martial character, and warfare was the area in which the people demonstrated their public spirit. "[W]e have now but those two things left, our arms and our virtue"; he wrote, "and if we yield up our arms, how shall we make use of our virtue" (III, 313). The only way to pursue civic greatness successfully, much less to survive in the predatory world, was to attain a large population and to arm it. Walter Ralegh summarized Bacon's view: "Certaine it is, (as Sir Francis Bacon hath iudiciously obserued) That a State whose dimension or stemme is small, may aptly serue to be foundation of a great Monarchie: which chiefly comes to passe, where all regard of domesticall prosperitie is laid aside; and euery mans care addressed to the benefit of his countrie."[32]

Bacon coupled this moral evaluation of the armed citizen with a social and political evaluation of civic greatness. First, to ensure that people were capable of cultivating valor, certain material standards should be met. Bacon opened his analysis by asserting that sedentary and indoor arts were detrimental to military character (VI, 448). This echoed Lipsius's argument (derived from the Roman military writer Vegetius) that professional soldiers should be selected from the manly professions.33 But in Bacon's hands it received a different ideological twist. Warlike people, Bacon wrote, were "a little idle" and they loved "danger better than travail" (VI, 448). They were not conducive to commerce and economic life and it was of crucial importance that they abstained from direct involvement in it. The success of "the ancient states of Sparta, Athens, Rome and others" had been based on slavery. Slaves, in other words, had taken care of "those manufactures." Because this was not a solution available in Bacon's own day, he suggested that this social problem could be solved by leaving "those arts chiefly to strangers" (VI, 449). If "delicate manufactures" were done by strangers, the bulk of the native people could be "handicraftsmen of strong and manly arts," "free servants," and above all "tillers of the ground" (VI, 449). Bacon conceived the armed citizen as a cultivator, a sturdy and free Roman farmer.

Moreover, to ensure that there was a large body of free farmers, it was important that taxes and subsidies should not be too high. For "taxes levied by consent of the estate," as in the Netherlands and England, "do abate men's courage less" (VI, 446). But it was even more important that the numbers of the nobility did not increase disproportionately to those of the common people. Should this happen, farmers would become dependent on landlords, with the fateful consequence that the number of soldiers would decrease dramatically. For if the farmer lost the ownership of his land, he would lose his "heart" and would become but the landlord's hireling: his arm would be his landlord's, and he would no longer fight for the common good. "Even as you may see in coppice woods"; Bacon wrote, using an analogy from forests, "if you leave your staddles too thick, you shall never have clean underwood, but shrubs and bushes" (VI, 446–7; I, 796–7). According to him, England had a proper infantry because Henry VII had realized the close connection between the economic position of the farmer and his ability to act as a soldier, and had decided with Parliament that all farms of twenty acres or more "should be maintained and kept up for ever" (VI, 93–5).34

Another and equally momentous factor in attaining and maintaining a valorous people – and thereby civic greatness – was to look after the political arrangement of the commonwealth. The greatness of a state, Bacon asserted, "consisteth in the temper of the government fit to keep subjects in heart and courage, and not to keep them in the condition of servile vassals" (VII, 49). Defending the naturalization of the Scots, Bacon told the House of Commons that the Scots and English were alike, they were not "tractable in government." Indeed, this quality was incident to all martial people, as was evident "by the example of the Romans." They were like "fierce horses," "of better service than others, yet are they harder to guide and manage" (X, 315; VI, 307). The attainment of civic greatness required free people who were not governed or directed at will.

Although Bacon did not enlarge on his idea of "the temper of the government," his discussion of the Anglo-Scottish union contains an important clue as to what he might have had in mind. In defending the union, he employed the staple example of the Roman citizenship, which consisted of several "liberties." The most important of these were *"Jus Suffragii"* – "the voice in Parliament, or voice of election of such as have voice in Parliament" – and *"Jus Petitionis"* – "answereth to place in counsel and office" (X, 97; VI, 448; VII, 661). This example enabled Bacon to argue against those who expressed fears of Scottish participation in English offices.[35] The Scots, in other words, should be able to participate in English offices and to have a voice in Parliament, because union and naturalization entailed these liberties. But an important corollary of the argument was the idea that citizenship entailed the capacity to vote and to hold office. Explaining what he had in mind, Bacon told the House of Commons that "all ability and capacity is either of private interest of *meum* and *tuum*, or of public service" (X, 309). And, as we have seen, Bacon argued later in the same speech that the English should not merely think of *"meum* and *tuum"* but should take up the loftier aims of civic greatness (X, 325). Rather than simply looking after their private property, the people should serve the public. "And the public," Bacon carefully added, "consisteth chiefly either in Voice, or in Office" (X, 309). A state which pursued civic greatness should, in other words, be organized so that it was certain not merely that the people were armed, but also that their ability to participate in the political life – through having voice in Parliament and opportunity for office – was secured.

Because of his official place as James I's nearest counselor, Bacon conceived himself as "a perfect and peremptory royalist." But his main political ideas cannot be identified with absolutism. On the contrary, he subscribed to the idea of the ancient constitution and sometimes even accepted the right of resistance. More importantly, his strong arguments for the active life, his sincere respect for the republican and aristocratic forms of government and his Machiavellian conception of civic greatness attest to his thorough familiarity with and indebtedness to the classical humanist and republican strands of political thought. In particular, Bacon's theory of *grandezza* was a genuinely Machiavellian theory of war, vigor, and instability, and set an important precedent for the militaristic aspects of mid-seventeenth-century republicanism.

NOTES

I should like to thank Quentin Skinner and Brian Vickers for commenting on an earlier version of this essay and Walter Johnson for revising my English.

1 Sommerville 1986, pp. 131, 134–7.
2 Sommerville 1986, pp. 117–18, 59–60.
3 When James summoned a new Parliament in 1614, he carefully followed Bacon's advice, see *Proceedings in Parliament 1614 (House of Commons)*, ed. Maija Jansson, Memoirs of the American Philosophical Society, vol. 172 (Philadelphia, 1988), pp. 17, 44.
4 Lord Ellesmere's argument is found in Knafla 1977, pp. 202–53 and in T. B. Howell, *A Complete Collections of State Trials* (London, 1816), II, cols. 659–96.
5 There is a striking contrast between Bacon's argument and those of Lord Ellesmere, who argued not only against George Buchanan's resistance theory but also for the absolutist notion of the king's legislative power, *State Trials*, II, cols. 690, 692–4.
6 "Aphorismi de jure gentium maiore sive de fontibus Justiciae et Juris," in Neustadt 1987, pp. 286–9.
7 VII, 416, 633, 760, and especially 369–71; VI, 159–60.
8 Martin 1992, pp. 134–40. Some scholars have made the further inference that the *New Atlantis* as it stands is in fact complete: Weinberger 1976; Wheeler 1990, 292–3.
9 Neustadt 1987, pp. 236–7; Box 1989b, pp. 125–46.
10 Albanese 1990, pp. 515–18; White 1968, pp. 226–7.

11 For the Ciceronian conception of a *scientia civilis*, see Skinner 1993.

12 For a succinct discussion, see Jardine 1974a, pp. 151, 161-3.

13 For the lack of the theoretical part of civil knowledge, see Wormald 1993, p. 168 ff.

14 Crane 1923; Fish 1972, pp. 78–80.

15 Box 1982; Jardine 1974a, pp. 227–8; Box 1989b, pp. 117–22.

16 See e.g., Tuck 1993, Burke 1969, Burke 1991, Salmon 1989.

17 See John F. Tinkler's Chapter 9.

18 Lipsius, *Six Bookes of Politickes or Civil Doctrine*, translated by William Jones (London, 1594), pp. 112–23.

19 For a more detailed discussion, see Ian Box's Chapter 10 and Peltonen 1995, ch. 3.

20 See also IX, 12–13. But cf. XI, 252–4, where Bacon argued that there were already too many grammar schools, which resulted in there being "more scholars . . . than the state can prefer and employ." He added that "the active part of that life not bearing a proportion to the preparative, it must needs fall out that many persons will be bred unfit for other vocations, and unprofitable for that in which they are brought up; which fills the realm full of indigent, idle, and wanton people, which are but *materia rerum novarum*."

21 Tuck 1993, p. 112.

22 See Tuck 1993, p. 114, for the fact that Bacon's writings got a favorable response in Venice.

23 Cf. I, 510; IV, 307, where he spoke about the "princes" of "free states [*republica libera*]."

24 For Lipsius, see *Six Bookes*, pp. 83, 139–59. In his *De militia Romana libri qvinqve, commentarivs ad Polybivm* (Antverpiae, 1598 [1st. ed. 1596]), especially pp. 12, 210–14, 285–91, 361, Lipsius argued for continuous training and hard discipline. Lipsius's *Poliocreticon sive de machinis, tormentis, telis libri qvinque* (Antverpiae, 1599 [1st. ed. 1596]) studied the Roman arms and fortifications in great detail. For Botero, see *The Reason of State* [1st. ed. 1589], translated by P. J. and D. P. Waley (London, 1956), pp. 117, 131–2, 144, 183.

25 Lipsius, *Six Bookes*, p. 144.

26 Lipsius, *Six Bookes*, pp. 82, 136; *Admiranda, siue, de magnitudine Romana libri quattuor* (Parisiis, 1598), pp. 56–162.

27 Botero, *Reason of State*, pp. 134, 150–1; idem, *A Treatise, Concerning the Causes of the Magnificencie and Greatnes of Cities*, translated by Robert Peterson (London, 1606 [1st. ed. 1588], pp. 6, 11–13, 48–50; idem, *Relations of the Most Famovs Kingdoms and Commonweales Thorovgh the World*, translated by Robert Johnson (London, 1608 [1st. ed. 1591–2]), sig. B3ᵛ–4ʳ.

28 Matthew Sutcliffe, *The Practice, Proceedings, and Lawes of Armes* (London, 1593), sig. B2ᵛ–C1ʳ, pp. 16–20.
29 Bacon used the term "reason of state" for the first time in 1584, see VIII, 47.
30 It should be noted that at times Bacon argued otherwise, see X, 269; XII, 37; XIII, 46; XIV, 126.
31 It is worth pointing out that elsewhere Bacon endorsed different views. Thus in his essay "Of seditions and troubles," which is highly reminiscent of Lipsius's account of the same issue (*Six Bookes*, pp. 194–7), one of the prime reasons of seditions was said to be poverty. This could be alleviated by, amongst other things, "the opening and well-balancing of trade" and "the cherishing of manufactures," VI, 410; see also VI, 422–3, 476; VIII, 157–9; V, 88–9.
32 *The Historie of the World* (London, 1614), V,iii,13, p. 496.
33 Lipsius, *Six Bookes*, p. 150.
34 It should be noted that Bacon blended this Machiavellian argument with one based on feudal inheritance, and wrote that "the state of free servants and attendants upon noblemen and gentlemen . . . are no ways inferior unto the yeomanry for arms. And therefore out of all question, the splendour and magnificence and great retinues and hospitality of noblemen and gentlemen, received into custom, doth much conduce unto martial greatness," VI, 447.
35 See Levack 1987, pp. 59–62.

12 Bacon's legacy

I INTRODUCTION

Posterity has been remarkably generous to Bacon. Yet this generosity has taken the form of a protracted debate and has been largely disguised under the cloak of a culturally tacit certitude. We are faced with that debate from the very moment we are intent to gauge Bacon's technical influence on the ensuing philosophical reflection and in particular in that field in which Bacon is most commonly remembered, namely the epistemological discussion which fills so large a period of Western speculation in the modern age. It is not for nothing that Bacon hails his own *Novum organum* as a new logic and saw himself as a legislator and discoverer of sorts. But, as will be shown, the exact tenor and merit of Bacon's purported discoveries is open to much dispute. Unshakably certain, on the other hand, is that the ethos he infused into modern science as something inherently related to social development remains by and large a substantial part of our categorial framework.

In Western culture the researcher, the scientist, the knower is no longer an insulated sage, and society as a whole rather than the individual has long been perceived as the true bearer of knowledge and the ultimate recipient of its fruits. This certitude is, historically speaking, the most solid and enduring part that the Baconian conception of knowledge has bequeathed to the self-images of the age. In other words, if the *technical* components of the Lord Chancellor's speculations on methods of scientific research may not inspire great historiographic enthusiasm today and some students have been anxious to expose their real or supposed decrepitude, the protracted vitality of the societal project that Bacon proposed to Western thought testifies to the decisive significance of his philosophy in the formation of Western values and aspirations, that is, in the fabric of Western rationality as a whole. Now, what is the connection, if any, between the *Novum organum* and the *New Atlantis*, that is, what is the link between Bacon the strict methodologist and Bacon the thinker about science and (or for) society? Granted that the thread running from one part of his discourse to the other might turn out to be extremely tenuous if the student exclusively focuses on the purely internal unfolding of scientific thinking. Nevertheless, if one holds that no ideology is or can ever be merely tangential to human science proper or that, as in Jürgen Habermas's conception, knowledge and interest should be regarded as an undivided category, then Bacon's mark in Western culture is still decisively present.[1]

No science can exist without a specific ethos and Francis Bacon was the first explicit and articulate theoretician of an ethics of science in the form of a message embodying values, visions, hopes, and rational expectations. For that very reason, our age has been aptly termed "the Baconian age," and the fusion of technological power and technocratic control over Nature and society stands for that disputed heritage.[2] I shall consider both aspects of Bacon's legacy in turn as they appear in the historical narrative, with different stresses and serving diverging and sometimes conflicting goals.

II BACON AND CARTESIANISM

Bacon's immediate reception in France shows that the comprehensive tenor of his plan for reform of philosophy was not exactly understood. This early stage of his fortunes already signals the long sequence of partial and distorted readings which, sometimes creative and sometimes dismissive, have accompanied the whole history of Baconianism. Descartes, for example, did recommend what he termed *la méthode de Vérulamius* as a kind of cautious and punctilious, theory-free and fact-gathering process which the prospective knower should resort to before advancing any hypotheses of his own. He even asserted that Bacon's method (i.e., the *historiae naturales et experimentales* to the exclusion of the rest) was the legitimate complement to his own and that both approaches, one a posteriori and the other a priori, could and should be duly conciliated.[3] This is indeed a glaring example of the highly selective reading Bacon's writings soon lent themselves to: the Cartesian project is by no means unaware of the practical vocation of human science, but fails to elaborate on the social and political implications that such a vision naturally entails.[4]

Nor did Marin Mersenne pay much attention to the more technical part of Francis Bacon's philosophy, though he devoted various passages of La vérité des sciences (1625) to the Lord Chancellor's general conception of philosophy, and stressed his critical import against Scholasticism. Mersenne, however, rejected Bacon's positive claims about new modes of knowing or the forms of explanation (roughly along proto-Corpuscularian lines) that he discerned in the pages of the Novum organum. The "aids" Bacon proposed to help man's understanding to transcend the realm of sense, that is, the whole canon of induction and experimentation, were dismissed as irrelevant, while, as Descartes had also done, the Baconian much-favored notion of historia naturalis et experimentalis or ordered inventory of data according to specific heads was hailed as a well-founded step in the pursuit of natural knowledge.[5]

Descartes and Mersenne's surprising silence about Bacon's key concept of induction was only partially remedied by Pierre Gassendi in his posthumous Syntagma philosophicum (1658). In this work Gassendi summarizes Bacon's logical doctrines and regards his gnoseological project as somehow germane to the Cartesian – at least in its starting point, namely the urge to construct a new philosophy from its very foundations (ab imis fundamentis). Yet he criticizes Bacon's stress on inductive procedure as a blind alley in the search for scientific truth. According to Gassendi, "induction is unable to prove anything except by virtue of the syllogism," which therefore has to find its proper place in the domain of methodological reflection.[6] Again, in the next generation Nicolas de Malebranche dwelled on the Baconian philosophy in La recherche de la vérité, but appeared to understand it as a powerful weapon against Scholasticism insofar as he relates Bacon's thoughts to the Skeptical critique.[7] All in all, these evaluations reveal that the classical idiolect of seventeenth-century philosophy is definitely not Bacon's idiolect: the doctrines expounded in the Novum organum or in the De augmentis were wholly peripheral, if not alien, to the great metaphysical debate which Descartes's speculations unleashed in Western philosophical culture. The oft-repeated mistake consisting in seeing in Bacon something like the father of British empiricism – a common misconception which can be traced back to Hegel's own *Vorlesungen über die Geschichte der Philosophie*[8] – can be easily exposed when one remembers that Locke, Berkeley, or Hume wholly partook of the philosophical outlook of a Descartes, a Mersenne, a Gassendi, or a Malebranche, and did not elaborate on, say, matters of method or rules of experimenting.[9] One can go even further and negate the existence of any such school as the British empiricist precisely on the grounds of the radical continuity as regards issues and approaches between Continental and insular thinkers of that period.[10] Further yet, Bacon did not espouse or openly recommend mathematically oriented patterns of reasoning and spurned the use of mathematics in physics; now the construction of modern physical science made full and fruitful use of them, be it in its Galilean, Cartesian, Keplerian, or Newtonian versions. Though students such as T. S. Kuhn regard this process as a merit of sorts insofar as Bacon can be thereby credited with having fathered the so-called experimental tradition in Western scientific culture,[11] we can already perceive in this separation the seeds of the later controversy as to whether the *Novum organum* did play any role in the emergence of modern physical science and its supposed unitarist methodology.[12]

III BACON IN SEVENTEENTH-CENTURY ENGLAND: THE EMERGENCE OF BACONIAN SCIENCE

While the pedagogical and institutional tenets of Bacon's reflections on science were almost entirely ignored by the Lord Chancellor's first readers on the Continent, political turmoil led the English to concentrate on those aspects of Bacon's philosophy which deal more closely with matters of societal values and the general organization of science – a science which was still to come. Thus the English Interregnum can be regarded as the first historical period in which Baconian key proposals gained full currency and from where they have sprung into our own age. The practical, philanthropic *élan* of much republican ideology in Cromwellian England has been traced back to Bacon's inspiration, as expressed in Jan Amos Comenius's pedagogical ideals or in Samuel Hartlib's recasting of utilitarian tenets. True, the source of John Webster's, William Petty's, or John Wilkins's stress on man's moral self-perfection by means of studying Nature as God's second book, or their reevaluation of the mechanical arts, may be ultimately found in religious thought, but the literary clothing they chose for such doctrines was thoroughly Baconian.[13]

These authors fully espoused Bacon's resolute conviction about the redeeming power of science as the most effective tool in assuaging man's sufferings and bettering his state. So, though Bacon's picture of an ideal commonwealth in the *New Atlantis* did not fully square with the mostly egalitarian persuasions shared by these thinkers, they nonetheless embraced the ideal of a fusion of earthly salvation with the mastery of Nature's forces in the benefit of society. As regards their methodological insights, these "low Baconians," in Hugh Trevor-Roper's phrase,[14] did not go beyond Descartes's or Mersenne's appreciation of Bacon's philosophy: the notion of *natural history* enjoyed pride of place in their perception of the Lord Chancellor's plans for delineating a new path to knowledge. Contrary to their more famous French counterparts, however, they regarded this fact-gathering approach to science as the epistemological mirror of men's equality before God. "Any" man was therefore in a position to contribute something to the fabric of empirical knowledge. Hence some historians like I. Bernard Cohen have aptly seen in this belief one of the abiding (though ideal) traits of the Western scientific outlook: no less than the "democratization of science" was the enduring result of this revolutionary approach.[15]

The English Restoration of 1660 saw the adding of institutional flesh to the programmatic bones already perceptible during the Interregnum. The situation, however, looks today far more complex than it used to be believed when the link between the institution of Salomon's House in Bacon's *New Atlantis* and the chartering of the Royal Society in 1662–3 was taken for granted. On the one hand, Royalist historians were anxious to conceal the achievements of Cromwellian Baconians, so that experimental science could be made politically unobjectionable once stripped of its revolutionary or seditious connotations, and hence could be linked to the established Church of England and the monarchical settlement. This is especially noticeable in Bishop Thomas Sprat's commissioned *History of the Royal Society*,[16] which goes to considerable lengths to stress the continuity between Bacon's figure as a loyal statesman and the pursuits of Charles II's gentlemen and virtuosi. On the other hand, Cartesian doctrines had been already introduced in England;

so the epistemological reflections of a Boyle, a Hooke, or a Newton had to elaborate methodological doctrines which, though avowedly but vaguely Baconian, went far beyond the Lord Chancellor's proposals in order to respect nationalistic polarizations in the philosophical debate of the second part of the seventeenth century.

The founding of the Royal Society represents both Bacon's deification as a philosopher and the final victory of the Baconian project of collaboration, utility, and progress in natural inquiries. In the words of its first secretary, Henry Oldenburg, the Society "aims at the improvement of all useful sciences and arts, not by mere speculations but by exact and faithful observations and experiments."[17] Thomas Sprat, the official historian of the Society, claims that its Fellows

have shown to the world this great secret, that Philosophy ought not only to be attended by a select company of refined spirits. As they desire that its productions should be vulgar, so they also declared that they may be promoted by vulgar hands. They exact no extraordinary preparation of learning: to have sound senses and truth is with them a suficient qualification. Here is enough business for minds of all sizes.[18]

This is but Sprat's characteristic rephrasing of Bacon's celebrated contention that his method "places all wits and understandings nearly on a level" (IV, 63). Further yet, the democratization of science of which Cohen spoke proceeds not only vertically, that is, up and down the social scale and the hierarchy of intelligences, but also horizontally. That is to say, perhaps for the first time in Christian history, science (or something approaching our notion of it) is saluted as a human endeavor to be kept rigorously apart from the pursuit of metaphysical or theological truths. No doubt there is a considerable amount of rhetoric in this claim, since Sprat's account is chiefly latitudinarian, but again the Baconian strict separation of the domains of scientific and religious knowledge as expressed in the *Novum organum* becomes crystallized in an institutional shape. In Hooke's own words, the business of the Royal Society was: "To improve the knowledge of natural things and all useful arts, manufactures, mechanic practices, engines and inventions by experiments – not meddling with divinity, metaphysics, morals, politics, grammar, rhetoric or logic."[19]

The exact character of the method propounded in Royal Society circles is more difficult to elucidate. Sprat couples a vague reference to experimentation (for which he fails to mention precise rules of the type laid down by Bacon in the second book of the *Novum organum*) with the general appeal to observation, patient fact-gathering and cautious (or nonexistent) theorizing. This is Sprat's for a time canonical summary of Bacon's method:

True philosophy must first of all be begun by a scrupulous and severe exami-nation of particulars; from them, there may be some general rules, with great caution, drawn: but it must not rest there; nor is that the most diffi-cult part of the course: it must advance those principles, to the finding of new effects through all the varieties of matter, and so both the courses must proceed orderly together; from experimenting to demonstrating, and from demonstrating to experimenting again.[20]

Robert Hooke's design to develop a "philosophical algebra," on the other hand, was presented from the start as a conscious attempt at elaborating Bacon's methodological insights. His formulations are scattered in various works. Defined by Bacon's nineteenth-century editor R. L. Ellis as "the best commentary on Bacon" (I, 25), the relevant passages in the *Micrographia* (1665) and the *Discourse of Earthquakes* (1668) are the most significant to this respect. Hooke asserts that all hope of human regeneration in matters of knowledge is to "proceed from the real, the mechanical, [and] the experimental philosophy," by virtue of which we may perhaps be enabled to dis-cern all the secret workings of Nature "almost in the same manner as we do those that are the productions of art, and are managed by wheels, and engines and springs that were devised by human wit."[21] For Hooke the right method for investigating Nature is the upshot of "solid histories, experiments and works"; his thirty-year-long geo-logical observation and classification is a clear paradigm of what his contemporaries regarded as Baconian inductive practice: laborious compilation of data and cautious and provisional theorizing. The lack of any guiding metaphysical presupposition – except the ubiqui-tous belief that Nature does everything by way of motion, bulk and figure, that is, the basic premise of mechanicism – is indeed the mark of a new style of scientific thinking, which can aptly illustrate Kuhn's conception about the emergence of the so-called Baconian sciences in the seventeenth century.[22]

Bacon's influence on Robert Boyle is somewhat more complex to

assess, for, contrary to Hooke, the polemical tenor of his most relevant writings on method and natural science displays a wealth of
metaphysical and theological concerns which make him partake,
against Sprat's vaunted desideratum, of the great philosophical debate carried on between Cartesians and anti-Cartesians of various
persuasions. His manner of exposition is heir to the rules laid down
in Bacon's *Parasceve*, that is, a straightforward account of the steps
followed in devising and performing an experiment. Thus, some of
Boyle's most technical passages are examples of a new literary genre,
the "written-up experiment" in Brian Vickers's felicitous phrase,[23]
which conveys a protocol of description of the devices employed, an
account of the phenomena to be investigated, a narrative of the
experiments in question, a detailed record of the results, and some
theoretical implications for further research.

Moreover, Boyle's requirements about publicity and reproducibil-
ity in the circumstances alleged – at least ideally or rhetorically[24] –
is of paramount significance, and this further documents the formation of a new cultural type: the European "scientist," as distinct
from the ancient sage, the Renaissance magus or the academic philosopher.[25] It is a matter of dispute, however, as to how far Boyle's
Baconianism (his, for example, is the transformation of Bacon *in-
stantia crucis* in the *Novum organum*, [IV, 180–90] into the more
modern-sounding and influential notion of "crucial experiment"[26])
can be legitimately squared with his resolute upholding of the corpuscular theory of matter. Some scholars aver that it is Descartes's
heritage rather than Bacon's that we encounter here.[27] Nevertheless,
some form or other of Corpuscularianism is common to all outstanding seventeenth-century thinkers – with the partial exception of
Leibniz – and in the case of Boyle one can reasonably wonder
whether he himself regarded that doctrine as the putative result of
experimental inquiry rather than as the a priori theoretical framework of research.[28] Be it as it may, the official Baconianism of a
Hooke or a Boyle – and of most members of the Royal Society or of
countless virtuosi through the land – is coupled with a criterion of
scientific acceptability which can hardly be reconciled with Bacon's
proclaimed ideals in the *Novum organum* and in the *De augmentis*.[29] Both Bacon and Descartes still belonged to the age in
which human *scientia* was perceived as inseparable from the old
requirement of demonstrative certainty.[30] Yet the Baconian tradition

is perhaps the first proponent, in the figures just considered, of a probabilistic and fallibilist criterion of knowledge which went on a par with the "emergence of probability" (in Ian Hacking's phrase) in Pascal's time.[31] In Bacon's own texts (the second book of the *Novum organum*), the notion of certainty is surprisingly linked to the concept of gradual induction, but both the term and the idea seem absent from Sprat's summary of Bacon's method or from Hooke's or Boyle's more detailed illustrations of scientific procedure. Yet, Bacon's espousal of certainty is hard to reconcile with the cooperation he recommended in matters of natural inquiry and with his historical apprehension of a collective human knower. Thus, the motto *veritas temporis filia* (*Novum organum*) is a self-defeating aspiration if the prospective inquirer claims that the long-awaited truth about anything has been finally discovered.[32]

Bacon's putative triumph, however, was nowhere more flamboyantly celebrated than in the widespread Baconian reading of Newton's *Principia* (1678) and *Opticks* (1704). Though the full implications of this interpretation, begun by Thomas Reid, were documented only in the nineteenth century, it is noticeable that from the very start the successes of Newtonian science was attributed to its author's faithful following of the rules laid down in the *Novum organum* some fifty or seventy years earlier. It is true that Newton does once refer to the "argument from induction" as a methodological principle, and that he dwells on the importance of the careful collection of particulars (i.e., Bacon's *historia naturalis*) and consecrates the use of the crucial experiment in the *Opticks*.[33] Yet Newton never mentions Bacon by name, and philosophers and historians of science have been almost unanimous in rejecting this time-honored reading as wholly uncongenial, not to say inimical, to the mathematical tradition to which Newton obviously belonged.[34] Nonetheless, Newton himself most probably knew of the Baconian interpretation of his science and, as far as we know, did not voice any objection to it in his lifetime, though the full attribution to the Baconian inspiration was chiefly due to his posthumous editors Collin MacLaurin, Roger Cotes, and Henry Pemberton. Perhaps the need for intellectual patronage and nationalistic polarizations made this choice inevitable in the context of English Restoration science. Besides, as Michel Blay has shown in careful detail, Newton's use of Baconian themes from the optical studies of 1672 onward appears to belong to the domain of *figures de rhétorique* or modes of presentation of scientific results in the heyday of the decidedly more Baconian Boyle and the earlier Royal Society's strong commitment to the Baconian program.[35]

IV   BACON AND THE FRENCH ENLIGHTENMENT

If a biased epistemological reading of Bacon is characteristic of British culture in the second half of the seventeenth century and early eighteenth century, the next step in the historical construal of Baconianism tended to emphasize the most overtly social and political facets of the Lord Chancellor's thought. For the eighteenth-century French *philosophes* the meaning of the concept Baconianism recaptured once again the revolutionary pathos it had reflected in Interregnum England. Though lavish in their panegyrics, French authors remained characteristically vague as to the real merits that Bacon's philosophy could claim as regards the real progress of knowledge. On the question whether modern science was or was not methodologically "Baconian" they were tellingly silent. A token figure again, Bacon is enthusiastically eulogized by D'Alembert as "le plus grand, le plus universel et le plus éloquent des philosophes," by Diderot as "ce grand génie," by Rousseau as "le plus grand, peut-être, des philosophes," by Condorcet as the discoverer of "la véritable méthode pour étudier la Nature." These and similar evaluations are perhaps the upshot of the acritical acceptance of Voltaire's questionable portrait of Bacon in his *Lettres sur les Anglais* of 1734. Confronted with Descartes, the Lord Chancellor is here depicted as the builder of the great scaffolding on which modern science (i.e., Newton's celestial mechanics) has been erected, thereby rendering useless the whole scaffolding. Though in the *Eléments de la philosophie de Newton* Voltaire does not fail to mention Bacon's concrete proposals in the *Novum organum* regarding possible experiments to inquire into the nature of the earth's attraction (IV, 185; I, 299), on the whole his encomium seems patronizingly hollow.

Why was Bacon truly great then? Because he was a putatively comprehensive social thinker. The humanitarian values of the Baconian project of a technologically exploitable science harnessed to society's needs weighed heavily on the scales of enlightened thought. As a collective subject, mankind has to reform itself through the redeeming powers of science, that is, reason at work, which is generally regarded as coextensive with moral betterment, the assuaging of suffering and toil by means of medicine and the mechanical arts, and especially the institution of a novel social order superseding feudalism and absolute monarchy. In this respect the *Baconbild* of the French *philosophes* is diametrically opposed to the one enshrined by the conservative perception of natural science proper to the Royal Society group and to Restoration England. More precisely, the Encyclopaedists revered Bacon as the eloquent and successful propagandist and ideologist of natural inquiry, but were intriguingly reticent about the epistemological value of his methodological insights. Thus, the entry "induction" in the *Encyclopédie* does not mention Bacon and, though his name fleetingly appears in the articles on "logique" and "encyclopédie," the abbé Pestré commits himself to a vague eulogy when dealing expressly with the issue "Baconisme ou philosophie de Bacon."[36]

At this stage of his fortunes, the Baconian reading of Newton's *Principia* seemed to have been acritically accepted, though Diderot took care to dissociate Bacon's name from that of Newton when in the second part of the century doubts began to be raised as to how valid was the project of an all-embracing geometrization of the natural world. In Diderot's Baconian-sounding *De l'interprétation de la Nature* of 1753 the method of the *historiae* or inventory of data is commended as the right approach in the investigation of life phenomena: once the plasticity of the species has been suspected, the rigidity of the Newtonian mathematical model would amount to a kind of antiscientific dogma because Nature's more dynamic processes in the animal and vegetal kingdoms could hardly be accommodated to that model of research.[37] All in all, however, the *philosophes'* appeal to Bacon's authority was the result of an ideological negotiation, that is, it took part without necessitating the otherwise expected familiarity with Bacon's texts. No wonder then that the first complete French translation of the *Novum organum* (by Antoine Lasalle) had to wait till 1800–3.

V VICTORIAN BACON: THE FATHER OF INDUCTIVE SCIENCE

It was no doubt in the first half of the nineteenth century when a recently awakened epistemological debate in England led philosophers to a serious and systematic scrutiny of Bacon's methodological precepts as something more directly and technically associated with the real procedure of scientific inquiries. In their different and sometimes conflicting ways John Herschel, William Whewell, and John Stuart Mill set the pace of evaluation and criticism of a voice no longer regarded as coming from a distant and therefore possibly legitimizing past, but from a living present. The general tenor of their appreciation is encapsulated in these enthusiastic tirades of Herschel's *Preliminary Discourse*:

It is to our immortal countryman Bacon that we owe the broad announcement of this grand and fertile principle; and the development of the idea that the whole of natural philosophy consists entirely of a series of inductive generalizations, commencing with the most circumstantially stated particulars, and carried up to universal laws, or axioms, which comprehend in their statements every subordinate degree of generality, and of a corresponding series of inverted reasoning from generals to particulars, by which these axioms are traced back to their remotest consequences, and of particular propositions deduced from them. . . .

It is not the introduction of inductive reasoning, as a new and hitherto untried process, which characterizes the Baconian philosophy, but his keen perception, and his broad and spirit-stirring, almost enthusiastic, announcement of its paramount importance, as the alpha and omega of science.[38]

Herschel is dwelling here on Bacon's most "exploitable" insights. These are: the inquirer's need to purge his understanding of prejudices of "opinion" and of "sense" before embarking on actual scientific research (something akin to Bacon's indictment against the "idols" that haunt man's mind), the concrete art of experimenting as illustrated by Bacon's "prerogatives instances," and in general the drawing of rules of philosophizing from the doctrines of method in the *Novum organum*. Yet there is a fundamental misunderstanding in this approach: Herschel sees no contradiction in writing that "in the study of Nature we should not be scrupulous as to *how* we reach knowledge of such general laws: provided only we verify them carefully once detected."[39] Now this means that what gives us the characteristic gist of scientific theories is not the rational plan of their discovery (i.e., the *ars inveniendi* of old) but the method we deploy in proving their mettle as purported explanations of the phenomena we set about to investigate. Now this hardly reflects Bacon's avowed intention as a methodologist, that is, to found a logic of scientific discovery which, if and when duly applied, should yield demonstratively true results.

The tensions between the apparently mechanical requirements of a rational method open to all men and the aristocratic demands of something called *genius* – a token figure of the Romantic culture to which early Victorians belonged – is further revealed by Bacon's arch-admirer William Whewell:

Scientific discovery must ever depend upon some happy thought of which we cannot trace the origin: some fortunate cast of mind, rising above all rules. No maxims can be given which inevitably lead to discovery. No precepts will elevate a man of ordinary endowments to the level of a man of genius; nor will the inquirer of truly inventive mind need to come to the teacher of inductive philosophy to learn how to exercise the faculties which Nature has given him.[40]

Likewise, John Stuart Mill, another neo-Baconian of sorts, voices the same sentiments at the start of his most famous work:

Logic is not the science of belief, not the science of proof, or evidence . . . The office of logic is to supply a test for ascertaining whether or not the belief is well founded. . . . Logic is the common judge and arbiter of all particulars investigations. It does not undertake to find evidence, but to determine whether it has been found. Logic neither observes, nor invents, nor discovers; but judges.[41]

Again, in the face of this evidence, what is the point of writing an unashamedly prescriptive methodology such as Bacon's? Let us recall his own words in the *Novum organum*:

But the course I propose for the discovery of sciences [*nostra vero inveniendi scientias ea est ratio*] is such as leaves but little to the acuteness and strength of wits, but places all wits and understandings nearly on a level. For as in the drawing of a straight line or a perfect circle, much depends on the steadiness and practice of the hand, if it be done by aim of hand only, but if with the aid of rule or compass, little or nothing; so is it exactly with my plan [*omnino similis est nostra ratio*]. (IV, 62–3; I, 172)

This can hardly fit in with the understanding of the unexpected turns that the inquiring mind took according to Bacon's nineteenth-century interpreters. For them, Bacon was decidedly not the author or propounder of an *ars inveniendi* – a cultural project whose credentials were no longer accepted by that time.[42] Rather, he had been the most successful forerunner of a logic of science insofar as his inductive procedure ought to be read as a posteriori mapping out of the unconscious process that scientific research followed in the mind of its (perhaps logically untutored) practitioner. Historiographically regarded, therefore, the emphasis falls on the analytical acumen that the doctrines in the *Novum organum* display rather than in the prescriptive strengths of its methodological proposals. This is perhaps the real sense of Whewell's enthusiastic eulogy:

The general Baconian notion of the method of philosophizing, that it consist in ascending from phenomena, through various stages of generalizations, to truths of the highest order, received, in Newton's discovery of universal mutual gravitation of every particle of matter, that pointed actual exemplification from want of which it had hitherto been almost overlooked or at least very vaguely understood.[43]

This partly explains Whewell's characterization of Bacon as the "supreme legislator of the republic of science, not only the Hercules who slew the monster that obstructed the earlier traveller, but the Solon who established a constitution fitted for all time."[44] But here we have a legislator whose merit, so to speak, has been to codify much previous common law, that is, the norms that science has followed according to "her natural impulses." That this is so can be documented from another quarter: for Herschel, Whewell, or Mill there could be no questioning about the essentially inductive character of science. But their notion of induction was not Bacon's. This misunderstanding helps us to illuminate the polemical background against which this for a time canonical *Baconbild* had been construed.

VI THE BEGINNING OF DENIGRATION

In fierce opposition to the historically far more accurate interpretation of Bacon's induction as an *ars inveniendi*, in 1855 the great Scottish physicist David Brewster had launched a demolishing campaign against the most entrenched of the epistemological dogmas of that time: the relation of Newton to Bacon. In his *Memories of the Life, Writings and Discoveries of Sir Isaac Newton* Brewster stressed that Newton's achievements were not only independent of the methodological doctrines advanced in the *Novum organum* but that, had Newton followed Bacon's precepts, he could not have achieved his

goals. Again, the Romantic notion of the creative genius who un-
bounds himself from all types of fetters is at work in Brewster's
characterization of Newton's achievements:

It is impossible to ascertain the relative importance of any facts, or even
determine if the facts themselves have any value at all, till the master fact
which constitutes any discovery has crowned the zealous efforts of the
aspiring philosopher . . . The impatience of genius spurns the restraints of
mechanical rules, and never will subject to the plodding drudgery of inductive discipline . . . Conscious of having added to science what has escaped
the sagacity of former ages, the ambitious discoverer . . . forms innumerable
theories to explain it, and he exhausts his fancy in trying its possible relations to recognized difficulties or unexplained facts.[45]

As can be readily seen, the tenor of Brewster's criticism attains
the very heart of the more sober evaluations proposed by his English
opponents: one notices that he is casting doubts on the value of the
"inductive discipline" in scientific matters, and is denying the putatively automatic character of the cognitive process by which the
researcher finally ascertains the crucial significance of a particular
phenomenon. The guiding idea (the "master fact") behind the whole
process has to be revealed first. But how? Brewster does not answer
this question directly, but one may surmise from the background to
the whole debate that the unaccounted-for role of the imagination
as something ostensively inimical to rules and precepts of any sort
is the key factor in the framing of scientific hypotheses. Now we
remember that in Bacon's analysis of the faculties of the human
soul the imagination was a capacity strongly to be warned against
and essentially rejected as conducive to irrational fancies: the prospective knower has to add weights to his understanding rather than
wings. Translated into more modern terms: in Brewster's view, Bacon's characterization of the cognitive process – even if we do not
interpret it as being an *ars inveniendi* – was radically faulty because
it left no room for the formation of hypotheses – a function of man's
imaginative capacities – and was systematically hostile to their elaboration. Be it as it may, the tensions of the debate reverberated into
the very appreciation of the great Victorian editors of Bacon's works.
Hence, in the *General Preface to the Philosophical Works*, R. L.
Ellis suspected that the Lord Chancellor's claims to philosophical
glory could no longer be unquestioningly maintained along the lines

of his methodological acumen as a true father of modern science: "It is neither to the technical part of his method nor to the details of his view of the nature and progress of science that his [i.e., Bacon's] fame is justly owing. His merits are of another kind. They belong to the spirit rather than to the positive precepts of his philosophy" (I, 64).

The second part of the nineteenth century was not slow to belittle even this general "spirit." In England Augustus de Morgan wrote in 1858 that "if Newton had taken Bacon for his master, not he, but somebody else would have been Newton";[46] and the renowned epistemologist William S. Jevons went even further in that he tried to encompass the whole history of Western science in this arresting verdict:

It would be an interesting work . . . to trace out the gradual reaction which has taken place in recent times against the purely empirical or Baconian theory of induction. Francis Bacon . . . asserted that the accumulation of facts and the orderly abstraction of axioms, or general terms from them, constitutes the true method of induction. Even Bacon was not wholly unaware of the value of hypothetical anticipation. In one or two places he incidently acknowledges it, as he remarks that the subtlety of Nature surpasses that of reason . . . Nevertheless, *Bacon's method may be estimated historically by the fact that it has not been followed by any of the great masters of science.* Whether we look to Galileo, . . . to Gilbert, . . . or to Newton and Descartes, Leibniz or Huygens . . . *we find that discovery was achieved by the opposite method of that advocated by Bacon.*[47]

Likewise in France and in Germany the second half of the century witnesses a similar ebb in Bacon's fortunes. In his celebrated *Introduction à l'étude de la médecine expérimentale* (which has been called by H. Bergson the *Discourse on method* of the nineteenth century), Claude Bernard emphasized the autonomous character of experimentation in science as independent from and prior to the publication of a corpus of precepts such as Bacon's *Novum organum*.[48] As to Justus von Liebig, whose role in the emergence of the novel notion of *technoscience* has been stressed by S. Toulmin, he rejected the supposed primacy of observation and induction and ridiculed Bacon as an ignorant *Wunderdoktor*.[49]

Forced to hazard a general evaluation of all these views, we may venture that the overall denigration of Bacon's figure is the historically explainable counterpart of the opinion it so blatantly opposes, namely Bacon's decisive role in bringing about the so-called Scientific Revolution and the techniques (as counterdistinct to the ethos) of modern physical science: rhetoric meets rhetoric on its own ground. For that very reason a sober and eclectic reminder like this brief observation by Paolo Rossi is highly in point: "One very obvious thing should not be forgotten: the science of the seventeenth and eighteenth century was at once Galilean, and Baconian, and Cartesian."[50]

VII EPILOGUE

It seems that in a significant sense, however, the general import of the late nineteenth-century verdict on Bacon's merits and especially of the cultural locus where his influence has to be investigated has not been radically altered in our century. The myth of inductivism as the proper method of natural science has been denounced and exposed countless times from various quarters.

Despite all these technical zigzags in the appreciation of Bacon's methodological relevance, no serious questioning of the chief Baconian ideal has been articulated through the history of Western philosophy since the seventeenth century. Thus, there has been a fair cultural consensus in that human betterment is not to be achieved through the self-perfection of the individual knower (as was the case in Antiquity) or through the religiously inspired organization of the Christian commonwealth (as in the Middle Ages). Bacon's insight that scientific knowledge is the main guide through the turmoil of history and of Nature and that science effectively can (and should) beget the reconciliation of man with himself and with the outside world became an anthropological certainty of European humankind relatively soon. In the words of the *Novum organum*:

The introduction of famous discoveries [*inventorum nobilium*] appears to hold by far the first place among human actions; and this was the judgment of the former ages. For to the authors of inventions they awarded divine honours; while to those who did good service in the state . . . they decreed no higher honours than heroic. And certainly if a man rightly compare the two, he will find that this judgment of antiquity was just. For the benefits of discoveries may extend to the whole race of man [*ad universum genus humanum*], civil benefits only to particular places; the latter last not beyond a few ages, the former through all time. . . .

Now the empire of man over things depends wholly on the arts and sciences. For we cannot command Nature except by obeying her [*Naturae enim non imperatur, nisi parendo*]. (IV, 113–14; I, 221–2)

Science is therefore conceived as a collective enterprise of which all can partake and whose fruits all can enjoy. Now since it is society that benefits itself from it, it is society, in the form of the State, that should finance it in a systematic way rather than in the form of a whimsical or sporadic patronage left to individuals' decisions. The inspiration for this vision of public advancement lies in the paradigm of the mechanical arts and their progressiveness; the goal of it is no other but the assuaging of human toil and suffering. Was that inspiration sound and has that goal been achieved?

As Gernot Böhme has convincingly argued, the great ideal bequeathed by Bacon to Western culture has been the notion of the "good" science.[51] Good, that is, insofar as it is useful or technologically exploitable. This needs elucidation: in Antiquity knowledge was generally regarded as good by itself, and a form of "neutral" knowledge was chiefly represented by technology. In Plato's *Gorgias*[52] the art of the physician can be directed toward restoring health or causing death, so the guiding of his practice had to resort to a stance other than medicine, which is a mere *technē*. True knowledge, on the other hand, was always good since it caused a moral benefit, that is, it enhanced the virtue of the knower by making him interiorize and partake of the alleged order and beauty of the world. For Bacon science is itself a moral good which has to be integrated into the fabric of society as a whole, though the ambivalence of the technocratic form of culture that lurks behind this aspiration is not clearly understood or unveiled. For example, in the *De sapientia veterum* (VI, 734) Bacon elaborated on the fable of Daedalus in order to deplore that the mechanical arts can be also put to vicious or deadly uses, but in the *Novum organum* and in other places artillery is repeatedly extolled as one of the signposts of human progress and ingenuity. Bacon wrote in 1603 that "the knowledge that we now possess will not teach a man even what to *wish*" (X, 87). In the list of wishes which he himself drew and which appeared appended to the *New Atlantis* in 1625 under the general rubric of the *Magnalia naturae* the "prolongation of life" appears on a par with the making of "instruments of destruction, as of war and poison" (III, 167). The reference to gunpowder (along with the printing press or the mariner's compass) had become a commonplace among European thinkers who, like Bacon, unhesitantly espoused the cause of the moderns against the ancients. Yet, his repeated allusion to artillery (and not to the peaceful uses of gunpowder) makes it possible to construe Bacon's insight as a decisive step in the gradual perception of the self-acting potentialities of technology; so science becomes autotelic. One would look in vain, however, for a systematic elaboration of a selective ethics of progress in Bacon's speculation: it is progress itself that has autonomously begotten its own ethics, as science has become research susceptible of self-correction in successful action rather than a corpus of statements purportedly revealing the innermost truth of things. For that reason Böhme points out that in good Baconian doctrine a science which led to the improvement of artillery or to the invention of artificial means of preserving food was equally good, because it was equally useful for the end required, that is, a purely technical challenge that research had proposed to meet.[53] Hence "good" science is not the antonym of "bad science" but of useless or rather idle knowledge; in this sense no critic of the Baconian *method* has been really a systematic critic of the Baconian *program* – which perhaps led to its most radical conclusions with the Positivist movement in the last century – until the revolt against its scientistic pretensions began to articulate itself from various quarters.[54] As we know, conventional wisdom has it that science and technology are good or at least neutral, though they can be put *to bad uses*. This is, however, a superficial analysis of the technocratic tenor that the Baconian program inevitably entails: the uses of "technoscience," in the term usually employed to reflect the cognitive constellation outlined in the nineteenth century according to Baconian guidelines, seem to be integrated and reabsorbed into the technical project itself, which therefore becomes autonomous and self-acting.

Still, sociologically speaking, the token value and the regulative function of such concepts as scientific progress identified with a betterment of man's moral condition, has continued unabated, despite the glaring contradictions revealed by the war industry (technologically oriented science *effectively* kills) and by ecological perplexities (technologically oriented science *effectively* destroys man's environment and creates no other).

A further cause of discomfort for the Baconian program has been the failure of a "scientific" organization of human society according to supposedly rational rules. Thus, despite its Hegelian philosophy of history, the Marxian project of construction of a heavenly city based on scientific reason and on the subjugation of Nature by man can be regarded as a recognizable heir to Bacon's program. In this case the Faustian dream has been fused with a messianic dialectic of history in which the final attainment of power by a class becomes the unexpected counterpart of technological success in the realm of natural knowledge, that is, it constitutes its mark of truth. That the embodiment of such an ideal has been so sorely disappointing is perhaps not so surprising if we remember that the tensions involved in the undisputed primacy of action were left unresolved from the very start: the man who is able to subject and subdue Nature is likely to do so by subjecting and subduing other men. The disen-chantment (*Entzauberung*) of the world with which Max Weber viv-idly characterized European culture in the modern age has been expressed in a plurality of fields. One of them was religious reform but not less significant in the domain of cognitive goals was the victorious image of Nature as a soulless mechanism, a vast store-house or an insensitive witness to be cross-questioned in the most severe fashion (IV, 94–5). Bacon's program is perhaps nowhere better depicted than in the forensic image of the stern judge who dictates his questions in order to extract manipulative directions with regard to his sole practical interests. This is the simile of the inquiring mind that Kant so enthusiastically adopted in the *Preface* to the second edition (1787) of his *Critique of Pure Reason*. If at long last the ethos of domination which pervades such inquisitorial dreams has led to the challenging of the most entrenched parts of the Ba-conian program and, with it, to an alternative representation of Na-ture, we may as well ask which of the two – Nature or man – has ultimately become the judge and which the frightened defendant. This poignant perplexity is perhaps the last metamorphosis of the Baconian legacy.

NOTES

1 Habermas 1978.
2 Böhme 1993, pp. 3–14; Schäfer 1993, pp. 95–151. Though Jürgen Mitel-

strass resorts to Leonardo's figure as providing a more apposite symbol, his characterization of a technologically based and a technologically oriented science also follows a Baconian inspiration. Cf. Mittelstrass 1992, pp. 11–73, and Mittelstrass 1982, pp. 37–64.

3 "Nous nous complétons, Vérulamius et moi. Mes conseils serviront à étayer dans ses grandes lignes l'explication de l'univers; ceux de Vérulamius permettront de préciser les expériences nécessaires," *Correspondance*, in *Oeuvres de Descartes*, ed. Ch. Adam and P. Tannery, I, p. 318; cf. also I, pp. 151–2; II, pp. 597–8; III, p. 307; cf. Milhaud 1921, pp. 213–27, and Lalande 1911. The whole question is well treated in Clarke 1982, pp. 17–24. Cf. also Pérez-Ramos 1988, pp. 7–31.

4 Cf. *Discours de la méthode*, Vième partie, ed. E. Gilson (Paris 1987), pp. 61f. Gilson considers that Descartes is annexing the Baconian ideal of science to his own, ibid., p. 450. Cf. in general Brown 1936.

5 *La vérité des sciences* (Paris, 1625; Stuttgart-Bad Cannstatt, 1969) I, XVI, pp. 205–11. Cf. also letter to Cornier: "Si vous voulez achever la traduction du *Sylva Sylvarum* . . . je crois que vous feriez une chose fort agréable à beaucoup de monde. Pour moi, je vous dirai que je n'estime pas tant en Bacon la curiosité de ses expériences comme les conséquences qu'il en tire, et la méthode avec laquelle il s'en sort," *Correspondance du P. M. Mersenne*, ed. P. Tannery et al. 14 vols. (Paris, 1932–50), I, pp. 611–12; Cf. also I, p. 593; II, p. 69. With the term "méthode" Mersenne is referring to Bacon's *historiae*. Cf. in general Lenoble 1971, pp. 326–35, 487, 588; Dear 1988, pp. 187f. The notion of "natural history" has been perhaps the most successful in the long history of Baconianism. Cf. Kambartel 1968, pp. 78ff.

6 *Syntagma philosophicum*, in *Opera omnia* (Lyon, 1658) Book I ("De Logicae Fine," ch. VI), pp. 55–66; 89–90. Gassendi contends that Bacon seeks a *fundamentum solidissimum* on which true philosophy can be erected. If Descartes has putatively found it in the *cogito*, Bacon has resorted to *res*. Cf. Popkin 1979, pp. 138–50; and Milton 1987, esp. pp. 58f.

7 *De la recherche de la vérité* (1674), ed. G. Rodis-Lewis, 3 vols. (Paris, 1962), I, pp. 512 ff., 531 ff.; II, pp. 544, 550. Cf. in general Penrose 1934, pp. 117–42, 187–204. Baconian ideas were also at work in the foundation of the *Académie Royale des Sciences* in 1666 under Colbert's auspices. Cf. Christiaan Huygens's unmistakably Baconian memorandum to Corbert in D'Elia 1985, pp. 181f.

8 *Vorlesungen über die Geschichte der Philosophie* III, *Werke*, ed. E. Moldenhauer and K. M. Michel (Frankfurt-am-Main, 1971), XX, pp. 76ff. Cf. Fischer 1856.

9 There is a notable exception, however. The outline of the rules em-

ployed in scientific research as described (or prescribed) by Hume in his *Treatise on Human Nature* reads like a rephrasing of Bacon's canon, Book I, Part III, XV. Cf. Pera 1982, pp. 31–5.

10 Cf. Norton 1981.

11 Kuhn 1977, esp. pp. 41–52.

12 Near contemporaries already deplored Bacon's lack of interest in mathematics. Cf. Seth Ward in *Vindiciae academiarum* (1654): "It was a misfortune to the world that my Lord Bacon was not skilled in mathematics, which made him jealous of their assistance in natural inquiries," cited in Crombie 1994, II, p. 983.

13 Hill 1965, pp. 85–130; Webster 1975, pp. 485–516. The term "Puritan," however, covers a wider spectrum of denominations than most authors seem to assume in these discussions. Cf. Hooykaas 1972; Ben-David 1971, pp. 74ff.; and Cohen 1985, pp.146ff.

14 Trevor-Roper 1967, pp. 224–93.

15 Cohen 1985, pp. 146ff.

16 *The History of the Royal Society of London* (1667), ed. J. I. Cope and H. W. Jones (London, 1959). Cf. Fisch and Jones 1951 and Wood 1980.

17 "It is our business, in the first place, to scrutinize the whole of Nature and to investigate its activity and powers by means of observations and experiments; and then in course of time to hammer out a more solid philosophy and ample amenities of civilisation" (Letter to van Dam 23 January 1663). *The Correspondence of Henry Oldenburg*, ed. A. R. and M. B. Hall (London, 1975-), II, pp. L3f. Cf. also Brooke 1991, pp. 82–116.

18 *History of the Royal Society*, Part 3, sect XL.

19 Cited in Hunter 1981, p. L46. Cf. *Novum organum* (IV, 66; I, 176) and *De augmentis* (IV, 341; I, 545). On the whole question of religion in connection with the new science, cf. Cohen 1990.

20 *History of the Royal Society*, p. 31. Induction is not even mentioned; cf. Malherbe 1984.

21 *Micrographia: or some Physiological Descriptions of Minute Bodies made by Magnifying Glasses. With Observations and Inquiries thereupon* (London, 1665). *The Preface*, cited in Vickers 1987, pp. 102f.

22 Kuhn 1977.

23 Vickers 1987, p. 45.

24 Shapin and Schaffer have shown the limited extent to which the notion of "publicity" was understood at the time in these debates: 1985, pp. 110–54.

25 Cf. Morris 1981; Ross 1962.

26 This occurs in *Defence of the Doctrine touching the Spring and Weight of the Air* (1662), when Boyle refers to Pascal's experiment on the Puy-de-Dôme as "an experimentum crucis (to speak with our illustrious

Verulam)," *Works*, ed. Thomas Birch (London, 1772), I, p. 151. Hooke first used the expression in *Micrographia* (1665), perhaps independently.

27 Cf. Sargent 1986, Sargent 1994, and Davis 1994.

28 Cf. Leibniz's *Nouveaux Essais sur l'entendement humain* (Paris 1966), ed. J. Brunschwig, IV, XII, p. 403. On Leibniz and Bacon cf. Robinet 1985.

29 Cf. IV, 39, 40, 50, 412; I, 151, 152, 160, 621–2.

30 Cf. van Leeuwen 1963 and Shapiro 1983.

31 Hacking 1975.

32 Cf. Kondylis 1986, pp. 74f.

33 Newton's early letter to the Royal Society (19 February 1672) published in *Philosophical Transactions*, VI, no. 80, pp. 3075–87, already contains a reference to the *experimentum crucis*, devised in order to prove that "light consists of rays differently refrangible." The *argumentum inductionis* appears in the "abandoned" philosophical Rule V in the drafts of the *Regulae philosophandi*. Cf. Koyré 1968, pp. 315–29.

34 Cf. Kuhn 1977. On the misunderstanding of reading Newton's methodology as a version of Baconianism cf. Mittelstrass 1972, esp. pp. 320–2.

35 Cf. Blay 1983, pp. 79–85 and Blay 1985.

36 Cf. "Baconisme ou Philosophie de Bacon" in *L'Encyclopédie* II, 8–10; "encyclopédie" in ibid. V, 635–49; "induction" in ibid. VIII, 686–90. Cf. Malherbe 1985a. Perhaps Bacon's greatest contribution was expressed in Diderot's image of *le philosophe éclectique*. Cf. Casini 1984.

37 Cf. Belaval 1952. Diderot's disenchantment with the Newtonian world-view is manifest in *L'interprétation de la Nature*, II-VI, in *Oeuvres Philosophiques*, ed. Paul Vernière (Paris 1961), pp. 178–84. The Baconian emphasis on natural history squares better with a changing universe than a rigid mathematical approach could do.

38 Herschel 1830, pars. XLVI, CV. Induction is described in par. XLV.

39 Herschel 1830, p. 164.

40 Whewell 1967, II, pp. 20f. Cf. also Lanaro 1987, pp. 54–80, and Fisch 1991, pp. 99–139.

41 Mill 1884, pp. 2–6. One has to notice, however, that in Book III (p.186) Mill does not hesitate to write that "Induction may be defined as the operation of *discovering* and proving general propositions" (my italics). On the other hand, Mill's canons are conceived as ways of investigating *and* discovering the cause of a given phenomenon, pp. 254ff.

42 Laudan 1981, pp. 181–91. The value of Bacon's method as an *ars inveniendi* or "logic of scientific discovery" has been analyzed by some philosophers from the standpoint of contemporary Popperianism: cf. Urbach 1987. For a review of such analyses cf. Pérez-Ramos 1991.

43 Whewell 1967, II, p. 275.

44 Whewell 1967, II, p. 227.

45 Brewster 1855, II, p. 404. This work is a revised version of the early *The Life of Sir Isaac Newton* (London 1831). The philosophical and scientific background to Brewster's views in relation to changing perceptions of Baconianism is aptly documented in Olson 1975, pp. 26–54 and 94–124.

46 Cited in Yeo 1985. A. de Morgan's assessment appeared in an article on "The Works of Francis Bacon" published in *The Athenaeum* in 1858.

47 Jevons 1877, pp. 506f. (my emphasis).

48 Bernard 1984, pp. 34, 88f., 311.

49 The notion of technoscience is outlined in Toulmin 1972. Von Liebig's tirades against Bacon appear in von Liebig 1863.

50 Rossi 1968–73, p. 172.

51 Böhme 1993, pp. 273ff.; Pérez-Ramos 1991, pp. 155f.

52 *Gorgias*, 511E.

53 Böhme 1993; cf. also Schäfer 1993, Whitney 1986, and Whitney 1989.

54 On the similarities between Bacon's and Comte's programs cf. Finch 1872. For an example of a systematic criticism of the pretensions of scientism cf. Adorno and Horkheimer 1972, or Jonas 1979, both with explicit references to Bacon's legacy.

BIBLIOGRAPHY

BACON'S OWN WORKS

The standard scholarly edition of Bacon's works is still *The Works of Francis Bacon*, edited by James Spedding, Robert L. Ellis, and Douglas D. Heath (London: Longman, 1857–74), 14 vols. (reprinted Stuttgart-Bad Cannstatt: F. Frommann Verlag, 1961–3 and New York: Garrett Press, 1968). Volumes 1–5 comprise philosophical works, 6–7 literary and professional works (including *De sapientia veterum*), and 8–14 comprise *The Letters and the Life of Francis Bacon*. There is a separate edition of the first seven volumes (Boston: Brown and Taggard, 1860–4) 15 vols. (reprinted St. Clair Shores: Scholarly Press, 1969).

Bacon wrote most of his philosophical writings in Latin, and the Spedding edition contains the translation of the most important of them. A translation of *Temporis partus masculus, Cogitata et visa*, and *Redargutio philosophiarum* can be found in Benjamin Farrington, *The Philosophy of Francis Bacon. An Essay on Its Development from 1603 to 1609* (Liverpool: Liverpool University Press, 1964). The Oxford University Press will produce a new scholarly edition of all of Bacon's works.

Easily accessible modern editions of individual works include: *The Advancement of Learning*, ed. G. W. Kitchin (London: Dent, 1973), *The Advancement of Learning*, ed. Arthur Johnson (Oxford: Clarendon Press, 1974), *The New Organon, and Related Writings*, ed. Fulton H. Anderson (Indianapolis: Bobbs-Merrill, 1960), *The Great Instauration and New Atlantis*, ed. Jerry Weinberger (Arlington Heights: AHM Publishing Corporation, 1980), *The Essayes or Counsell, Civill and Morall*, ed. Michael Kiernan (Oxford: Oxford University Press, 1985), *The History of the Reign of Henry the Seventh*, ed. F. J. Levy (New York: Bobbs-Merrill, 1972).

Although the Spedding edition contains the bulk of Bacon's writings, new manuscript material has come up, some of which have been published. Graham Rees (assisted by Christopher Upton) published *De viis mortis* in

Francis Bacon's Natural Philosophy: A New Source, BSHS Monographs no. 5 (St. Giles, 1984). A text with a translation of Aphorismi de jure gentium maiore sive de fontibus justiciae et juris is to be found in Mark S. Neustadt, The Making of the Instauration: Science, Politics, and Law in the Career of Francis Bacon. (Ph.D. diss., The Johns Hopkins University, 1987). Speeches which Bacon devised for a court festivity in 1592 have been published in 1870 by James Spedding in A Conference of Pleasure and even more fully by Frank J. Burgoyne in Collotype Facsimile & Type Transcript of an Elizabethan Manuscript Preserved at Alnwick Castle, Northumberland (London, 1904), which also contains Bacon's composition for the Queen's day in 1595 and some other minor works. Bacon's advice to Fulke Greville has been printed in Vernon F. Snow, "Francis Bacon's Advice to Fulke Greville on Research Techniques," Huntington Library Quarterly, XXIII (1960), 369–78 and his "A Direccon for the Readinge of Histories with Profitt" has been printed in David Bergeron, "Francis Bacon: An Unpublished Manuscript," The Papers of the Bibliographical Society of America, LXXXIV (1990), 397–404. Bacon's argument in Slade's case can be found in J. H. Baker, "New Light on Slade's Case," Cambridge Law Journal, XXIX (1971), 51–67, reprinted in idem, The Legal Profession and the Common Law (London: The Hambledon Press, 1986), pp. 401–8.

A new edition of Bacon's literary works, with commentaries, has been published in the "Oxford Authors" series, Francis Bacon, edited by Brian Vickers (Oxford: Oxford University Press, 1996).

Letters not found in The Letters and the Life have been printed in several different places: B. Brogden Orridge, Illustrations of Jack Cade's Rebellion . . . Together with Some Newly-Found Letters of Lord Bacon (London, 1896); E. R. Wood, "Francis Bacon's 'Couisin Sharpe,'" Notes and Queries, CXCVI (1951), 248–9; Robert Johnson, "Francis Bacon and Lionel Cranfield," Huntington Library Quarterly, XXIII (1960), 301–20; Daniel R. Woolf, "John Seldon [sic], John Borough and Francis Bacon's History of Henry VII 1621," Huntington Library Quarterly, XLVII (1984), 47–53.

BIBLIOGRAPHY OF SECONDARY SOURCES

Abbri, Ferdinando. 1984. "Bacon, Boyle e le 'forme' della materia," in Fattori 1984a, pp. 5–27.

Achinstein, Sharon. 1988. "How to Be a Progressive without Looking Like One: History and Knowledge in Bacon's New Atlantis," Clio, XVII, 249–64.

Adorno, Theodor W., and Max Horkheimer. 1972. Dialectic of Enlightenment, trans. J. Cumming. New York: Seabury.

Albanese, Denise. 1990. "The *New Atlantis* and the Uses of Utopia," *ELH*, LVII, 503–28.

Alexander, Peter. 1985. *Ideas, Qualities and Corpuscles. Locke and Boyle on the External World*. Cambridge University Press.

Anderson, Fulton H. 1948. *The Philosophy of Francis Bacon*. Chicago: The University of Chicago Press.

1962. *Francis Bacon: His Career and His Thought*. Los Angeles: University of Southern California Press.

Anderson, Judith H. 1984. *Biographical Truth: The Representation of Historical Persons in Tudor-Stuart Writing*. New Haven: Yale University Press.

Anglo, Sydney. 1966. "The Reception of Machiavelli in Tudor England: A Re-assessment," *Il Politico*, XXXI, 127–38.

Ariew, Roger. 1990. "Christopher Clavius and the Classification of Sciences," *Synthese*, LXXXII, 293–300.

Aughterson, Kate. 1990. "Awakening from a Deep Sleep: The Heuristic Status of Tropes in the Writings of Francis Bacon." D.Phil. diss., University of Oxford.

1992. " 'The Waking Vision': Reference in the *New Atlantis*," *Renaissance Quarterly*, XLV, 119–39.

Baldwin, T. W. 1944. *Shakespere's Small Latine and Lesse Greeke*, 2 vols. Urbana: University of Illinois Press.

Barnouw, Jeffrey. 1979. "The Experience of Bacon's *Essays*: Reading the Text vs. 'Affective Stylistics,' " *Proceedings of the Ninth Congress of the International Comparative Literature Association*, II, 351–7.

1981. "The Separation of Reason and Faith in Bacon and Hobbes, and Leibniz's *Theodicy*," *Journal of the History of Ideas*, XLII, 607–28.

Belaval, Yvon. 1952. "La crise de la géométrisation de l'univers dans la philosophie des Lumières," *Revue Internationale de Philosophie*, VI, 337–55.

Ben-David, Joseph. 1971. *The Scientist's Role in Society*. Englewood Cliffs: Prentice-Hall.

Benjamin, Edwin B. 1965. "Bacon and Tacitus," *Classical Philology*, LX, 102–10.

Bergeron, David M. 1990. "Francis Bacon: An Unpublished Manuscript," *Papers of the Bibliographical Society of America*, LXXXIV, 397–404.

Bergson, Henri. 1946. *La Pensée et le mouvant*. Paris: P.U.F.

Bernard, Claude. 1984. *Introduction à l'étude de la médecine expérimentale* (1st published 1865), ed. F. Dagognet. Paris: Flammarion.

Berns, Laurence. 1978. "Francis Bacon and the Conquest of Nature," *Interpretation*, VII, 1–26.

Berry, Edward I. 1971. "History and Rhetoric in Bacon's Henry VII," in

Stanley E. Fish (ed.), *Seventeenth-century Prose: Modern Essays in Criticism*. New York: Oxford University Press, pp. 281–308.

Bierman, Judah. 1963. "Science and Society in the *New Atlantis* and Other Renaissance Utopias," *Publications of the Modern Language Association*, LXXVIII, 492–500.

1971. "New Atlantis Revisited," *Studies in the Literary Imagination*, IV, no.1, 121–41.

Blay, Michel. 1983. *La conceptualisation newtonienne des phénomènes de la couleur*. Paris: Vrin.

1985. "Remarques sur l'influence de la pensée baconienne à la Royal Society: pratique et discours scientifiques dans l'étude des phénomènes de la couleur," *Etudes Philosophiques*, 359–74.

Bloch, Olivier. 1971. *La Philosophie de Gassendi*. The Hague: Martinus Nijhoff.

Blodgett, E. D. 1931. "Bacon's *New Atlantis* and Campanella's *Civitas solis*: A Study in Relationships," *Publications of the Modern Language Association*, XLVI, 763–80.

Blumenberg, Hans. 1957. "Nachahmung der Natur: Zur Vorgeschichte der schöpferischen Menschen," *Studium Generale*, X, 266–83.

1983. *The Legitimacy of the Modern Age*, trans. R. M. Wallace. Boston: M.I.T. Press.

Boas, Marie. 1951. "Bacon and Gilbert," *Journal of the History of Ideas*, XII, 466–7.

Bock, Hellmut. 1937. *Staat und Gesellschaft bei Francis Bacon: Ein Beitrag zur politischen Ideologie der Tudorzeit*. Berlin: Junker und Dunhaupt.

Böhme, Gernot. 1993. *Am Ende des Baconschen Zeitalters*. Frankfurt-am-Main: Suhrkamp.

Boss, Jeffrey. 1978. "The Medical Philosophy of Francis Bacon (1561–1626)," *Medical Hypotheses*, IV, 208–20.

Bouwsma, William J. 1976. "Changing Assumptions in Later Renaissance Culture," *Viator*, VII, 421–40.

Bowen, Catherine Drinken. 1963. *Francis Bacon: The Temper of a Man*. London: Hamish Hamilton.

Box, Ian. 1982. "Bacon's *Essays*: From Political Science to Political Prudence," *History of Political Thought*, III, 31–49.

1989a. "Medicine and Medical Imagery in Bacon's 'Great Instauration,' " *Historical Reflections*, XVI, 351–65.

1989b. *The Social Thought of Francis Bacon*. Lewiston: The Edwin Mellen Press.

1992. "Politics and Philosophy: Bacon on the Values of War and Peace," *The Seventeenth Century*, VII, 113–27.

Bradford, Alan T. 1983. "Stuart Absolutism and the 'Utility' of Tacitus," *Huntington Library Quarterly*, XLVI, 127–55.

Brewster, David. 1855. *Memoirs of the Life, Writings and Discoveries of Sir Isaac Newton*. Edinburgh: Constable and Co.

Briggs, John C. 1989. *Francis Bacon and the Rhetoric of Nature*. Cambridge Mass.: Harvard University Press.

Brooke, J. H. 1991. *Science and Religion. Some Historical Perspectives*. Cambridge University Press.

Brown, Harcourt. 1936. "The Utilitarian Motif in the age of Descartes," *Annals of Science*, I, 182–92.

Bundy, Murray W. 1930. "Bacon's True Opinion of Poetry," *Studies in Philology*, XXVII, 244–64.

Burch, C. N. 1928. "The Rivals," *Virginia Law Review*, XIV, 507–25.

Burke, Peter. 1969. "Tacitism," in T. A. Dorey (ed.), *Tacitus*. London: Routledge, pp. 149–71.

———1991. "Tacitism, Scepticism, and Reason of State," in J. H. Burns (ed.), *The Cambridge History of Political Thought 1450–1700*. Cambridge University Press, pp. 479–98.

Busch, Wilhelm. 1895. *England under the Tudors: King Henry VII* (first published in German in 1892), trans. Alice M. Todd. London: A. D. Innes.

Bush, Douglas. 1962. *English Literature in the Earlier Seventeenth Century*. Oxford University Press.

Cardwell, Kenneth William. 1986. "*Inquisitio rerum ipsarum*: Francis Bacon and the Interrogatrion of Nature." Ph.D. diss., University of California, Berkeley.

———1990. "Francis Bacon, Inquisitor," in Sessions 1990b, pp. 269–89.

Carruthers, Mary J. 1990. *The Book of Memory: A Study of Memory in Medieval Culture*. Cambridge University Press.

Casini, Paolo. 1984. "Diderot et le portrait du philosophe éclectique," *Revue Internationale de Philosophie*, 148/9, 35–45.

Clark, Stuart. 1974. "Bacon's *Henry VII*: A Case-Study in the Science of Man," *History and Theory*, XIII, 97–118.

Clarke, Desmond. 1982. *Descartes' Philosophy of Science*. Manchester: Manchester University Press.

———1992. "Descartes' Philosophy of Science and the Scientific Revolution," in John Cottingham (ed.), *The Cambridge Companion to Descartes*. Cambridge University Press, pp. 258–85.

Clericuzio, Antonio. 1984. "Le transmutazioni in Bacon e Boyle," in Fattori 1984a, pp. 29–42.

Close, A. J. 1969. "Commonplace Theories of Art and Nature in Classical

Antiquity and in the Renaissance," *Journal of the History of Ideas*, XXX, pp. 467–86.

Coates, Alice M. 1971. "Francis Bacon's Gardening," *Journal of the Royal Horticultural Society*, XCVI, 462–6.

Cochrane, Rexmond C. 1958. "Francis Bacon and the Architect of Fortune," *Studies in the Renaissance*, V, 176–95.

Cocking, John M. 1984. "Bacon's View of Imagination," in Fattori 1984, pp. 43–58.

Cogan, Marc. 1981. "Rhetoric and Action in Francis Bacon," *Philosophy and Rhetoric*, XIV, 212–33.

Cohen, I. Bernard 1985. *Revolution in Science*. Cambridge Mass.: Harvard University Press.

(ed.) 1990. *Puritanism and the Rise of Modern Science: The Merton Thesis*. New Brunswick: Rutgers University Press.

Cohen, L. Jonathan. 1980. "Some Historical Remarks on the Baconian Conception of Probability," *Journal of the History of Ideas*, XLI, 219–31.

Coleman, Janet. 1992. *Ancient and Medieval Memories*. Cambridge University Press.

Colie, Rosalie L. 1955. "Cornelis Drebbel and Salomon de Caus: Two Jacobean Models for Salomon's House," *Huntington Library Quarterly*, XVIII, 245–60.

1956. "*Some Thankfulnesse to Constantine*": *A Study of English Influence Upon the early works of Constantijn Huygens*. The Hague: Martinus Nijhoff.

Collingwood, R. G. 1949. *The Idea of History*, ed. T. M. Knox. London: Oxford University Press.

Copenhaver, Brian. 1978. "The Historiography of Discovery in the Renaissance: The Sources and Composition of Polydore Vergil's *De inventoribus rerum I–III*," *Journal of the Warburg and Courtauld Institutes*, XLI, 191–214.

1988a. "Translation, Terminology and Style in Philosophical Discourse," in Charles B. Schmitt and Quentin Skinner (eds.), *The Cambridge History of Renaissance Philosophy*. Cambridge University Press, pp. 77–110.

1988b. "Astrology and Magic," in Charles B. Schmitt and Quentin Skinner (eds.), *The Cambridge History of Renaissance Philosophy*. Cambridge University Press, pp. 264–300.

Coquillette, Daniel R. 1992. *Francis Bacon*. Edinburgh: Edinburgh University Press.

Crane, Ronald S. 1923. "The Relation of Bacon's *Essays* to His Program for the Advancement of Learning," in *Schelling Anniversary Papers*. New York: Century, pp. 87–105. (Reprinted in Vickers 1968a.)

Cressy, David. 1981. "Francis Bacon and the Advancement of Schooling,"
   History of European Ideas, II, 65–74.

Croll, Morris. 1923. "Attic Prose: Lipsius, Montaigne, Bacon," in *Schelling
   Anniversary Papers*. New York: Century, pp. 117–50. [Reprinted in
   Style, Rhetoric and Rhythm. Essays by Morris W. Kroll, ed. J. M. Patrick
   et al. Princeton: Princeton University Press, 1966, pp. 167–202.]

Crombie, Alistair C. 1994. *Styles of Thinking in the European Tradition*, 3
   vols. London: Duckworth.

Crowther, J. G. 1960. *Francis Bacon: The First Statesman of Science*. London: The Cresset Press.

Curtis, M. H. 1959. *Oxford and Cambridge in Transition, 1558–1642*. Oxford: Oxford University Press.

Daniel, Stephen H. 1982. "Myth and the Grammar of Discovery in Francis
   Bacon," *Philosophy and Rhetoric*, XV, 219–37.

Davies, David W., and Elizabeth S. Wrigley (eds.). 1973. *A Concordance to
   the Essays of Francis Bacon*. Detroit: Gale Research Company.

Davis, Edward B. 1994. " 'Parcere Nominibus': Boyle, Hooke and the Rhetorical Interpretation of Descartes," in Michael Hunter (ed.), *Robert
   Boyle Reconsidered*. Cambridge University Press, pp. 157–75.

Davis, J. C. 1981. *Utopia and the Ideal Society: A Study of English Utopian
   Writing 1516–1700*. Cambridge University Press.

Davis, Natalie Zemon. 1988. "*AHR Forum: The Return of Martin Guerre*:
   'On the Lame,' " *American Historical Review*, XCIII, 572–603.

Davis, Walter R. 1966. "The Imagery of Bacon's Late Work," *Modern Language Quarterly*, XXVII, 162–73.

Dean, Leonard. 1941. "Sir Francis Bacon's Theory of Civil History–Writing,"
   ELH, VIII, 161–83. [Reprinted in Vickers 1968a.]

Dear, Peter. 1988. *Mersenne and the Learning of the Schools*. Ithaca: Cornell University Press.

Debus, A. G. 1967. "Fire Analysis and the Elements in the Sixteenth and
   Seventeenth Centuries," *Annals of Science*, XXIII, 127–47.

   1973. "Motion in the Chemical Texts of the Renaissance," *Isis*, LXIV, 5–17.

De Caprio, Vincenzo. 1978. "Retorica e ideologia nella *Declamatio* di
   Lorenzo Valla sulla donazione di Costantino," *Paragone*, no. 338,
   36–56.

Deleule, Didier. 1984. "Experientia-experimentum ou le mythe du culte de
   l'expérience chez Francis Bacon," in Fattori 1984a, pp. 59–72.

   1985. "L'éthique baconienne et l'esprit de la science moderne," in Malherbe and Pousseur 1985, pp. 53–77.

D'Elia, Alfonsina. 1985. *Christian Huygens: Una biografia intellettuale*.
   Milan: Franco Angeli.

De Mas, Enrico. 1969. "Vico's Four Authors," in Giorgio Tagliacozzo (ed.),

Giambattista Vico: An International Symposium. Baltimore: The Johns Hopkins Press, pp. 3–14.

1984. "Scienza e creazione – studio sul tema trinitario e sulla terminologia biblica nel corpus baconiano," in Fattori 1984a, pp. 73–90.

Dibon, Paul. 1984. "Sur la reception de l'oeuvre de F. Bacon en Hollande dans la première moitié du XVIIᵉ siècle," in Fattori 1984a, pp. 91–115.

Dickie, William M. 1922. "A Comparison of the Scientific Method and Achievement of Aristotle and Bacon," *Philosophical Review*, XXXI, 471–94.

1923. " 'Form' and 'Simple Nature' in Bacon's Philosophy," *Monist*, XXXIII, 428–37.

Ducasse, C. J. 1960. "Francis Bacon's Philosophy of Science," in E. H. Madden (ed.), *Theories of Scientific Method: The Renaissance through the Nineteenth Century*. Seattle: University of Washington Press, pp. 50–74.

Duhem, Pierre. 1954. *Le système du monde*. 10 vols., 2nd. ed., Paris: Librairie Scientifique Hermann et Cⁱᵉ.

Eagle, Roderick L. 1950. "Bacon's Licence to Travel Beyond the Seas," *Notes and Queries*, CXCV, 334.

1952. "Dr. Whitgift's Accounts of Francis and Anthony Bacon at Trinity, Cambridge," *Notes and Queries*, CXCVII, 179–80.

Eiseley, Loren. 1962. *Francis Bacon and the Modern Dilemma*. Lincoln: The University of Nebraska.

Elena, Alberto. 1991. "Baconianism in the Seventeenth-Century Netherlands: A Preliminary Survey," *Nuncius*, VI, 33–47.

Elsky, Martin. 1989. *Authorizing Words: Speech, Writing, and Print in the English Renaissance*. Ithaca: Cornell University Press.

Emerton, Norma E. 1984. *The Scientific Reinterpretation of Form*. Ithaca: Cornell University Press.

Epstein, Joel J. 1970. "Francis Bacon and the Issue of Union, 1603–1608," *Huntington Library Quarterly*, XXXIII, 121–32.

1977. *Francis Bacon: A Political Biography*. Athens: Ohio University Press.

Farrington, Benjamin. 1949. *Francis Bacon: Philosopher of Industrial Science*. New York: Henry Schuman.

1953. "On Misunderstanding the Philosophy of Francis Bacon," in E. Ashworth Underwood (ed.), *Science, Medicine, and History: Essays . . . in Honour of Charles Singer*. London: Oxford University Press, I, pp. 439–50.

1964. *The Philosophy of Francis Bacon: An Essay on its Development from 1603 to 1609 with New Translations of Fundamental Texts*. Liverpool: Liverpool University Press.

1971. "Francis Bacon after His Fall," *Studies in the Literary Imagination*, IV, no. 1, 143–58.

Fattori, Marta. 1980. *Lessico del "Novum Organum" di Francesco Bacone.* 2 vols. Roma: Edizioni dell' Ateneo.

1983. " 'Nature semplici' in Francesco Bacone," *Nouvelles de la république des lettres,* no. 1, 1–33.

(ed.). 1984a. *Francis Bacon, terminologia e fortuna nel XVII secolo.* Roma: Edizioni dell' Ateneo.

1984b. *"Phantasia* nella classificazione baconiana delle scienze," in Fattori 1984a, pp. 117–37.

1984c. *"Spiritus* dans l'*Historia vitae et mortis* de Francis Bacon," in M. Fattori and M. Bianchi (eds.), *Spiritus IV: Colloquio internazionale.* Lessico intellettuale Europea, XXXII, pp. 283–323.

1985. "Le *Novum Organum* de Francis Bacon: problèmes de terminologie," in Malherbe and Pousseur 1985, pp. 79–92.

Fell, London. 1973. "The Classical Four Causes in the Renaissance Art of Law, Legislation, Sovereignty, and the State in Marsilius of Padua, Corasius, and Bodin." Ph.D. diss., Columbia University.

Ferguson, Arthur B. 1975. "The Non-Political Past in Bacon's Theory of History," *Journal of British Studies,* XIV, no. 1, 4–20.

Finch, A. Elley. 1872. *On the Inductive Philosophy: Including a Parallel between Lord Bacon and Auguste Comte as Philosophers.* London: Longmans.

Fisch, H. and H. W. Jones. 1951. "Bacon's Influence on Sprat's *History of the Royal Society,"* *Modern Literary Quarterly,* XII, 399–406.

Fisch, Menachem. 1991. *William Whewell: Philosopher of Science.* Oxford: Clarendon Press.

Fischer, Kuno. 1856. *Franz Bacon von Verulam: Die Realphilosophie und ihr Zeitalter.* Leipzig: Brockhaus.

Fish, Stanley E. 1972. "Georgics of the Mind: The Experience of Bacon's *Essays,"* in Stanley E. Fish, *Self-Consuming Artifacts: The Experience of Seventeenth-Century Literature.* Berkeley and Los Angeles: University of California Press, pp. 78–155.

Fletcher, Harris F. 1956. *The Intellectual Development of John Milton.* Urbana: University of Illinois Press, 2 vols.

Fores, Michael. 1982. "Francis Bacon and the Myth of Industrial Science," *History of Technology,* VII, 57–75.

Frank, Robert G., Jr. 1980. *Harvey and the Oxford Physiologists.* Berkeley and Los Angeles: University of California Press.

Funkenstein, Amos. 1986. *Theology and the Scientific Imagination from the Middle Ages to the Seventeenth Century.* Princeton: Princeton University Press.

Fussner, F. Smith. 1962. *The Historical Revolution: English Historical Writing and Thought 1580–1640.* London: Routledge.

Garber, Daniel. 1992. *Descartes' Metaphysical Physics*. Chicago: University of Chicago Press.

Garin, Eugenio. 1965. *Italian Humanism: Philosophy and Civic Life in the Renaissance*, tr. P. Munz. Oxford: Blackwell.

Garner, Barbara Carman. 1970. "Francis Bacon, Natalis Comes and the Mythological Tradition," *Journal of the Warburg and Courtauld Institutes*, XXXIII, 264–91.

Gaskell, Philip. 1979. "Books bought by Whitgift's Pupils in the 1570s," *Transactions of the Cambridge Bibliographical Society*, VII, 284–93.

Geldsetzer, Lutz. 1985. "L'induction de Bacon et la logique intensionnelle," in Malherbe and Pousseur 1985, pp. 159–78.

Gilbert, N. W. 1960. *Renaissance Concepts of Method*. New York: Columbia University Press.

Gillespie, Gerald. "Scientific Discourse and Postmodernity: Francis Bacon and the Empirical Birth of 'Revision,' " *Boundary 2*, VII, no. 2, 119–48.

Gilmore, Myron P. 1963. "The Renaissance Conception of the Lessons of History," in Wallace K. Ferguson et al. (eds.), *Facets of the Renaissance*. New York: Harper and Row, pp. 73–101.

Ginzburg, Carlo. 1976. "High and Low: The Theme of Forbidden Knowledge in the Sixteenth and Seventeenth Centuries," *Past and Present*, no. 73, 28–41.

Giuliani, Alessandro. 1962. "The Influence of Rhetoric on the Law of Evidence and Pleading," *The Juridical Review*, 216–51.

Gouk, Penelope M. 1984. "Music in Francis Bacon's Natural Philosophy," in Fattori 1984a, pp. 139–54.

Grafton, Anthony. 1983. *Textual Criticism and Exegesis*, vol. I of *Joseph Scaliger: A Study in the History of Classical Scholarship*. Oxford: Clarendon Press.

Grafton, Anthony, and Lisa Jardine. 1986. *From Humanism to the Humanities: Education and the Liberal Arts in Fifteenth- and Sixteenth-Century Europe*. London: Duckworth.

Gray, Hanna H. 1963. "Renaissance Humanism: The Pursuit of Eloquence," *Journal of the History of Ideas*, XXIV, 497–514.

Green, A. Wigfall. 1966. *Sir Francis Bacon*. New York: Twayne Publishers.

Greenleaf, W. H. 1964. *Order, Empiricism and Politics: Two Traditions of English Political Thought 1500–1700*. London: Oxford University Press.

Green-Pedersen, Niels J. 1984. *The Tradition of the Topics in the Middle Ages: The Commentaries on Aristotle's and Boethius' "Topics."* München and Wien: Philosophia Verlag.

Gregory, J. C. 1938. "Chemistry and Alchemy in the Natural Philosophy of Sir Francis Bacon 1561–1626," *Ambix*, II, 93–111.

Grendler, Paul F. 1988. "Printing and Censorship," in Charles B. Schmitt and Quentin Skinner (eds.), *The Cambridge History of Renaissance Philosophy*. Cambridge University Press, pp. 25–53.

1989. *Schooling in Renaissance Italy: Literacy and Learning, 1300–1600*. Baltimore: Johns Hopkins University Press.

Griffiths, G. S. "The Form of Bacon's Essays," *English*, V, 188–93.

Gruman, G. J. 1966. *A History of Ideas about the Prolongation of Life: The Evolution of Prolongevity Hypotheses to 1800*. Transactions of the American Philosophical Society, New Series, LVI, part 9.

Guibbory, Achsah. 1975. "Francis Bacon's View of History: The Cycles of Error and the Progress of Truth," *Journal of English and Germanic Philology*, LXXIV, 336–50.

Habermas, Jürgen. 1978. *Knowledge and Human Interests*, trans. J. J. Shapiro. London: Heinemann.

Hacking, Ian. 1975. *The Emergence of Probability*. Cambridge University Press.

1983. *Representing and Intervening*. Cambridge University Press.

Hall, Clifford. 1985. "Bacon and the Corruption Issue: Some Legal Aspects of Steward's Case," *Journal of Legal History*, VI, 201–13.

1989. "Some Perspectives on the Use of Torture in Bacon's Time and the Question of His 'Virtue,' " *Anglo-American Law Review*, XVIII, 289–321.

Hall, Joan Wylie. 1985. "Bacon's Triple Curative: The 1597 *Essayes, Meditations*, and *Places*," *Papers on Language and Literature*, XXI, 345–58.

Hall, Marie Boas. 1963. "In Defense of Bacon's Views on the Reform of Science," *Personalist*, XLIV, 437–53.

Hall, T. S. 1971. "Life, Death and the Radical Moisture: A Study of Thematic Pattern in Medieval Medical Theory," *Clio Medica*, VI, 3–33.

Hannah, Robert. 1926. *Francis Bacon, the Political Orator*. New York: Century.

Harrison, C. T. 1933. "Bacon, Hobbes, Boyle, and the Ancient Atomists," *Harvard Studies and Notes in Philology and Literature*, XV, 191–218.

Harrison, John L. 1957. "Bacon's View of Rhetoric, Poetry, and the Imagination," *Huntington Library Quarterly*, XXIX, 107–25. (Reprinted in Vickers 1968a.)

Harvey, E. Ruth. 1975. *The Inward Wits: Psychological Theory in the Middle Ages and the Renaissance*. London: The Warburg Institute.

Hattaway, Michael. 1978. "Bacon and 'Knowledge Broken': Limits for Scientific Method," *Journal of the History of Ideas*, XXXIX, 183–97.

Heath, Terrence. 1971. "Logical Grammar, Grammatical Logic, and Humanism in Three German Universities," *Studies in the Renaissance*, XVIII, 9–64.

Helgerson, Richard. 1992. *Forms of Nationhood: The Elizabethan Writing of England*. Chicago: University of Chicago Press.

Heltzel, Virgil B. 1948. "Young Francis Bacon's Tutor," *Modern Language Notes*, LXIII, 483–5.

Herschel, John. 1830. *Preliminary Discourse on the Study of Natural Philosophy*. London: Longman.

Hesse, Mary. 1962. "Hooke's Development of Bacon's Method," *Proceedings of the Tenth International Congress of the History of Science*, 265–8.

1964. "Francis Bacon," in D. J. O'Connor (ed.), *A Critical History of Western Philosophy*. London: Collier-Macmillan, pp. 141–52. (Reprinted in Vickers 1968a.)

Hill, Christopher. 1965. *The Intellectual Origins of the English Revolution*. Oxford: Oxford University Press.

Hind, A. M. 1964. *Engraving in England in the Sixteenth and Seventeenth Centuries*, vol. III, M. Corbett and M. Norton (eds.). Cambridge University Press.

Hintikka, Jaakko. 1974. *Knowledge and the Known*. Dordrecht: Reidel.

Hogan, John C., and Mortimer D. Schwartz. 1983. "On Bacon's 'Rules and Maximes' of the Common Law," *Law Library Journal*, LXXVI, 48–77.

1985. "A Translation of Bacon's Maxims of the Common Law," *Law Library Journal*, LXXVII, 707–18.

Holdsworth, W. S. 1933. "Francis Bacon's Decisions," *Law Quarterly Review*, CXCIII, 61–9.

Hooykaas, R. 1958. *Humanisme, science et réforme: Pierre de la Ramée (1515–1572)*. Leiden: E. J. Brill.

1972. *Religion and the Rise of Modern Science*. Edinburgh and London: Scottish Academic Press.

Horkheimer, Max, and Theodor Adorno. 1972. *Dialectic of Enlightenment*, trans. John Cumming. New York: Seabury.

Horton, Mary. 1973. "In Defence of Francis Bacon: A Criticism of the Critics of the Inductive Method," *Studies in the History and Philosophy of Science*, IV, 241–78.

1982. "Bacon and 'Knowledge Broken': An Answer to Michael Hattaway," *Journal of the History of Ideas*, XLIII, 487–504.

Hovey, Kenneth Alan. 1985. " 'Diuinitie, and Poesie, Met': The Baconian Context of George Herbert's Divinity," *English Language Notes*, XXII (3), 30–9.

1990. "Bacon's Parabolic Drama: Iconoclastic Philosophy and Elizabethan Politics," in Sessions 1990b, pp. 215–36.

Howell, A. C. 1946. "*Res et Verba*: Words and Things," *ELH*, XIII, 131–46.

Howell, W. S. 1956. *Logic and Rhetoric in England, 1500–1700*. Princeton: Princeton University Press.

Huffman, William H. 1988. *Robert Fludd and the End of the Renaissance*. London: Routledge.

Hulse, Clark. 1988. "Spenser, Bacon, and the Myth of Power," in Heather Dubrow and Richard Strier (eds.), *The Historical Renaissance: New Essays on Tudor and Stuart Literature and Culture*. Chicago: The University of Chicago Press, pp. 315–46.

Hunter, Michael. 1981. *Science and Society in Restoration England*. Cambridge University Press.

———. 1988. "Promoting the New Science: Henry Oldenburg and the Early Royal Society," *History of Science*, XXVI, 165–81.

Hunter, Michael, and Paul B. Wood. 1986. "Towards Solomon's House: Rival Strategies for Reforming the Early Royal Society," *History of Science*, XXIV, 49–108.

Jaeger, W. 1947. *The Theology of the Early Greek Philosophers*. Oxford: Clarendon Press.

Jardine, Lisa. 1974a. *Francis Bacon: Discovery and the Art of Discourse*. Cambridge University Press.

———. 1974b. "The Place of Dialectic Teaching in Sixteenth-Century Cambridge," *Studies in the Renaissance*, XXI, 31–62.

———. 1990. "*Experientia literata* or *Novum Organum*? The Dilemma of Bacon's Scientific Method," in Sessions 1990b, pp. 47–67.

Jardine, Nicholas. 1984. *The Birth of History and Philosophy of Science: Kepler's "A Defence of Tycho against Ursus" with Essays on Its Provenance and Significance*. Cambridge University Press.

Jevons, William. 1877. *The Principles of Science: A Treatise on Logic and Scientific Method* (1st published 1874). London: Macmillan.

Johnson, Robert C. 1960. "Francis Bacon and Lionel Cranfield," *Huntington Library Quarterly*, XXIII, 301–20.

Jonas, Hans. 1979. *Das Prinzip Verantwortung. Versuch einer Ethik für die technologische Zivilisation*. Frankfurt-am-Main: Suhrkamp.

Jones, Richard Foster. 1961. *Ancients and Moderns: A Study of the Rise of the Scientific Movement in Seventeenth-Century England*, 2nd ed. St. Louis: Washington University Studies.

Kambartel, Franz. 1968. *Ehrfahrung und Struktur: Bausteine zu eine Kritik des Empirismus und Formalismus*. Frankfurt-am-Main: Suhrkamp.

Kargon, Robert. 1963. "John Graunt, Francis Bacon, and the Royal Society: The Reception of Statistics," *Journal of the History of Medicine*, XVIII, 337–48.

Kelley, Donald R. 1974. "Clio and the Lawyers: Forms of Historical Consciousness in Medieval Jurisprudence," *Medievalia et Humanistica*, n.s. V, 25–49.

Kelly, H. A. 1965. "The Deployment of Faith and Reason in Bacon's Approach to Knowledge," *The Modern Schoolman*, XLII, 265–85.

Kessler, Eckehard. 1988. "The Intellective Soul," in Charles Schmitt and

Quentin Skinner (eds.), *The Cambridge History of Renaissance Philosophy*. Cambridge University Press, pp. 485–534.

Kiernan, Michael (ed.). 1985. *Sir Francis Bacon: The Essayes or Counsels, Civill and Morall*. Cambridge: Harvard University Press.

Kirkwood, James J. 1965. "Bacon's *Henry VII*: A Model of a Theory of Historiography," *Renaissance Papers*, 51–5.

Klaaven, Eugen M. 1977. *Religious Origins of Modern Science*. Grand Rapids: Eerdmans.

Klein, Jürgen, 1987. *Francis Bacon oder die Modernisierung Englands*. Anglistische und Amerikanistische Texte und Studien, Band 4.

Klibansky, R., E. Panofsky, and F. Saxl. 1964. *Saturn and Melancholy. Studies in the History of Natural Philosophy, Religion and Art*. London: Nelson.

Knafla, Louis A. 1977. *Law and Politics in Jacobean England*. Cambridge University Press.

Knights, L. C. 1946. "Bacon and the Seventeenth-Century Dissociation of Sensibility," in L. C. Knights, *Explorations*. London: Chatto and Windus, pp. 92–111.

Kocher, Paul. 1953. *Science and Religion in Elizabethan England*. San Marino: Huntington Library Publications.

   1957. "Francis Bacon on the Science of Jurisprudence," *Journal of the History of Ideas*, XVIII, 3–26. (Reprinted in Vickers 1968a.)

   1958. "Francis Bacon and His Father," *Huntington Library Quarterly*, XXI, 133–58.

Kohl, Benjamin G. 1974. "Petrarch's Prefaces to *De viris illustribus*," *History and Theory*, XIII, 131–44.

Kondylis, Panajotis. 1986. *Die Aufklärung im Rahmen des neuzeitlichen Rationalismus*. Munich: Ernst Klett.

Kosman, L. A. 1964. "The Aristotelian Background of Bacon's *Novum Organum*." Ph.D. diss., Harvard University.

Kotarbinski, Tadeusz. 1935. "The Development of the Main Problem in the Methodology of Francis Bacon," *Studia philosophica. Commentarii societatis philosophicae Polonorum*, I, 107–17.

Koyré, Alexandre. 1968. *Etudes newtoniennes*. Paris: Presses Universitaires de France.

Kraus, Oskar. 1926. *Der Machtgedanke und die Friedensidee in der Philosophie der Engländer: Bacon und Bentham*. Zeitfrage aus dem Gebiete der Soziologie, III Reihe, 1. Heft.

Kremer-Marietti, Angèle. 1985. "*Philosophia prima et scala intellectus*, concepts en devenir chez Bacon et chez Comte," in Malherbe and Pousseur 1985, pp. 179–99.

Kristeller, Paul Oskar. 1979. *Renaissance Thought and Its Sources*, ed. Michael Mooney. New York: Columbia University Press.

1988. "Humanism," in Charles Schmitt and Quentin Skinner (eds.), *The Cambridge History of Renaissance Philosophy*. Cambridge University Press, pp. 113–37.

Kristof, Ladis K. D. 1978. "Francis Bacon and the Marxists: Faith in the Glorious Future of Mankind," in G. L. Ulman, *Society and History. Essays in Honor of Karl August Wittfogel*. The Hague: Mouton, pp. 233–57.

Krook, Dorothea. 1955. "Two Baconians: Robert Boyle and Joseph Glanvill," *Huntington Library Quarterly*, XVIII, 261–78.

Kuhn, Thomas S. 1977. *The Essential Tension*. Chicago: University of Chicago Press.

Kusukawa, Sachiko. 1995. *The Transformation of Natural Philosophy: The Case of Philip Melanchthon*. Cambridge University Press.

Laird, W. R. 1986. "The Scope of Renaissance Mechanics," *Osiris*, n.s. II, 43–68.

Lakatos, Imre. 1974. "Popper on Demarcation and Induction," in P. A. Schilpp (ed.), *The Philosophy of Karl Popper*. La Salle: Open Court.

Lalande, André. 1911. "Sur quelques textes de Bacon et de Descartes," *Revue de métaphysique et de morale*, XI, 296–311.

Lanaro, Giorgio. 1987. *La teoria dell'induzione in William Whewell*. Milan: Franco Angeli.

1989. "Il genio e le regole: Osservazioni su Whewell e l'immagine di Bacone nel primo ottocento," *Rivista di Storia della Filosofia*, XLIV, 37–67.

Larsen, Robert E. 1962. "The Aristotelianism of Bacon's *Novum Organum*," *Journal of the History of Ideas*, XXIII, 435–50.

Laudan, Laurence. 1966. "The Clock Metaphor and Probabilism: The Impact of Descartes on English Methodological Thought (1650–65)," *Annals of Science*, XXII, 73–103.

1981. *Science and Hypothesis*. Dordrecht: Reidel.

Leary, John E., Jr. 1994. *Francis Bacon and the Politics of Science*. Ames: Iowa State University Press.

Le Doeuff, Michèle. 1984. "Bacon chez les grands au siècle de Louis XIII," in Fattori 1984a, pp. 155–78.

1990a. "Hope in Science," in Sessions 1990b, pp. 9–24.

1990b. "Man and Nature in the Gardens of Science," in Sessions 1990b, pp. 119–38.

(ed. and tr.). 1991. Francis Bacon, *Du progrès et de la promotion des savoirs*. Paris: Gallimard.

Lemmi, C. W. 1933. *The Classical Deities in Bacon: A Study in Mythological Symbolism*. Baltimore: The Johns Hopkins Press.

Lenoble, Robert. 1969. *Histoire de l'idée de nature*. Paris: Albin Michel.

1971. *Mersenne ou la naissance du mécanisme*. Paris: Vrin.

Levack, Brian P. 1987. *The Formation of the British State. England, Scotland, and the Union 1603–1707.* Oxford: Oxford University Press.

Levine, Joseph M. 1983. "Natural History and the History of the Scientific Revolution," *Clio,* XIII, 57–73.

1987. *Humanism and History: Origins of Modern English Historiography.* Ithaca: Cornell University Press.

Levy, F. J. 1967. *Tudor Historical Thought.* San Marino: Huntington Library.

1986. "Francis Bacon and the Style of Politics," *English Literary Renaissance,* XVI, 101–22.

(ed.). 1972. *The History of the Reign of King Henry the Seventh,* by Francis Bacon. New York: Bobbs-Merrill.

Linden, Stanton J. 1974. "Francis Bacon and Alchemy: The Reformation of Vulcan," *Journal of the History of Ideas,* XXXV, 547–60.

Livesey, Steven J. 1989. *Theology and Science in the Fourteenth Century: Three Questions on the Unity and Subalternation of the Sciences from John of Reading's Commentary on the Sentences.* Leiden: E. J. Brill.

Lohr, Charles H. 1988. "Metaphysics," in Charles Schmitt and Quentin Skinner (eds.), *The Cambridge History of Renaissance Philosophy.* Cambridge University Press, pp. 537–638.

Low, Anthony. 1983. "New Science and the Georgic Revolution in Seventeenth-Century English Literature," *English Literary Renaissance,* XIII, 231–59.

Luciani, Vincent. 1947. "Bacon and Machiavelli," *Italica,* XXIV, 26–40.

McCabe, Bernard. 1964. "Francis Bacon and the Natural Law Tradition," *Natural Law Forum,* IX, pp. 111–21.

McCanles, Michael. 1975. "Myth and Method in the Scientific Philosophy of Francis Bacon," in Michael McCanles, *Dialectical Criticism and Renaissance Literature.* Berkeley and Los Angeles: University of California Press, pp. 14–51.

1990. "From Derrida to Bacon and Beyond," in Sessions 1990b, pp. 25–46.

McCreary, E. P. 1973. "Bacon's Theory of the Imagination Reconsidered," *Huntington Library Quarterly.* XXXVI, 317–26.

McCutcheon, Elizabeth. 1972. "Bacon and the Cherubim: An Iconographical Reading of the *New Atlantis,*" *English Literary Renaissance,* II, 334–55.

McIntosh, Marjorie K. 1975. "Sir Anthony Cooke: Tudor Humanist, Educator and Religious Reformer," *Proceedings of the American Philosophical Society,* CXIX, 233–50.

McLuhan, Marshall. 1974. "Bacon: Ancient or Modern?," *Renaissance and Reformation,* X, 93–8.

McMullin, Ernan. 1985. "Openness and Secrecy in Science: Some Notes on Early History," *Science, Technology and Human Values,* X, 14–23.

1992. "Introduction: The Social Dimensions of Science," in Ernan McMullin (ed.), *The Social Dimensions of Science*. Notre Dame: University of Notre Dame Press, pp. 1–26.

McNamee, Maurice B. 1950. "Literary Decorum in Francis Bacon," *Saint Louis University Studies*, Series A, vol. I, 1–52.

1971. "Bacon's Inductive Method and Humanistic Grammar," *Studies in the Literary Imagination*, IV, no. 1, 81–106.

McVaugh, M. 1974. "The *Humidum Radicale* in Thirteenth-Century Medicine," *Traditio*, XXX, 259–83.

Macciò, M. 1962. "A proposito dell'atomismo nel *Novum organum* di Francesco Bacone," *Rivista critica di storia della filosofia*, XVII, 188–96.

Maddison, R. E. W. 1969. *The Life of the Honourable Robert Boyle, FRS*. New York: Barnes and Noble.

Maitland S. R. 1847/1848. "Archbishop Whitgift's College Pupils," *The British Magazine*, XXXII, 361–79, 508–28, 650–6; XXXIII, 17–31, 444–63.

Malherbe, Michel. 1984. "L'induction baconienne: De l'échec metaphysique à l'échec logique," in Fattori 1984a, pp. 179–200.

1985a. "Bacon, l'*Encyclopédie* et la Révolution," *Etudes Philosophiques*, 387–404.

1985b. "L'expérience et l'induction chez Bacon," in Malherbe and Pousseur 1985, pp. 113–33.

1986. "L'induction des notions chez Francis Bacon," *Revue internationale de philosophie*, XL, 427–45.

1988. "L'histoire naturelle inductive de Francis Bacon," *Estudios sobre Historia de la Ciencia y de la Tecnica*, I, 49–66.

1990. "Bacon's Critique of Logic," in Sessions 1990b, pp. 69–87.

Malherbe, Michel, and Jean-Marie Pousseur (eds.). 1985. *Francis Bacon science et méthode*. Paris: J. Vrin.

Mandelbaum, Maurice. 1964. *Philosophy, Science and Sense Perception*. Baltimore: The Johns Hopkins University Press.

Margenau, Henry. 1961. "Bacon and Modern Physics: A Confrontation," *Proceedings of the American Philosophical Association*, CV, 487–92.

Margolin, Jean-Claude. "L'idée de nouveauté et ses points d'application dans le *Novum Organum* de Bacon," in Malherbe and Pousseur 1985, pp. 11–36.

Martin, Julian. 1992. *Francis Bacon, the State, and the Reform of Natural Philosophy*. Cambridge University Press.

Marwil, Jonathan L. 1976. *The Trials of Counsel: Francis Bacon in 1621*. Detroit: Wayne State University Press.

Melzer, Arthur M. 1993. "The Problem with the 'Problem of Technology,'" in Arthur M. Melzer, Jerry Weinberger, and M. Richard Zinman (eds.), *Technology in the Western Political Tradition*. Ithaca: Cornell University Press, pp. 287–322.

Merton, Robert K. 1961. "Singletons and Multiples in Scientific Discovery: A Chapter in the Sociology of Science," *Proceedings of the American Philosophical Society*, CV, 470–86.

Messeri, Marco. 1985. *Causa e spiegazione: La fisica di Pierre Gassendi.* Milan: Franco Angeli.

Mikkeli, Heikki. 1992. *An Aristotelian Response to Renaissance Humanism: Jacopo Zabarella on the Nature of Arts and Sciences.* Helsinki: Societas Historica Finlandiae.

Milhaud, Gaston. 1921. *Descartes savant.* Paris: Alcan.

Mill, John Stuart. 1884. *A System of Logic, Ratiocinative and Inductive.* London: Longman.

Millen, Ron. 1985. "The Manifestation of Occult Qualities in the Scientific Revolution," in M. J. Osler and P. L. Farber (eds.), *Religion, Science and Worldview: Essays in Honour of Richard S. Westfall.* Cambridge University Press, pp. 185–216.

Milton, J. R. 1987. "Induction before Hume," *British Journal for the Philosophy of Science*, XXXVIII, 49–74.

Minogue, Kenneth. 1983. "Bacon and Locke: Or Ideology as Mental Hygiene," in Anthony Parel (ed.), *Ideology, Philosophy and Politics.* Waterloo: Wilfrid Laurier University Press, pp. 179–98.

Mittelstrass, Jürgen. 1972. "The Galilean Revolution: The Historical Fate of a Methodological Insight," *Studies in the History and Philosophy of Science*, II, 297–328.

1982. *Wissenschaft als Lebensform.* Frankfurt-am-Main: Suhrkamp.

1992. *Leonardo-Welt. Über Wissenschaft, Forschung und Verantwortung.* Frankfurt-am-Main: Suhrkamp.

Momigliano, Arnaldo. 1966. "Ancient History and the Antiquarian," *Studies in Historiography.* London: Weidenfield and Nicolson.

Mommsen, Theodor E. 1942. "Petrarch's Conception of the 'Dark Ages,' " *Speculum*, XVII, 226–42.

Mondolfo, Rodolfo. 1969. *Il verum factum prima di Vico.* Naples: Guida.

Monfasani, John. 1988. "Humanism and Rhetoric," in A. Rabil, Jr. (ed.), *Renaissance Humanism: Foundations, Form and Legacy*, 3 vols. Philadelphia: University of Pennsylvania Press, III, pp. 171–235.

Morris, M. N. 1981. "Science as *Scientia*," *Physis*, XXIII, 171–96.

Morrison, James C. 1977. "Philosophy and History in Bacon," *Journal of the History of Ideas*, XXXVIII, 585–606.

Mouton, Johann. 1983. "Reformation and Restoration in Francis Bacon's Early Philosophy," *The Modern Schoolman*, LX, 101–12.

1987. " 'The Masculine Birth of Time': Interpreting Francis Bacon's Discourse on Scientific Progress," *South African Journal of Philosophy*, VI, 43–50.

1990. " 'The Summary Law of Nature': Revisiting Bacon's Views on the Unity of the Sciences," in Sessions 1990b, pp. 139–50.

Nadel, George H. 1966. "History as Psychology in Francis Bacon's Theory of History," History and Theory, V, 275–87. (Reprinted in Vickers 1968a.)

Neustadt, Mark S. 1987. "The Making of the Instauration: Science, Politics, and Law in the Career of Francis Bacon." Ph.D. diss., The Johns Hopkins University.

Newman, W. R. 1994. "Boyle's Debt to Corpuscular Alchemy," in Michael Hunter (ed.), Robert Boyle Reconsidered. Cambridge University Press, pp. 107–18.

Noreña, Carlos G. 1970. Juan Luis Vives. The Hague: Martinus Nijhoff.

Norton, D. F. 1981. "The Myth of British Empiricism," History of European Ideas, I, 331–4.

Olivieri, Grazia Tonelli. 1991. "Galen and Francis Bacon: Faculties of the Soul and the Classification of Knowledge," in Donald R. Kelley and Richard H. Popkin (eds.), The Shapes of Knowledge from the Renaissance to the Enlightenment. Dordrecht: Kluwer Academic Publishers, pp. 61–81.

Olson, Richard. 1975. Scottish Philosophy and British Physics, 1750–1800. A Study in the Foundations of the Victorian Scientific Style. Princeton: Princeton University Press.

O'Malley, John W. 1988. "Grammar and Rhetoric in the pietas of Erasmus," Journal of Medieval and Renaissance Studies, XVIII, 81–98.

Ong, Walter J. 1958. Ramus, Method, and the Decay of Dialogue. Cambridge Mass.: Harvard University Press.

Orsini, Napoleone. 1936. Bacone e Machiavelli. Genoa: Emiliano degli Orfini.

Ovitt, George Jr. 1983. "The Status of the Mechanical Arts in Medieval Classifications of Learning," Viator, XIV, 89–105.

Pagel, Walter. 1958. Paracelsus: An Introduction to Philosophical Medicine in the Era of the Renaissance. Basel: Karger.

1960. "Paracelsus and the Neoplatonic and Gnostic Tradition," Ambix, VIII, 125–66.

1967. William Harvey's Biological Ideas. Basel: Karger.

Panofsky, Erwin. 1924. Idea: Ein Beitrag zur Begriffsgeschichte der älteren Kunsttheorie. Leipzig and Berlin: Teubner.

Park, Katherine. 1984. "Bacon's 'Enchanted Glass,' " ISIS, LXXV, 290–302.

1988. "The Organic Soul," in Charles Schmitt and Quentin Skinner (eds.), The Cambridge History of Renaissance Philosophy. Cambridge University Press, pp. 464–84.

Park, Katherine, and Eckehard Kessler. 1988. "The Concept of Psychology," in Charles Schmitt and Quentin Skinner (eds.), *The Cambridge History of Renaissance Philosophy*. Cambridge University Press, pp. 455–63.

Paterson, Timothy H. 1987. "On the Role of Christianity in the Political Philosophy of Francis Bacon," *Polity*, XIX, 419–42.

1989. "The Secular Control of Scientific Power in the Political Philosophy of Francis Bacon," *Polity*, XXI, 457–80.

Patrick, J. Max. 1971. "Hawk versus Dove: Francis Bacon's Advocacy of a Holy War by James I against the Turks," *Studies in the Literary Imagination*, IV, no. 1, 159–71.

Peltonen, Markku. 1992. "Politics and Science: Francis Bacon and the True Greatness of States," *Historical Journal*, XXXV, 279–305.

1995. *Classical Humanism and Republicanism in English Political Thought 1570–1640*. Cambridge University Press.

Penrose, S. B. L. 1934. *The Reputation and Influence of Francis Bacon in the Seventeenth Century*. New York: Columbia University.

Pera, Marcello. 1982. *Hume, Kant e l'induzione*. Bologna: Il Mulino.

Pérez-Ramos, Antonio. 1985. "Bacon in the Right Spirit," *Annals of Science*, XLII, 603–11.

1988. *Francis Bacon's Idea of Science and the Maker's Knowledge Tradition*. Oxford: Oxford University Press.

1990a. "And Justify the Ways of God to Men," *Studies in History and Philosophy of Science*, XXI, 323–39.

1990b. "Francis Bacon and astronomical inquiry," *British Journal for the History of Science*, XXIII, 197–205.

1991. "Francis Bacon and the disputations of the learned," *British Journal for the Philosophy of Science*, XLII, 577–88.

1993. "Francis Bacon and Man's Two-faced Kingdom," *The Renaissance and Seventeenth-Century Rationalism*, ed. G. H. R. Parkinson, vol. IV of the *Routledge History of Philosophy*. London: Routledge, pp. 140–66.

Popkin, Richard H. 1979. *History of Scepticism from Erasmus to Spinoza*. Berkeley and Los Angeles: University of California Press.

1988. "Theories of Knowledge," in Charles Schmitt and Quentin Skinner (eds.), *The Cambridge History of Renaissance Philosophy*. Cambridge University Press, pp. 668–84.

Pousseur, Jean-Marie. 1984. "La distinction de la *ratio* et de la *methodus* dans le *Novum organum* et ses prolongements dans les rationalisme cartésien," in Fattori 1984a, pp. 201–22.

1985. "Méthode et dialectique," in Malherbe and Pousseur 1985, pp. 93–111.

1986. "De l'interprétation: Une logique pour l'invention," *Revue internationale de philosophie*, XL, 378–98.

1988. *Bacon, inventer la science.* Paris: Belin.

1990. "Bacon, a Critic of Telesio," in Sessions 1990b, pp. 105–17.

Preus, J. Samuel. 1979. "Religion and Bacon's New Learning: From Legitimation to Object," in F. Forrester Church and Timothy George (eds.), *Continuity and Discontinuity in Church History. Essays Presented to G. H. Williams.* Leiden: E. J. Brill, pp. 267–84.

Primack, Maxwell. 1962. "Francis Bacon's Philosophy of Nature." Ph.D. diss., The Johns Hopkins University.

1967. "Outline of a Reinterpretation of Francis Bacon's Philosophy," *Journal of the History of Philosophy,* V, 123–32.

Principe, L. R. 1994. "Boyle's Alchemical Pursuits," in Michael Hunter (ed.), *Robert Boyle Reconsidered.* Cambridge University Press, pp. 91–106.

Prior, Moody E. 1954. "Bacon's Man of Science," *Journal of the History of Ideas,* XV, 348–70. (Reprinted in Vickers 1968a.)

Quinton, Anthony. 1980. *Francis Bacon.* Oxford: Oxford University Press.

Raab, Felix. 1964. *The English Face of Machiavelli: A Changing Interpretation 1500–1700.* London: Routledge.

Rabb, Theodore K. 1969. "Francis Bacon and the Reform of Society," in Theodore K. Rabb and Jerrold Seigel (eds.), *Action and Conviction in Early Modern Europe.* Princeton: Princeton University Press, pp. 163–93.

Rashid, Salim. 1985. "Dugald Stewart: 'Baconian' Methodology and Political Economy," *Journal of the History of Ideas,* XLVI, 245–57.

Rattansi, P. N. 1968. "The Intellectual Origins of the Royal Society," *Notes and Records of the Royal Society of London,* XXIII, 129–43.

Ravetz, J. R. 1972. "Francis Bacon and the Reform of Philosophy," in Allen G. Debus (ed.), *Science and Society in the Renaissance. Essays in Honor of Walter Pagel,* 2 vols. New York: Neale Watson, II, pp. 97–119.

Rees, Graham. 1975a. "Francis Bacon's Semi-Paracelsian Cosmology," *Ambix,* XXII, 81–101.

1975b. "Francis Bacon's Semi-Paracelsian Cosmology and the *Great Instauration,*" *Ambix,* XXII, 161–73.

1977a. "The Fate of Bacon's Cosmology in the Seventeenth Century," *Ambix,* XXIV, 27–38.

1977b. "Matter Theory: A Unifying Factor in Bacon's Natural Philosophy?," *Ambix,* XXIV, 110–25.

1979. "Francis Bacon on Verticity and the Bowels of the Earth," *Ambix,* XXVI, 202–11.

1980. "Atomism and 'Subtlety' in Francis Bacon's Philosophy," *Annals of Science,* XXXVII, 549–71.

1981. "An Unpublished Manuscript by Francis Bacon: *Sylva Sylvarum* Drafts and Other Working Notes," *Annals of Science,* XXVIII, 377–412.

1984a. "Bacon's Philosophy: Some New Sources with Special Reference to the *Abecedarium novum naturae*," in Fattori 1984a, pp. 223–44.

1984b. "Francis Bacon and *spiritus vitalis*," in M. Fattori and M. Bianchi (eds.), *Spiritus IV: Colloquio internazionale*. Lessico intellettuale Europeo, XXXII, pp. 265–81.

1984c. "Francis Bacon's Biological Ideas: A New Manuscript Source," in Brian Vickers (ed.), *Occult and Scientific Mentalities in the Renaissance*. Cambridge University Press, pp. 297–314.

Rees, Graham, assisted by Christopher Upton. 1984d. *Francis Bacon's Natural Philosophy: A New Source*. The British Society for the History of Science. Monographs 5.

Rees, Graham. 1985. "Quantitative Reasoning in Francis Bacon's Natural Philosophy," *Nouvelles de la république des lettres*, 27–48.

1986. "Mathematics and Francis Bacon's Natural Philosophy," *Revue internationale de philosophie*, XL, 399–426.

1990. "The Transmission of Bacon Texts: Some Unanswered Questions," in Sessions 1990b, pp. 311–23.

Reif, P. 1969. "The Textbook Tradition in Natural Philosophy," *Journal of the History of Ideas*, XXX, 17–32.

Reiss, Timothy J. 1982. *The Discourse of Modernism*. Ithaca: Cornell University Press.

Renaker, David. 1990. "A Miracle of Engineering: The Conversion of Bensalem in Francis Bacon's *New Atlantis*," *Studies in Philology*, LXXXVII, 181–93.

Renaldo, John J. 1976. "Bacon's Empiricism, Boyle's Science, and the Jesuit Response in Italy," *Journal of the History of Ideas*, XXXVII, 689–95.

Rice, Eugene F., Jr. 1958. *The Renaissance Idea of Wisdom*. Cambridge Mass.: Harvard University Press.

Rickert, Corinne. 1956. "An Addition to the Canon of Bacon's Writings," *The Modern Language Review*, LI, 71–2.

Robertson, J. 1912. "Bacon as a Politician," *Contemporary Review*, CII, 338–49.

Robinet, André. 1985. "La refonte de la refonte: Leibniz face à Bacon," *Etudes Philosophiques*, 375–86.

Roller, Duane H. D. 1953. "Did Bacon Know Gilbert's *De magnete*?," *ISIS*, XLIV, 10–13.

Ross, Sydney. 1962. "*Scientist*: The Story of a Word," *Annals of Science*, XVIII, 65–85.

Rossi, Paolo. 1968. *Francis Bacon: From Magic to Science*, trans. Sacha Rabinovitch. London: Routledge.

1970. "Truth and Utility in the Science of Francis Bacon," in Paolo Rossi,

Philosophy, Technology, and the Arts in the Early Modern Era, trans. Salvator Attanasio. New York: Harper, pp. 146–73.

1971a. "Bacone e la Bibbia," in Paolo Rossi, *Aspetti della rivoluzione scientifica.* Napoli: Morano, pp. 51–82.

1971b. "Venti, maree, ipotesi astronomiche in Bacone e in Galilei," in Paolo Rossi, *Aspetti della rivoluzione scientifica.* Napoli: Morano, pp. 151–222.

1973. "Baconianism," in Philip Wiener (ed.), *Dictionary of the History of Ideas.* New York: Charles Scribner's Sons, pp. 172–9.

1974. "Note Baconiane," *Rivista critica di storia della filosofia,* XXIX, 32–51.

1975. "Hermeticism, Rationality, and the Scientific Revolution," in Marta Luigi Righini-Bonelli and William R. Shea (eds.), *Reason, Experiment and Mysticism in the Scientific Revolution.* New York: Science History Publications, pp. 247–73.

1984. "Ants, spiders, epistemologists," in Fattori 1984a, pp. 245–60.

1991. "Mnemonical Loci and Natural Loci," in Marcello Pera and William R. Shea (eds.), *Persuading Science: The Art of Scientific Rhetoric.* Canton: Science History Publications.

Rossky, W. 1958. "Imagination in the English Renaissance: Psychology and Poetic," *Studies in the Renaissance,* V, 49–73.

Salamun, Kurt. 1975. "Bacons Idolenlehre aus der Sicht der neueren Ideologiekritik," *Archiv für Rechts- und Sozialphilosophie,* LXI, 529–56.

Salmon, J. H. M. 1989. "Seneca and Tacitus in Jacobean England," *Journal of the History of Ideas,* L, 199–225.

Sargent, Rose-Mary. 1986. "Robert Boyle's Baconian Inheritance: A Response to Laudan's Cartesian Thesis," *Studies in History and Philosophy of Science,* XVII, 469–86.

1989. "Scientific Experiment and Legal Expertise: The Way of Experience in Seventeenth-Century England," *Studies in History and Philosophy of Science,* XX, 19–45.

1994. "Learning from Experience: Boyle's Construction of an Experimental Philosophy," in Michael Hunter (ed.), *Robert Boyle Reconsidered.* Cambridge University Press, pp. 57–78.

Schäfer, Lothar. 1993. *Das Bacon-Projekt: Von der Erkenntnis, Vernutzung und Schonung der Natur.* Frankfurt-am-Main: Suhrkamp.

Schmidt-Biggemann, Wilhelm. 1983. *Topica Universalis: Ein Modellgeschichte humanistischer und barocker Wissenschaft.* Hamburg: Felix Meiner Verlag.

Schoeck, R. J. 1953. "Rhetoric and Law in Sixteenth-Century England," *Studies in Philology,* L, 110–27.

Sessions, William A. 1970. "Francis Bacon and the Negative Instance," *Renaissance Papers*, 1–9.

1976. "Mutations of *pietas litterata*," *Renaissance Papers*, 1–10.

1990a. "Francis Bacon and the Classics: The Discovery of Discovery," in Sessions 1990b, pp. 237–53.

(ed.). 1990b. *Francis Bacon's Legacy of Texts: The Art of Discovery Grows with Discovery*. New York: AMS Press.

Sewell, Elizabeth. 1969. "Bacon, Vico, Coleridge, and the Poetic Method," in Giorgio Tagliacozzo, *Giambattista Vico: An international symposium*. Baltimore: The Johns Hopkins University Press, pp. 125–36.

Shapin, Steven, and Simon Schaffer. 1985. *Leviathan and the Air-Pump: Hobbes, Boyle, and the Experimental Life*. Princeton: Princeton University Press.

Shapiro, Barbara J. 1975. "Law Reform in Seventeenth-Century England," *American Journal of Legal History*, XIX, 280–312.

1980. "Sir Francis Bacon and the Mid–Seventeenth-Century Movement for Law Reform," *American Journal of Legal History*, XXIV, 331–62.

1983. *Probability and Certainty in Seventeenth-Century England*. Princeton: Princeton University Press.

1991. "Early Modern Intellectual Life: Humanism, Religion and Science in Seventeenth-Century England," *History of Science*, XXIX, 45–71.

Siegl, Edmund. 1983. *Das Novum organum von Francis Bacon: Skizze einer induktivistischen Philosophie*. Innsbruck: Universität Innsbruck.

Simonds, Roger T. 1986. "Bacon's Legal Learning: Its Influence on his Philosophical Ideas," in I. D. McFarlane (ed.), *Acta Conventus Neo-Latini Sanctandreani: Proceedings of the Fifth International Congress of Neo-Latin Studies*. Binghampton: Medieval and Renaissance Texts and Studies, pp. 493–501.

Siraisi, Nancy. 1990. *Medieval and Early Renaissance Medicine: An Introduction to Knowledge and Practice*. Chicago: University of Chicago Press.

Skinner, Quentin. 1993. " 'Scientia Civilis' in Classical Rhetoric and in the Early Hobbes," in Nicholas Phillipson and Quentin Skinner (eds.), *Political Discourse in Early Modern Britain*. Cambridge University Press, pp. 67–93.

Slaughter, Mary. 1982. *Universal Languages and Scientific Taxonomy in the Seventeenth Century*. Cambridge University Press.

Snider, Alvin. 1988. "Francis Bacon and the Authority of Aphorism," *Prose Studies*, XI, 60–71.

Snow, R. E. 1967. "The Problem of Certainty: Bacon, Descartes, and Pascal." Ph.D. diss., Indiana University.

Snow, Vernon F. 1960. "Francis Bacon's Advice to Fulke Greville on Research Techniques," *Huntington Library Quarterly*, XXIII, 369–78.

Solomon, Julie Robin. 1987. "Between Magic and Travel: Francis Bacon and the Theatres of Human Knowing." Ph.D. diss., University of Pennsylvania.

——— 1991. " 'To Know, to Fly, to Conjure': Situating Baconian Science at the Juncture of Early Modern Modes of Reading," *Renaissance Quarterly*, XLIV, 513–58.

Sommerville, J. P. 1986. *Politics and Ideology in England 1603–1640*. Harlow: Longmans.

Steadman, John M. 1971. "Beyond Hercules: Bacon and the Scientist as Hero," *Studies in the Literary Imagination*, IV, no. 1, 3–47.

Stephens, James. 1975. *Francis Bacon and the Style of Science*. Chicago: The University of Chicago Press.

Stillman, Robert E. 1989. "The Jacobean Discourse of Power: James I and Francis Bacon," *Renaissance Papers*, 89–99.

Stone de Montpensier, Roy L. 1968. "Bacon as Lawyer and Jurist," *Archiv für Rechts- und Sozialphilosophie*, LIV, 449–83.

Tasche, Frank, and Gerhard P. Knapp. 1971. "Methodik und Intention: Zum Wissenschaftsbegriff von Francis Bacon," *Zeitschrift für Philosophische Forschung*, XXV, 293–306.

Tillman, James S. 1975. "Bacon's Georgics of Science," *Papers on Language and Literature*, XI, 357–66.

——— 1976. "Bacon's *Ethos*: The Model Philosopher," *Renaissance Papers*, 11–19.

Tinkler, John F. 1987. "The Rhetorical Method of Francis Bacon's *History of the Reign of King Henry VII*," *History and Theory*, XXVI, 31–52.

——— 1988a. "Humanist History and the English Novel in the Eighteenth Century," *Studies in Philology*, LXXXV, 510–37.

——— 1988b. "Praise and Advice: Rhetorical Approaches in More's *Utopia* and Machiavelli's *The Prince*," *The Sixteenth Century Journal*, XIX, 187–207.

——— 1988c. "The Splitting of Humanism: Bentley, Swift and the Battle of the Books," *Journal of the History of Ideas*, XLIX, 453–72.

Tittler, Robert. 1976. *Nicholas Bacon: The Making of a Tudor Statesman*. Athens: University of Ohio Press.

Torrini, Maurizio. 1984. "Il *topos* della meraviglia come origine della filosofia tra Bacone e Vico," in Fattori 1984a, pp. 261–80.

Toulmin, Stephen. 1972. *Human Understanding*. Oxford: Oxford University Press.

Trevor-Roper, Hugh. 1962. "Francis Bacon after Four Centuries," *Encounter*, XVIII, no. 2, 73–7.

——— 1967. *Religion, the Reformation and Social Change*. London: Macmillan.

Tuck, Richard. 1993. *Philosophy and Government 1572–1651*. Cambridge University Press.

Urbach, Peter. 1982. "Francis Bacon as a Precursor to Popper," *British Journal for the Philosophy of Science*, XXXIII, 113–32.

1987. *Francis Bacon's Philosophy of Science: An Account and a Reappraisal*. La Salle: Open Court.

van den Daele, Wolfgang. 1977. "The Social Construction of Science: Institutionalization and Definition of Positive Science in the Latter Half of the Seventeenth Century," in Everett Mendelsohn et al. (eds.), *The Social Production of Scientific Knowledge*: Dordrecht: D. Reidel, pp. 27–54.

van Helden, Albert. 1983. "The Birth of the Modern Scientific Instrument, 1550–1700," in John G. Burke (ed.), *The Uses of Science in the Age of Newton*. Berkeley and Los Angeles: University of California Press, pp. 49–84.

van Leeuwen, H. G. 1963. *The Problem of Certainty in English Thought (1630–1690)*. The Hague: Martinus Nijhoff.

von Liebig, Justus. 1863. "Lord Bacon as Natural Philosopher," *Macmillan's Magazine*, VII, 237–49, 257–67.

von Wright, G. H. 1951. *A Treatise on Induction and Probability*. London: Routledge.

Vasoli, Cesare. 1968. *La dialettica e la retorica dell'Umanesimo: "Invenzioni" e "Metodo" nella cultura del XV e XVI secolo*. Milan: Feltrinelli.

Viano, C. A. 1954. "Esperienza e natura nella filosofia di Francesco Bacone," *Rivista di filosofia*, XLV, 291–313.

Vickers, Brian (ed.). 1968a. *Essential Articles for the Study of Francis Bacon*. Hamden: Archon Press. (Reprinted in 1972, London: Sidgwick and Jackson.)

Vickers, Brian. 1968b. *Francis Bacon and Renaissance Prose*. Cambridge University Press.

1971. "Bacon's Use of Theatrical Imagery," *Studies in the Literary Imagination*, IV, no. 1, 189–226. (Reprinted in Sessions 1990b.)

1978. *Francis Bacon*. Harlow: Longman.

1981. "Rhetorical and Anti-rhetorical Tropes: On Writing the History of *Elocutio*," *Comparative Criticism*, III, 105–32.

1983. " 'The Power of Persuasion': Images of the Orator, Elyot to Shakespeare," in J. J. Murphy (ed.), *Renaissance Eloquence: Studies in the Theory and Practice of Renaissance Rhetoric*. Berkeley: University of California Press, pp. 411–35.

1984a. "Analogy versus Identity: The Rejection of Occult Symbolism, 1580–1680," in Brian Vickers (ed.), *Occult and Scientific Mentalities in the Renaissance*. Cambridge University Press, pp. 95–163.

1984b. "Bacon's So-Called 'Utilitarianism': Sources and Influences," in Fattori 1984a, pp. 281–313.

1985. "The Royal Society and English Prose Style: A Reassessment," in *Rhetoric and the Pursuit of Truth: Language Change in the Seventeenth and Eighteenth Centuries.* Los Angeles: William Andrews Memorial Library, pp. 1–76, at pp. 26–41.

1987. *English Science, Bacon to Newton.* Cambridge University Press.

1988a. *In Defence of Rhetoric.* Oxford: Clarendon Press.

1988b. "Rhetoric and Poetics," in Charles Schmitt and Quentin Skinner (eds.), *The Cambridge History of Renaissance Philosophy.* Cambridge University Press, pp. 715–45.

1991a. "Bacon among the Literati: Science and Language," *Comparative Criticism,* XIII, 249–71.

1991b. "Pour une véritable histoire de l'éloquence," *Etudes littéraires,* XXIV, 121–52.

1992. "Francis Bacon and the Progress of Knowledge," *Journal of the History of Ideas,* LIII, 495–518.

(ed.). 1996. *Francis Bacon.* Oxford: Oxford University Press.

Vleeschauwer, H. J. de. 1958. "Autour de la classification psychologique des sciences," *Mousaion,* no. 27.

Walker, Daniel P. 1972. "Francis Bacon and *Spiritus*," in Allen G. Debus (ed.), *Science, Medicine and Society: Essays in Honor of Walter Pagel.* New York: Neale Watson, 2 vols., II, pp. 121–30.

1984. "Spirits in Francis Bacon," in Fattori 1984a, pp. 315–27.

Wallace, Karl R. 1943. *Francis Bacon on Communication and Rhetoric.* Chapel Hill: The University of North Carolina Press.

1956. "Aspects of Modern Rhetoric in Francis Bacon," *Quarterly Journal of Speech,* XLII, 398–406.

1957. "Discussion in Parliament and Francis Bacon," *Quarterly Journal of Speech,* XLIII, 12–21. (Reprinted in Vickers 1968a.)

1961. "Bacon's Conception of Rhetoric," in Raymond F. Howes (ed.), *Historical Studies of Rhetoric and Rhetoricians.* Ithaca: Cornell University Press, pp. 114–38.

1967. *Francis Bacon on the Nature of Man.* Urbana: University of Illinois Press.

1971. "Chief Guides to the Study of Bacon's Speeches," *Studies in the Literary Imagination,* IV, no. 1, 173–88.

Walton, Craig D. 1971. "Ramus and Bacon on Method," *Journal of the History of Philosophy,* IX, 289–302.

Warhaft, Sidney. 1958a. "The Anomaly of Bacon's Allegorizing," *Papers of the Michigan Academy of Science, Arts, and Letters,* XLIII, 327–33.

1958b. "Science against Man in Bacon," *Bucknell Review*, VII, 158–73.

1963. "Bacon and the Renaissance Ideal of Self-knowledge," *Personalist*, XLIV, 454–71.

1971. "The Providential Order in Bacon's New Philosophy," *Studies in the Literary Imagination*, IV, no. 1, 49–64. (Reprinted in Sessions 1990b.)

Watanabe, Masao. 1992. "Francis Bacon: Philanthrophy and the Instauration of Learning," *Annals of Science*, IL, 163–73.

Webster, Charles. 1970. *Samuel Hartlib and the Advancement of Learning*. Cambridge University Press.

1975. *The Great Instauration: Science, Medicine, and Reform 1626–1660*. London: Duckworth.

1982. *From Paracelsus to Newton: Magic and the Making of Modern Science*. Cambridge University Press.

Weinberger, Jerry. 1976. "Science and Rule in Bacon's Utopia: An Introduction to the Reading of the *New Atlantis*," *American Political Science Review*, LXX, 865–85.

1985. *Science, Faith, and Politics: Francis Bacon and the Utopian Roots of the Modern Age*. Ithaca: Cornell University Press.

Weisheipl, James A. 1965. "Classification of the Sciences in Medieval Thought," *Medieval Studies*, XXVII, 54–90.

1978. "The Nature, Scope and Classification of the Sciences," in David C. Lindberg (ed.), *Science in the Middle Ages*. Chicago: University of Chicago Press, pp. 461–82.

West, Muriel. 1961. "Notes on the Importance of Alchemy to Modern Science in the Writings of Francis Bacon and Robert Boyle," *Ambix*, IX, 102–14.

Westfall, Richard. 1958. *Science and Religion in Seventeenth-Century England*. New Haven: Yale University Press.

Westman, R. S., and J. E. McGuire. 1977. *Hermeticism and the Scientific Revolution*. Los Angeles: William Andrews Clark Memorial Library.

Wheatley, J. M. O. 1961. "Bacon's Redefinition of Metaphysics," *Personalist*, XLII, 487–99.

Wheeler, Harvey. 1956. "The Constitutional Ideas of Francis Bacon," *Western Political Quarterly*, IX, 927–36.

1983a. "The Invention of Modern Empiricism: Juridical Foundations of Francis Bacon's Philosophy of Science," *Law Library Journal*, LXXVI, 78–122.

1983b. "Science out of Law: Francis Bacon's Invention of Scientific Empiricism," in Dalmas H. Nelson and Richard L. Sklar (eds.), *Toward a Humanistic Science of Politics: Essays in Honor of Francis Dunham Wormuth*. Lanham: University Press of America, pp. 101–44.

1990. "Francis Bacon's *New Atlantis*: The 'Mould' of a Lawfinding Commonwealth," in Sessions 1990b, pp. 291–310.

Wheeler, Thomas. 1955. "Sir Francis Bacon's Concept of the Historian's Task," *Renaissance Papers*, 40–6.

1957a. "Bacon's Henry VII as a Machiavellian Prince," *Renaissance Papers*, 111–17.

1957b. "The Purpose of Bacon's *History of Henry the Seventh*," *Studies in Philology*, LIV, 1–13.

Whewell, William. 1831. "Review of Herschel's *Preliminary Discourse on the Study of Natural Philosophy*," *London Quarterly Review*, XLV, 374–407.

1958. *Novum Organum Renovatum* (1st published 1858). London: Frank Cass.

1967. *The Philosophy of the Inductive Sciences* (1st published in 1840), eds. L. Laudan and G. Buchdahl. London: Frank Cass.

Whitaker, Virgil K. 1933. "Bacon and the Renaissance Encyclopedists." Ph.D. diss., Stanford University.

1962. *Francis Bacon's Intellectual Milieu*. Los Angeles: William Andrews Clark Memorial Library. (Reprinted in Vickers 1968a.)

1970. "Bacon's Doctrine of Forms: A Study of Seventeenth-Century Eclecticism," *Huntington Library Quarterly*, XXXIII, 209–16.

1971. "Francesco Patrizi and Francis Bacon," *Studies in the Literary Imagination*, IV, no. 1, 107–20. (Reprinted in Sessions 1990b.)

White, Hayden V. 1978. *Tropics of Discourse*. Baltimore: The Johns Hopkins University Press.

White, Howard B. 1957. "The English Solomon: Francis Bacon on Henry VII," *Social Research*, XXII, 457–81.

1958a. "Bacon, Bruno, and the Eternal Recurrence," *Social Research*, XXV, 449–68.

1958b. "Bacon's Imperialism," *American Political Science*, LII, 470–89.

1968. *Peace among the Willows: The Political Philosophy of Francis Bacon*. The Hague: Martinus Nijhoff.

1970. "Bacon's *Wisdom of the Ancients*," *Interpretation*, I, 107–29.

Whitney, Charles. 1984. "Cupid Hatched by Night: The 'Mysteries of Faith' and Bacon's Art of Discovery," in Peter S. Hawkins and Anne H. Schitter (eds.), *Ineffability: Naming the Unnamable from Dante to Beckett*. New York: AMS Press, pp. 51–64.

1986. *Francis Bacon and Modernity*. New Haven: Yale University Press.

1989. "Francis Bacon's *Instauratio*: Dominion of and over Humanity," *Journal of the History of Ideas*, L, 371–90.

1990. "Merchants of Light: Science as Colonization in the *New Atlantis*," in Sessions 1990b, pp. 255–68.

Wicher, H. B. 1986. "Nemesius Emesenus," *Catalogus Translationum et Commentarium*, VI, 31–72.

Wiley, Margaret. 1950. "Francis Bacon and a Land Unknown," in Margaret Wiley, *Creative Skeptics*. London: George Allen and Unwin, pp. 47–94.

1971. "Francis Bacon Induction and/or Rhetoric," *Studies in the Literary Imagination*, IV, no. 1, 65–79.

Witt, Ronald G. 1982. "Medieval 'Ars Dictaminis' and the Beginnings of Humanism: A New Construction of the Problem," *Renaissance Quarterly*, XXXV, 1–35.

Wolff, Emil. 1910–13. *Francis Bacon und seine Quellen*. Literarhistorische Forschungen, Hefte XL, LII. (Reprinted in 1977, Nendeln, Lichtenstein: Kraus.)

Wood, E. R. 1951. "Francis Bacon's 'Cousin Sharpe,' " *Notes and Queries*, CXCVI, 248–9.

Wood, Neal. 1983. *The Politics of Locke's Philosophy*. Berkeley: University of California Press.

Wood, P. B. 1980. "Methodology and Apologetics: Thomas Sprat's *History of the Royal Society*," *British Journal for the History of Science*, XIII, 1–26.

Woolf, Daniel R. 1984. "John Seldon [*sic*], John Borough and Francis Bacon's *History of Henry VII*, 1621," *Huntington Library Quarterly*, XLVII, 47–53.

1987. "Erudition and the Idea of History in Renaissance England," *Renaissance Quarterly*, XL, 11–48.

Wormald, B. H. G. 1993. *Francis Bacon: History, Politics and Science, 1561–1626*. Cambridge University Press.

Yates, Frances. 1966. *The Art of Memory*: Chicago: University of Chicago Press.

Yates, Frances A. 1984. "Bacon's Magic," in Frances A. Yates, *Ideas and Ideals in the North European Renaissance*. London: Routledge, pp. 61–6.

Yeo, Richard. 1985. "An Idol of the Market-Place: Baconianism in Nineteenth Century Britain," *History of Science*, XXIII, 251–98.

Zedelmaier, Helmut. 1992. *Bibliotheca Universalis und Bibliotheca Selecta: Das Problem der Ordnung des gelehrten Wissens in der frühen Neuzeit*. Köln: Böhlau Verlag.

Zeitlin, J. 1928. "The Development of Bacon's *Essays* with Special Reference to the Question of Montaigne's Influence upon Them," *Journal of English and Germanic Philology*, XXVII, 496–519.

Zetterberg, J. Peter. 1982. "Echoes of Nature in Salomon's House," *Journal of the History of Ideas*, XLIII, 179–93.

INDEX